A COMPULSION
FOR ANTIQUITY

Cornell Studies in the History of Psychiatry

A series edited by

Sander L. Gilman
George J. Makari

A full list of titles appears at the end of the book.

A COMPULSION FOR ANTIQUITY

Freud and the Ancient World

RICHARD H. ARMSTRONG

CORNELL UNIVERSITY PRESS
ITHACA AND LONDON

Cornell University Press gratefully acknowledges a grant from the University of Houston, which aided in the publication of this book.

First published 2005 by Cornell University Press
First printing, Cornell paperbacks, 2006

Printed in the United States of America

Library of Congress Cataloging-in-Publication Data

Armstrong, Richard H.
    Compulsion for antiquity : Freud and the ancient world /
Richard H. Armstrong.
        p.   ;   cm. — (Cornell studies in the history of psychiatry)
    Includes bibliographical references and index.
    ISBN-13: 978-0-8014-4302-2 (cloth : alk. paper)
    ISBN-10: 0-8014-4302-4 (cloth : alk. paper)
    ISBN-13: 978-0-8014-7333-3 (pbk. : alk. paper)
    ISBN-10: 0-8014-7333-0 (pbk. : alk. paper)
        1. Freud, Sigmund, 1856–1939.   2. Psychoanalysis—History.
    3. Civilization, Ancient.   [DNLM: 1. Freud, Sigmund,
    1856–1939.   2. Freudian Theory.   3. History.   4. Memory.
    5. Mythology.   6. Psychoanalysis—history.   7. Western World—
    history.   WM 460 A737c 2005]   I. Title.   II. Series.
    RC503.A75 2005
    150.19'52—dc22
                                                    2004023902

Cornell University Press strives to use environmentally responsible suppliers and materials to the fullest extent possible in the publishing of its books. Such materials include vegetable-based, low-VOC inks and acid-free papers that are recycled, totally chlorine-free, or partly composed of nonwood fibers. For further information, visit our website at www.cornellpress.cornell.edu.

Cloth printing   10 9 8 7 6 5 4 3 2
Paperback printing   10 9 8 7 6 5 4 3 2 1

Jeder hat noch in den Alten gefunden, was er brauchte oder wünschte; vorzüglich sich selbst.

Everyone has found in the ancients whatever he needed or wished for; especially himself.

—FRIEDRICH SCHLEGEL, *Athenäums-Fragmente 15*

For the kings of my heart, Carlos and Felipe

And for the Dawn of my new life

> Who is she that shines through like the dawn,
> Beautiful as the moon,
> Radiant as the sun,
> Awesome as bannered hosts?
> —*Song of Songs*, 6.10

CONTENTS

ACKNOWLEDGMENTS

■

This book was not written in ideal circumstances, but it owes its existence to the help of many people and institutions who made the job of writing it significantly easier. Initial research was undertaken in Greece, Austria, and London, thanks to a grant from the University of Houston, which later assisted in the publication of this book through a subvention grant. I am very happy to thank my home institution for its financial support. I wish also to thank the staff of the National Libraries in Athens and Vienna for their professionalism and kind assistance. Throughout the project, I also benefited from the generosity of the staff at both Freud Museums (London and Vienna); they include Michael Molnar, Erica Davies, Keith Davies, and Lydia Marinelli. Christfried Tögel, Peter Swales, Peter Rudnytsky and Norman Holland, four other Freud scholars of the battleship class, were extremely helpful in providing me with information, offprints, commentary, and criticism. Last but certainly not least, Sander Gilman patiently waited for the final draft of this book and helped to provide an excellent venue for its publication. My considerable debt to his scholarship will be amply acknowledged below throughout the footnotes.

Bill Bowman at Gettysburg College was very helpful to me on matters of Austrian history. Lida Triantafillidou and Fivos Verdelis were my generous hosts in Athens. In Houston, I was helped on matters German and Freudian by John Vincent, Hannah Decker, Hildegard Glass, David Mikics, Cary Nathenson and Katrin Völkner; on classical matters I enjoyed the wise counsel of Dora Pozzi, Francesca D'Alessandro Behr, and Casey Dué-Hackney. The superb library staff at the University of Houston so catered to my at times kinky requests for rare material that I am compelled by gratitude and honor to thank some of them by name: Keiko Horton, Jeff Fadell, and Michelle Stone. Thanks go locally also to Bill Parsons at Rice University, whose work on Freud and religion opened a whole new vista that I hope to pursue at a later date.

I had the luxury of sharing my ideas with audiences on several occasions at the American Philological Association, the Pacific Ancient and Modern Literature Association, the Comparative Drama Conference, the College of William and Mary, Trinity University (San Antonio), The University of Texas at San Antonio, Rice University, and Emory University. As I was finishing the manuscript, I had the splendid opportunity to discuss its themes in a National Endowment for the Humanities sponsored seminar at SUNY Potsdam, and I wish to thank the participants for a wonderful four weeks of discussion: David Curry, Galen Pletcher, Caroline Downing, Arlene Stillwell, Anne Malone, Joe Di Giovanna, Art Clark, and Rick Williams. Lastly, in the final stages of the project, I stumbled upon (or rather, was stumbled upon by) the research seminar *Archive der Vergangenheit* at the Humboldt Universität zu Berlin, where I was invited to come and share in a week's worth of timely discussion. I wish to thank, in particular, Dr. Knut Ebeling and Professor Stefan Altekamp for a very stimulating Berlin sojourn.

I wish to thank my sons Carlos and Felipe for never letting me forget that psychology, if it is to have any real value beyond pathological taxonomies, must be rooted in loving interaction. Far from a distraction, they were a real inspiration for my research.

I am very grateful to Herman Rapaport and Teresa Jesionowski for their sound editorial advice, and to Cornell University Press as a whole for their professionalism and efficiency.

And finally, I must thank my PowerBook G3 MacIntosh laptop for the considerable abuse it has sustained with mechanical equanimity. It has survived against incredible odds and has never complained, not even after I dumped a mug of hot coffee on its keyboard.

R.H.A.

A COMPULSION
FOR ANTIQUITY

INTRODUCTION

∎

Disturbing Acropolis

> Every choice human being strives instinctively for a citadel and a secrecy
> where he is saved from the crowd, the many, the great majority where
> he may forget "men who are the rule," being their exception—except-
> ing only the one case in which he is pushed straight to such men by a still
> stronger instinct, as a seeker after knowledge in the great and exceptional
> sense.
>
> —NIETZSCHE, *Beyond Good and Evil*

On September 4, 1904, Sigmund Freud put on his best shirt and climbed
atop the Acropolis of Athens in the company of his brother, Alexander.[1]
In the course of the hours the two brothers spent on the site, he experienced what he later termed a derealization [*Entfremdungsgefühl*], a
thought expressed in the astonishing words: "So all this really *does* exist,
just as we learnt at school!" (SE 22:241). The thought was astonishing,
because he knew he had never doubted the existence of the ancient world;
it was thus not just a simple derealization, but a disturbance of memory.
For thirty-two years he mulled over this curious sensation, until he finally
wrote a short essay on it which traced this feeling to the guilt he and his
brother felt in "making it all the way" to Athens; that is, in "going farther" than their father.[2] Filial piety, aroused by the sense of oedipal triumph, had turned Athens into an unreal city out of respect for the dead
Jewish father for whom Athens would not have meant very much. In as-
cending the Acropolis, the two successful sons not only achieved the
touristic conquest of another cultural capital (as they had "conquered"
Rome three years before), but gave proof of their own "cultural capital"
as well educated Europeans. Their father was a Central European in the

geographical sense, a modest Jewish businessman from a Galician *shtetl* who knew Hebrew better than he did German. But the sons had become *centrally* European and stood that September day at the primal scene of European identity.

We take it quite for granted that the Acropolis should serve as the cynosure of a particular Western European faith in ancient history, as the physical center of a historical consciousness that continues to inform the liberal democratic tradition to this day. But the physical reconstitution of Athens as a modern European capital was a nineteenth-century achievement, brokered by Western European powers and the Bavarian monarchy that formed the first government of modern Greece.[3] After the Greek Revolution (1821–1829), the Acropolis itself was deliberately reconstructed to be an official classical ruin instead of the Turkish fortress it had been since 1456. Particularly under the influence of the German architect Leo von Klenze (1784–1864), it had its medieval and Turkish structures gradually removed, including the mosque which had been tucked inside the Parthenon (Bastéa 2000, 100–104). Freud was thus experiencing a disturbance of memory on a much disturbed site of memory, and it seems appropriate, perhaps even inevitable, that his ultimate means of laying this complex experience to rest was to invoke an oedipal reading of it, tucking it safely away within the armature of his own scientific theories. The Oedipus complex had long been Freud's disturbing acropolis by the time he wrote his essay. Though the Oedipus scenario began as an observation on typical dreams, it became the dynamic center of his entire theory of the neuroses, of the socialization of the individual, and later of the origins of "religion, morals, society, and art" (*Totem and Taboo*, SE 13: 156). It became in effect his citadel and sacred center from which he would not budge. As he once put it quite aggressively, the Oedipus complex was "the shibboleth that distinguishes the adherents of psychoanalysis from its opponents," invoking the Hebrew password from Judges 12:6 (*Three Essays on the Theory of Sexuality*, SE 7:226 n. 1). Whether this citadel of theory was ultimately his immortal Acropolis or his desperate Masada remains a matter of considerable debate.

This book is an attempt to delve into the relationship between the two narratives I have here introduced: the narrative of antiquity's deployment in Western European identity, and the narrative of Freud's developing science of the mind. The first is a matter of the reception of Greek, Roman, Near Eastern and Egyptian cultures; the second falls squarely into the newer field of Freud studies, which includes psychoanalysis's historical scenario of gestation and growth as much as it does its claims to ther-

apeutic efficacy and scientific truth. The easy way to link the two is by
way of the even newer field of mnemohistory, as has been done with regard to Freud's Moses by the eminent Egyptologist Jan Assmann, whose
work has been a great stimulus and inspiration for my own (1992, 1997,
2000a, 2000b, [1996] 2002). Mnemohistory allows us to examine the
work done on the archive of antiquity by such figures as Freud, without
turning the question simply into a matter of "where Freud went wrong."[4]
For the history of memory is not a matter of mere transmission of information; rather it is the history of *acts* of remembrance, or what I shall
loosely call "memory work." As Assmann says, in mnemohistory "[t]he
past is not simply 'received' by the present. The present is 'haunted' by
the past and the past is modeled, invented, reinvented, and reconstructed
by the present" (1997, 9). Since Freud's science of the mind is largely an
art of memory, the question of remembering the ancients fits snugly into
the general contour of the memory work of the couch. I thus feel confident that this book not only has an easily recognizable discursive objective, but also an identifiable audience, since the interest in the processes
of cultural and individual memory has increased vastly over the past thirty
years, a phenomenon that is in part responsible for keeping Freud in the
crosshairs of academic debate (Crews et al. 1995; Mollon 2000).

Since I deal here as much with the memory of Freud as the memory
of antiquity, I might well characterize this study as a tale of two archives:
the ancient archive, which expanded considerably in his lifetime, and the
Freud archive, which has become increasingly more available to the general public during mine.[5] How, more exactly, are the two to be linked?
Freud's "A Disturbance of Memory on the Acropolis" suggests at least
three lines of investigation for tracing the role antiquity plays in his life
and works. First, there is the intriguing historical question of Freud's own
social group, the Jewish *Bildungsbürgertum* of the Austro-Hungarian Empire, which passed from the absorbing marginality of traditional Jewish
life, through the homogenizing institution of the classical high school or
Gymnasium, and thence onward to the university and the liberal professions of law, medicine, and journalism.[6] Being raised in a liberal era when
democratic ideals were seriously—though ultimately ineffectually—entertained, Freud's generation of Jewish professional men was to experience an ugly awakening to the fact that political anti-Semitism would dog
them and hamper their careers in spite of their education and talents. In
the end, this anti-Semitism in its most virulent form under the Nazis
would seek to annihilate those of them who remained after the Anschluss

with Germany in 1938, and this drove Freud and his family from Vienna to London, a mere two years after writing the Acropolis essay. The story of this Jewish "marooned mandarinate" and the role of classical education in its formation was an integral part of the research for this book; but it became such an important topic in itself that I ultimately decided to put that material aside for a whole separate volume. There I shall treat in adequate demographic and historical detail the extraordinary odyssey of these Jewish Europeans who came to form the backbone of intellectual life in Vienna and their relation to the political and educational deployments of the ancient world. For now, however, we must bracket that line of investigation and move on.

The second line of investigation *is* addressed by the present book, and I do not think I have put the cart before the horse by giving it priority over the first. What is the relationship between Freud's interest in the ancient world and the substance of psychoanalysis? If we care at all about the Freud scenario, it is because we remain engaged in some way with the legacy of his thought, not just the anecdotal details of his life. A classicist might well police Freud's works to detect errors, distortions, and omissions vis-à-vis the archive of antiquity and simply dismiss Freud as a dilettante with an irrepressible taste for classical trappings.[7] Such police work is a necessary if tedious feature of disciplinary agency—for it is not a matter of indifference that Freud often makes gratuitous and even erroneous references to the ancient world. So the burden of proof would lie with the person who would prefer to show psychoanalysis to be something more than a case of the modern "misappropriation" of a classical heritage that exists in a pristine state somewhere else (like Oxford, for example).

This book consequently hovers around Freud's couch; that is, it takes the analytic encounter as the paradigm from which I will work my theme. As we look at the prolonged "scientific improvisation" Freud sustains in founding a new science of the mind, we will see how utterly necessary the archive of the ancient world becomes to his burgeoning enterprise, and this in a way that goes well beyond mere name-dropping in reference to Oedipus and Narcissus.[8] We will see that his improvisation is given form through constant reference to the historical disciplines that mediate the knowledge of antiquity, disciplines that offer him methodologies, analogies, evidence, and consolation. We will see how his master narrative of civilization actualizes his interest in different eras of human history according to the pressures and the politics of his improvising. We will see how being a Jew, in particular, conditioned his constant recourse to the ancient world, and how this recourse is no traditionalist retreat to a safe

haven of Jewish identity, but something more complex and psychologically more intriguing.

But there is still a third line of investigation that follows upon the second. How can the cultures of antiquity be put in meaningful dialogue with
psychoanalysis itself? For only in this way would we see why the topic of
psychoanalysis and ancient culture should remain of interest once the
questions of historical filiation are settled. The disciplinary police work
of the classicist may help to convince the psychoanalyst that Freud over-
stated his case in reading the archive of ancient cultures. But another,
bolder project then suggests itself, which is to show how the archive of
ancient culture not only had a vague "impact" on the development of
Freud's thought (the typical "reception" question), but how psychoanalysis itself reflects more deeply the cultural logic, the values, the textual
maneuvers and nuances, and even the psychological interests of the ancient world. In other words, the question is not whether psychoanalysis
truly is the master discourse with which to unlock the real meaning of antiquity; it is rather how psychoanalysis still participates in the uncanny
after-work generated by the archive of ancient culture.

To put this in a provocative form, the question would be whether psychoanalysis is the return of repressed antiquity, distorted to be sure by
modern desire, yet still bearing the telltale traces of the ancient archive.
If in some sense this is the case, then would not our growing distance from
the archive of antiquity (a fact of mass education, at least in the United
States) also imply that we are in the process of losing our grip on psychoanalysis itself, as Freud conceived it? Jacques Lacan once said that
"the Oedipus complex cannot run indefinitely in forms of society that are
more and more *losing the sense of tragedy*" ([1966] 1977, 310; my emphasis). This suggests that at least some of the classic ruptures of modernism
are deeply implicated in their dialogue with antiquity, that the ancient
past came to have a particular deployment—its great moment of modernity one could say—that it has since lost in the age of Prozac.[9] We are
thus losing our grip on both our ancients and our moderns, our "classic
moderns" who unmasked for us the *ancien régime* of consciousness and
limpid rationality by summoning Oedipus and Dionysus from the Tartarus of European memory.

This third line of inquiry was also a part of the research for this book,
and though it too had to be mostly deferred for reasons of economy, it
will still make itself known here on important occasions. But I wish to
stress that in some ways it represents the most important avenue for interdisciplinary contact between psychoanalysis and the study of ancient

cultures, since it provides a significant challenge to *both* fields. In this regard, Jan Assmann's *Moses the Egyptian* (1997) remains an exemplary achievement, since it situates Freud's Egyptian Moses within a history of European discourse on Egypt, while at the same time it makes use of a psychoanalytically informed view of traumatic memory to draw a real link between Moses and the heretic pharaoh Akhenaten, though it is not Freud's link.[10] The value of this ongoing project of confrontation is worth stressing here, for it shows how it is not enough to dismiss Freud for misreading, as most classicists feel he does, the ancient archive. Freud's method of reading has a greater resiliency and relevance than is allowed by the standard critiques of him offered by disciplinary police-men. At the same time, it shows those coming from the psychoanalytic perspective that the rich resonance between Freud and the ancient archive is not proof that he is inevitably right in his theories of Western civilization. For we are often seeing a common ideology at work more than a timeless truth, as Assmann shows by placing Freud's Egyptian Moses within a tradition of thinking that reveals Freud to be uncannily in tune with a long line of predecessors, most of whom he had not read.

From the outset, then, I wish to locate my inquiry into Freud's rela-tions with the ancient world as a fragment of a greater whole, and one undertaken in the spirit of immanent critique that has animated many of the more robust readings of Freud over the past fifty years.[11] I am not consciously attempting a vindication of either Freudian theory or some true vision of the ancient world. Like most people, I read Freud critically, and I am both intrigued and horrified by the peculiar social dynamic of the early psychoanalytic movement, in which a new language of psycho-logical insight became quite often a blunt weapon in struggles for power and priority. At the same time, my need to explicate Freud's compulsion for antiquity obviously shows the trace elements of transference which one might expect in any sustained treatment of a controversial figure, a "great man of history." At times I seem eager to expose his game, at oth-ers I praise his uncanny genius, but I take this ambivalence to be part of the territory. Any immanent critique of Freud must by definition use the tools he forged or at least popularized (such as the concept of ambiva-lence) in order to pick away at the edifice of his work. Yet, the ironies thus produced are hopefully neither shallow nor cheap. Indeed, the whole work of analysis could be described as one long education in self-irony, so this project could even lay some claim to continuing the analytic en-terprise through the detection of its *historical* ironies.

If such an operation inevitably stinks of intellectual patricide, we can at least assert that to kill Freud as the Father is to free him to return to the position of being the father, the historical individual who founded this discourse with all its blindness and insight, and not the impossible colossus he often balloons into under the storm and stress of cultural debate.[12] Like it or not, Freud has become a figure of memory, not just a figure of history, and in this way he has achieved the status (if not the stature) of other world-historical Jews, like Jesus, Moses, and Marx. As we move farther and farther away from the twentieth century, the kind of Freud we will have to live with will depend on the quality of our own memory work as Post-Freudians. In the last three decades of Freud studies, it seems that we have often had to choose between the extremes of either Freud the Fraud or Freud the Secular Tsaddik; we have seen vociferous debates on the Freudian legacy that take an almost ritualized form of profound ambivalence.[13] In fact, as a figure of memory, Freud appears like the Year Daemon of the Cambridge Ritualists: when he is "Victorian," patriarchal, sexist, naively "scientistic" if not openly dishonest, we kill him off with righteous indignation, only to welcome him again as "modern" (or even proto-postmodern), polymorphously perverse, bisexually aware, anti-homophobic, brutally honest, and wickedly suspicious of authority. I think we can safely predict that this dual quality of overlord and underdog will keep his ghost abroad in academia for some time to come, particularly given the Freudian archive's cross-fertilization of sexuality and textuality. What more could an academic want by way of a theme?

This book is divided into three parts. The first and longest introduces Freud's compulsion for antiquity and illustrates it in terms of a series of case studies. The second part focuses on the relationship between Freud's psychoanalytic memory work and its contemporary discourses of history and then traces the institutional implications of part 1. The final part is a concluding chapter that discusses Freud's emergent master narrative of human history as it relates to the ancient world.

As to citations, all references to Freud's work are to James Strachey's *Standard Edition*. A much chided translation, it is still indispensable for being the only *critical* edition of Freud's complete works, and I shall have cause to underscore how some later additions to his texts tell a story of their own.[14] For the German texts, I have consulted both the *Gesammelte Werke* and the *Studienausgabe*, the latter incorporating insights from the *Standard Edition*. For reasons of economy, citations from Freud's voluminous correspondence are made with reference to the editor's name. Unless otherwise credited, all translations are my own.

PART I

Collision and Collusion
in the Archives

On the one hand, no one has illuminated better than Freud what we have called the archontic principle of the archive, which in itself presupposes not the originary *arkhê* but the nomological *arkhê* of the law, of institution, of domiciliation, of filiation. No one has analyzed, that is also to say, deconstructed, the authority of the archontic principle better than he. No one has shown how this archontic, that is, paternal and patriarchic, principle only posited itself to repeat itself and returned to re-posit itself only in parricide. It amounts to repressed or suppressed parricide, in the name of the father as dead father. The archontic is at best the takeover of the archive by the brothers. The equality and the liberty of brothers. A certain, still vivacious idea of democracy.

But on the other hand, in life as in his works, in his theoretical theses as in the compulsion of his institutionalizing strategy, Freud repeated the patriarchal logic. He declared, notably in *The Rat Man*, that the patriarchal right (*Vatterrecht*) marked the civilizing progress of reason. He even added to it in a patriarchic higher bid, even where all his inheritors, the psychoanalysts of all countries, have united themselves as a single man to follow him and to raise the stakes. To the point that certain people can wonder if, decades after his death, his sons, so many brothers, can yet speak in their own name. Or if his daughter ever came to life (*zôê*), was ever anything other than a phantasm or a specter, a Gradiva *rediviva*, a Gradiva-Zoe-Bertgang passing through at Berggasse 19.

—JACQUES DERRIDA, *Archive Fever*

CHAPTER 1

◾

Compulsive Situations

> Someday a clever psychologist will recount the history of this most di-
> sastrous illusion; he will recount the history of what we have always
> revered as "ancient" [*antik*] since the days of the Gothic style. There are
> few tasks which would be more instructive for an intimate understand-
> ing of the Western soul, from Kaiser Otto III (the first victim of the
> South), to Nietzsche (the last).
>
> —Spengler, *The Decline of the West*

Freud's compulsion for antiquity ties together for us his cognitive style
and personality with the unfolding narrative of psychoanalysis as a new
therapeutic regime and a scientific discourse. I am less interested in finding the ultimate psychological mechanism behind this compulsion than
in plotting its effects within Freud's life and works. I make no surprising
revelations about his personal life, nor do I trace this compulsion to a primal trauma, such as his relocation from the rural Moravian town he was
born in to the bustle and squalor of Vienna where he grew up.[1] Although
I resist such *ad hominem* explanations in their most reductive forms, I still
leave considerable room for the personal and the biographical, because
the reduction of Freud's compulsion to a mere effect of discourse would
also be unsatisfactory. Freud's commitment to and involvement with the
ancient world is, as Freud would say, overdetermined; it is the precipitate
of numerous psychological and discursive compromises.

   In this chapter I situate Freud's compulsion within its general European context. Then in chapter 2 I anatomize the compulsion in a way that
will be further unpacked and illustrated throughout the rest of the book.
Situating Freud's compulsion entails a basic recognition that a powerful

interest in the ancient world is hardly an inexplicable anomaly for a classically educated intellectual steeped in the currents of nineteenth-century materialism and deterministic explanation. Nonetheless, there is a great deal in the peculiar blend of Freud's compulsion that cannot be seen as typical of anything but psychoanalysis. Explanations based on milieu and education can only take us so far, and we must understand how thoroughly Freud reshuffles and transforms inherited ways of thinking.

From our post-Freudian perspective, it is obviously difficult to examine Freud without using the very tools he gave us, so I will now take as a model throughout this chapter someone with a compulsion for antiquity whom Freud himself came to analyze. In his 1907 analysis of the archaeologist Norbert Hanold from Wilhelm Jensen's novella *Gradiva*, Freud was able to sleuth the ruses of repressed desire in Hanold's fascination with a figure of antiquity, the gracefully stepping girl depicted in a bas-relief whom he names "Gradiva." Norbert's compulsive interest in this figure leads him to imagine that she was a girl of Greek descent who perished in the ashes of Pompeii, and he impulsively decides to go there, only to encounter his lost love from childhood, Zoe Bertgang. Though the mysterious attraction of the figure seems to dissolve into the reality of Zoe, I take heart from the fact that Freud *does not* in the end dispel Norbert's profession of archaeologist as being itself a delusion or mere substitute satisfaction along the same lines.

In analyzing Hanold's first dream, Freud finds the desire to be an eye-witness of the catastrophe in Pompeii "understandable in any archaeologist"; but this is coupled with the repressed desire to lie with the woman he loved, which points to the problematic nature of Norbert's repression of his sexuality in the interests of serious study (*Delusions and Dreams in Jensen's* Gradiva, SE 9:93). Norbert's compulsive interest in Pompeii is thus intensified *in part* by his erotic urges, but not explained away by their revelation. For there are two orders of desire that operate in him: the will to history that takes the path of sublimation through research, and the repressed desire for Zoe Bertgang, a desire that ultimately needs to be consciously addressed if he is to keep his grip on reality. His scholarly interests are not just a pretext for his erotic motives; as Freud says, "the unconscious determinants could not effect anything that did not simultaneously satisfy the conscious, scientific ones" (SE 9:52). Thus Norbert's compulsion is a compromise between science and the erotic, forming an erotic science we might say, whose fantasy-formation is all the richer for serving two masters, though this leads to a pathological extreme. Luckily the hero of this tale is able to rediscover his lost love on the site of Pompeii, and she acts in turn as both analyst and love-object, freeing him from the delusional force of his repressed desire and returning his love. This *eros ex machina* allows Jensen to tie up his archaeological romance with a conventional happy ending, but it also allows Freud to insert psychoanalysis as symbolically present in the plot (SE 9:87–90). However, Norbert remains the archaeologist he was before: "we shall take our wedding trip to Italy and Pompeii," he exclaims at the end (Jensen [1903] 1956, 234).

As Freud would later do in his analysis of Leonardo da Vinci (1910), he sexualizes Norbert's "drive for research" (*Forschertrieb*) without using this as the means to invalidate the very idea of research; for such activity in its ideal constitution forms the small sphere of free sublimation that qualitatively differentiates the quest for knowledge from both the neurotic inhibitions of religion and the brooding, unfree ruminations of "neurotic compulsive thinking" (*Leonardo da Vinci and a Memory of His Childhood*, SE 11:80).[2] While the "drive for research" is to be considered neither as belonging to the elementary instinctual components nor as exclusively sexual, it is first awakened in children by sexual problems and gets its first real deployment there, as Freud argued two years before in *Three Essays on the Theory of Sexuality* (1905, SE 7:194–195). "Its activity corresponds on the one hand to a sublimated manner of obtaining mastery, while on the other hand it makes use of the energy of scopophilia" (SE 7:194). Thus the will to know is clearly linked to a sublimated will to power, and is tied in its most elementary stage to the pleasures of the gaze and the mysteries of sex.

The moral of the story of Norbert Hanold is that the drive for historical knowledge may be powerful or even compulsive, but it is not in itself pathological. It combines the compulsive force of drive or instinct on the one hand and the ideal of sublimated mastery on the other, an *askesis* for which one must be psychologically prepared.[3] But part of that psychological preparation is to develop the awareness that in the archive of antiquity one confronts the very sexuality that the sublimating drive for professional advancement and "objective knowledge" seeks to repress or co-opt, which is itself a return to the sexual interest that activates the will to know in childhood. This is made poignantly clear in the very first paragraph of Jensen's story by the intense aesthetic pleasure his protagonist derives from a sculpted female figure that he "possesses" in a plaster copy in his study (like the one Jensen owned and the one Freud later acquired), and that unconsciously returns him to his childhood sexual object. Norbert would seem to be the ideal disinterested observer of artifacts, as he is both economically independent and—so it seems—emotionally self-sufficient. And yet the sensuous immediacy of an ancient bas-relief returns him to a world of human nature he had disciplined himself to ignore. As Freud put it, the story deals with a young archaeologist "who had surrendered his interest in life in exchange for an interest in the remains of classical antiquity, and who was now brought back to real life by a roundabout path which was strange but perfectly logical" (SE 9:10).

Let us take a moment to consider the "logic" of Norbert's return to "real life" from a broader perspective, for in a way it reads like an allegory of cultural reception. Jensen's novella is just one example of a long tradition of European confrontations with the ancient archive in which a modern regime of repressive self-mastery is confounded by the "natural" excellence and hedonic provocation suggested by artifacts and ancient texts. Given the historical tenor of Christian sexual mores and the Jewish abhorrence of idolatry, the traces of alternative sexualities that persist in the ancient archive create a situation whereby the study of ancient culture brings on a veritable "return of the repressed." The repressed which returns is not just a matter of sexual interests and indulgences, but also the compulsive fascination with the sensuous image itself and the insistent immediacy of its hedonic properties. Consider the words of an English monk encountering a marble Venus (perhaps the Capitoline Venus) around 1200 in Rome: "The image is made from Parian marble with such wonderful and intricate skill, that she seems more like a living creature than a statue; indeed she seems to blush in her nakedness, a reddish tinge coloring her face, and it appears to those who take a close look that blood flows in her snowy complexion. Because of this wonderful image, and perhaps because of some magic spell that I am unaware of, I was drawn back three times to look at it despite the fact that it was two *stadia* from my inn" (cited in Barkan 1999, 46).

The ancient tradition of figural art, in particular, constantly provokes a reconsideration of the body and its pleasures from an historically Archimedean point, a point that promises a unified view of human nature seemingly detached from the arbitrary, time-bound prohibitions of culture. Whether the modern repressive regime is real or imaginary is not the issue, nor do we have to settle the question of whether the ancients were truly "better at sex" or more in tune with human nature in some sense than we moderns.[4] The point is that the detour through antiquity *historically* has authorized an alternative view of human nature and human sexuality that provided a convenient point from which to interrogate the Judeo-Christian tradition and its bodily regimes. This view grew significantly in importance with the elaboration of an autonomous characterization of the aesthetic realm, which allowed for the discursive containment of the hedonic mischief inherent in the ancient archive, as well as the ideological transformation of objects of cult into objects of art (cf. the "fig leaf" phenomenon).[5] To situate Freud historically will therefore require us to acknowledge this positioning of the ancient archive within the hedonic contours of modern Western thought. Freud is after all one of our greatest theorists of the pleasure principle, and with Jensen's story he is attempting his first major incursion into the aesthetic realm armed with psychoanalytic knowledge. So his choice of Jensen's text represents an elective alignment with a particular trajectory of European thought we must consider at this point.

The aestheticization of ancient culture in the eighteenth and nineteenth centuries effectively helped to bypass the historical antipathy between pagan and Christian (an antipathy still alive in the very term "pagan," which marginalizes polytheism to the peripheral *pagi*, the outlying rural districts), and instead created the discursive means to uphold the sensuous immediacy and naked human truth embodied in the material and textual remains of antiquity. When Hegel says, for example, "In Greek Beauty the Sensuous is only a sign, an expression, an envelope, in which Spirit [*Geist*] manifests itself," he tucks the sensuous safely back in line with the rational, while still allowing the sensuous to *signify* in relation to a universal history ([1899] 1956, 239). In fact, though histories of Western thought ground European rationalism in the Greek Logos, we can also say that the enduring importance of the Greek tradition has equally been to return significance to *aesthesis*, to the sensuous and the hedonic via Greece's role as an aesthetic ideal. Thus Hegel's historical reinvention of the Greek Spirit as that which transforms the natural into the spiritual (*das Geistliche*) tacitly authorizes the modern Spirit to regress along the same path; that is, to reacquaint itself with the "natural" and desublimate itself by means of a return to the cultural emanations of the Greeks, emanations that stood in a proper balance between nature and intellect ([1899] 1956, 239). The study of antiquity thus provides a kind of productive self-alienation for the modern mind. "This world [of classical antiquity]," Hegel wrote in 1809, "separates us from ourselves, but at the same time it grants us the cardinal means of returning to ourselves: we reconcile ourselves with it and thereby find ourselves again in it, but the self which we then find is the one which accords with the tone and universal essence of mind" (cited in Rudnytsky 1987, 153).

In their sensuous-rational balance, the "Greeks" come to form a historical buffer from the grotesqueries of "the Orient" and the ascetic excesses of the Middle Ages, and remembering the Greeks becomes a means of recentering one's view of history and humanity. In a phrase that is pregnant with historical significance for the emergent culture of bourgeois Europe, Hegel defines the Greek character as *Individuality conditioned by Beauty*, an ideal of free agency and hedonic self-possession ([1899] 1956, 238).[6] And in a phrase by Wilhelm von Humboldt, architect of Prussia's highly influential educational reforms ([1793] 1968, 275), the Greek character is representative of "the original character of humankind overall." This is a phrase that stands behind the entire ideology of the German *Gymnasium*, which schooled Freud along with most German and Austrian intellectuals. In more ways than one, then, the ancient archive enables us to glimpse naked human nature, and this from a good century before the advent of Freud's oedipal truths.

The combination of "flesh and the ideal," or the coupling of an aesthetic pleasure principle to a universalizing view of human nature present in the ancient archive, is a feature of European thought that begins most markedly with Johann Joachim Winckelmann's works on Greek culture in the eighteenth century. His *History of the Art of Antiquity* (1764) and *Thoughts On the Imitation of Greek Works in Painting and Sculpture* (1755) were foundational for the development of both art history and archaeology as academic disciplines, and he himself remained a figure of great interest throughout the nineteenth century (Potts 1994; Ferris 2000, chapter 1). Winckelmann's view of ancient Greece might be termed the vision of a gaze; that is, a qualitative characterization of the Greek gaze as constituting the authority of Greek art, which first represented the true essence of beauty.[7] Blessed with a temperate climate, a sound nervous constitution, the opportunity to view plenty of naked youth, and political freedom of expression, the Greeks consequently produced an art that fully reflects the ideal of *Schönheit* that is forever worthy of imitation. The combination of pleasure, freedom, and authority in this vision allowed for classical *Bildung*, in the wake of Winckelmann, to become itself a locus of freedom and aesthetic consciousness within the European imaginary, and yielded a wide variety of not just imitations of the antique, but also *sexual* personae, from the roguish heterosexual of Goethe's *Roman Elegies*, to the Olympian dominatrix of Sacher-Masoch's *Venus in Furs*, the enlightened homosexual apologist of André Gide's *Corydon*, and, of course, Norbert Hanold, the archaeologist and foot-fetishist redeemed from his repression through the bas-relief (no pun intended) that returns him to his childhood love.

However, what the ancient archive affords is not a simple aesthetic ideology but rather a *synaesthesis*, a complex synthetic understanding wherein many features of sense and inference, of experience and discourse come into play.[8] To return to our model: as Norbert wanders through Pompeii, images from his various museum visits and scraps of myth and ancient poetry run through his head, "Thus, under the glowing sun of the Campagna, there was a mythological-literary-historical-archaeological juggling in his head" (Jensen [1903] 1956, 183). "Antiquity" thus represents a nexus of discursive and physical relations, not a monolithic object nor even a single discursive realm. It is a "juggling" of found objects caught up in various webs of interaction (tourism, aristocratic and later nationalistic collecting, bourgeois economies of reproduction and distribution) and of texts construed through various social and professional networks (schooling of the classical canon, contemporary novels, plays, scholarly monographs, and even pornography).

This synaesthetic understanding moves not only between the domains of the visual and the verbal, or the tactile and the visual, but also between the temporal domains of the living and the dead, the ancient and the modern, as is suggested by the imaginative force that works within Norbert Hanold with such compulsion. The charming enigma of Gradiva's angled foot sends him out into the world of the living to observe what he can of ladies' feet, casting him for the first time into the problematic interchanges of seduction and rebuff, but also leading him to understand the uniqueness of the sculpture's gait through his "pedestrian investigations." As Goethe wrote in the *Roman Elegies*, being open to erotic experience on classical soil infuses antiquity with new understanding, instead of distracting one from it:

> Und belehr' ich mich nicht, indem ich des lieblichen Busens
> Formen spähe, die Hand leite die Hüften hinab?
> Dann versteh' ich den Marmor erst recht; ich denk' und vergleiche,
> Sehe mit fühlendem Aug', fühle mit sehender Hand.
> (5.7–10)

> [And am I not studying while I observe the shape
> of lovely breasts, and as my hand slides down her hips?
> Only then do I understand the marble correctly; I ponder and compare,
> See with a feeling eye, feel with a seeing hand.]

It would be a mistake to assume that this "carnal knowledge" of the ancient archive is meant as mere irony, as a joke that invalidates historical understanding. For if consciousness is a feature of embodied subjects, *bodily egos* as Freud calls them, then sexuality is a genuine mode of understanding, even of historical understanding, due to its receptivity to the traces of human desire in the cultural archive.[9] It is only by forcing this issue with the European bourgeois that one avoids the *truly* embarrassing irony of a Norbert Hanold, who remains so disassociated from the specificity of his own desire that he falls out of time.

The synaesthesis that the ancient archive affords must be indexed to its material insistence; i.e., the archive's open appeal to the senses which implicates it in bodily experience, and its availability to the gaze as objects of observation and knowledge. And yet, we must take adequate account of how deeply historicized this synaesthesis is, and how this conditioned its manifestations already in Winckelmann's *History of The Art of Antiquity* (1764). For the twin forces that uphold the ancient archive are the gaze and *narration* (or in the case of *Gradiva*, the narration of a gaze).[10] The Greek ideal offered at once both the naïve immediacy of nature—readily available to the imagination through its figural art—and the narrative nexus of history, *historía* itself conveniently being a product of Greek inquiry in the fifth century BCE. It offered the self-evident revelation of human nature at the same time that it represented a *process*, an achievement, the "Greek miracle" that forever differentiated Western civilization from Egypt and the Near East in the standard narratives of the time. This Greek ideal was especially important to secular culture, which with the decline of Christian views of history lacked a centering narrative that differentiated Western Christendom from its Others. Thus the great discursive gambit effected by the modern European elaboration of the ancient archive was to tie empirical nature to a narrative of culture that took Greece as its *arkhê*, its origin and ruling principle, and metaphorized it as its own precocious childhood—a metaphor Freud himself would be unable to avoid.

One could say, then, that Greece became the center of a "family romance" in European intellectual life, a means of uniting the emergent secular cultures by providing a narrative frame for these cultures' departures (from the Orient, from Nature, from the Middle Ages) and returns (to Nature, to aesthetic pleasure, to heroic nationalism). "Among the Greeks," as Hegel said, "we feel ourselves immediately at home, for we are in the region of Spirit" ([1899] 1956, 223). This statement effectively discloses the domestic ideology of the West, which adopts Greek antiquity and "remembers it" as its own youth in order to feel present to itself in historical time—even when the modern subjects in question are the descendants of Germanic barbarians or Jews—and institutionalizes the recapitulation of Greek and Roman culture (albeit in a very limited form) for its own children in the *Gymnasium*, *lycée*, and the British Public School. The modern European *Geist* thus both colonizes ancient Greece and is colonized by it, creating a "region of Spirit" in which it is "at home."[11]

However, the ancient archive fascinates and entices not just because of its moments of presence, like the charming insistence of Gradiva's gait caught forever in stone, but also because of its absences, its fragmentation and temporal *dis*-location, its quality of being otherwise and otherwhere, and therefore unavailable as a totality. As Freud knew very well, history's many gaps and lacunae are what invite us to supplement, to reconstruct—in sum, to engage our historical fantasy the way Norbert readily envisions a whole family background and social context for his mysterious ancient maiden.[12] Thus part of what feeds the compulsive interest in the past through this synaesthetic understanding is the very need for synthesis and constant reorganization, for *narrative renewal*. For while the gaze feeds on insistent objects, narrative thrives on persistent absences.

The most obvious instance of this relationship between narrative and visual enterprises in Freud's case is his essay on the Moses of Michelangelo, where he solves a visual enigma in the statue's posture by means of telling the story leading up to the point represented in the work ("The Moses of Michelangelo," SE 13:211–238). But Freud's own historical moment further intensified the narrative drive to reorganize the past, because it was a moment when nature itself had become thoroughly historicized through the doctrine of evolution. For this reason, then, the particular shape that Freud's own compulsion for antiquity takes is strongly manifested in his transformation of narrative forms, something we shall take as a point of departure for part 2. His compulsion will take him from the narratives of Greek, Roman, and Egyptian antiquity further back to Darwinian scenarios of the early human family, where human culture first emerges from the world of animal instinct, and even further still to the first emergence of organic life. Part of his claim for the unique necessity of psychoanalytic knowledge is its very ability to straddle the disparate domains of natural and cultural history.

Thus Freud stands before an ancient archive that has already been prearranged as a narrative nexus and a locus of sensuous experience that beckons for acts of synaesthesis, reconstruction, and renewal. Like

Gradiva's gait, the archive is both self-evident and enigmatic, expressive and yet concealing, triggering a cognitive urge to complete the story, to piece together causes and effects, and to supplement the fragmentary. It seems only fitting that we should place Freud himself in a situation analogous to Norbert's first journey to the Italian museums. Consider Freud's ruminations in Italy as he ponders in 1898 the Roman finds on display in Aquileia, among which are, he reports:

> Several priapic statues: a Venus indignantly turning away from her newborn child after having been shown his penis; Priapus as an old man, whose genitals are being covered by a silenus and who henceforth can give himself over to drink; a priapic stone ornament of the penis as a winged animal, which has a small penis in the natural place, while the wings themselves end in a penis. Priapus stood for permanent erection, a wish fulfillment representing the opposite of psychological impotence. (Masson 1985, 308)

Here we see Freud, *Wissenschaftler* and bourgeois tourist, confronted with protruding facts which seem obscenely obvious and yet enigmatic in their obviousness: for what does a winged penis mean exactly?[13] The scandal of the phallic artifact's unambiguous natural *reference* is what calls for an answer as to its *significance*—why refer to the penis symbolically at all, unless some hidden agenda of desire is being served?[14] Freud's approach to the ancient archive presupposes a process of development that makes an encounter with ancient sexuality *historically* significant and not simply titillating, since the stylizations of desire and the forms of repression vary in their intensity over time. Freud sees the apparent scandal as an opportunity for understanding human nature, and works to decode, like others before him, what must be "a very natural symbol of a very natural and philosophical system of religion, if considered according to its original use and intention" ([1786] 1894, 15).[15] Freud's interpretation converts the literal phallic self-reference of the priapic object into an expression of wish fulfillment, in league with his own burgeoning understanding of the mind's "endopsychic myths" (Masson 1985, 286). In this way, he makes himself at home among the *disjecta membra* before him.[16] In this synaesthetic moment in the museum, we witness the elaboration of a historical consciousness that works from both sense and inference toward an embodied truth situated between the individual lifespan in all of its empirical immediacy (i.e., his scrupulous museum observations recorded for his fellow scientist Wilhelm Fliess, his experience as a doctor with disorders of desire, his own sexual experience) and the species' lifespan in its awesome, primitive depths and civilized heights.

To sum up so far, long before Freud, the ancient archive was a space of synaesthetic interaction in modern European thought, a realm of imaginary freedom and eros tied to highly valued norms of culture— which continues to fascinate even the post-modern mind, to judge from the amount of work on ancient sexuality produced in the wake of Michel Foucault.[17] For Freud as for many thinkers in the nineteenth century, historical consciousness is itself an expression of freedom, even when it bears an admixture of other determinants and ought not to be exaggerated into a basis for radical free will (see chapter 10). The exposure of unconscious motives in one's fascination with the ancient archive does not lead to a dismissal of this fascination as mere *projection*; for Freud, it rather establishes a genuine psychological *connection*, the discovery of a common unconscious ground that expands the import of research, intensifies its power, and validates its outcomes.

The crucial proviso in this Freudian agenda, however, is that the unconscious connection be made *through the intervention of psychoanalysis*, which, like Zoe's intervention, will guarantee a return to reality instead of the further elaboration of projected fantasies. This empowerment of the subjective and the psychological remains Freud's radical challenge to the field of history—and, it must be said, the basis of history's resistance to Freud. At the same time, it also reveals the pathos of Freud's desire to seek legitimation through constant appeals to the historical *Wissenschaften*, which can only legitimate his own operations if he is first allowed to transform their disciplinary procedures—a matter we shall explore throughout part 2 below. But this also implies that my own investigation must address Freud's challenge by dropping *neither* the personal contingencies of desire to which he is so attuned *nor* the general configurations of discourse—of "science," of the historical *Wissenschaften* — in which he operates, lest I lose track of what makes the Freud scenario itself so compelling. In this sense, any study of Freud remains an exercise in emulation and needs to work the same dimensions of canvas.

My point here in relation to *Gradiva* is that we are not empowered even by Freud himself to reduce a compulsive interest in the past to a *simple* unconscious plot in the present, even when we suspect this is the real direction of his approach, given the apparent dissolution of Gradiva into Zoe Bertgang. In the paradigmatic instance of Norbert Hanold, Freud shows himself to be quite capable of conceiving of a strong will to history that is not itself a delusional activity, even when his main thesis is to expose the "dreams and delusions" that trouble his subject. For there is a remainder of interest, a desire to know the past that never dissolves itself completely into unconscious motives, and which compels us to move beyond history-as-substitute-satisfaction into history as a process of genuine consciousness, as a form of memory work that might even require us to labor *against* the pleasure principle and delve into the Faustian abysses of cultural and/or personal trauma. Norbert Hanold's delusional situation, after all, can be read as a failure of historical consciousness, not an indictment of it. It is a failure to address the radical specificity of his *own* history, the traces of his own desire which lead him to Pompeii as if in pursuit of an ancient quarry. The expansion of his will to history to include his own past is precisely the cure effected by Zoe, who plays along with his delusion in order to lead him from ancient Rome back to contemporary Germany, by way of their bodily presence on the site of Pompeii. This interaction reorients him as an embodied, desiring subject whose research interests remain intact though transformed, and whose foot fetish now finds fulfillment in a consensual relationship.[18]

As if to illustrate the historical remainder, Freud's last word on *Gradiva* in his 1912 postscript is simply a dry scholarly clarification that the relief is in the Museo Chiaramonti, that it is from the "zenith of Greek art" and is therefore not Roman as Jensen says (though Gradiva is thus Greek, as Norbert intuited), and that it is a fragment that belongs with others in Florence and Munich. These fragments altogether represent three figures of the Horai, "the goddesses of vegetation, and the deities of the fertilizing dew who are allied to them" (SE 9:95). Very subtly, the sexual theme of growth and fertilization remains entwined around this historical "information," but the sexuality arises from the ancient archive itself and not the troubled mind of Norbert Hanold. It is a "fact" inherent in the archive, waiting to be construed in the next synaesthesis.[19] And in the event, Freud construed it the following year in "The Theme of the Three Caskets" (1913; SE 12: 297–298), by which time the Horai merged with the Moirai (Fates) and the Great Mother, and the search once again was for the *femme fatale*, the Gradiva *rediviva*.

Complications

Norbert's example is not only a convenient model for how we might view Freud's compulsion for antiquity as part of a longer history of confrontations with the ancient archive. It was the model *Freud* chose for his first extended essay on a literary work from the psychoanalytic point of view. This concerns the *double* narrative I am explicating—the narrative recounting the European investment in antiquity coupled to that of Freud's unfolding psychoanalytic enterprise. Freud's essay is very much such a double-jointed text[20] and recapitulates Jensen's story in considerable detail, while it also situates psychoanalysis in relation to the creative arts and science at large. The compulsive richness of Freud's own fantasy can be seen in how he adopts this second-rate archaeological novella as the ground on which to stake out his claims for a new scientific view of dreams and fantasies.[21] Freud effectively makes of Jensen's narrative a kind of motet by spinning out a psychoanalytic counterpoint to the story of Norbert and Zoe, retelling the story of a troubled young archaeologist's quest for happiness at the same time he pleads his own case for a psychological hermeneutics that stands in opposition to "strict science" (SE 9:7).

On one level of his interpretation, he takes the classic psychoanalytic approach of delving into Norbert's childhood in order to show how his dreams and delusions "were not capricious products of his imagination, but determined, without his knowing it, by the store of childhood impressions which he had forgotten, but which were still at work in him" (SE 9:31). Thus inevitably archaeology itself, which was both the cause and the means of escaping his erotic feelings, suggested the return of the repressed passion for Zoe in the figure of an antique sculpture. But on another level, Freud is demonstrating that a new science has arisen which vindicates ancient, superstitious beliefs in the meaning of dreams, a science that takes as its ally the creative writers whose knowledge of the mind is "far in advance of us everyday people, for they draw upon sources which we have not yet opened up for science" (SE 9:8). So this essay is itself a first serious breaking of the ground for his extended application of psychoanalysis to the creative arts and culture at large, a move that promises to open a vast archive of human truths for the first time to an articulate scientific understanding.

The choice of a Pompeiian fantasy for this ground-breaking is hardly fortuitous, since, as Freud himself remarks, "There is, in fact, no better analogy for repression, by which something in the mind is at once made inaccessible and preserved, than burial of the sort to which Pompeii fell a victim and from which it could emerge once more through the work of spades" (SE 9:40).[22] Freud praises Jensen for thus choosing Pompeii as the setting for Norbert's personal archaeology, since it puts together in picturesque fashion a particular mental process in the individual and a unique event from the history of mankind. But he is most grateful for the powerful analogy that this combination suggests, one that serves to kick the theory of repression into a higher register of operation, well beyond Norbert's fictitious personal problems (SE 9:40). This register is, as he would describe it the following year, "wherever archaic modes of thought have predominated or persist—in the ancient civilizations, in myths, fairy tales and superstitions, in unconscious thinking, in dreams and in neuroses" ("Character and Anal Eroticism," SE 9:174). In other words, Freud's motet subtly orchestrates the link between individual and cultural analysis in a way that puts his own work in a paramount position, far in advance of "strict science," which "does not as yet suspect the importance of repression," and yet on firmer empirical ground than the intuitive creative genius, who cannot explicate his uncanny truths within the armature of proper *Wissenschaft* (SE 9:53–54).

When Freud thus adopts Jensen as an ally in 1907, it is because he himself needs allies, not the other way around; yet rhetorically he brilliantly twists the situation to make it seem as though he is coming to Jensen's aid: "Does our author stand alone, then, in the face of united science? No, that is not the case (if, that is, I may count my own works as part of science), since for a number of years—and, until recently more or less alone—I myself have supported all the views that I have here extracted from Jensen's *Gradiva* and stated in technical terms" (SE 9:53). It is here that the archaeological romance of Jensen gives way to the *empirical romance* of Freud, the lonely researcher who has labored long and made findings about the human soul which he discovers to his surprise are confirmed in imaginative writings (SE 9:54). The literary writer and the scientist have worked by different methods, but "the agreement of our results seems to guarantee that we have both worked correctly" (SE 9:92). Jensen's archaeological romance was written by the author's attending directly to his own unconscious, discovering the laws of that realm he cannot explicate but that he can mimic in his creations. Freud, on the other hand, works by "conscious observation of abnormal mental processes in other people so as to be able to elicit and announce their laws" (SE 9: 92). So from this motet emerge two figures of authority: the author Jensen, unconscious manipulator and maker of psychologically valid fantasies, and the author Freud, lawgiver of the unconscious who works in the light of *Wissenschaft* and empirical observation, though his workstation is far ahead of "strict science," out on the remote frontiers of research.[23]

Hence when I invoke the phrase "Freud's compulsion for antiquity" I allude to his continued attraction to the complex topography I have just outlined: the conventional view of antiquity ensconced as a cultural and aesthetic assemblage (like the sculptured figure of Gradiva, a copy of which hung above Freud's analytic couch); the serious professional study of antiquity with its ascetic ideals of faithful reconstruction and objective understanding (as we see in Norbert's unquestioned legitimacy as a *Forscher*, or Freud's "final word" in the post-script); and more broadly, the archive of antiquity which psychoanalysis promises to unlock as if for the first time for true psychological understanding, and with which psychoanalysis stands in a strange form of solidarity. When Freud declares himself a "partisan of antiquity and superstition," he does so because the archive of antiquity resonates with his own psychological project far better than "strict science" which, as he claims, ridicules the idea that dreams have meaning (SE 9:7). If his compulsion for antiquity is vindictive, this is because he sees that the ancient archive vindicates and confirms his theories where modern science does not, because of the latter's own negligence and arrogance. Thus at the heart of Freud's ultra-modernist enterprise of unmasking the *Scheinwelt* of consciousness lies an anti-modernity that remains one of Freud's most alluring contradictions. By constantly gesturing toward the archive of antiquity while, at the same time, brokering his scientific advances, he presents us with an agenda whose motto seems to be: *Forward into the Past!*

Habitus and Discursive Incontinence

Just as Freud does not reduce Norbert Hanold's devotion to archaeology to a mere displacement of his erotic interests, I do not wish to whittle Freud's lifelong engagement with the ancient world down to a reductive biographical plot, even though it might make a more interesting story to do so. I prefer to outline the compulsion overall as a nexus of effects emanating from what the sociologist Pierre Bourdieu calls *habitus*, or the socialized repertoire of actions and reactions that underwrite individual agency without "causing" it in a mechanical sense. These systems of durable, transposable dispositions extend far beyond purposive theorizing into the minutiae of everyday social praxis—here there come to mind Freud's personal rituals surrounding his collection of antiquities; the nexus of gift-giving that quite often involved the exchange of antiquities or books with friends, colleagues and analysands (e.g., it was probably his follower Wilhelm Stekel who suggested Jensen's *Gradiva* to him);[24] his personal taste in prints, illustrations, and reproductions, as well as in reading material for his off-hours; his theater-going; and his travel destinations to classical sites and museums with their own rigors and rituals of on-site performance. Such activities outstrip any obvious professional or theoretical necessity, and reveal an abiding set of preferences and autotelic activities, refuges and fetishes, fantasies and practical strategies that can be seen as a coherent pattern *without* assuming they must have a single conscious aim or single unconscious cause. As Bourdieu says,

> Each agent, wittingly or unwittingly, willy nilly, is a producer and a reproducer of objective meaning. Because his actions and works are the product of a *modus operandi* of which he is not the producer and has no conscious mastery, they contain an "objective intention," as the Scholastics put it, which always outruns his conscious intentions. The schemes of thought and expression he has acquired are the bases for the *intentionless invention* of regulated improvisation. ([1972] 1977, 79)

Thus Freud's compulsive interest in antiquity is part of a complex social network that has a particular time and place, a network he both inhabits and creates through his social and scientific improvisation, his elective affinity with other secular Jewish *Bildungsbürger*, his interactions with mostly bourgeois patients, and even the subtler stylizations of his ambition (his choice of Latin mottos, for example) targeted for a faceless public at large.

My construal of this compulsive interest, then, will attempt to raise it out of the isolation of the anecdotal, the quirky, and the idiosyncratic in order to trace its socio-historical relations and lines of communication, and to ascribe to it an "objective intentionality" that is not to be totalized as a mere symptom, a deeper syndrome, or a single coherent strategy. "Antiquity," as we have seen, is fundamentally an act of ongoing synaesthesis, and it remains for Freud a scene of intersection, a locus where fantasy and historical truth collide, where class interests and individual desire find a curious détente, and where personal memory and the cultural archive confront one another. Since I construe antiquity as a dynamic space of interaction, the concept of *habitus* serves me well with its inclusive breadth and sociological focus. Bourdieu's insistence that *habitus* should be seen as a repertoire out of which social improvisation emerges is especially apt, since there is much improvisation in Freud's life as both a secular Jewish paterfamilias and the founder of a suspicious new science

of the mind. Part of the discreet charm of the bourgeois Freud is his negotiation of radical new ideas from within a framework of a fairly conservative family life and a vestigial old-world respect for hierarchy and
authority. He clearly had what Bourdieu calls "the taste for order," even
when his own sense of order generates a meta-order that stands in a certain tension with his times ([1984] 1988, 49).

My recourse to *habitus* is similar to Sarah Winter's deployment of it in
her excellent study, *Freud and the Institution of Psychoanalytic Knowledge*
(1999), where she invokes it as a means of overcoming the exclusively psychological emplotment that characterizes the psychoanalytic approach to
historical problems. She states that her invocation of *habitus* is itself a theoretical necessity because it represents many of the things Freud's own
project tries to downplay in order to put psychoanalytic knowledge to
the fore:

> To understand the cultural authority and political effects of psy-
> choanalysis historically, it is necessary to interrogate the scientific,
> cultural, and professional rationales of psychoanalysis as a form of
> knowledge that takes shape in response to and also gives direction to
> cultural demands for psychological expertise. The ways in which
> Freud answers and reformulates such demands are grounded in what
> we can cogently call his *habitus*—his familial, educational, social, and
> cultural formation—at the intersection of class, culture, and history.
> I seek to demonstrate that psychoanalysis emerges in crucial ways as
> the product of Freud's particular embodiment and reworking of his-
> tory. In fact, the things that *habitus* designates are precisely those
> social and historical "circumstances" that Freud's project of institu-
> tionalization requires be consistently marginalized in order to assert
> the priority and explanatory power of a psychoanalytic, psychologi-
> cal classification of subjectivity. (Winter 1999, 15)

My project differs from Winter's in that my exclusive concern is with the
archive of antiquity and its discursive relationship with psychoanalysis as
an ongoing improvisation by its founder.

As Winter rightly emphasizes, Freud's schooling in a classical *Gymnasium* obviously played a large role in the creation of this *habitus*, but it is
important not to assume the curriculum in itself explains the phenomenon of Freud's compulsion in the manner of simple cause to effect.[25] The
professional classicist can readily understand from dismal experience how
plenty of *Gymnasium* students went on to forget, quite happily, whatever

they learned about the Greek aorist or the Latin passive periphrastic. What needs explaining is why and how Freud *retained* his fascination with the ancient world after the ordeal of his *Matura* examination in 1873 (which marked his "ripeness" for going on to university study). It is specifically Freud's trajectory as a secular Jew through this curriculum that should interest us, though in this study I shall be unable to enter into it in the full detail it merits. But Freud's compulsion to return to the study of antiquity transcends the mere repetition of a "schoolboy psychology," since it impinges on the adult prerogatives of travel, collecting, museum-going, theater attendance, and most importantly, the formation of his scientific theory and praxis—all of which suggests a shifting set of choices, problems and responses that transcend the primal scene of his *Gymnasium* socialization. As I show throughout the chapters that follow, Freud's compulsion has everything to do with his ongoing need to model his expanding scientific enterprise, to find analogies and evidence that support a theory of the mind which grew out of relatively modest efforts at therapy.

Here it is important to put Freud's scientific improvising in relation to the discursive volatility of his times, since psychoanalysis is only one manifestation of a general explosion of new approaches to antiquity that occurred during his adult life. So great were the changes, in fact, that they have proved too vast to characterize in a synthetic reception study in the way books have been written on the French Baroque, the German *Klassik*, or even the Victorian era.[26] There was such a welter of new information about the ancient world and new forms of interpreting it during this period (1870–1933) that the only clear paradigm seems to be one of a Babelic confusion, a crisis of abundance. T. S. Eliot gave a good description of this confusion in the course of a review of Gilbert Murray's translation of *Medea*, which showed Murray to be "a very insignificant follower of the pre-Raphaelite movement" in spite of the fact that Murray was himself one of the most "modern" classicists around.

As a Hellenist, he is very much of the present day, and a very important figure in the day. This day began, in a sense, with [E. B.] Tylor and a few German anthropologists; since then we have acquired sociology and social psychology, we have watched the clinics of Ribot and Janet, we have read books from Vienna and heard a discourse of Bergson; a philosophy arose at Cambridge; social emancipation crawled abroad; our historical knowledge has of course increased; and we have a curious Freudian-social-mystical-rational-istic-higher-critical interpretation of the Classics and what used to be called the Scriptures. [. . .] A number of sciences have sprung up in an almost tropical exuberance which undoubtedly excited our admiration, and the garden, not unnaturally, has come to resemble a jungle. Such men as Tylor, and Robertson Smith, and Wilhelm Wundt, who early fertilized the soil, would hardly recognize the resulting vegetation; and indeed, poor Wundt's *Völkerpsychologie* was a musty relic before it was translated. ([1920] 1967, 75–76).

Freud's early life experience coincides remarkably well with the dawning of Eliot's bewildering "present day," which was a period of violent and sudden transition from the world of imperial monarchies to one of mass democratic movements.

As a product of the elite *Gymnasium* system, Freud was exposed to the humanistic values of the eighteenth century, the age of Winckelmann, Lessing, Herder, Goethe, and Schiller. He was perhaps atypical in the extent to which he "bought the program" of instruction, retaining an emotional loyalty to *Griechentum und Goethezeit*, Hellenism and the Goethean Age, well into his last years of life. But already in his final three years of *Gymnasium* (1871–1873), the intellectual climate was changing rapidly. Darwin's *Descent of Man* and E. B. Tylor's epoch-making *Primitive Culture* both appeared in 1871 (the same year in which the unified German *Reich* was officially declared in the Hall of Mirrors at Versailles). Nietzsche's *Birth of Tragedy* appeared in 1872, as did Victor Carus' German translation of *The Descent of Man*. In 1873, the year Freud finished the *Gymnasium* and took his *Matura* examination, Heinrich Schliemann dug up "Priam's Treasure" at Troy and the World Exhibition was being held in Vienna—in fact, in the Prater, virtually at Freud's backdoor in Leopoldstadt. One can well understand why a young man setting off to university in such times would feel the world was ripe for radical change and reinterpretation.

In his maturity, Freud was a highly creative thinker and synthesized with sometimes reckless abandon a great deal of the intellectual currents of his day: archaeology, critical historiography, philology, ethnography, and the history of religions—just to name a few of the pertinent discourses which he brought to bear on issues that arose originally from his therapeutic field of concern. The fact that Freud's discursive incontinence was sometimes wide of the mark does not diminish his importance to me in the least. On the contrary, through his reckless syntheses he better shows the sheer *conceptual velocity* that marks the transition from the liberal bourgeois era of the late nineteenth century to the dire and alarming circumstances of the twentieth. Rather than chiding Freud, as do so many anti-Freudians, for not fully embodying twentieth-century standards of scientific procedure or norms of feminist consciousness or sensitivity to socio-economic difference, I prefer to see the disjunction between his nineteenth-century bourgeois mentality and his radical conceptual innovations as *proof* of his creative and critical power, as evidence of his ability to think beyond the bourgeois European frame of reference that plays "second nature" to the primary world of instincts he hypothesizes. I find I am thus in agreement with Arnold Davidson, whose "How to Do the History of Psychoanalysis: A Reading of Freud's *Three Essays on the Theory of Sexuality*" (2001, chapter 3) drives home the point that the gap between mentality and conceptual innovation can be taken as the healthy sign of a creative thinking that does not yet grasp the import of its own work, rather than as the symptom of ideological stupidity.

> Automatisms of attitude have a durability, a slow temporality, which does not match the sometimes rapid change of conceptual mutation. Mental habits have a tendency toward inertia, and these habits resist change that, in retrospect, seems conceptually required. Such resistance can take place not only in a scientific community but even in the individual who is most responsible for the conceptual innovation. [. . .] But given the divergent temporality of new concepts and the formation of new mentalities, it is no surprise that Freud's mental habits never quite caught up with his conceptual articulations. The attitudes that comprise a mentality are sufficiently impervious to recognition, so much like natural dispositions, that many decades may intervene before habit and concept are aligned. (2001, 91)

Part of what makes Freud so intriguing as a theorist is what he himself considered his intuitive and compulsive mode of working. He once admitted to Joseph Wortis that he did not have difficulty writing "because I have usually not written until a thing was ripe and I felt *a real compulsion to express myself*" ([1954] 1975, 152; my emphasis). This pattern seems evident in many works, such as *Totem and Taboo*, in which he clearly worked from the conclusion backwards toward the evidence.[27] This methodology is certainly convenient for an ambitious improviser, but it guarantees even more that its products will display the contradictions inherent in bold conceptual initiatives that cannot quite outpace the old mentalities from which they emerge. Freud's own contradictions and shortcomings thus bear for me what he would call *historical truth*, that is, a truth about the conflicting circumstances of their utterance that can be separated for my purposes from the question of their substantive truth as scientific theories.

In sum, Freud's compulsion for antiquity is to be situated historically and sociologically within the particular circumstances not only of his classical schooling, but more importantly within the explosive changes brought about by the Darwinian revolution, the growing visibility of ethnographic and anthropological discourse, the professionalization of historiography and archaeology, and the ever-expanding public appetite for sweeping historical narrative, all this against the background of an ancient archive already established as a locus of synaesthetic (and even sexual) understanding. We might characterize this set of changes as the nineteenth century's confrontation with the radical *newness* of the past, a past that seemed to erupt suddenly and scandalously into the public imaginary, revealing an unsuspected backward extension of time well beyond what human history recounts, while tossing out material enigmas for the mind to ponder, like the archaeopteryx, winged phallic artifacts, and snake-handling, bare-breasted Minoan goddesses.

A fundamental aspect of modernity is that it entails a radical reorientation to the past, a shift from the traditional stance of reception and repetition to a paradigm of investigation, public argument, and quite often disenchantment and scandal. After all, to be truly "modern" in the scientific terms of embracing evolution meant professing one's *antiquity* as a member of a primate species. This was a newly discovered antiquity that went well beyond Bishop Ussher's famously precise dating of creation from October 23, 4004 BC (*Annales Veteris et Novi Testamenti* [1650–54]), and it is still being calculated to this day. The modern scientific view of the unity of humanity was predicated not on its being made in the image of God, but on its *hominidity*, i.e., the fact of its animal origin and basic instinctual make up, which "destroyed man's supposedly privileged place in creation" (SE 16: 285). Freud's psychoanalytic revolution followed along the Darwinian pattern of scandalous prehistory that refuses to ennoble us through its recourse to origins. By exposing the fiction of rational hegemony and the scandalous origins of our precious moral judgments and taboos, psychoanalysis disturbs the peace of this world, a fact of which Freud was quite proud (*Introductory Lectures on Psychoanalysis*, SE

16: 285).[28] So any assessment of Freud's compulsion for antiquity must at least allude to the pandemic crisis of historical memory in the nineteenth century from which Freudian memory work emerges and which stylizes the forms of its understanding (Terdiman 1993; Schleifer 2000a). Well up to the end of his life, Freud sought in the clinical reality of the neurotic nothing less than the archaic constitution of the species, or even an antiquity beyond the species.[29] As he said in one of his last jottings, "With neurotics it is as though we were in a prehistoric landscape—for instance, in the Jurassic. The great saurians are still running about; the horsetails grow as high as palms" ("Findings, Ideas, Problems," SE 23:299).

CHAPTER 2

∎

Compulsive Anatomy

Although my approach to Freud's compulsion for antiquity is aimed at the historical and biographical details of his life, it is also keenly interested in its discursive effects. Yoking biographical narrative to the analysis of scientific theories can be cumbersome and problematic, hence the need for a serviceable model that will allow us to balance these objectives in a nuanced and yet economical way. I wish now to introduce such a model for Freud's compulsion, which is divided into three conceptual dimensions through which antiquity regularly intervenes in the Freudian archive. As I will show in detail in a series of studies, I see these three dimensions as distinct in purely heuristic terms, but not in their real operations. They are neither rigidly discrete nor mutually exclusive, but interact to a considerable degree, even to the extent of melding into one another. In fact, the nature of their interaction is the real source of their importance. But by anatomizing the compulsion into three heuristically distinct modes of analysis, we will come to appreciate more readily and more rapidly the interaction between situation and discourse. The three dimensions are: the *personal*, the *analogical*, and the *evidentiary*.

The first dimension has the admittedly banal designation of the *personal*, which accommodates the biographical and historical specificity of Freud's life, and yet is *not* to be equated with the private, the unrevealed or the non-public. This dimension arises from the details of his personal trajectory—like his schooling and his private collection, his travels to sites and museums, the gifts he gave to intimates, the personal space he filled at Berggasse 19, his recreations and his fantasies, his misrepresen-

tations and his pretensions. One thinks of his study, crammed with artifacts and books about antiquity, and how the collection spilled out into
his consulting room, some of it hanging conspicuously over the famous
analytic couch.[1] But just as the extension of this collection into his own
worksite is very telling of the *lack* of a distinction between his intimate
and his professional lives, the fact that the collection does not extend to
his *family's* living area at Berggasse 19 says a great deal of the construction of privacy, professionalism, and privilege inherent in the disposition
of his rooms.

In a famous statement to his friend Stefan Zweig, Freud cited this collection, his recreational reading in archaeology, and his travels as evidence that he is a complex character and not just a workaholic and dutiful
paterfamilias, as Zweig's literary portrait of him suggested: "I have made
many sacrifices for my collection of Greek, Roman, and Egyptian antiquities, and have actually read more archaeology than psychology; [. . .]
up to the war [sc. WWI] and once since I had to be in Rome for days or
weeks at least once a year, and so on. I know from miniatures that the for-
mat requires the artist to simplify and omit, but then a false image is easily brought about" (Stefan Zweig 1989, 154–155). Part of the true image
or "big picture" of Freud, then, would be by his own assertion this compulsive hobby of antiquity that stands clearly as *something apart from* his
professional arena of concerns, while still intimately occupying the same
space. The motto of this recreational Freud can be found in a letter he
wrote to his fiancée in 1886, in which he describes his visit to the
Pergamene sculptures in the Royal Museum of Berlin: "one can't always
be a doctor" (Ernst Freud 1960, 211).

We have clear evidence that Freud disassociated his recreational self
from the professional persona of Berggasse 19 in a letter he wrote to Sándor Ferenczi on October 2, 1910 after their vacation together in Sicily
that September.[2] Responding to a letter from Ferenczi, Freud remarks:

> Your letter has reminded me of the fact that I am the same per-
> son who picked papyrus in Syracuse, fought with the railway per-
> sonnel in Naples, and bought antiquities in Rome. My identity has
> been restored. It is strange how easily one succumbs to an inclina-
> tion to isolate the formations of personality. (Brabant et al. 1993–
> 2000, 1:215)

Tension had arisen on their journey precisely because Ferenczi had expected constant intellectual stimulation and Freud was not in the mood

to pose as the Master; he simply wished to engage in what he later called "wallowing in nature and antiquity" (McGuire 1974, 360). In their correspondence after the journey, they found it necessary to talk out this matter. "So I was probably mostly quite an ordinary old gentleman, and you, in astonishment, realized the distance from your fantasy ideal," Freud remarked (Brabant et al. 1993–2000, 1:215).

At the same time, however, it is clear from the same journey that Freud never entirely left considerations of work at home. Writing to Jung from Rome on September 24, he explained the personal benefit of the trip in purely psychoanalytic terms:

> The trip has been very rich and has supplied several wish-fulfillments that my inner economy has long been in need of. Sicily is the most beautiful part of Italy and has preserved unique fragments of the Greek past, infantile reminiscences that make it possible to infer the nuclear complex. (McGuire 1974, 353)

He adds, moreover, that "a number of scientific notions I brought with me have combined to form a paper on paranoia," a reference to his paper on the Schreber case, in which he would come to ruminate on a "basic language" (*Grundsprache*) of the paranoiac's obsession ("Psycho-Analytic Notes on an Autobiographical Account of a Case of Paranoia," SE 12:23; cf. Freud's letter to Jung of October 1, 1910, in McGuire 1974, 358). While in the Schreber case Freud meant this "basic language" to refer to a "nuclear complex" that the paranoiac can experience consciously only in distorted form, he later used the term "basic language" to refer by extension to symbolic expressions common to dreams, myths, linguistic idioms, and artistic creations (*Introductory Lectures on Psycho-Analysis*, SE 15:166). This suggests that the "infantile reminiscences" of Greek culture in Sicily were a visual metaphor for the fragmented survivals of an archaic mode of expression, the lost language of the unconscious.

The fact is, a great many of Freud's "vacations" were busman's holidays spent writing the works for which he is known, works that could not all be written during the pressured months of daily analysis and other professional activities. A vivid image of the proximity between work and recreation can be found in a letter to Wilhelm Fliess which Freud wrote as he was finishing the *Interpretation of Dreams* during his vacation (August 1, 1899): "My old and grubby gods, of whom you think so little, take part in the work as paperweights for my manuscripts" (Masson 1985, 363). This seems a perfectly ironic image of how the past weighs down upon the present in his work, but it also shows the intimate Freud who brings his antiquities along on holiday for consolation and amusement as he completes one of his most ambitious works. The theme of consolation is particularly important in the personal dimension, as it reflects a deep resonance within his disposition toward antiquity that stretches from his maturity and old age (one thinks of Freud the embattled intellectual writing at his desk lined with ancient figurines, as immortalized in Max Pollack's 1914 etching) all the way back to his school days, when he sat proudly as first in his class year after year. As he said on the occasion of the fiftieth anniversary of his *Gymnasium*, he distinctly recalled that there he received "my first glimpses of an extinct civilization (which in my case was to bring me as much consolation as anything else in the struggles of life)" ("Some Reflections on Schoolboy Psychology," SE 13:241). His open acknowledgment of the role recreational fantasy plays in one's interest in the past allowed him to speculate critically on the psychological motivations of historiography.

However, psychoanalysis being what it is, the personal dimension is far from synonymous with Freud's private life, or even the private as a concept overall—i.e., that secret realm of the self that does not emerge in official discourse. The personal, as Freud deploys it, regularly appears in the public world, and is even a vital part of that public world. Take for example the ancient intaglio rings given to the members of the Secret Committee, who were the paladins in the fight to keep the science unified and pristine after the defections of Carl Jung, Alfred Alder, and Wilhelm Stekel (1911–1913), and whose power stemmed from their intimacy with Freud. Freud the ring-giver marked them with this special token of regard, which—as Hanns Sachs, one of the ring-bearers, later commented—"reminded us that our mutual relations had the same center of gravity. It made us feel that we belonged to a group within the group although without any formal ties or the attempt to become a separate organization" (1946, 153). Freud, bearing his own intaglio ring of Jupiter, provided the center of gravity by establishing a relation of privileged personal trust and intimacy which was tied to a very public concern with scientific authority, unity, and strategic advancement.

One should also consider the myriad intrusions of his private collection into his written works, like the Etruscan cinerary urn that appears in the *Interpretation of Dreams* to illustrate the doctrinal truth that every dream is a wish (SE 4:124). Or we could mention the quasi-magical rituals involving the destruction of an artifact as a sacrifice in order to make a thank offering or to avert some danger, which he discusses in *The Psy-*

chopathology of Everyday Life (SE 6:169–170). From such examples, it is obvious that what emerges from the Freudian archive in the "personal" dimension is not just what was, initially at least, withheld from public utterance, but also what was uttered in public *under the sign of the personal* to serve a larger discursive objective. Such deployments of the personal form a gesture of intimacy toward the reader and work to establish a rhetorical voice that embraces ruthless self-honesty and even personal risk. Freud's self-revelations vary in their tone, at times sounding like nervous confessions, while other times they bristle with a flourish of unabashed ambition or even arrogance. How, for example, does one characterize Freud's confession of a childhood fixation on Hannibal in the *Interpretation of Dreams*? (SE 4:197–198). Is this the ironic parallax of adult hindsight, mocking the cruel judgment of a young boy who is disappointed that his father is not a great hero? Or is the boy's judgment to be understood as representing the adult Freud's as well, such that he is candidly revealing to us his own "father complex" in a spirit of pitiless self-analysis? Or is it the defiant gesture of a combative Jew toward gentile readers who he imagines will be hostile to his novel ideas? Or is it all of the above?

To complicate matters even further, how shall we characterize the "personal" material we know Freud adduced in his writings as belonging to another, when it is highly likely that this material was in fact *his own*? His early paper "Screen Memories" includes just such a presentation of personal material in the guise of another, as is well known among Freud scholars today (1899, SE 3:303–322). A more controversial instance of this involves Freud's analysis of a misremembered line from Vergil's *Aeneid* (4.625) in *The Psychopathology of Everyday Life* (SE 6:8–11), where he creates a literary dialogue between himself and another Jewish intellectual that is an ideal miniature of psychoanalytic interpretation. There is a growing consensus of opinion that this other Jew is really a construct, that the parapraxis was Freud's own, and, to follow the argument of Peter Swales, that he is actually disclosing-without-disclosing his own concerns relating to an affair with Minna Bernays, his sister-in-law, whom he had allegedly impregnated (1982).[3] Here antiquity is implicated in a very complex scenario where the private and problematic realm of sexuality is put on display as a "personal" revelation through a very public pseudo-analysis.

In sum, the personal dimension in this model is not synonymous with the private or the biographical *precisely because we are talking about psychoanalysis and not just a certain Viennese, one Sigmund Freud.* The personal is not an addendum or a gloss on Freud's work, the way the life of Wittgenstein might be seen in relation to his philosophical writings.[4] The personal for Freud is a central element of his scientific concern that stands in dynamic relation to a whole array of supra-personal ambitions and interests. From the personal emerges the very evidence Freud requires for his new science, and its emergence is delicately predicated on the quality of the interpersonal relationship fostered in the analytic situation. Moreover, a distinctive feature of psychoanalysis which I will regularly discuss is Freud's bifocal interest in the macrohistorical and the individual, a prominent aspect of his cognitive style which has caused serious worries for loyal Freudians in the past, because it shows his tendency toward speculation on a grand scale, particularly through the topic of phylogenetic inheritance.

The passage from the individual focus of the couch to the grander historical themes of his work is the focus of chapter 7 below, but I should mention here and now that my approach to the personal is itself bifocal. On the one hand, I will historicize Freud's own attitudes and experiences vis-à-vis antiquity in order to show how they conform to or deviate from common nineteenth- or twentieth-century patterns, thus filling out the personal in relation to a larger context, mentality, or *habitus*. On the other hand, I will work with the personal at the discursive level within Freud's writings, to show how the very category itself fits into a larger project where individual analysis and macrohistorical analysis stand in a strangely complementary relation much of the time. This latter move effectively deconstructs the discursive category of the personal in relation to the discrete realm of private experience, putting it instead in dynamic relation to the social, the public, the *pre*-personal (a fact often missed by Freud's social-oriented critics). Such a deconstruction is inevitable from within psychoanalysis's own investigative logic, if we consider that Freud's overall project might be termed an attempt to create *a science of the personal*, or the incursion of a universalizing discourse of human psychology into the radical specificity of individual experience and sexual object choice.[5]

The next dimension is the *analogical*. If the personal is in a sense the dimension of intimacy, self-revelation, and risk, we might say that the analogical is the mode of flirtation and free play, that is, the somewhat irresponsible and suggestive discursive behavior that promises much but refuses to follow through in extensive detail—often for good reason. A moment of analogy is often the marker of Freud's need to assert a claim of legitimacy for his new science, and as such it is often a great indicator

of his deepest worries and largest ambitions. Freud's compulsion for analogical expression, in general, extends far beyond the topic of antiquity,
and it is pervasive throughout the long chronology of his works.[6] One
need only look to the final chapter of *Studies on Hysteria* (1893–1895) to
see how readily he flits from one simile to the next quite early in his career. In a parenthetical aside, he admits:

> (I am making use here of a number of similes, all of which have
> only a very limited resemblance to my subject and which, moreover,
> are incompatible with one another. I am aware that this is so, and I
> am in no danger of over-estimating their value. But my purpose in
> using them is to throw light from different directions on a highly
> complicated topic which has never yet been represented. I shall
> therefore venture to continue in the following pages to introduce
> similes in the same manner, though I know this is not free from ob-
> jection.) (SE 2: 291)

Analogy is a mode with obvious advantages for an intuitive thinker who
makes rapid connections without sweating the details. Ludwig Wittgenstein attests to its valuable role in conceptual innovation: *Ein gutes Gleich-
nis erfrischt den Verstand* ["A good simile refreshes the understanding"]
([1977] 1984, 1). Thus we can understand why up to the very end of his
life, Freud remained comfortable in the analogical mode in spite of its
obvious pitfalls and limitations: "Let me give you an analogy; analogies,
it is true, decide nothing, *but they can make one feel more at home*" (*New Introductory Lectures on Psycho-Analysis*, SE 22:72; my emphasis). Feeling at
home for Freud means literally surrounding oneself with ancient artifacts
and books of historical scholarship; so it should not surprise us when his
analogies tend toward such themes.

It is typical in any moment of Freudian discourse that an analogy is ostensibly proffered as a momentary construct, something to be discarded
after a point is made lest one get caught up in the mire of reification. Over
time, however, one can see emergent patterns in his analogies that dis-
close something more like parallel discursive operations which are clearly
not fleeting illustrations. For example, the analogy that psychoanalysis as
a clinical procedure is like archaeological excavation or epigraphic decipherment is consistent over a considerable stretch of time, from 1893 to
1937. Analogies between the methodologies of critical historiography
and the analysis of individual memory also recur, suggesting that Freud's
positioning of his new science within—and between—the typology of

natural and historical sciences *depends* on a certain structure of identification with historiography, one which reveals Freud's tendency toward
recursive analogies.

In a recursive analogy, one begins with the formal statement that psychoanalysis is *like* another field, say critical historiography. But then one
asserts the methodological innovation of psychoanalysis, promising that
this new science gives insight into the psychological motivations of an
historian or a whole cultural era. Gradually one inverts the analogy to
show how historiography reveals an operation similar to a feature from
psychoanalysis, like the screen memory or the family romance. Historiography then becomes rewritten in psychoanalytic terms, rather than
serving as the latter term in the equation: A is like B. The end result is
that the whole analogical relationship can collapse into a relation of *identity*, that is, psychoanalysis is in the end put forward as *a method of historiography*, not an operation *analogous* to historiography. And it is here that
we often find the analogical is just a moment in discourse that gradually
slides into the evidentiary, shifting from the order of suggestive speculation to the order of hard proof.

In fact, the relationship between the analogical and the *evidentiary* is
so close that we should turn to the latter now without delay. Most questions in science come down to matters of evidence and its interpretation,
and Freud's discourse is typically overloaded with evidentiary concerns.
What makes antiquity directly relevant in the evidentiary realm on a constant basis is in fact a *biological* dogma of the age; namely, the doctrine of
recapitulation propounded in full-blown ideological form by Ernst
Haeckel (1834–1919), who played the part of St. Paul for the evolutionary gospel when the Darwinian revolution hit German-speaking Europe.[7] The theory is simple: ontogeny recapitulates phylogeny, or the
development of the individual organism repeats in abbreviated form the
historical evolution of its species.[8] This simple doctrine has more drastic
consequences the farther it is extended. For one thing, it creates a bifur-
cation into the macrohistorical and the microhistorical arrayed as parallel lines of concern that reinforce one another, and here we see how this
enables the personal to be enlisted in grand universal narratives (and vice
versa).

The result is a whole new construal of evidence based on a set of equiv-
alences: the infantile becomes *archaic and pre-historic;* neurotic regressions
are equal to *ancient beliefs and practices,* primitive rituals are *survivals* and
are thus equal to things *ancient and infantile;* dreams can be associated in
their imagery with myths and vice versa. This effectively means that

Freud has suddenly moved to expand the body of evidence to a considerable degree, in keeping with the quadrilateral arrangement: neurotic = infantile = archaic = primitive. Thus Freud finds it very significant that a neurotic patient's obsessive image of his father as a "father-arse"—the naked lower part of a body with arms and legs but no head—has a mythological parallel in certain Baubo figurines from the ancient cult of Demeter, which similarly show a belly with limbs and a face but no head ("A Mythological Parallel to a Visual Obsession," SE 14:337–338). He finds a corroboration for the assumption that dreams of flying are really about the sensation of erection in the existence of ancient phallic amulets that sport wings (*The Interpretation of Dreams*, SE 5:394). Here the ancient artifacts are valuable evidence in that they suggest a line of psychic continuity that would place random mental events like obsessive images and dreams in a larger category of universal but archaic modes of thought that are exposed through regressions like dreaming and neurosis.

Not only does Freud use this recapitulatory dogma, also known as the "biogenetic law," to expand the body of evidence, he also derives from it the means to change the *very rules of evidence* in historical argument. The most important of these means is the theory of repression—not repression conceived as an individual defense mechanism, but as a macrohistorical phenomenon operant in whole historical epochs. Repression leads to the weird sisters symbol, symptom, and slip—a trio that empowers the psychoanalytic interpreter by the mere fact of their enigmatic intrusion— and allows for a symptomatic reading of entire cultures. For example, once neurotic rituals and religious rituals are no longer *analogous* but are conceived in recapitulatory terms, the search for similarities ends and becomes, rather, the search for *traces of the past* in the present. Metaphor is replaced by metonymy, that is, by relations of contiguity and historical causation. For example, the formal similarity of totemism to certain childhood phobias becomes instead "The Return of Totemism in Childhood" (chapter 4 of *Totem and Taboo*). All of history then can be read from the analyst's couch, since the rules of historical evidence have now been changed in a decisive manner to the analyst's favor. "The mental life of human individuals, when subjected to psychoanalytic investigation, offers us the explanations with the help of which we are able to solve a number of riddles in the life of human communities or at least to set them in a true light" (*Introductory Lectures on Psycho-Analysis*, SE 15:168).

Conversely, the intrusions of historical themes in individual analysis also change the nature and construal of the self's evidence. When confronted, for example, by a series of enigmatic images (a draught board, a dagger, a sickle, a scythe) produced by a fourteen-year-old patient, Freud solves the riddle of the boy's psychic situation by reading them in the light of Greek mythology (except that he is wrong about the details). He thus produces a perfectly Freudian conflict between the boy and his father, complete with the threat and counter-threat of castration, based on a mythic model from the cultural archive that empowers the coherent construal of a set of seemingly random evidence (*The Interpretation of Dreams*, SE 5:618–619). On a grander scale, once the "true meanings" of *Oedipus Tyrannus* and *Hamlet* were revealed by Freud, these texts accrued a clear paradigmatic influence on the interpretation of clinical data. Indeed, many of Freud's harsher critics cite the intrusion of the oedipal paradigm as Freud's primal and most egregious scientific error, the "displacement of evidence by theory" (Spence 1994) or even a downright "assault on truth" (Masson 1984). Just consider the curious wording of this statement from the *Introductory Lectures:* "Analysis *confirms* all that the legend describes [*Sie weist ihn so auf, wie ihn die Sage erzählt*]. It shows that each of these neurotics has himself been an Oedipus or, what comes to the same thing, has, as a reaction to the complex, become a Hamlet" (SE 16:335; my emphasis). Antiquity is thus not only relevant by being sucked into Freud's evidentiary field through recapitulatory logic; it also informs the general narrative contours of one of his central elements of developmental and nosological theory.

The relation of the evidentiary to the analogical is established, we might say, by virtue of the fact that recapitulation is itself a *reification* of analogical thinking.[9] For the biogenetic law is essentially a form of reasoning by morphological similarities, resemblances established by the visual comparison of embryonic specimens (which Haeckel notoriously doctored in his highly popular illustrations). Hence, the two dimensions not only intersect, they appear quite often to be virtually identical, though it is very important to see that Freud would on occasion like to maintain a hygienic distinction between them. One can also see quite easily how the evidentiary and the personal intersect, since so much of the evidence that psychoanalysis deploys is *self-evidence*, that is, the empirical facts of selfhood (*specific* dreams, slips, symptoms belonging to particular individuals) that are thought to support psychoanalytic truth. Here again, the personal is never just a matter of private experience, since all "private" experience is now at the heart of an *empirical* science and forms the epistemological cutting edge of Freud's enterprise. Every babbling analysand not only divulges valuable scientific evidence in her personal discourse for the operations of the unconscious; she may, through the mysterious workings of the biogenetic law, uncover some relic of the human past as well.

The intersection of the personal, the analogical, and the evidentiary in the figures of the analyst and the analysand is what grounds the unfolding narrative of discovery and authority that I have termed Freud's empirical romance. It is not my intention to expose the "falsehood" of psychoanalysis's claims to being a true empirical science by referring to this paradigm as a "romance." A laboratory scientist might well consider the analytic encounter as Freud conceived it to be "pseudo-empirical" from the standpoint of experimental methodology. But the importance of the empirical for Freud lies not in what can be replicated in the laboratory, but what is uniquely *experienced* between the analyst and the analysand: the phenomena of transference and resistance.[10] Because his historical hermeneutic is drawn from an experiential situation, Freud flatly refuses to consider the theory of repression as a premise; it is instead a *finding*, "a theoretical inference legitimately drawn from innumerable observations" ("On the History of the Psycho-Analytic Movement," SE 14:17). Resistance and transference are therefore "facts of observation which emerge whenever an attempt is made to trace the symptoms of a neurotic back to their sources in his past life" (SE 14:17). They are first and foremost experiential precipitates of clinical memory work and they thoroughly condition Freud's convictions about both the empirical foundations and the historical validity of his enterprise.

It is thus this experience (Greek *empeiria*, whence "empirical" derives) of living memory that Freud takes to be the empirical basis of his science. Like the "family romance," the empirical romance is a tale of legitimation, an attempt at self-authentication by means of a new genealogy (for Freud gladly discloses his scientific progenitors and heroic ancestors, like Copernicus, Darwin, or Jean-Martin Charcot, after whom he named his first-born son, thus incorporating him literally into his own genealogy). Only, unlike the bogus aristocratic parentage of the family romance, the empirical romance authenticates ultimately with exclusive reference to the authority of Nature herself as an observable and self-evident Truth. Such truth was the stated goal of the seventeen-year-old Freud at the outset of his scientific studies: to peer into Nature's multi-millennial dossiers, to discover something of her eternal process, and to share it with whoever wants to learn.[11]

In this regard, it is important to see that Freud's foundational act of self-analysis functions as a kind of parthenogenesis in the narrative of the psychoanalytic movement. In other words, the *primum mobile* in this empirical romance is human nature observing itself in the specific instance of Sigmund Freud. As Frank Sulloway has argued, "The myth of the hero and the myth of Freud as pure psychologist stand as the two great pillars around which traditional psychoanalytic history has long cultivated its inspiring image of Freud," which in turn provided the means to create a unique ideological system (1992, 487). In fact, Sulloway makes the bolder claim that there is "no other theory in the history of scientific thought that can rival psychoanalysis for such an elaborate system of self-reinforcing defenses" (1992, 487). Donald Spence has further argued that the rhetorical function of Freud's self-analysis is to serve "as one of the principle exhibits in the psychoanalytic collection of specimens" which "will never yield all its secrets and continues to call for reanalysis and reinspection" (1994, 97). As Spence shows in vivid detail, the legend of the self-analysis gets increasingly elaborate as one reads the versions by Ernest Jones, Kurt Eissler, and Peter Gay, who, in the absence of further evidence, are free to recount the feat of *katabasis* and to ascribe to it all kinds of heroic qualities (1994, 99–105). "This act of patient heroism has never been repeated," Gay confidently asserts (cited in Spence 1994, 117).

Thus standing at the head of this unfolding scientific improvisation is a narrative of self-origination that enforces the notion of psychoanalysis's unique epistemic rupture with all previous forms of knowing. As one proponent has written,

> Because of its theory of the unconscious, which obliges it to investigate phenomena that the sciences, religions, and philosophies have always excluded from their field of vision, and to attach extreme importance to what other disciplines have disregarded, psychoanalysis can claim to rest entirely on its own feet, to be its own law and criterion of truth. Radically independent—it is not a prolongation of any other discipline and requires no outside help for its development—it is for every disciple and every patient, regardless of intellectual horizon, an absolute beginning. (Robert 1977, 135)

Thus for its most zealous proponents, the first year of Freud's self-analysis is effectively Year One on a revolutionary calendar, a watershed in human thought from which there is no turning back. But just as the French Revolution relied heavily on its republican heroes from the ancient past, the Freudian revolution could not manage its ruptures with tradition without also engineering its returns.

I realize that my attention to so many points of reference at once in the model I have proposed might give the appearance of a crowded agenda, so I now offer six case studies that integrate the personal, the analogical, and the evidentiary, and which demonstrate why this is a coherent and economical approach to Freud's compulsion for antiquity. I deliberately select these samples from critical features and junctures in Freud's career, since only such "high stakes" scenarios are worth considering, if we are to take the compulsion for antiquity as a central aspect of his life and thought, and not just an amusing personal preference. We begin with Freud's disturbing acropolis itself, the paradigm of oedipal desire, which will help to characterize the psychoanalytic movement overall in reference to its dominant myth and icon, with specific attention to the way the oedipal pattern tightly imbricates the three dimensions. From there we shall consider as our second case study Freud's first serious attempt at historical biography, his analysis of Leonardo da Vinci, which is instructive in part for the way in which it *fails* to achieve the tight imbrication that the oedipal paradigm so successfully accomplishes. It turns out to be the mother's desire that causes this failure, and this has wide-ranging implications.

The third and fourth case studies—taken from the first edition of *The Interpretation of Dreams*, and his later invocation of Empedocles at the very end of his life,—will be considered next in conjunction with one another, since they display Freud's deployment of antiquity as an alternative tradition on which he relies when his own theories seem at odds with the scientific establishment. The need for such an alternative tradition shows that, despite the great promise of self-authentication inherent in the empirical romance, the need for a legitimating genealogy never disappears, since the empirical moment for psychoanalysis inherently points toward the anecdotal isolation of individual experience. Thus Freud's invocation of Greek predecessors points to his need to deepen the empirical romance historically, to show that others have seen the same things he has seen, and that his historical advantage is simply that he possesses the scientific armature that can fully address the reality of what he sees.

Lastly, my fifth and sixth case studies are likewise presented together in chapter 6, and both stem from Freud's *Introductory Lectures on Psychoanalysis*. These last studies show how strongly the analogical dimension works to redress the inherent problem of the evidentiary for any public "demonstration" of psychoanalysis, which is a science that cannot be demonstrated like a vacuum pump or a chemical reaction. It is precisely in the public forum of the lecture (or more accurately, the textual *repre-*

sentation of the public lecture) that we see Freud attempting to pursue the paradigm of public science that is his scientific and political ideal; yet at the same time we see how much of psychoanalysis is kept from the public view because its empirical moment (the analytic encounter) is highly personal in nature and cannot be observed by a third party. At the same time, the semantic occlusion of psychoanalysis's evidence—that is, its encryption due to the workings of repression—implies that there is ultimately *nothing* self-evident about the self's evidence, since dreams, symptoms, and parapraxes require laborious exegesis. Hence the public spectacle of archaeology—with its paradigms of material excavation and decipherment—becomes a master-trope for psychoanalytic science, since it provides a means of distracting us from the fact that we are dealing with the assurance of things hoped for and the conviction of things not seen. Which is to say, we are being indoctrinated into a faith (cf. Hebrews 11.1).

CHAPTER 3

■

The Theban Paradigm

SOPHOCLES

Viele versuchten umsonst *das Freudigste freudig* zu sagen,
  Hier spricht endlich es mir, hier in der Trauer sich aus.

SOPHOCLES

Many have assayed in vain to speak joyfully [*freudig*] of the most joyful
[*Freudigste*];
  Here amidst sadness at last, I hear it so clearly conveyed.
—HÖLDERLIN, *Epigrams*

Let us begin with an analysis of the central case of Oedipus. Freud's fascination with Oedipus grows out of personal experience with the text—his reading of *Oedipus Tyrannus* in high school, his attendance of performances of it in Paris and Vienna—coupled with the personal and professional crisis of the late 1890s that led to the development of psychoanalysis as we know it.[1] The first document to mention his interpretation of the Sophoclean work in 1897 shows that the connection between the universal claims of his theory and his personal self-revelation is close to appearing downright causal: *because* he has discovered oedipal feelings in himself, he leaps to the conclusion that *everyone* must have them.[2] This suggests a cogent personal reason why Oedipus increased in significance over the years, leading to the elaboration of the original Oedipus situation as it modestly appears in the *Interpretation of Dreams* into the "nuclear complex" of the neuroses during the years 1907–1910. Later still the oedipal theory ballooned into the macrohistorical thesis of *Totem and Taboo*, a book that grew out of a personal strug-

gle with Carl Jung over the use of the past and the direction of the psychoanalytic movement.[3]

But in the *public* arguments in favor of a universal complex, Freud's
self-analysis is understandably subtracted from the evidentiary array. Instead, the text of *Oedipus Tyrannus* itself is adduced at some length in *The
Interpretation of Dreams* as corroboratory evidence for common dreams of
an incestuous and/or parricidal nature (SE 4:261–264). However, the
play is adduced not merely for its narrative content, but also as a dramatic
performance whose significance is to be judged by the extraordinary *effect* it has on the modern audience. Later in the *Introductory Lectures* (Lecture 21), Freud appeals to this text again as an experience: "I hope many
of you may yourselves have felt the shattering effect of the tragedy in
which Sophocles has treated the story" (SE 16:330).[4] Here Freud operates on a dual level of the evidentiary: the audience reaction proves the
relevance of this ancient material to his very modern psychological concerns, while the great antiquity of the myth reinforces the notion that
something primeval, deeply human, and universally true must be contained in the plot, something he will then unpack effectively for the first
time in history.[5] The scenario of ancient drama thus allows for an effective combination of an empirical approach with a historical one. As I have
argued elsewhere, Freud's reading of *Oedipus Tyrannus* effectively turns
the play's surprising success on the modern stage (something he had witnessed himself in Paris and Vienna) into a riddle; namely, why should
such an ancient play move a modern audience when its theme of oracles
and fate is so objectionable to the modern mind? (See especially SE
16:330–332.) Freud's oedipal theory presents itself as the answer to this
riddle, an explanation for the self-evident but enigmatic truth that the
play has a powerful effect on Parisians and Viennese, and not just Athe-
nians of the fifth century BCE (Armstrong 1999b).

Indeed, Freud's reading fundamentally shifts the evidentiary status of
the figure of Oedipus from the ancient pattern of being a particularly
egregious example of human calamity to being a paradigm of universal
experience.[6] To the ancient world, Oedipus was indeed a paradigm of dis-
aster, but one that was *uniquely* horrible, caught up in circumstances of
extreme specificity that could hardly be repeated. When the chorus of
Oedipus Tyrannus reflects on Oedipus' downfall in the fourth stasimon
(1186–1221), it makes of his destiny a universal example (παράδειγμα)
only in so far as his fall from such a height to such a depth implies that *no*
mortal is likely to be happy.

ἰὼ γενεαὶ βροτῶν,
ὡς ὑμᾶς ἴσα καὶ τὸ μη-
δὲν ζώσας ἐναριθμῶ.
τίς γάρ, τίς ἀνὴρ πλέον
τᾶς εὐδαιμονίας φέρει
ἢ τοσοῦτον ὅσον δοκεῖν
καὶ δόξαν γ᾽ ἀποκλῖναι;
τὸν σόν τοι παράδειγμ᾽ ἔχων,
τὸν σὸν δαίμονα, τὸν σόν, ὦ
τλᾶμον Οἰδιπόδα, βροτῶν
οὐδὲν μακαρίζω.

(Oedipus Tyrannus 1186–1195)

O generations of mortals,
how I count your lives as nothing.
For what man, what man attains
a happiness that is more than just mere seeming
which shines and then declines.
Having your fate, *your* fate as an example,
O wretched Oedipus,
I count nothing blessed in lives of men.

The Sophoclean chorus makes it clear that the fate of Oedipus is *his* uniquely by their thrice-repeated pronoun "your" (**ton son** *toi paradeigm' ekhôn* / **ton son** *daimona,* **ton son,** *ô*). Oedipus is evidence of human nature in the sense of a worst-case scenario, not in the sense of collective suffering, like the plague that strikes all the Thebans at the outset. He may be in a remote sense the *cause* of their suffering, but what they suffer is not the same as the particular transgressions of his fate. The broad trajectory of his life with its meteoric rise and precipitous fall calls into question the scale of human values *in spite* of the singularity of his experience (much the same was said before by Aeschylus' chorus in *Seven Against Thebes,* lines 772–791). The chorus' deep sympathy arises more from their gratitude for his previous service against the Sphinx than for any common ground they have with his horrific deeds, which leave them stunned.

How far exactly does this worst-case scenario apply in the ancient world? How would the Jews of antiquity construe the evidence of Oedipus? Among the Hellenized Jewry of Alexandria, Oedipus was still the paradigm of a wide-ranging catastrophe, but one affecting Greeks and not Jews, thanks to the wisdom of Moses, who himself laid down the law against incestuous union in the Torah. According to Philo (ca. 20 BCE to ca. 50 CE), Moses did this in order to repudiate the practices of the Persians, whose magistrates would openly marry even their own mothers and produce children whom they considered the noblest of men. Philo then adds:

> These enormities [sc. of incest] formerly took place among the Greeks in the case of Oedipus, the son of Laius, and the actions were committed out of ignorance and not voluntarily, and yet that marriage brought on such a host of evils that nothing was wanting to make up the amount of the most complete wretchedness and misery, for there ensued from it a continual succession of wars, both domestic and foreign, which were bequeathed like an inheritance from their fathers and ancestors to their children and descendants; and there were destructions of cities which were the greatest in Greece, and destructions of embattled armies, and slaughter of nations and of allies which had come to the assistance of either side, and mutual slaughter of the most gallant leaders in each army, and irreconcilable enmities about sovereignty and authority, and fratricides, by which not only the families and countries of the persons immediately concerned were utterly extinguished and destroyed, but the greater portion of the whole Greek nation also, for cities which were previously populous now became desolate and void of inhabitants, and were left as a memorial of the calamities of Greece, and a miserable sight for all beholders. (1993, 595; = *De specialibus legibus* 3.3.15–16)

This is certainly a national catastrophe (though this hyperbolic version seems unique to the Jews, exaggerated no doubt for rhetorical effect), but not a *universal* condition thanks the exceptional nature of Jewish Law. Oedipus is evidence of what is avoided through the legacy of Moses' preemptive wisdom, and this is cause for the Jews, unlike the Sophoclean chorus, to rejoice. The Jews can see in Oedipus something that will *never* happen to them as long as they cleave to the Law, thus giving them no cause to entertain the archaic pessimism of the Greeks.

But Oedipus becomes for Freud the evidence that both *documents* the universal historical truth of oedipal desire (at least for fifth-century BCE

Athens) and *instantiates* this oedipal truth by reawakening the realm of the repressed in the spectators through the theatrical effect of *Oedipus Tyrannus*.

> The Greek legend seizes upon a compulsion which everyone recognizes because he senses its existence within himself. Everyone in the audience was once a budding Oedipus in fantasy [*Jeder der Hörer war einmal im Keime und in der Phantasie ein solcher Ödipus*] and each recoils in horror from the dream fulfillment here transplanted into reality [on the stage] with the full quantity of repression which separates his infantile state from his present one. (Masson 1985, 272)

In this very crucial way, the oedipal truth of Sophocles' drama is in Freud's view *self-evident*, at least to those few who are willing to forego the misrecognition of Oedipus' crimes as uniquely his (for the play's effect depends upon the distancing this misrecognition affords—a *dusanagnôrisis* instead of an *anagnôrisis;* otherwise, there would be no pleasure in it). It is self-evident both in the nature of the crimes that are finally revealed and in the response that it evokes in the audience, who feel it in their innermost selves.

The self-evident nature of Oedipus' crimes is not to be taken for granted. Part of Freud's intransigent argument for the Oedipus complex is simply to affirm the literal nature of the myth's meaning: it really *is* a tale of incest and patricide, nothing more, nothing less. It is neither at base an allegory of nature, as classical scholars of the time suggested, nor is it a pious reflection on the awesome power of the gods (which Freud dismisses as a ruse of secondary revision, a mere rationalization of the latent content [*Interpretation of Dreams*, SE 4:264]).[7] In this way, Freud's insistence on a literal reading of the plot replicates the unique feature of the oracle that Oedipus desperately seeks to invalidate, since in a most unusual manner, the oracular predictions of his "parrincest" come true *literally*, whereas most Delphic oracles that seem so blatantly disturbing on the surface turn out to be true in only a figurative sense. Oedipus thus suffers in a "tragedy of specificity" whereby the victims of his actions are the specific people he has gone out of his way to avoid, and these crimes have been *specified* unambiguously from the outset to no avail.

So a peculiar feature of Freud's deployment of the play as evidence is his dogged insistence that Oedipus' individual destiny must be accepted as a contingent yet universal *fact* that, in being a common event to all members of the species ("[e]very new arrival on this planet is faced by the task of mastering the Oedipus complex" [*Three Essays on the Theory of Sexuality*, SE 7:226 n. 1]), effectively has the compulsive force of fate.[8] The child's contingent circumstances within the family coincidentally reproduce the oedipal situation, and thus lead the child to repeat Oedipus' "tragedy of specificity" through the structural limitations of object choice. What was once considered fate (*daimôn*) is now considered chance (*tuchê*), but the end result is the same. As Sarah Winter has argued very convincingly, this cooptation of tragic destiny positions psychoanalytic truth itself as a tragic necessity that inevitably evokes resistance, yet which ultimately cannot be denied (1999, chapter 2). The "evidence" of tragedy thus comes to characterize more broadly the disturbing cognitive revolution of psychoanalysis, which pushes us toward the *anagnôrisis* that repression so deftly evades. As Freud said somewhat melodramatically, "Like Oedipus, we live in ignorance of these wishes, repugnant to morality, which have been forced upon us by Nature, and after their revelation we may all of us well seek to close our eyes to the scenes of our childhood" (SE 4:263).

This evidentiary deployment of *Oedipus Tyrannus* situates the analogical in turn, since the play about the riddle-master who must solve the riddle of himself becomes a formal analogy with the process of psychoanalysis right from the start, and the figure of Oedipus becomes the literal icon of the psychoanalytic movement (SE 4:262). The analysand who approached Freud's couch saw the framed reproduction of Ingres' "Oedipus and the Sphinx" (1808) hanging just to the right, an item from Freud's personal collection that prompted the patient to be prepared to solve the enigmas of human life in the course of this encounter (see figure 1). On one occasion early in his practice, Freud even awarded a copy of it to an analysand who had helped him solve the enigma of his own railway phobia (Masson 1985, 392). Versions of this picture were reproduced in a medallion presented to Freud in 1906 (for his fiftieth birthday), in a personal bookplate in 1910 (figure 2), and as the logo of the Internationaler Psychoanalytischer Verlag (figures 3 and 4), the official press for the propagation of psychoanalytic truth during the years 1919–1938, where the logo began to convey not just the sense of a group identification, but implicitly the authoritative stamp of an *imprimatur, nihil obstat.*[9] The figure of Oedipus thus literally became symbolic capital for the movement, that is, the means of honoring its founder as a chief riddle-solver and powerful man. The Greek inscription on the medallion states: "he who knew the famous riddles and was a most powerful man,"

Figure 1. Ingres, *Oedipus and the Sphinx* (1808). A reproduction hung over Freud's couch in Berggasse 19.

Figure 2. Bookplate designed for Freud ca. 1910, based on the medallion presented to him in 1906 by his early followers. The Greek verse is from Sophocles' *Oedipus Tyrannus*, and reads, "who knew the famous riddles and was a most powerful man." (By permission of the Freud Museum, London)

a line from *Oedipus Tyrannus* (1525). The figure was also the means for Freud himself to signal possession of the cultural capital of his library (immodestly repeating the very same verse), and the movement's means of marking the commodities it produced for the marketplace with a distinctive emblem that conveyed its guiding myth with iconic immediacy.

Ingres' painting is evocative of many things that one can readily associate with the ambitions of the psychoanalytic movement. Its basic iconography replicates the ancient vase paintings of Oedipus and the Sphinx, such as the one on an Athenian red-figured hydria that Freud owned (Gamwell and Wells 1989, 94–95). But Ingres' classical nude figure of Oedipus appears to be interacting with the smallish, visibly female yet feline sphinx in a way that recalls not so much a vulnerable man trembling before a hideous monster as it does the confident analyst before the female hysteric, that wretch whose body itself has become an eerie symbolic enigma. The image also reminds us of the tremendous optimism of the biological *Wissenschaft* of the times, which stood before what Ernst

Figures 3 and 4. Two versions of the Logo of the Internationaler Psychoanalytischer Verlag, based on the painting "Oedipus and the Sphinx" by Ingres.

Haeckel called the "world-riddle" with a fearless sense of being able to solve the millennial puzzles of nature (1905). Freud's own interpretation of this scene tellingly conflates the manly, heroic resistance to the beast with the childhood scenario Oedipus comes to represent. For although Oedipus is like the analyst—or better yet, Freud the archetypal *self-analyst*—the riddle he is solving is the very first one presented to every child, the one that awakens the "instinct for research": the question of where babies come from. In fact, it was a good five times in print that Freud declared this to be the real meaning of the riddle of the Sphinx.[10] So the scene represents the mature psychoanalytic hero as a *revenant* of the inquisitive boy who first came to inquire about the mysteries of sex and thus began his career in "research." [11]

Like the ancient iconographic tradition, the psychoanalytic movement preferred to keep this image of Oedipus as their icon, neglecting the catastrophic consequences of what was to follow upon his ruthless pursuit of the truth. Sándor Ferenczi, in a zealous early article on the symbolism of Sophocles' play, interprets Oedipus as the symbol of the reality principle itself, and this in Faustian terms that come close to capturing the painful essence of his plight, yet still fail to follow through with the consequences of the analogy.

The reality principle, however, the Oedipus in the human soul, does not allow the seductions of pleasure to keep him from penetrating into even a bitter or a horrible truth, it estimates nothing so lowly as to be not worth testing, it is not ashamed to seek the true psychological nucleus of even superstitious prophecies and dreams, and learns to endure the knowledge that in the inmost soul aggressive and sexual instincts dwell that do not pause even at the barriers erected by civilization between the son and his parents. ([1912] 1956, 269)

This ignores the obvious fact that the same probing spirit leads Oedipus in a fit of paranoia to accuse Creon and Tiresias of a plot to overthrow him, that the knowledge of his incest drives him to attempt *conscious* matricide (avoided only by Jocasta's suicide), and that later he lays a dire curse upon his own sons.[12] By the same logic of analogy, the political and personal dissensions of the movement reflect the paranoia, misogyny, and filial rivalry of the myth, just as Freud's exile, death, and burial in London might be said to reflect the later fate of Oedipus at Colonus (something Freud himself suggests with his private references to his daughter as "Anna-Antigone" [Ernst Freud 1970, 106]).

The inherent danger in the analogy, then, is that it remains unclear just how the figure of Oedipus can safely be taken as *foundational*, as an icon of a discursive practice that has real claims to order, authority, and stable social relations. Ferenczi clearly felt that the establishment of oedipal self-analysis for *all* scientists would render the development of the various sciences, "which today is an endless series of energy-wasting revolutions and reactions," smoother, more insightful, and more profitable ([1912] 1956, 257). In hindsight it seems almost comical that there could have been such a vision of a scientific *pax Freudiana*, where the "fortunate possessors of the Freudian psychology (which like a mental picklock provides a ready key to so many locks that have till now been considered impossible to open)" would save scientists from projecting elements of their own personality into their work ([1912] 1956, 258). The real, fractious outcome of the psychoanalytic movement seems rather to have proved the opposite: that projection is inherently a part of *psychoanalytic* theorizing. Such an outcome could be seen to reflect all too well the nature of its own myth, for the Thebaid is no Aeneid. Rather than the foundational narrative of a *domus* destined to rule, the Thebaid is the long saga of a *devota domus*, a doomed household where paternity is highly problematic in the scheme of history, as much a curse as a marker of distinction.[13] Psychoanalysis disturbs the sleep of the world, as Freud says. But we might just as well adopt his legendary remark upon coming to America and say that like Oedipus, Freud brought a plague upon his people.[14]

The incongruous nature of Oedipus' two characteristics—that is, that he is, on the one hand, a pariah, an incestuous patricide, and, on the other, an intellectual hero and the savior of Thebes—is responsible for the fact that psychoanalysis takes his tragic plight literally as the human condition while also brazenly making him its intellectual icon. So rather than suggesting that Freud and company simply misread the ancient archive, I prefer to underscore how they in fact replicate the features of the Oedipus myth's composite development, at least, to the extent that this can be known. For the Sphinx episode, which in Greek iconography, beginning in the fifth century BCE, becomes the *defining* moment in the myth, appears to be a later addition to the story of contested kingship and childhood wounding that would represent the oldest version of the tale (Edmunds [1983] 1995, 147–173).[15] Only during the Athenian "enlightenment" of the latter fifth century did Oedipus become the *intellectual* hero, the riddle solver; and the tragic nature of his fate in the Sophoclean drama can be read as a critique of the hubris inherent in such an "enlightenment," since Athens went careening into defeat and political cynicism by the end of the century (a reading of the play well presented by Bernard Knox [1957]). The mythic "Thebes" we know is really the invention of Athens, its Other created in the space of the social imaginary and conveniently staged in the Theater of Dionysus (Zeitlin 1990). Thebes is the Dionysian unconscious of Athens, to make a sound bite of it; the two find their open dialogue only out in the suburbs in the sanctuary of the furies at Colonus.

Thus if Freud's oedipal icon ultimately invites a deconstruction of the movement's project with its limping dialectic of enlightenment, then we might argue that his choice of text was all too perfect for the nature of his enterprise. The disturbing acropolis of oedipal theory was indeed misrecognized as the foundation of a new kingdom of the ego—hence those voices crying out in the desert in the middle of the twentieth century denouncing the conformist vapidities of American ego psychology. But psychoanalysis's real disturbing truth, "the self's radical ex-centricity to itself with which man is confronted," is precisely what is at stake whenever it is enlisted in imperial projects to turn neurotics into model citizens (Lacan [1966] 1977, 171). This certainly explains why someone who claims to guard the flame of the Freudian text in the ascetic manner of Jacques Lacan would have to become vestal, *vates* and *nabi* all in one—a virgin textualist, an oracle monger, and an Old Testament prophet—refusing to relinquish psychoanalysis's uncompromising attitude toward psychic compromises for the sake of greater social "relevance" and facile readability. Such a true believer cannot abide the idolatrous sacrifices made on the altar of the ego:

> But neither does it suffice to associate oneself with the moralistic tartufferies of our time or to be forever spouting something about the "total personality" in order to have said anything articulate about the possibility of mediation.
>
> The radical heteronomy that Freud's discovery shows gaping within man can never again be covered over without whatever is used to hide it being profoundly dishonest. (Lacan [1966] 1977, 172)

We might say, then, that the only honest job left *after* the oedipal self-revelations that shook the twentieth century from its slumber would be the office of Tiresias, who is no hero of the polis and no help against the Sphinx.

By coupling in so tight a fashion the personal, the evidentiary, and the analogical dimensions in the development of psychoanalysis, the figure of Oedipus inevitably became the center of *resistance* to Freud and his orthodox cabal on the part of the dissenters. For if the empirical romance relates how Freud, the oedipal self-analyst, came to realize the perennial truth of Sophocles' play and expanded this kernel of wisdom into a whole field of scientific endeavor, then any attack on Freud that hopes to dismantle the new science with thoroughness must reach Freud through Sophocles and expose his telltale misreading of the text. The detected misreading consequently becomes the evidence for exposing a corresponding analogical error in the practice of psychoanalysis, and Freud, like the Sphinx, is undone in one fell gesture of interpretation.[16] This is, I freely admit, a condition of oedipal textuality from which I myself cannot escape even at this writing.[17]

Thus it is no surprise that Otto Rank, who came closer than anyone to being a "true son" to Father Freud (including almost becoming his son-in-law), should have gradually shifted from following the oedipal agenda with scrupulous care in his massive *The Incest Theme In Literature and Legend* ([1912] 1992) to tearing it down after his break with the movement throughout his later writings. Already in *The Trauma of Birth* ([1924] 1993, 143–146), the precipitating cause of Rank's break with Freud, he makes the situation of the Oedipus complex *secondary*, a mere repetition of the *primal* trauma of birth which is represented by Oedipus' confrontation with the Sphinx, "the strangler" (from Greek *sphingō*, "to constrict"). Though Freud himself had interpreted the riddle of the Sphinx to mean, "Where do babies come from?" Rank's implicit criticism is that he failed to see how the hero must overcome the birth anxiety (asphyxia being one of its most anxiety-provoking components) on the way back to the mother, such that the sexual Oedipus complex can only be achieved through first overcoming the birth trauma and the primal fear of the mother. In a sense this follows the sequence of the myth, since only by solving the riddle of the Sphinx does Oedipus "win" his mother's body.[18]

In several books after his departure from the fold, Rank returns again and again to the theme of Oedipus, eventually developing a reading of *Oedipus Tyrannus* in a way that shows his own plight as a renegade son formerly tantalized by the prospect of replacing the Father. In his 1932 *Art and Artist*, he chides the movement for taking artistic evidence of the Oedipus complex as proof of its ubiquity instead of as evidence for the powerful reaction the creative personality has to this motif, for this approach led to a banalization of the creative personality that stymied psychoanalytic art criticism, his particular field of expertise ([1932] 1989, 63–65). Arguing instead for the creative capacities enlivened by the oedipal struggle, he extends this to a new reading of the Oedipus myth in existential terms as "the deliberate affirmation of the existence forced upon us by fate. That which is dimly but unequivocally preordained for the hero by his birth, in the mythical account, he deliberately makes his own by embodying it in action and experience" ([1932] 1989, 65). One can read this as a covert recognition that Rank's own creative rebellion from the Freudian fold is thus fulfilling an oedipal destiny which he now openly accepts as a self-willed life project. In a transformation through analogy, the tragic necessity of Freudian self-knowledge gives way to the positive self-assertion of Rankian "will therapy," which no longer seeks to break down the analysand's "resistances" to the analyst's dire truths, but rather to cultivate "the creative expression of the total personality" ([1941] 1958, 49–50).

In *Modern Education* (1932), however, Rank took a different tack, asking within the framework of patriarchy not just "What is a Father?" but, rather poignantly for his position, "What is a son?" He characterizes the culture of Europe up to the First World War as the dying embers of a dominant father ideology, in which psychoanalysis came to play the role of offering a transitory therapeutic effect by *temporarily* replacing the missing Father. "In this sense, Psychoanalysis is as conservative as it appeared revolutionary; for its founder is a rebellious son who defends the paternal authority, a revolutionary who, from fear of his own rebellious son-ego, took refuge in the security of the father position, which however was already ideologically disintegrated" (1931, 191–192). Here it is highly relevant to note that Rank had deliberately rejected his own father (changing his name from Rosenfeld to Rank) and was taken in by Freud and the movement as a virtual adopted son.[19] Once this second set of family relations failed him, he sought to annul the dead-end implications of filial ambivalence by a further transformation of the myth. In a convoluted reaction to Freud's reading of Oedipus, Rank comes to stress the theme of willful self-possession that pushes the oedipal conflict *beyond* the eternal dialectic of fathers and sons; now Oedipus' sin turns out to be his desire to be immortal by denying all paternal and filial relations entirely and begetting himself anew through a return to the mother.

> For as little as the father wants to continue to exist only in his sons, just as little has the son an inclination to play only the part of a successor to the father. In this sense Oedipus rebels likewise against the role of son as against that of father and not as son against his father. This double conflict in the individual himself who wants to be neither father nor son, but simply Self, is portrayed in the myth in all its features. (1932, 193–194)

There is a certain weariness in Rank's long argument in support of this, where he seems like a rat in a maze, trying to uphold the individual impulse that makes Oedipus' agency a glorious failure while at the same time evading the complex of fatherhood and filiation that so clouds his own position as former heir to the Kingdom of Oedipus, the psychoanalytic movement. Yet Rank's compulsive need to address and redress the story of Oedipus is further proof of how well Freud had welded together his analogical and evidentiary gestures with the personal relations of the enterprise. Even in his desire simply to be himself, Rank must find his ground in Thebes in order to feel he has his feet firmly beneath him.

This is just one example among a great many of how Freud's oedipal science forged a mythic *habitus* which so thoroughly conditioned the nature of psychoanalytic knowledge that to this day critiques of Freud inevitably become oedipal critiques, attacking him in terms he set out for us like an enduring curse upon his descendants. As Jay Greenberg has aptly put it, "a particular explanation of the Oedipus complex has become the Oedipus complex" (1991, 18). Thus as late as 1997, we find Daniel Boyarin's provocative reading of Freud's turn to oedipal theory in terms of "homosexual panic" still recapitulating the same Freudian imbrication of the personal, the analogical and the evidentiary.

> In short, not only was the new theory of psychoanalysis essentially an act of repression/overcoming, but the Oedipus model itself ought to be interpreted as a repression of homoerotic desire. In Freud, the fundamental ideas of human sexual development are a sort of screen or supervalent thought for a deeper but very threatening psychic constituent that Freud had found in his own hysteria but that had then panicked him: the desire for "femaleness," for passivity, to be the object of another man's desire, even to bear the child of another man. The analysand in whom Freud came to disbelieve was thus himself. (1997, 208)

In Boyarin's reading, Oedipus was a beard of gentile virility adopted to bury deep anxieties about masculinity and Jewishness, for in adopting the Oedipus model Freud "is unconsciously fantasizing that he is not the circumcised Schelomo, son of Jakob, but the uncircumcised and virile Greek Oedipus, son of Laius, just as earlier he had consciously fantasized that he was Hannibal, son of the heroic Hamilcar, and not the son of his 'unheroic' Jewish father" (1997, 242). The gothic horror of incest and patricide is infinitely preferable to the even greater horror of gender trouble and passivity in this view, and Freud chose to close his eyes to the painful self-knowledge by adopting the emblematic figure of self-blindedness. It is a pity that Boyarin did not attend better to the evidentiary dimension of his own argument, however, since Laius was reputedly the inventor of pederasty in parts of the mythic tradition. In fact, his death at the hands of his own son fulfills a curse put on him for having raped a young man he loved who later committed suicide.[20] Moreover, Oedipus, in finding out he is in fact a member of the Royal House of Thebes, turns out to have Semitic ancestry by way of its founder, Cadmus the Phoenician.[21] Had he noted these facts, Boyarin's argument would then have had its most incisive Freudian feature: the return of the repressed via the very means used to conceal it ("Notes upon a Case of Obsessional Neurosis," SE 10:225). For Thebes was neither as straight nor as Aryan as Freud thought.

It is rather telling that Rank and Boyarin raise two figures to challenge Freud's Theban paradigm: the mother and the homosexual. These two figures pose an overt threat to the model of masculine rivalry immortalized in the oedipal model, and they loom large in the next case study I shall present: namely, the case of Leonardo da Vinci.

CHAPTER 4

■

Leonardo's Gay Science

This first psychoanalytic pathography [. . .] will serve as a model for all time. The explanation of your philosophy of life made the deepest impression on me: willful subordination to the rule of Ἀνάγκη.

—FERENCZI TO FREUD, 1910
(BRABANT ET AL. 1993–200, 1:181)

Antiquam exquirite matrem.
[Seek out your ancient mother.]

—VERGIL, *Aeneid* 3.96

Freud's study of Leonardo, *Eine Kindheitserinnerung des Leonardo da Vinci* (1910, SE 11:63–137) was his first serious historical-biographical foray, but also his last. The interaction of our three dimensions is not as carefully imbricated in this study as in the Theban paradigm, and this produces some troublesome confusion, suggesting that Freud's own agenda in the study is itself overcrowded.[1] I shall dwell on this confusion in some detail, however, because it reveals some telltale features of the psychoanalytic agenda that impinge upon Freud's compulsive enlistment of antiquity.

The Leonardo study bears extensive reading for the fractures of the oedipal paradigm it discloses, as well as the tensions that allude to psychoanalysis's self-understanding and its future directions, particularly in relation to gender theory. Although it is often seen as an exceptional text, I shall argue that in some ways it can be realigned and read as a key for understanding Freud's personalized genealogy of empirical science. It is also a suggestive text in that it demonstrates Freud's shifting recourse to ancient Egypt, on the one hand, and ancient Greece, on the other hand, in the elucidation of individual psychology. As such, we shall begin with a careful examination of how the highly personal focus on Leonardo involves the cultures of remote antiquity by reason of both evidence and analogy.

The Enigma of Genius

Fundamentally, Leonardo's personality is the enigma Freud sets out to explain, and it is clear that Freud undertakes this as yet another groundbreaking enterprise that will expand the scope of psychoanalytic endeavors, just as his study of Jensen had done.[2] Unlike a standard literary biography, this pathographic study of the Great Man of History sets out to show the value of Freud's science of the personal by taking an unsentimental look at the subject's early childhood and sexual experience. Already in the first section of the study, he declares the answer to the riddle of Leonardo's character: "The core of his nature, and the secret of it, would appear to be that after his curiosity had been activated in infancy in the service of sexual interests he succeeded in sublimating the greater part of his libido into an urge for research" (SE 11:80–81). But unlike Norbert Hanold, who is brought back to life and love through Zoe Bertgang, Leonardo's sexuality remained atrophied and problematic, a highly sublimated form of homosexuality, according to Freud's reconstruction.

On one level, we could read the Leonardo study as a *tour de force* of novel gestures on the evidentiary plane, since Freud clearly stakes a great deal on showing the subtlety with which psychoanalysis can handle the smallest fragments of evidence and yet reach wide-ranging conclusions. His point of departure is the single recollection of childhood that can be documented for Leonardo's life, the bizarre memory of how a bird (actually a kite [*nibbio*], but Freud takes it to be a vulture through a mistranslation) came down to him as he lay in his crib, opened his mouth with its tail, and struck him many times against his lips with this very same tail (SE 11:82). Leonardo simply took this occurrence as an omen that he was destined to take a strong interest in such birds, a prospective interpretation that is in keeping with a long tradition in biography since antiquity concerning portents that occur to a great man in his infancy. Freud, however, redefines and refines this anecdote, first turning it from an infantile memory into an adult *fantasy* projected back onto childhood and then using the "evidence" of this fantasy to establish a biographical "fact": that Leonardo lived his first years alone with his mother, an unmarried peasant woman whose excessive affection had a powerful influence on his psychosexual development.

Already in this gesture we can see the conflicting agenda Freud is advancing: on the one hand, the *critical analysis* of memory in relation to "facts"—for he asserts that this odd occurrence simply cannot have happened as Leonardo remembers it—and, on the other hand, the *reconstruction* of memory that leads instead to other, more significant "facts." Freud justifies this evidentiary maneuver with an explicit analogy to ancient historiography and the elaboration of legendary history, and this analogy in itself is highly significant to my investigation; however, I defer my full discussion of it to chapter 8 below. For now it is enough to note that personal memory is called radically into question in this study, but any radical doubts about the possibility of recalling the past are assuaged by the importation of the critical principles of ancient studies. In other words, if memories are like personal myths or legends, then we should approach them like those professionals who study myths and legends.

So to understand fully the audacity of the Leonardo study, one must first grasp that it all hangs on Freud's conversion of one memory into a fantasy that, unlike the veridical recollection of a simple event, betrays the complex signification of desire with its successive elaborations. The paucity of other evidence (for there simply *is* no evidence that Leonardo ever lived alone with his birth-mother in the first years of his life, or that she over-stimulated him in the manner Freud alleges) is swept aside by the assumption that this one memory-fantasy *must* reflect the most important feature of Leonardo's early development and will therefore lead us to solve the enigma of his personality. Freud thus balances a great deal on one tenuous set of evidentiary assumptions:

> If it is true [*Wenn es richtig ist*] that the unintelligible memories of a person's childhood and the phantasies that are built on them *invariably emphasize* the *most important elements* of his mental development, then it follows that the *fact* which the vulture phantasy confirms [*die durch die Geierphantasie erhärtete Tatsache*], namely that Leonardo spent the first years of his life alone with his mother, will have been of decisive influence on the formation of his inner life. (SE 11:92; my emphasis)

Having converted the memory into a fantasy, Freud is now free to interpret it in the condensed manner of a dream. The bird's tail condenses the
nipple longed for by the nursing child with the imaginary phallus of the
mother, and the fantasy is now sexualized in a manner that has a pro-
nounced, passive homosexual character. The question is: why is the
mother displaced by a vulture in his fantasy?

Through his analogy between individual memory and legendary history, Freud establishes the idea that our early memories are effectively a
personal mythology, a self-narrative creatively elaborated to conceal as
much as reveal the essence of our development. But now his recourse to
mythology shifts from the analogical to the evidentiary mode in a manner so abrupt it seems at first like a free-association: "At this point a
thought comes to the mind from such a remote quarter that it would be
tempting to set it aside" (SE 11:88). He relates that the Egyptian hiero-
glyph of the vulture stands for "mother," and that the Egyptians worshipped a vulture-headed mother goddess by the name of Mut ("Mother,"
which bears a striking resemblance to the German *Mutter*, as he hastens
to point out), who was "usually represented by the Egyptians with a phallus" (SE 11:94).[3] Initially this Egyptian connection to Leonardo's fantasy
is drawn in source-historical terms: Leonardo read somewhere (perhaps
in Horapollo's *Hieroglyphica* or in the Church Fathers) about the vulture's
peculiarity of having only the female sex and yet of being able to reproduce itself, and this information fed back into the adult recollection of
his childhood. Leonardo's later reading transformed some early memory into a fantasy of being a vulture-child, a virgin birth like Christ (SE
11:90).

Thus far Freud deploys a conventional historical methodology by citing probable background evidence for particular beliefs. But then he
muddies the picture considerably by shifting the status of the vulture-
complex back and forth between an evidentiary and an analogical footing. Mythological figures like Mut show how androgyny can represent
"the primal creative force of nature" (which itself explains phallic mother
figures in ancient cults according to some scholars); but the psychoanalyst's knowledge of children's sexual theories further explains how the initial assumption of every child (i.e., boy) is that the mother has a penis (SE
11:95). So it would now appear that the universal infantile theory is the
origin for the mythological image of the phallic mother, and that psychoanalytic evidence has cleared up another historical riddle, namely, why
phallic mother goddess cults existed in antiquity.

Only Freud greatly confuses the issue by saying that "impressive analogies from biology have prepared us to find that the individual's mental development repeats the course of human development in an abbreviated form; and the conclusions which psychoanalytic research into the child's mind has reached concerning the high value set on the genitals in infancy will not therefore strike us as improbable" (SE 11:97). This rather suggests the opposite: the existence of phallic cults in antiquity now serves as evidence for Freud's oddly phallocentric theory about children's sexual knowledge. He invokes Richard Payne Knight's *A Discourse on the Worship of Priapus* (1786) to make the point that in the primeval days of the human race "the genitals were the pride and hope of living beings," as opposed to prudish modern mores, and he asserts that the "indelibility that is characteristic of all mental traces" insures that this primeval attitude still has survivals today (SE 11:97). According to this, children are just little savages, *revenants* of a primitive culture. But, then, are they? Freud's own conclusion is stated this way: "The child's assumption that his mother has a penis is thus the *common source* from which are derived the androgynously-formed mother goddesses such as the Egyptian Mut and the vulture's *coda* in Leonardo's childhood phantasy" (SE 11:97; my emphasis). Here the Egyptians are just little children, and the analogy becomes recursive to a point where the distinction between evidence and explanatory similitude simply falls apart.[4] Are children just Egyptians, or were the Egyptians just children? What is Mut to Leonardo, or Leonardo to Mut?

This confusion over the exact relationship between psychology and mythology (which is itself a wavering between the evidentiary and the analogical) is instructive, for it shows that psychoanalysis as Freud practices it here cannot be an "individual psychology" apart from a "cultural psychology"; for the evidence of the individual seems arbitrary or bewildering if read as some kind of idiolect. Freud wishes to construct from it a more universal language of experience, though in a way that foregoes all previous "biographical" languages. The ancient manner of reading a memory such as Leonardo's would be to take the bird's strange action as reflecting a teleology *within* the individual's life and explainable in those terms alone, as Leonardo himself clearly did when he said that, "It seems that I was always destined [*che sia mio destino*] to write so distinctly about the kite" (cited in SE 11:82). Just as bees were said to have coated the infant Plato's lips with honey as a portent of his eloquence, Leonardo's "writing so distinctly about the kite" was foretold by the feather (i.e., the quill pen) placed between his lips, the bodily locus of eloquence. But Freud's search for meaning casts its net much more broadly than the

scope of the individual life and seeks to condense far more into this portent: suckling, fellatio, the exclusivity of the mother-infant bond, the
deleterious consequences of excessive maternal affection, homosexuality,
the sexual theories of children, creativity and the drive for scientific
knowledge, and even the smile of Mona Lisa. The importation of mythology therefore follows a pattern of interpretive conquest, adding a deep
temporal dimension to an already ambitious undertaking and further universalizing the scope of inquiry.

We might even characterize Freud's deployment of recapitulation as a
symptom of his compulsive need to speak *beyond* individual memory and
capitalize on the resources of a vaster cultural archive, yet doing so in a
manner that still foregrounds the individual, "empirical" focus of the analytic situation. In fact, right at the end of the study there is clear evidence
that Freud sees individual experience in terms of experiment and he co-
opts a citation by Leonardo that seems to suggest any scientist should feel
humble before the complexity of nature: "*La natura è piena d'infinite ragioni che non furono mai in isperienza* [Nature is full of infinite causes that
were never in (human) experience]" (SE 11:137). Here nature and human
experience seem incommensurable in a way that does not sound optimistic (the only scientific principle one could draw from this is the "principle of surprise"). Yet Freud uses this to stake out his turf in science by
pleading for the unique causal force of childhood experience in the formation of the adult personality, and this childhood experience is the region psychoanalysis carefully maps through the analytic encounter. His
conclusion to the study clearly links the experimental verification of natural processes with the uniqueness of individual circumstance: "Every
one of us human beings corresponds to one of the countless experiments
in which these '*ragioni*' of nature force their way into experience" (SE
11:137). Thus the singularity of individual experience—that particular-
ity which once made the individual *ineffable* (*individuum est ineffabile*, as
the Scholastic maxim goes)—is now counted as experimental verification
of universal causes and effects. Even Leonardo can in a sense be studied
as a locus of natural causation.

Freud assumes that the epistemological advantage of the analytic encounter is that it focuses on the analysand as a "concrete universal," a
specimen combining the ontological certainty of the individual with the
discursive availability of the universal.[5] As in *Gradiva*, Freud is trying to
convince us that psychoanalysis has a lot to say about human culture as
well as human nature, and he does so explicitly by showing how a great
genius need not be seen as some preternatural miracle, but rather as

someone who is "subject to the laws which govern both normal and pathological activity with equal cogency," the laws, that is to say, which psychoanalysis discovers, verifies, and codifies (SE 11:63). As with his reading of Sophocles' *Oedipus Tyrannus*, Freud demystifies the notion of "fate" (what Leonardo called *mio destino*) and inserts instead the "laws" of Nature that govern us all and have the same compulsive force as fate. The contingent circumstances of Leonardo's over-indulgent mother *fixed his erotic destiny* as a homosexual, and now a host of personal idiosyncrasies can be recognized as a coherent nexus that weaves together his own *Schicksalstragödie*, "the factors which have stamped him with the tragic mark of failure" (SE 11:131). The infantile fantasies of the great Leonardo are clearly established in an order of natural knowledge, as are, along the way, certain fantasies of the Egyptians—which is to say, certain infantile fantasies of the human race. It is not hard to see why Carl Jung, who later theorized the collective unconscious, said upon reading this essay: "The transition to mythology grows out of this essay from inner necessity, actually it is the first essay of yours with whose inner development I felt perfectly in tune from the start" (McGuire 1974, 329). Within two years this harmony would be permanently lost.[6]

Dreams of an Analyst

It is quite obvious by now that the personal dimension of my model is deeply implicated in the Leonardo study in that Freud is seeking to explain a great personality and to show in this first example how psychoanalysis can contribute to the study of historical biography with its *scientific* view of the personal. As he pleads at the end of the work, this is what sets off his pathography from the hagiographic accounts written by conventional biographers. Throughout, he employs defensive rhetoric concerning his scandalous discussions of Leonardo's intimate life in the interests of science (SE 11:130). But his criticism of the conventional biographer's identification with/idealization of the subject can equally be applied to himself, since he appears to have a personal investment in Leonardo that goes well beyond a mere scientific case study. Since Freud's science of the personal arises from the intersubjective encounter of analysis, we must now read the "personal" from the side of the beholder to see how Freud's own personality is implicated in the study and where this implication takes us.

From his letters of the time, it is clear that the Leonardo study, like

many of his boldest works, came as a flash of intuition right as he was trying to find a way to take a hold of biography for the movement. To Jung
he writes: "The riddle of Leonardo da Vinci's character has suddenly become clear to me. That would be a first step in the realm of biography.
But the material concerning L. is so sparse that I despair of demonstrating my conviction intelligibly to others" (McGuire 1974, 255). In the
event, as we have seen, he turned this sparseness into a virtue by assuming what little remains *must* be both essential and sufficient, and the absence of other evidence let his imagination have full rein. His work on
the study filled the very few moments of leisure left to him after the long
hours of daily analytical practice, and he even characterized it as a play-
ful occupation formed as a reaction *against* his work routine (McGuire
1974, 310). Work fills his days, but "[o]therwise I am all Leonardo," he
tells Jung (McGuire 1974, 301).

This work, then, was gestated in a zone between the serious practice
of science and the pleasures of pure recreation; can it be a mere coincidence that Freud's primary enigma to solve is Leonardo's vacillation between artistic creativity and scientific research? Or that he admits his
study is open to serious criticism for being merely a "psychoanalytic
novel," which would make it a fantasy based on the fantasy of Leonardo
(SE 11:134)? If we read Freud's reading of Leonardo's memory *as* a fantasy of Freud's, some striking things emerge. For one thing, there is a
suspicious resonance between the tendentious way Freud interprets Leonardo's fantasy and his own childhood dream of his mother's "death" discussed earlier in *The Interpretation of Dreams* (SE 5:583–584), in which
he saw his "beloved mother" being carried by people with bird's beaks
and laid upon a bed. The birdman figures were, he recalled, most likely
inspired by falcon-headed gods from an Egyptian funerary relief depicted
in the Philippsohn Bible he read as a child (SE 5:583). His sudden connection to the Egyptian Mut in analyzing Leonardo's memory might well
be an association to his own *liebe Mutter* and the anxiety-dream from his
seventh or eighth year; for there is otherwise remarkably little reason for
Egypt to enter into the Leonardo analysis (especially given that the bird
in Leonardo's memory is *not* a vulture). "Egypt" signifies thus not just the
childhood of Leonardo or that of the human race, but also *Freud's* childhood. The instability of the evidentiary and analogical status of Mut
seems more understandable when we analyze her presence in the text by
adding the personal dimension from Freud's point of view, which thrusts
her into the childhood scenario in advance of clear connecting logic.

Freud's complex sexual interpretation of Leonardo's memory can also be seen as a reflection of the earlier analysis of his own dream, which hints that the birdmen who placed his mother on the bed are linked to the slang term *vögeln* (literally, "to bird," but meaning "to screw" [SE 5:583]); in fact, he returns to this word explicitly in the Leonardo study (SE 11:125). Thus the anxiety in the dream was not over his mother's death, but rather, as he interprets it, was due to the repression of "an obscure and evidently sexual craving that had found appropriate expression in the visual content of the dream" (SE 5: 584).[7] Moreover, there are certain resonances between his reading of Leonardo's "two mothers" and his own experience of being raised by his mother and a Czech nursemaid, as well as his sexual initiation by the latter.

So we might well suspect that Freud's ambitious attempt to reconstruct Leonardo's childhood from a single memory is a projection of his self-analysis onto a historical figure. There are moments in the text that certainly invite such a reading. From this passage, the personal outlook and the professional gaze seem welded together in Freud's attempt to "see things" in Leonardo's queer vision:

> If we examine with the eyes of a psychoanalyst [*mit dem Auge des Psychoanalytikers*] Leonardo's phantasy of the vulture, it does not appear strange for long. *We seem to recall having come across the same sort of thing in many places, for example in dreams;* so that we may venture to translate the phantasy from its own special language into words that are generally understood. The translation [*Übersetzung*] is then seen to point to an erotic content. (SE 11:85; my emphasis)

By means of this linguistic analogy, Freud assumes that the eccentricity of an individual's mental images can be redressed through their promotion to a linguistic order that is supra-individual, thus banishing anxieties about an inaccessible "private language" unavailable to a universalizing science.[8] But do we see here in this instance the translation from an idiolect into a standard language, or rather the translation from one idiolect into another, i.e., based on the lexicon of Freud's personal experience?

For Freud, the common obscene extension of the word "tail" to mean "penis" in many languages (in fact, the Latin word *penis* meant primarily "tail" and was a kind of euphemism for the direct obscenity *mentula*) is sufficient evidence of a universal sexual significance in the scene, and clearly oral stimulation is overtly involved in the memory. So a "translation" of the scene in terms of fellatio is the least outrageous maneuver from the linguistic point of view. Under the influence of the "seduction theory," someone might be tempted to assume this is a screen memory masking sexual abuse by a male relative. Its evidentiary status in that regard seems much easier to uphold. Does the shadow of Laius the pederast then fall over Leonardo's crib? Would this explain his alleged homosexuality?

As it turns out, the evidentiary gap that Freud rushes to fill so readily and decisively for Leonardo's fate is rather the *absence of the mother* in this recollection, not the father. According to the Freudian rules of evidence, it is precisely the mother's absence that points to her centrality in the scene, and his complex reconstruction of the oral pleasures of fellatio with the experience of suckling helps to bridge the gap between the manifest image and its latent content. Yet as we have seen, it is at this juncture that he invokes the powerful mother goddess Mut to establish the presence of the marginal peasant woman Caterina through the convenient picture-language of Egyptian hieroglyphics. But this convenient linguistic solution brings with it sinister implications, as it introduces the self-sufficient paradigm of the "phallic" mother whose authority threatens the phallic mastery of the male. As Madelon Sprengnether observes, "Having once evoked the image of the powerful Egyptian mother goddess, Freud cannot quite banish her or contain her influence over his text" (1990, 79). Since this issue touches upon *both* the invocation of antiquity as a body of evidence *and* the analogical paradigm of masculine, oedipal science, I shall now address Freud's complex navigation of the gender trouble he creates for himself in unpacking Leonardo's fantasy. As we shall see, this moment in the 1910 study has profound implications for how we might view Freud's later work.

Egypt and Exodus

Egyptian mythology was always highly attractive to Freud for its syn-cretic—or perhaps we should say *accretive* — nature. Lacking cogent models for his notions of condensation and the *revenant* (a figure who returns in the guise of another), it is clear that complex figures like Mut acquired an exemplary status in his mind. "A special feature of the Egyptian pantheon was that the individual gods did not disappear in the process of syncretization. Alongside the fusion of gods the individual divinities continued to exist in independence" (SE 11:94). The Egyptian pantheon thus serves itself as an analog of memory and the dynamic condensation/preservation of mnemic material, and Freud is especially enticed by the phenomenon of Mut's condensation of maternal and masculine characteristics, which suggests mnemic holdovers from childhood sexual theories.[9] But this same combination creates the alarming paradigm of female self-sufficiency, a threat to the phallic order that is the Freudian norm whereby the female is seen as derivative, castrated, and dependent. Thus the absence of Leonardo's father, which might be expected to create the pre-oedipal idyll of the boy's complete enjoyment of his mother, instead creates for Freud the disturbing scenario of female domination and aggression, which effectively emasculates the boy (see SE 11:117, discussed below). The problem with using mythological evidence, as we have already seen in the case of Oedipus, is that myths work with a narrative logic of their own that cannot safely be contained by the rationalizing discourse of *Wissenschaft*. Myth always exceeds the grasp of discrete propositions about the world, and its invocation by other discourses quite often leads to a seepage that can function to undermine the very propositions that it was supposed to support.

There is certainly reason to see a threat in Mut, whose cult is worth discussing in more detail at this point. Mut's cult shows very well the process of fusion Freud describes. It grew particularly during the period of the New Kingdom (1539–1075 BCE) to absorb a variety of other powerful goddess-figures, like Sekhmet, the leonine goddess representing the punitive power of the sun (she is referred to as the "Eye of Re" in her capacity to bring terrible justice). In a Ptolemaic manuscript of the *Book of the Dead*, there is a spell (no. 164) that clearly shows how Mut-Sekhmet-Bastet holds the creative power of life and death over all orders of being. The spell's salutation is an apotheosis of the maternal principle.

> Hail to thee, Sekhmet-Bastet, (eye) of Re, mistress of the gods, plume-wearer, lady of bright red linen, mistress of the white crown and the red crown [the double crown of Upper and Lower Egypt], *sole one superior to her father, (thou) to whom no gods (can) become superior* [. . .] manifestation of the mistress and lady of tombs, Mut in the horizon of the sky, contented of heart (yet) lover of conflict. Strife and peace are in thy grasp. Thou shalt be standing at the prow of thy father's bark overthrowing the evil-natured one while *thou puttest truth at the prow of his bark.* Thou art the consuming flame— unduplicated later [. . .].
>
> Praise to thee, *who art stronger than the gods;* joy to thee. The Ogdoad [the great 8 divinities] (and) the living souls who are in their coffins are praising thy dignity. *Thou art their mother; thou art their*

creator, who makes for them the place of rest in the mysterious nether world and keeps bones sound, so that they are preserved from terror. Thou <makest> them divine in the seat of eternity, preserving them from the (judgment) hall of the evil one [. . .] . (Allen 1974, 160; my emphasis)

The mummies cradled in their coffins are protected by this great mother, and the spell involved here requires one to employ an image of Mut with three heads (one human, one a vulture's, and one of Pakhet, "She Who Scratches," a lion-goddess from Middle Egypt), a phallus, wings, and a lion's claws. The effect of the spell is that the deceased "shall be divine among the gods in the god's domain and shall not be kept away forever and ever" (Allen 1974, 161).

This image of a life-giving mother suggests a feminine order where the laws of maternal Nature take precedence over all, combining not only the cosmic powers of life and death, but also the temporal powers of state. In texts from the Eighteenth Dynasty, she is called Mut the Great, Mistress of Heaven, Mistress of All the Gods, and Mistress of the Two Lands, the latter being the official title of the queen of Egypt (Lesko 1999, 138). She was often depicted in human form wearing the double crown (*peschent*) of Egypt, worn *only* by the pharaoh and *not* his wife; she was in fact the only goddess to be so depicted as Mistress of Crowns. So there is a dimension to Mut that clearly suggests the feminine accession to power, quite literally in the case of the woman pharaoh Hatshepsut, who brought the cult of Mut into prominence when she herself wore the double crown, which was itself a considerable aberration in dynastic history.

The image of Mut draws on what we can term the pre-oedipal idyll of the *alma mater*, the nourishing mother who sustains the continuity of delicate new life with the older, dying, and dead generations; in the mortuary cult of Egypt, this is melded with the role of preserver for the afterlife. But the very fact that Mut presides over life leads obviously to ambivalent feelings (such ambivalence, it must be said, is a structural characteristic of most polytheistic religions and their mythologies). "*Strife* and peace are in thy grasp," as the text says.[10] The greater her power to protect, the greater she is to be held in awe, even fear. The greater her power to bestow life in the next world, the more she is to be feared for withholding it. In the later New Kingdom, traitors were burned alive on the great brazier of Mut, an unusual concession to maternal vengeance (Lesko 1999, 148).

My reason for drawing out these historical details is that it is precisely in interaction with such great goddesses that one can trace *Freud's* ambivalence toward maternal power, as several feminist scholars have shown. Diane Jonte-Pace (2001) has recently read Freud's cultural texts in the light of a "counterthesis" that stands in tension with the oedipal masterplot, while still being a fragmented yet integral part of his thought. In this counterthesis, Freud engages in non-oedipal speculations on death and the fantasy of immortality in relation to the mother, and these ideas appear most visibly in his writings on religion. They are certainly very present in the cult of Mut, which he seems to have introduced so casually into Leonardo's past in part through the influence of his own experience.

I wish now to illustrate further the tension between the oedipal thesis and the rather different maternal plot in the Leonardo study, because it confirms Jonte-Pace's characterization of a floating counterthesis rather well, even if she herself made little use of it. But it also explains the inconsistencies in Freud's account of the Italian master and his parents' role in shaping his personality, which Freud regularly constructs with recourse to ancient mythology. In his desire to raise the Acheron of the unconscious, Freud ransacked the archive of antiquity for mythical correlates of his theories; but one cannot easily put back the netherworld forces once they are roused.

Madelon Sprengnether has very poignantly located Freud's uneasiness with the pre-oedipal mother in the matter of the mother's desire, which is always felt to be mysterious and unknowable, and is most often ignored in Freud's texts (1990). In fact, Freud presents femininity and feminine desire overall as a *historical* problem akin to the decipherment of hieroglyphics. "Throughout history people have knocked their heads against the riddle of the nature of femininity—*Häupter in Hieroglyphenmützen* [heads in hieroglyphic bonnets]" (Freud cites from Heinrich Heine's *Nordsee;* SE 22:113). Much of Leonardo's destiny seems tied to the intensity of his mother's desire, which in Freud's reconstruction (again, a reconstruction we have no reason to concede as anywhere near accurate) was unimpeded by the father's interdiction. But Freud's characterization of Caterina vacillates between "the tender and kindly mother who had nourished him" (SE 11:122) and the "poor forsaken mother" who "by the too early maturing of his erotism robbed him of a part of his masculinity" (*New Introductory Lectures on Psycho-Analysis*, SE 11:116–117). As Sprengnether points out, the Leonardo essay represents Freud's most explicit depiction of the mother-son relationship, and yet the study "assumes the character of a cautionary tale about the dangers of mother love" (1990, 75).[11]

The danger of mother love is its apparent propensity to emasculate, but the details of this procedure are far from clear. For one thing, we have great cause to wonder by what process the mother's awakening of Leonardo's eroticism early in life *robbed* him of his masculinity, and the strange answer is that she infected the boy with her own desire. Unable to imagine the consequences of a male child left completely in the clutches of feminine power, Freud asserts that

> The child's love for his mother cannot continue to develop consciously any further; it succumbs to repression. The boy represses his love for his mother: he puts himself in her place, identifies himself with her, and takes is own person as a model in whose likeness he chooses the new objects of his love. In this way he has become a homosexual. (SE 11:100)

Just what triggers this repression *in the absence* of the father is a mystery; it simply just happens. But the shift in mythic paradigm is clear: instead of the incestuous crime of Oedipus, the boy "finds objects of his love along the path of *narcissism*, as we say; for Narcissus, according to Greek legend, was a youth who preferred his own reflection to everything else and who was changed into the lovely flower of that name" (SE 11:100). Thus a second analogical paradigm from Greek mythology aids Freud in engineering the child's exodus from the overwhelming Mut and Egypt, a land where incest was regularly accepted in the royal family, as Freud knew very well (*Introductory Lectures on Psycho-Analysis*, SE 16: 335). Lest he become totally absorbed into the Great Mother, the boy saves himself through masculine self-objectification.

But Leonardo's life is not simply a tragedy of gender; he does not remain Narcissus, but must become a syncretic Narcissus-Oedipus if he is to serve as a hero in Freud's empirical romance. For we are reminded right from the start that Leonardo is a culture hero and a man of great genius, "one who is among the greatest of the human race" as Freud says in his very first sentence (SE 11:63). The key to Leonardo's character is not homosexuality *per se*, but rather his almost thorough *sublimation* of his homosexuality; yet even that is not sufficient to salvage the culture hero in Freud's mind. Therefore, mapped onto the plot of Narcissus we find a reassertion of the oedipal paradigm, belatedly it seems, and in a fashion far from coherent.[12] In the syncretism of Narcissus-Oedipus we can see the tension between counterthesis and thesis that Jonte-Pace finds endemic in Freud's thought. On the one hand, the dominance of the mother gives Leonardo a precocious zest for research, limitless physical affection, and delusions of immortal grandeur (i.e., being a virgin birth like the Christ child). On the other hand, the model of the father becomes decisive for his attempted mastery of nature as spurred on by male rivalry. The details of Leonardo's father complex are well worth examining here, since they impinge directly upon the empirical romance.

As often happens in Freud's works, it is hard to tell whether the Father is a problematic presence or a creative and necessary absence. Initially, Freud claimed that being fatherless led Leonardo to address the "riddle of the Sphinx," since he was in the unusual situation of having only his mother and was thus forced to brood on the origin of babies with "special intensity" (SE 11:92). By his very absence, the father became the *telos* of such reasoning: "and so at a tender age [Leonardo] became a researcher, tormented as he was by the great question of where babies come from and *what the father has to do with their origin*" (SE 11:92; my emphasis). Thus Leonardo's position of having no father led him to play Oedipus and puzzle the riddle of life, and this lays the foundation for his later development as a researcher. His very first quest was to find out *not* "What does my mother want?" but, rather, "What does a father do?"

But later Freud seems compelled to insert the dynamic of a *present* father in order to generate the conflict he requires, so he reverts to the model of masculine sexual rivalry that balloons into an entire life project: "No one who as a child desires his mother can escape wanting to put himself in his father's place, can fail to identify himself with him in his imagination, and *later to make it his task in life to gain ascendancy over him*" (SE 11:120; my emphasis). Apparently we are simply to forget now that Leonardo had put himself *in his mother's place*. Thus when Leonardo moves in with the man who fathered him, he also moves from being Narcissus to being Oedipus, falling into "the normal relationship of rivalry" over his *step*mother and the normative male desire to be and be rid of the Father, which is thus set out as the life-task (SE 11:121).

This later father-identification has one unwholesome effect, since Leonardo-Oedipus comes to play Laius to his own creative works, of which he is the "father": "He created them and then cared no more about them, just as his father had not cared about him" (SE 11:121). But his antipathy toward his father had the positive effect of making him a truly independent scientific researcher, since unlike most people he was not afraid to challenge authority, which is just the inheritor of the paternal mystique that so impresses the young child.

Thus he became the first modern natural scientist, and an abundance of discoveries and suggestive ideas rewarded his courage for being the first man *since the time of the Greeks* to probe the secrets of nature while relying on observation and his own judgment. But in teaching that authority should be looked down on and that imitation of the 'ancients' [*Alten*] should be repudiated, and in constantly urging that the study of nature was the source of all truth, he was merely repeating—in the highest sublimation attainable by man— the one-sided point of view which had already forced itself on the little boy as he gazed in wonder on the world. If we translate scientific abstraction back again into concrete individual experience, we see that the "ancients" and authority simply correspond to his father, and nature once more becomes the tender and kindly mother who had nourished him. (SE 11:122; my emphasis)

Here Greek self-assertion overcomes a nebulous tradition of "the ancients" (the Egyptians?), and the Greeks themselves are clearly implicated in the empirical romance for being the first to rely solely on the senses and their own judgment. In his tragically untimely way, Leonardo reacquired the Greek gaze.[13] What is odd in this assertion is that one of the "ancients" Leonardo rejected was most assuredly Aristotle, a Greek well known for his epistemological reliance upon the senses and whose philosophical authority formed the backbone of Thomism, the official Catholic doctrine of the Counter-Reformation.

Thus in Freud's model of science, true scientific research is quintessentially oedipal, an anti-authoritarian grab at mother nature for one's own sensuous knowledge and enjoyment. It seems odd that Freud so insists on linking Leonardo's status as a scientific precursor to his alleged rivalry with his father, his desire to *out-Herod Herod* as he says (quoting tellingly from the other oedipal master-text, *Hamlet*), given Freud's initial insistence on the father's irrelevance to Leonardo's mental development as compared to his mother's overpowering affection. Yet we might explain this dogmatic reassertion of Oedipus if we refer back to Daniel Boyarin's suggestion that Freud's flight to the oedipal paradigm was itself a case of "homosexual panic" over the Fliess affair (1997, 208). Rather than casting his culture hero as a passive homosexual enslaved to an Egyptian *Mutter* (like a Hebrew, we might say in following Boyarin's linkage of the passive-feminine-Jewish), Freud suddenly shifts the tale from Egyptian Thebes (where Mut's impressive temple complex stands) to Boeotian Thebes of the Seven Gates, where the mother is simply a prized object passed on to victorious men. Just as Leonardo's secret of success lies in the *sublimation* of his homoerotic desire in the interest of "research," so too Freud's timely reinsertion of the oedipal paradigm will lead to scientific *immunity* to "feminine passivity" through masculine rivalry sublimated into empirical science.[14] So the counterthesis of a powerful mother who spurs on the first drive for research with her overwhelming physical attention is in the end conjured away by the oedipal design of the assertive male who wrings Nature's truths from her through the masterful discipline of his gaze and his reason.

The Law of the Mother

Yet Leonardo's life is discussed in *tragic* terms, as I mentioned before, and this is the last feature of the text that requires our attention, since it reflects what Sándor Ferenczi took to be Freud's philosophy of life when he read the Leonardo study (Brabant et al. 1993–2000, 1:181). Clearly his contemporary readers, in other words, were able to see the personal dimension that implicated Freud in this work at least at the level of secular ideology. We have seen that the phallic assertiveness of the oedipal paradigm seems to be a corrective for the pre-oedipal model of male passivity before an all-powerful female. Leonardo's research is thus interpreted as probing into kindly Mother Nature in violation of paternal authority. But as Freud comes to characterize the older Leonardo in his proto-secular reflections on the universe, it is clear that the gender roles are now re-characterized, even reversed, and the counterthesis seems to reassert itself after having been so carefully conjured away.

> The reflections in which he has recorded the *deep wisdom* of his last years of life breathe the resignation of the human being who subjects himself to Ἀνάγκη [Necessity], *to the laws of nature*, and who expects no alleviation from the goodness or grace of God. There is scarcely any doubt that Leonardo had prevailed over both dogmatic and personal religion, and had by his work of research removed himself far from the position from which the Christian believer surveys the world. (SE 11:125; my emphasis)

It is telling that when he characterizes this mature empirical hero, he paints his submission to the feminine realm of *die Natur* (which is, we know, ultimately *die Mutter*, Mut) as subjection to the grammatically feminine Ἀνάγκη [Necessity], implying the stoic and manly acceptance of a tragic fate that foregoes the consolations of a kindly *Father* god. The consoling reconciliations of paternal culture must be given up in the face of an overpowering feminine order, the "laws" of maternal nature.

Thus in spite of all the pretense to phallic mastery suggested by his tales of heroic self-assertion, the ultimate philosophy of Freud's science, as it appears ventriloquized through Leonardo's "deep wisdom" [*tiefe Weisheit*], is a form of resignation: the acceptance of a position of masochistic *passivity* before a feminine authority, Mother Nature. We must come to accept the "facts" of nature as "an inevitable fate" (cf. *Introductory Lectures on Psycho-Analysis*, SE 15:208). In the oedipal paradigm, the foundation of the resignation is cultural, not natural: the paternal law and threat of castration lead to the renunciation of incestuous desire. In the traditional religious resolution of the oedipal dynamic, the child is led to "complete submission to the will of God the Father" ("A Religious Experience," SE 21:171). But as Freud seems to suggest, a secular, scientific point of view requires us to forego submission to paternal power in order to understand the coercion of the *maternal* law. "Like Oedipus, we live in ignorance of these wishes, repugnant to morality, which have been *forced upon us by Nature*" (SE 4:263; my emphasis). Here the oedipal scenario seems readable not primarily as a reconciliation with the Father (its socially desired outcome), but as a painful acceptance of Mother Nature's law of desire that has been "forced upon us" like the probing tail of the vulture or the excessive affections of Caterina. That this recognition of maternal law seems a contradiction to the other, patriarchal aspect of Freud's thought has long been noted. Speaking of Freud's cultural writings, Sprengnether observes, "There is something like a Penelope principle at the heart of these texts, which seems to unravel what it creates. It is femininity, as embodied in the preoedipal mother, the specter that continues to inspire both awe and dread, that Freud associates with this condition" (1990, 119).

Freud's recourse to myth cannot save him from a certain inconsistency in this regard, for while Greek myth, in particular, reflects the castrating imposition of patriarchal order that is taken as normative, at the same time it preserves a feminine realm of fate for the individual that places the life-lot entirely in the hands of the Moirai, the spinners of personal destiny. Hence it seems symptomatic that around the time Freud forged his own patriarchal myth of the primal horde in *Totem and Taboo* (1911–1912), which greatly marginalizes feminine agency in history, he simultaneously wrote "The Theme of the Three Caskets" (1913, SE 12: 291–301) in which he characterized the three Moirai or fates as cultural precipitates of the Mother. A man's life is bounded by the three "inevitable relations" he has with a woman: the mother who gives him birth and becomes his first love-object, the woman he marries after his mother's image, and the Mother Earth that receives him when he dies. The Moirai reflect this trinity, which forms a cycle of departure and return to the Mother's body (SE 12: 301).[15]

But we can also use Freud's analysis of the Moirai to characterize his view of the scientific *Weltanschauung* that he believes Leonardo professed. The Moirai, Freud argues, are products of decomposition. They were a reaction-formation within Greek mythology, the "result of a discovery that warned man that he too is a part of nature and therefore subject to the immutable law of death" (SE 12:299). They are the analog in human life to the Horai, or the three Seasons, in the realm of nature, the "guardians of natural law and of the divine Order which causes the same thing to recur in Nature in an unalterable sequence" (SE 12:297). Only unlike the Horai, the Moirai are largely negative in character because they represent the humiliation of human egotism before the natural order. "The ineluctable severity of Law and its relation to death and dissolution, which had been avoided in the charming figures of the Horae, were now stamped upon the Moerae, as though men had only perceived the full seriousness of natural law when they had to submit their own selves to it" (SE 12:298). Again we see the theme of fundamental ambivalence vis-à-vis feminine figures and the natural world: the positive knowledge of natural regularities (Horai) and the negative submission to ineluctable natural laws (Moirai).

By Freud's own admission, the dour characterization of human life as submission to an impersonal "fate" is simply an embittered reaction on the part of male culture (for ultimately his point of view in "The Three Caskets" is just *für den Mann*) insofar as it is subject to the laws of feminine Nature. The bitterness of this response cannot be hidden by the ruses of the mythic tradition. The inveigling alterations in the tradition change the third sister, death, into the goddess of love, and convert the compulsion of the sisters' power over the individual into a free personal choice between them, according to Freud. The man in the myth is thus depicted as *choosing* the fairest, who is really Death. Such alterations were easily effected in the tradition, Freud asserts, because they were prepared for by "an ancient ambivalence" embodied in the earlier figures of the great Mother-goddesses, to whom there remained "a primaeval line of connection": "The great Mother-goddesses of the oriental peoples, however, all seem to have been both creators and destroyers—both goddesses of life and fertility and goddesses of death" (SE 12: 299). Thus a mere two years after the essay on Leonardo, Freud himself traced a clear line of development from Mut to Ἀνάγκη, that is, from the Great Mother in her ambivalent power of life and death over the individual to the culturally distilled Necessity, whose laws are one with the fabric of Nature. He effectively diagnosed his own secular "philosophy of life" as a recognition of maternal necessity behind the façade of male self-assertion.

As Madelon Sprengnether suggests, once Freud had evoked the name of the mother goddess in his Leonardo study, he could never quite contain her influence, and the "spectral mother" continued to haunt him—well beyond that text, as we can see (1990, 79).[16] Similar to Leonardo who was haunted by his mother's memory, Freud seems compelled in his scientific improvisation to face up to the Mother in her awesome and primeval power and to convince us to accept her "laws." At the same time, however, the "probing" of such laws is cast as a quest for phallic mastery over the Mother that rebels against the cultural "laws" of the castrating Father, even when Mut suggests to us a pattern of female self-sufficiency (for *she* bears the phallus) that robs the male of his masculinity and points to his irrelevance. Patricide and incest, we might say, seem a mere sideshow to a worse fate, namely, passivity and objectification before a no-longer-passive-and-objectified Woman. For there is in Freud's Leonardo-fantasy the disturbing counterthesis *not* of probing into nature, but of *being probed*, opened, and penetrated by a feminine agency with its own power, its own desire, and with clear links to death (i.e., the vulture and Mut as cradler of bones).

There are symptomatic moments in Freud's later work when this counterthesis seems to be responsible for certain disturbances in his otherwise oedipal argument. For example, we can cite the way Freud chose to read the image of Oedipus before the female Sphinx in the wake of Rank's heretical assertion that the primal trauma of life is birth anxiety, not the "Phocal" crime of phallic rivalry over the mother object. For while Rank was perfectly willing to see Oedipus as needing to overcome his fear of the Sphinx/Mother's power before he can desire her as a sexual object (i.e., that the birth trauma must be mastered *before* the oedipal rivalry can even occur), Freud chose instead to read the Sphinx as simply a symbolic encounter with *the Father,* in spite of a long tradition of iconography going back to antiquity that depicts the Sphinx in feminine form.

> The hero [Oedipus] commits the deed [patricide] unintentionally and apparently uninfluenced by the woman; this latter element is however taken into account in the circumstance that the hero can only obtain possession of the queen mother after he has repeated his deed upon the monster *who symbolizes the father.* ("Dostoevsky and Parricide," SE 21:188; my emphasis)

We have seen the curious way in which Freud already masculinizes the Sphinx's power in the Leonardo study, when Leonardo's urge to answer the riddle of where babies come from (Freud's translation of the Sphinx's riddle) boils down to discovering *what the father has to do with it.* This is effectively the primal scene of the empirical romance, as Freud relates, since it is the *terminus a quo* that dates the activation of the "drive for research," the compulsive *Wissensdrang* that leads to natural science. Yet instead of a free investigation of the mother's nature, Freud sees it rather as positing the question of paternal agency, which in Leonardo's case was conspicuous by its absence. Freud's ideological maneuver, which will color the entire enterprise of this new science, effectively turns the empirical romance (in essence, a gender-neutral tale of how we know things in a human body) into a *paternal* romance, a tale that comes to elaborate the Father as the source and origin, but also as the gap the son will fill and as the pattern of his desire.[17] Once the *pater* becomes the *arkhê* of Freud's scientific Logos, he effectively erases any distinction between archaeology and patriarchy.

As I argue in the final chapter of this book, Freud's conflation of archaeology and patriarchy shows clear continuity between his work of 1910 and that of the late 1930s. For while "Egypt" in the Leonardo study represents both the *return* to a pre-oedipal, emasculating *Mutter* and a triumphal *exodus* via oedipal science, "Egypt" in *Moses and Monotheism* is a return to patriarchal monotheism and its proto-scientific abstractions that bravely overcome the sensuous, feminine excesses of polytheism. By their historical and foundational act of killing their Egyptian "father" Moses, the Hebrews not only instantiate Freud's spin on oedipal truth (that patricide and incest are preferable to bondage to the Mother), they also bind themselves to Freud's paternal romance for all time and celebrate its culture of guilt and abstraction. The only fitting answer Freud could formulate to the spectral mother that haunted him was a spectral Father he mythically created in *Totem and Taboo* and then elevated in *Moses and Monotheism* into the Great Man of History (which, as the old feminist pun goes, thereby becomes merely *his* story).

CHAPTER 5

■

The Cunning of Tradition

> You taught me that a kernel of truth lurks behind every absurd popular belief.
>
> —FREUD TO FLIESS (MASSON 1985, 193)

Like Shelley, Freud would seem to have all good maverick scientists believe that we are all Greeks whenever we take up the standard of "a freer or superior view of the world" and liberate ourselves from the dead weight of tradition through the self-grounded authority of the scientific method (*Studies on Hysteria*, SE 2:282). It is here we can see quite clearly the inherent crisis of legitimation that Freud's weird science creates and must constantly address: *throw out the authorities and submit to my authority*. In the realm of theory, Freud's authority rests on the sheer weight of convincing evidence he can deploy based on his analytic practice, and yet this evidence is highly problematic in being radically personal and specific to the close confines of the analytic encounter. Thus his recourse to the empirical is itself more a matter of allusion than demonstration, as we shall see in the next four case studies. Yet he appeals to the empirical in more than one way, for along with his knowledge of case histories, he deploys other figures in the empirical romance, such as Leonardo, who not only serves as a suitable subject for analysis, but, as we have seen, also plays a part in the genealogy of empirical science itself. Just as Freud had extracted from Jensen both the case history of Norbert Hanold and the intuitive authority of the creative writer, so too with the Leonardo study he distilled both an elegant case history and an uncanny genius, only this time it was a genius who could play by Freud's own rules of scientific observation and not just creative inspiration. We might even say that the twin authorities of science and creativity from the *Gradiva* study find their ideal union in Leonardo himself.

Freud clearly is engaged in a process of tracing a genealogy for his kind of science, even when his science seems to deviate quite drastically from the normative *Naturwissenschaft* of his time.[1] Leonardo also went against the grain of the authoritative science of his day, and in doing so, as Freud said, he showed himself to be an exponent of "Greek" empiricism. In what seems like an instance of doublethink, Leonardo ignored the "ancients" and followed the "Greeks." The pattern here is the seemingly contradictory one of "progress as return," and in my next two case studies, I will show how this pattern can be traced from beginning to end in Freud's psychoanalytic career, first in *The Interpretation of Dreams* and then in his writings from the very end of his life when Empedocles emerges as the spectral father of the dual instinct theory.

The Ancient Language of Dreams

From the start, the embattled rhetorical voice of *The Interpretation of Dreams* casts itself as speaking from a place in a tradition at odds with contemporary scientific orthodoxy. The very style and organization of this founding tome of psychoanalysis show that Freud appeals to a readership that goes well beyond his scientific colleagues, and his rebellious spirit is conveyed through the Vergilian motto of the work: *flectere si nequeo superos, Acheronta movebo* ["If I cannot bend the gods above, I'll raise up Hell below"]. According to his own characterization, his views are not acceptable to "official science." He declares the very possibility that dreams can be interpreted is something completely rejected as a chimera by philosophers and psychiatrists of the day, and yet he states:

> But I have come to learn better. I have had to realize that here is another of those not infrequent cases where an ancient, stubbornly held popular belief seems to have come closer to the truth of things than the judgment of contemporary science. I have to maintain that dreams really do possess a meaning, and that a scientific method of dream-interpretation is possible. ([1900] 1999, 80 = SE 4:100)[2]

Psychoanalysis, then, represents a third something between the blurry convictions of antiquity and the outright blindness of modern science and philosophy. Freud's predecessor and antitype in this arrangement is the ancient dream interpreter, who followed either the method of comprehensive symbolic exegesis (as Joseph did with Pharaoh's dream of the seven kine) or that of "decoding" the dream elements individually. He expresses a certain respect for the ancient dream analyst Artemidorus of Daldis (second century CE), who showed great sensitivity in his *Oneirocritica* for the fact that dream symbols are not univocal, but rather change their meaning according to the dreamer ([1900] 1999, 79–80).[3] This method, in fact, inherently approaches Freud's own in its concern with individual associations and its manner of interpreting *en detail* and not *en masse* ([1900] 1999, 83). But Artemidorus also presents a problem in that "for the decoding method, everything would depend on whether the 'key,' the dream-book, is reliable. And of that there is no guarantee whatever" ([1900] 1999, 80 = SE 4: 99–100). In his first edition, Freud was at pains to avoid casting his own work as such a facile "key" for superficial interpretation (what the Germans call *Deutelei* instead of *Deutung*), and he quickly moves at this point to insist on his empirical basis. "For many years I have been occupied with unraveling certain psychopathological structures, hysterical phobias, obsessional ideas, and the like, for therapeutic purposes [. . .]" ([1900] 1999, 80). This leads to a lengthy discussion of the details of Freud's clinical method, especially concerning its preparation of the analysand's mind.

So it would seem that Freud has successfully differentiated himself from Artemidorus through the rigor of his scientific data and approach. Only a few paragraphs later, it is clear that this is *not* so, since he is unable to use most of his data. Although he can lay claim to having analyzed "more than a thousand dreams at least" in his practice, these all come from neurotic patients, which means that the reader will not be inclined to see this sampling as representative of the species ([1900] 1999, 83). Freud wants to approach the dream as a symptom ([1900] 1999, 81), but he is aware that the only way to do so based on his clinical evidence would be to introduce "an over-lengthy preamble for each dream, going deep into the nature and aetiological conditions of the psychoneuroses" ([1900] 1999, 83). So ultimately the key specimens he will provide for us turn out to be his own dreams, and he resorts to them "as an abundant and convenient fund of material coming from a more-or-less normal person and relating to a variety of occasions in daily life" ([1900] 1999, 83). Suddenly his body of evidence is a body of *self*-evidence, and he blithely dismisses the objection that such evidence is arbitrary with the statement that "in my judgment, the conditions for self-observation are more favorable than the conditions for the observation of others" ([1900] 1999, 83).

By enforcing the empirical paradigm of reliable self-observation, Freud thus hopes to banish any fear that his dream book's analyses are derived from an "unreliable key" that imposes tendentious patterns of meaning unconnected to the specificity of the dreamer, since in the dreamer's desire lies the key to his whole theory. His thick descriptions of the circumstances surrounding each specimen dream are the antidote to the poisonous accusations of arbitrary and facile decipherment, i.e., the kind of interpretation presented by the "dream book" of antiquity. And yet, even in this more "scientific" procedure, his modern dream book cannot banish the specter of the ancient text, since his division into preamble, dream text, and analyzed lemmata reproduces the appearance of an ancient text with its commentary, a procedural analogy that is made *explicit* in his statement that the dream must be approached as "Holy Writ" (*The Interpretation of Dreams*, SE 5:514). (This in turn recalls one of his dream-sources, the Philippsohn Bible with its German translation next to the Hebrew, its commentary, and its illustrations.) More importantly, Freud's sudden conflation of the personal with the evidentiary very cleverly exploits the inherent violation of privacy it requires. For the assumption is: if Freud will thus embarrass himself by disclosing the details of his life in the interests of science, then his examples *must* be true and reliable, for why else would he do such a thing? As he says coyly, "And I trust I may assume that in the reader, too, *an initial interest in the indiscretions I shall have to commit* will very soon give way to an absorption solely in the psychological problems they serve to illuminate" ([1900] 1999, 84; my emphasis). Freud thus cajoles the reader into accepting his "reliable" indiscretions as valid illustrations of his scientific theory, and yet we have no reason *not* to suspect that this self-evidence can be just as easily tainted as any other, consciously or not.

Clearly, then, "reliability" is an issue that haunts the text, and Artemidorus the ancient interpreter cuts an ambivalent figure for Freud as his predecessor. On the one hand, there is much in Artemidorus' technique that Freud can admire; yet, on the other hand, Artemidorus is also taken to represent an arbitrary and unscientific method of interpretation that relies wholly upon the interpreter's ability to convince the dreamer of the validity of his interpretation without recourse to a scientific basis. Freud's continuing interest in Artemidorus is evident in the fact that he kept returning to the *Oneirocritica* in footnotes he added to the text in subsequent editions, specifically in 1911 and 1914 (SE 4:98, note 1; 4:99, note 1). On the positive side, Freud takes one of his most concise examples of dream interpretation from Artemidorus, an example that illustrates the vital link between the linguistic and the visual in the dream process (*Oneirocritica* 4.24; cf. Plutarch, *Life of Alexander* 24.5). During his long and difficult siege of Tyre, Alexander the Great dreamed he saw a satyr dancing on his shield. This disturbing vision was made clear to him by his seer Aristander of Telmessus, who saw in the satyr (*saturos*) the encouraging message: *sa Turos*, "Tyre is yours." This is an example Freud so liked that he added it in a footnote to *The Interpretation of Dreams* in 1911, and he referred to it a few years later in his *Introductory Lectures* (1915–1916), in spite of the fact that one could easily dismiss it as a clever instance of a courtier's wit. "The interpretation," he says in the *Lectures*, "which has a sufficiently artificial appearance, was *undoubtedly the right one* [*Die Deutung, die gekünstelt genug aussieht, war unzweifelhaft die richtige*]" (SE 15:236; my emphasis). The right one, that is, for illustrating Freud's theory of wish fulfillment and the regression of verbal meaning into visual images.

Things become more complicated in his footnote of 1914. Here it is clear that he identifies with Artemidorus even more strongly than in the first edition, but this leads to the inevitable narcissism of difference.

Artemidorus of Daldis [. . .] has left us the most complete and painstaking study of dream-interpretation as practiced in the Graeco-Roman world. As Theodor Gomperz [Freud's friend and one of the greatest classical scholars of the nineteenth century] points out, he insisted on the importance of basing the interpretation of dreams on *observation and experience*, and made a rigid distinction between his own art and others that were illusory. The principle of his interpretative art, according to Gomperz, is identical with magic, *the principle of association*. A thing in a dream means what it recalls to the mind—*to the dream-interpreter's mind, it need hardly be said*. An insuperable source of arbitrariness and uncertainty arises from the fact that the dream-element may recall various things to the interpreter's mind and may recall something different to different interpreters. The technique which I describe in the pages that follow differs in one essential respect from the ancient method: it imposes the task of interpretation upon the dreamer himself. It is not concerned with what occurs to the *interpreter* in connection with a par-

ticular element of the dream, but with what occurs to the *dreamer*.
(SE 4:98, note 1; my emphasis)

Thus Artemidorus is a worthy predecessor in that he relied on an empirical basis, "observation and experience," and understood the principle of
mental association so crucial to Freud's method. But he accuses Artemidorus of imposing his own associations on the dreamer's dream, something Freud assures us he himself never does. And yet as we have just seen,
Freud's prime specimens are his own dreams, cases where in fact the
dreamer's associations are the same as the interpreter's. Effectively he
wins this game by changing the very nature of the contest, turning it into
a trial of *self-exegesis*.

What is more, later editions of the *Interpretation of Dreams* begin to
contradict the very project Freud outlined in the first edition by including more and more material on *universal dream symbols*, i.e., a "key" suggesting a set of univocal meanings for such things as hats, nail files, cigars,
stair cases, etc. This section of the book in later editions (VI.E "Representation by Symbols") shows Freud's uneasy accommodation to the idea
of fixed symbols, largely under the influence of Wilhelm Stekel, a follower whose *Die Sprache des Traumes* (1911) took psychoanalysis danger-
ously close to the principles of ancient dream interpretation.[4] In fact, a
side-by-side comparison of the later editions of *The Interpretation of
Dreams* with Artemidorus is quite revealing of this convergence, since it
shows how Freudian sexual symbolism can appear as arbitrary as Artemi-
doran symbolism, and how it simply inverts the signifier and the signified. That is, for Artemidorus the penis is a symbol for just about
everything, while for Freud just about everything is a symbol for the penis. Of the penis in dreams, Artemidorus says:

The penis (*to aidoion*) corresponds to one's parents, on the one hand,
because it has a relationship with the seed. It resembles children, on
the other hand, in that it is itself the cause of children. It signifies a
wife or a mistress, since it is made for sexual intercourse. It indicates
brothers and all blood relatives, since the interrelationship of the
entire house depends upon the penis. It is a symbol of strength and
physical vigor, because it is itself the cause of these qualities. That
is why some people call the penis "one's manhood" (*andreia*). It corresponds to speech and education because the penis [like speech] is
very fertile. Indeed, when I was in Cyllene, I also saw a statue of

Hermes which was made, by natural analogy [λόγῳ τινὶ φυσικῷ], into nothing other than a penis.

Furthermore, the penis is also a sign of wealth and possessions because it alternately expands and contracts and because it is able to produce and to eliminate. It signifies secret plans in that the word *mêdea* is used to designate both plans and a penis. It indicates poverty, servitude, and bonds, because it is also called "the essential thing" (*anankaion*) and is a symbol of necessity (*anankê*).

The penis signifies, moreover, the enjoyment of dignity and respect. For the enjoyment of all one's civil rights (*epitimia*) is also called *aidôs* [which can mean "one's shame/genitals" as well as "respect, awe"]. Therefore, if the penis is present and it stays in its proper place, it signifies that whatever is represented by the penis will remain in its present state. If the penis grows larger, what it represents will increase; if the penis is taken away, what it represents will be lost. If the penis is doubled, it signifies that everything will be doubled, with the exception of a wife or a mistress; these will be lost. For it is impossible to use two penises at the same time. (*Oneirocritica* 1.45; 1974, 38–39)

To this we can compare parts of the later editions of *The Interpretation of Dreams:*

Children in dreams often stand for the genitals; and, indeed, both men and women are in the habit of referring to their genitals affectionately as their "little ones." Stekel is right in recognizing a "little brother" as the penis. Playing with a little child, beating it, etc., often represent masturbation in dreams. To represent castration symbolically, the dream-work makes use of baldness, hair-cutting, falling out of teeth and decapitation. If one of the ordinary symbols for a penis occurs in a dream doubled or multiplied, it is to be regarded as a warding-off of castration. The appearance in dreams of lizards—animals whose tails grow again if they are pulled off—has the same significance. Many of the beasts which are used as genital symbols in mythology and folklore play the same part in dreams: e.g. fishes, snails, cats, mice (on account of the pubic hair), and above all those most important symbols of the male organ—snakes. [. . .] A quite recent symbol of the male organ in dreams deserves mention: the airship [i.e., Zeppelin], whose use in this sense is justified by its connection with flying as well as sometimes by its shape. (SE 5:357)

This comparison reveals two very similar phallocentric visions, but with the crucial difference that Freud's version takes the penis as a necessarily repressed signified, not a potent signifier through which a great many social signifieds can be expressed.[5] In reducing the realm of symbols largely to the theme of sexuality, Freud's dream book appears even more arbitrary than Artemidorus', particularly in its recurring obsession with images of castration.

The figure of Artemidorus, then, can only be understood properly in Freud's text if we range it alongside the figure of Wilhelm Stekel, who broke with Freud in the period that also saw the departures of Alfred Adler and Carl Jung (1911–1913). Freud returns to Artemidorus in part because he returns to Stekel in later editions, and through both he wrestles with the problem that universal symbolism is an attractive means of increasing the significance of psychoanalysis for understanding the human psyche, though it also threatens to undermine psychoanalysis's scientific status. On the one hand, Freud is convinced that dream symbolism "is not peculiar to dreams, but is characteristic of unconscious ideation, in particular among the people, and it is to be found in folklore, and in popular legends, linguistic idioms, proverbial wisdom, and current jokes, to a more complete extent than in dreams" (SE 5:351). It thus forms part of a larger pattern, an "ancient but extinct mode of expression, of which different pieces have survived in different fields" of the psyche, and which psychoanalysis is uniquely able to decipher (*Introductory Lectures on Psycho-Analysis*, SE 15:166). Years later, he will not be able to conceal the fact that he feels the analyst has the *authority* to impose his own associations when it comes to dream symbolism. "Since *we* know how to translate these symbols and the dreamer does not, in spite of having used them himself, it may happen that the sense of a dream may at once become clear to us as soon as we have heard the text of the dream, even before we have made any efforts at interpreting it, while it still remains an enigma to the dreamer himself" (*New Introductory Lectures on Psycho-Analysis*, SE 22:13; original emphasis). This is effectively what Freud did in analyzing the memory/fantasy of the vulture from Leonardo's childhood, which as we saw he "translates" symbolically with reference to Mut, the vulture-headed goddess.

However, the devil is in the details of actually specifying these symbols and their respective meanings, since the results look all too familiar: i.e., like the dream book of antiquity, alive and well in *Die Sprache des Traumes*. "Regard for scientific criticism forbids our returning to the arbitrary judgment of the dream-interpreter, as it was employed in ancient times and seems to have been revived in the reckless interpretations of Stekel" (SE 5:353). Freud is all too aware that his own form of mental associationism could be read as simply a modern form of superstition, and his ambivalence toward Stekel's intuitive gift as a dream interpreter is a symptom of this deeper anxiety. As I discuss further in chapter 7 below, this is precisely why he steers clear of the temporal realm with which ancient interpretation was most concerned: the future.

In sum, we see in *The Interpretation of Dreams* that psychoanalysis takes on a role of mediator between established science and ancient tradition. Freud relies heavily on the notion that ancient cultures and the *Volk* contain secrets about the psyche that must not be disregarded, yet his exploitation of these secrets is for the benefit of *Wissenschaft*, and effectively he pleads his case to the reader so that he may be allowed into the scientific hierarchy that seems quick to exclude him. The suspicion that there is a Romantic tinge to Freud's vindication of folk wisdom is confirmed toward the end of his book, when he deploys Goethe's concept of *das Dämonische* to describe the realm of the unconscious: "But the respect ancient peoples paid to dreams is a tribute, based on a true psychological intimation, to the untamed, indestructible elements in the human soul, the *daemonic* powers that produce the dream-wish and that we rediscover in our Unconscious" ([1900] 1999, 406). Antiquity thus offers Freud a body of evidence and true beliefs—through a glass darkly, to be sure—which help him fight his battle with the scientific establishment. As we saw above in chapter 1, this battle continues as he extends the scope of his science from dreams to the creative arts in his study of Jensen's *Gradiva* (1906), in which he declares at the start, "The author of *The Interpretation of Dreams* has ventured, in the face of the reproaches of strict science, to become a partisan of antiquity and superstition" (*Delusions and Dreams in Jensen's Gradiva*, SE 9:7).

From Psychology to Cosmology

At the end of his career, we find this pattern repeated when Freud appears to have become a heretic *within his own church* by bringing out the concept of a death drive (*Todestrieb*), which, he admitted, "found little sympathy" and was not really accepted even by psychoanalysts ("Analysis Terminable and Interminable," SE 23:244). Initially, he was aware that this made his science sound like a philosophical system, specifically like Schopenhauer's, though some suspect what he really suppresses is any recognition of his former followers' theories of aggression and bipolarity (*New Introductory Lectures*, SE 22:107).[6] But Freud later came to embrace the idea that he was simply reviving the theory of the Presocratic philosopher Empedocles of Acragas (ca. 495–435 BCE).[7] It seems very telling that Freud was made "all the more pleased" to find his own theory "in one of the great thinkers of ancient Greece," and he even admitted that he could never be certain whether what he took for his own creation might not be "an effect of cryptamnesia" based on his wide reading in earlier years (SE 23:244–245). This confession of cryptamnesia is disturbing if one considers how Freud effectively dodges any question of indebtedness to his followers Adler or Stekel—or for that matter, to the German philosophers Schopenhauer and Nietzsche—by freely embracing Empedocles as the spectral father of his dual instinct theory. Like the Roman poets of old, Freud deems it honorable to plagiarize from the Greeks, as long as one is the first to do so.

Following the scholar Wilhelm Capelle's characterization, Freud introduces Empedocles in "Analysis Terminable and Interminable" (1937) as a Greek Faust; this puts Empedocles suspiciously in line with a gallery of ego ideals, like Leonardo (the "Italian Faust") and Goethe, to whom Freud often returned for personal consolation.

> The activities of his [Empedocles'] many-sided personality pursued the most varied directions. He was an investigator and a thinker, a prophet and a magician, a politician, a philanthropist and a physician with a knowledge of natural science. He was said to have freed the town of Selinunte from malaria, and his contemporaries revered him as a god. His mind seems to have united the sharpest contrasts. He was exact and sober in his physical and physiological researches, yet he did not shrink from the obscurities of mysticism, and built up cosmic speculations of astonishingly imaginative boldness. (SE 23:245)

It is clear that there is a high degree of identification at work here, since the combination of empirical sobriety and imaginative boldness is exactly what characterizes the overall project of metapsychology in Freud's mind. As he says in *Beyond the Pleasure Principle*:

In any case it is impossible to pursue an idea of this kind except by repeatedly combining factual material with what is purely speculative and thus diverging widely from empirical observation. The more frequently this is done in the course of constructing a theory, the more untrustworthy, as we know, must be the final result. But the degree of uncertainty is not assignable. One may have made a lucky hit or one may have gone shamefully astray. (SE 18:59)

As with Artemidorus, Freud seems caught between a desire to embrace his predecessor in defiance of those of his contemporaries who mock him and the desire to overcome a rival theorist, no matter how ancient. "Born as he was at a time when the realm of science was not yet divided into so many provinces, some of his theories must inevitably strike us as primitive," Freud assures us (SE 23:245). This would lead us to expect that any similarity between Freud's theory and Empedocles' would be treated as coincidental. But Freud maintains the analogical difference with his Greek predecessor only with great difficulty, and the similarity quickly collapses into identity.

This collapse seems predicted from the start. "But the theory of Empedocles which especially deserves our interest is one which *approximates so closely* to the psychoanalytic theory of the instincts that *we should be tempted to maintain that the two are identical,* if it were not for the difference that the Greek philosopher's theory is a cosmic phantasy while ours is content to claim biological validity" (SE 23:245; my emphasis). Since Freud's theory is grounded in the concept of instinct, he feels secure that his own theory has "some sort of biological basis" (SE 23:246). And yet elsewhere he shows himself equally aware that in his own time the instincts are themselves just a kind of mythology (*New Introductory Lectures,* SE 22:95). Many years earlier he had even criticized how instinct theory was deployed at the outset of his own movement. "Everyone assumed the existence of as many instincts or 'basic instincts' as he chose, and juggled with them like the ancient Greek natural philosophers with their four elements," which is to say, like Empedocles, who first theorized the four elements (*Beyond the Pleasure Principle,* SE 18:51). So the "biological validity" he claims, as he knows, is only a provisional advantage over his Presocratic ancestor, not a transcendental ground of truth.

The manner in which Freud ultimately characterizes the relationship between the two theories is not similarity but "reemergence" (*wieder auftauchen*), as if psychoanalysis is merely channeling a current of cosmic truth first divined by the magus of Acragas.

The two fundamental principles of Empedocles—φιλία and νεῖκος [love and strife]—are, both in name and function, the same as our two primal instincts, *Eros* and *destructiveness*, the first of which endeavours to combine what exists into ever greater unities, while the second endeavours to dissolve those combinations and to destroy the structures to which they have given rise. We shall not be surprised, however, to find that, on its re-emergence after two and a half millennia, this theory has been altered in some of its features. (SE 23:246)

When Freud concludes this discussion by saying, "And no one can foresee in what guise the nucleus of truth [*Wahrheitskern*] contained in the theory of Empedocles will present itself to later understanding," he gives his own theory the status of a provisional update on a nuclear truth from long ago. Freud thus betrays such an odd reverence for ancient *origination* in this case that he is perfectly willing to give up any claim to *originality*. It is enough to vindicate an ancient theory with new evidence, just as psychoanalysis "confirms" the legend of Oedipus.

Freud's attraction to Empedocles is understandable. Writing in Homeric hexameters, Empedocles successfully grounded his theory in the rhetorical voice of the mythological tradition, something Freud could admire in that it brings scientific theory closer in line with the "primary process" thinking of mythology, the "secular dreams of youthful humanity" ("Creative Writers and Day-Dreaming," SE 9:152). Just as Sophocles lived in an age when the oedipal Truth lay closer to the surface in traditional narrative, enabling him to write the psychological masterpiece *Oedipus Tyrannus*, so too did Empedocles hit upon a primal reality that centuries of civilization would carefully bury under tartuffery and denial. Empedocles' thought was also palatable to Freud no doubt because of its "modern ideas," such as "the gradual evolution of living creatures, the survival of the fittest and a recognition of the part played by chance (τύχη) in that evolution" (SE 23:245).[8]

In fact, in spite of his mystical side, Empedocles fits well into the scheme of the empirical romance for his insistence on the value of "the present" and the observable: πρὸς παρεὸν γὰρ μῆτις ἀέξεται ἀνθρώποισιν ("the human mind grows as it encounters what is present"—Diels-Kranz fr. 106/Inwood 93). Perhaps it was Empedocles' belief in the transmigration of souls that led Freud to suggest his psychoanalysis was just a later reincarnation of Empedocles' "nuclear truth." The fact is that Freud had visited Empedocles' birthplace of Agrigento in 1910 and had re-

marked on how well preserved the Greek past is in Sicily: "infantile reminiscences that make it possible to infer the nuclear complex" (McGuire
1974, 353). This journey might be part of what was forgotten in his
"cryptamnesia." As Freud's friend Theodor Gomperz observed, "The
modern traveler who visits Girgenti [= Agrigento] is reminded at every
step of Empedocles, for the beautiful piety of the Italians, fostered by the
continuity of their civilization, takes no account of chronological barriers" ([1901] 1939, 1:227).

Whatever his reasons were for aligning psychoanalysis so closely with
Empedocles, his recourse to this figure fits a pattern we have seen: a disturbance in his theorization leads him to adopt a figure of antiquity as he
works toward his solutions. When his seduction theory of the neuroses
collapses, he adopts Sophocles (or at least his Oedipus). As he begins to
stake a great deal on the decipherability of meaning in dreams, he adopts
Artemidorus in opposition to "strict science." And when he begins to see
Eros as only part of the story of instinctual life, he adopts initially Plato,
then Empedocles to introduce Death.[9] But each adoption also requires a
degree of disavowal, so Sophocles is cast as a poet who knows not what
he says, Artemidorus is an interpreter who projects his own interpretations, and Empedocles is (effectively) a writer of science fiction. In each
instance, however, there is progress through a return to a "nuclear truth,"
a *Wahrheitskern* from the days of "youthful humanity." This seems to
rhyme well with the overall *habitus* of seeking fundamental truths at the
origins, be it in early childhood or early civilization.[10]

The return to ancient *Greek* culture is hardly insignificant in each
case—most emphatically in the case of Empedocles, whom Freud calls
"one of the grandest and most remarkable figures in the history of Greek
civilization" (SE 23:245). As I have already mentioned, the recourse to
figures of antiquity often hides a more troubling and proximate relation.
Sophocles' Oedipus, as some suggest, came along in time to save Freud
from troubling doubts concerning Wilhelm Fliess, his own father Jakob,
or even his mother Amalie.[11] Artemidorus, as we have seen, clearly resonates with the bothersome interpretive sophistry of Wilhelm Stekel;
therefore, additions to *The Interpretation of Dreams* that refer to Stekel are
matched with additions referring to Artemidorus. As I have also mentioned, Empedocles may well mask the figures of Stekel, Adler, Schopenhauer and/or Nietzsche.

So another element of *habitus* may well be the recourse to Greek antiquity as a vocabulary of *avoidance* and not just foundational truth. If I may
introduce a structural analogy of my own, Freud's gallery of Greek wor-

thies functions similarly to the architecture of the Vienna Parliament, the greatest neo-classical edifice on the *Ringstrasse*. This building deploys classical figures and motifs in order to hide the utter lack of a democratic tradition in the Austro-Hungarian Empire, and also to avoid the troubling complications inherent in monumentalizing *any* reference to the real histories of the Empire's numerous competing nationalities. As even Hitler noted, the Vienna Parliament was a disturbing acropolis because its eternal Hellenic forms concealed the tragicomic dysfunctionality of the government.[12] Its hyperbolic classical style suggests an attempt to achieve unity through collective amnesia, and it is by no means the only such example of a classicism deployed to repress native historical memory. This classical "edifice complex" can be seen in operation in our own Lincoln Memorial in Washington, D.C., which attempts to commemorate our greatest civil conflict without including a single image of an African-American (Savage 1994). So this architectural analogy teaches us that figures of memory like Sophocles, Artemidorus, and Empedocles are equally figures of forgetting.

An Occentric Theory

In this connection, there is one last act of oblivion I wish to suggest in relation to Empedocles, because it takes us back to Freud's disturbing Acropolis experience and a significant feature of his later personal life. I suggest that part of what Freud confronts in Empedocles is his uneasiness toward mysticism and, in particular, toward Romain Rolland, the scholar of religions in whose honor he had written his Acropolis essay in 1936. Freud readily admitted that the dual instinct theory is redolent of Schopenhauer (*New Introductory Lectures*, SE 22:107), and this raises the question of Freud's feelings toward Eastern mysticism, something quite present in Schopenhauer's cultural references to the doctrine of Maya and, more importantly, something in which Romain Rolland tried actively to interest Freud.

As opposed to the endless self-centered machinations of the libido, the death drive does not assume the imperative nature of the principle of individuation. Freud posits that the dominating tendency of mental life is "to reduce, to keep constant or to remove internal tension due to stimuli," and this is obviously in operation in the pleasure principle (since Freud's primary model of pleasure is neurological discharge), but also in death, the ultimate relaxation of all tensions within the mind (*Beyond the*

Pleasure Principle, SE 18:55). In this regard, knowledge of the death drive begins to resemble the renunciation of will that attained a high importance in Schopenhauer's thought, and which came close to the "oceanic feeling" propounded by Rolland. Schopenhauer said, "knowledge of the whole, of the inner nature of the thing-in-itself [. . .] becomes the *quieter* of all and every willing. The will now turns away from life; it shudders at the pleasures in which it recognizes the affirmation of life. Man attains to the state of voluntary renunciation, resignation, true composure and complete will-lessness" (cited in Safranski [1987] 1989, 235). As Rudiger Safranski observes, Schopenhauer's "greatest dream [. . .] was the denial of the will, its disappearance. He dreamed it by combining, as no one before him, the Western tradition of mysticism with the teachings of Eastern wisdom" ([1987] 1989, 346). His encounter with Eastern wisdom made him critical of the Jewish tradition upon which Christianity was founded; as he said of the Upanishads, "how the mind is here cleansed and purified of all Jewish superstition that was early implanted in it, and of all philosophy that slavishly serves this!" (cited in Safranski [1987] 1989). This orientalist enthusiasm represents the replacement of one ancient tradition for another, the Indian taking the place of the Jewish.[13]

Freud certainly did not ignore the great spiritual tradition of India. In *Beyond the Pleasure Principle* (1920), he referred to the "Nirvana principle" in discussing death instincts, and when he adduced Plato's myth of the three sexes to end his discussion, he freely entertained the notion that the Platonic myth may well be derived from an Indian source, since a similar myth can be found in the Upanishads (SE 18:58, note 1). It is clear, then, that he had a degree of knowledge and interest in Eastern thought as it was received in Europe at the time, even before his relationship began with Rolland in 1923. One of his last jottings from 1938 also shows his continued interest in the phenomenon of mysticism in general: "Mysticism is the obscure self-perception of the realm outside the ego, of the id" ("Findings, Ideas, Problems," SE 23:300). When Freud says that Empedocles "did not shrink from the obscurities of mysticism," this may point to an intimation of the unconscious workings of the death drive as "obscurely perceived" in the Greek's cosmological theory (cf. the "daemonic" self-perceptions of folk wisdom mentioned above in *The Interpretation of Dreams*). Freud shared an interest in Empedocles with Rolland, who had written a biography of the Greek philosopher in 1918, claiming him as the poet-visionary who opened the Mediterranean mind "to the oceanic perspectives of the infinite God" (cited in Parsons 1999, 97). Which is to say, Empedocles would therefore have been the first

Westerner to address that "oceanic feeling" Rolland felt at the heart of all religion, a feeling Freud felt lacking in himself, as he publicly claimed in *Civilization and Its Discontents* (SE 21:65).

In one of the most important recent books on Freud and religion, William Parsons has reconstructed Freud's relationship with Rolland in some detail precisely as it concerns the "oceanic feeling" (1999). In Parsons' subtle interpretation, Freud's oedipal reading of his Acropolis experience was his way of escaping from any serious consideration of mystical experience along Rolland's lines of thought, placing it instead firmly on the ground of psychoanalytic *Wissenschaft* and the family dynamic of oedipal rivalry (1999, 85). It is worth recalling here that Freud's initial title for his essay was "Unbelief [*Unglaube*] on the Acropolis," as if to proclaim his disbelief in mystical experience (Vermorel and Vermorel 1993, 537). We might see his appropriation of Empedocles the following year (1937) in a similar light, since Freud adduces this figure with overt reference to his "modern ideas" as well as his quainter ones, like the transmigration of souls. However, Freud pointedly omits any reference to Empedocles' theory of the "holy mind" of an immaterial god, which "darts through the whole cosmos with swift thoughts" (Diels-Kranz fr. 134/Inwood 110). Freud has no interest in presenting the religious side of this Greek predecessor in detail, just as he had made a proto-secular hero of Leonardo.

The case of Empedocles, I suggest, shows the long-term effects of *habitus* in that it reveals Freud's desire to ground his empirical romance in a decidedly *Western* tradition of thought, as conceived in opposition to an Eastern other. This sense of "occentricity" is quite plain in a letter Freud wrote to Rolland in January of 1930:

> I shall now try with your guidance to penetrate into the Indian jungle from which until now an uncertain blending of Hellenic love of proportion [σωφροσύνη], Jewish sobriety, and philistine timidity have kept me away. I really ought to have tackled it earlier, for the plants of this soil shouldn't be alien to me; I have dug to certain depths for their roots. But it isn't easy to pass beyond the limits of one's nature. (Cited in Parsons 1999, 176)

Freud very tellingly characterizes himself here as a Helleno-Jewish rationalist with certain "philistine" limitations, particularly when confronted with the "Indian jungle" of Eastern thought. His conflation of wild Indian nature with the spiritual complexity of Indian culture is a symptom of his dread, and, I suggest, returns us to Freud's early cultural orientation to classical culture *and* to the empirical romance that played itself out in the long-term development of his life.[14]

One of the important books Freud devoured as a *Gymnasium* student was Henry Buckle's whiggish *History of Civilization in England*, a book which follows Winckelmann in its upholding of the historical exceptionalism of the Greek gaze in relation to nature.[15] I dwell on Freud's reading of Buckle because it captures the positivistic assumptions that undergird Freud's own philosophy of history, such as it is. Buckle's "General Introduction" makes much of the contrast between the exotic and overpowering character of nature in India, versus the moderate climate of the Hellenic world, and how this determined the very different thought-worlds that thus arose.

> In Greece, Nature was less dangerous, less intrusive, and less mysterious than in India. In Greece, therefore, the human mind was less appalled, and less superstitious; natural causes began to be studied; physical science first became possible; and Man, gradually waking to a sense of his own power, sought to investigate events with a boldness not to be expected in those other countries, where the pressure of Nature troubled his independence, and suggested ideas with which knowledge is incompatible. (Buckle [1857] 1934, 100)

Clearly, then, the Acropolis of Athens is no place to be having mysterious experiences like *derealizations*, when Greece seems historically the epicenter of the reality principle in Western thought. The scenario of the son "waking to a sense of his own power" would seem far more appropriate than any wooly-headed "oceanic feeling," hence the oedipal outcome of Freud's self-analysis in relation to his "disturbance of memory."

Hence also, I conclude, the return to Empedocles when the death instinct becomes an integral part of Freud's metapsychology. This return seems to fulfill something Freud had read in the 1890s as he began his psychoanalytic adventure. Jacob Burckhardt said in his cultural history of Greece, which Freud read assiduously, that "All subsequent objective perception of the world is only elaboration on the framework the Greeks began. We see with the eyes of the Greeks and use their phrases when we speak" ([1898–1902] 1998, 12). Though the existence of Empedocles' theory seems to serve Freud's need to corroborate so bold an assertion as the *Todestrieb* with evidence from sober Greece (or in this case, Greater Greece), it is clear the personal dimension is rich with conflicts and their attempted resolutions that find a "compromise formation" in the magus of Acragas. Freud can indulge the flights of his own speculation through a venerable "empirical mystic," while keeping his distance from the Eastern-inspired mysticism of Rolland or Schopenhauer (and to open another old wound, C. G. Jung).

This has special importance for us, since the *Todestrieb* itself is the ultimate hypostasis of Freud's compulsion for antiquity. It is, as he defines it, "a need to restore an earlier state of things" (SE 18:57), the organic principle that renders into action what the *Forschertrieb* attempts to render into knowledge, i.e., the need to *know* the earlier state of things, such as where babies come from. At that moment of theorization in *Beyond the Pleasure Principle*, Freud knew very well there was no such thing as evidence, only myth. Originally he deployed the Platonic myth of the three sexes to suggest the hypothesis that "living substance at the time of its coming to life was torn apart into small particles, which have ever since endeavoured to reunite through the sexual instincts" (SE 18:58). At the time, he noted in reference to Plato's myth that "what is essentially the same theory is already to be found in the Upanishads" (SE 18:58), giving it an even more venerable antiquity than Plato's fourth-century text. But with Empedocles he found a proto-scientist who dwelt happily in a world where myth and science still communed with one another in the bright light of the Sicilian landscape, and not in the murky depths of the Indian jungle. What he lost in terms of chronological depth and Indian profundity, he gained in Greek "love of proportion"; that is, the fearful symmetry of Love and Death.

CHAPTER 6

▪

Conquest and Interpretation

Ὦ παῖ, [. . .] ζήτει σεαυτῷ βασιλείαν ἴσην·
Μακεδονία γάρ σε οὐ χωρεῖ.

"Boy, seek out a kingdom equal to yourself;
Macedonia cannot hold you."
Philip II to his son Alexander
—PLUTARCH, *Life of Alexander*

Last in my consideration of case studies are two formal analogies from the *Introductory Lectures* of 1915–17 that show how the analogical is often used in order to address a *crisis of evidence* caused by Freud's radical rewriting of evidentiary rules. This time, tension stems from the fact that Freud is ostensibly addressing medical students at the university who are proponents of conventional empirical science. At the same time, the published versions of the lectures are targeted for a general public that Freud seems much more interested in convincing. (Indeed, the *Introductory Lectures* were among his best-selling works.) Thus when he encodes references to the students' medical training, we see he has an opportunity to put the medical establishment on trial before the *reading public* as he presents the revelations and findings of his new Truth. In fact, from the beginning he openly dissuades the medical student from adopting the profession of analyst. "As things stand at present, such a choice of profession would ruin any chance he might have of success at a University, and, if he started in life as a practising physician, he would find himself in a society which did not understand his efforts, which regarded him with distrust and hostility, and unleashed upon him all the evil spirits lurking within it" (SE 15:16). The reading public cannot help but see the lecturer as a bold and embattled underdog delivering an *apologia* to a hostile, or at best, indifferent crowd. In this sense, there is always a double audience referred to when he begins each lecture with *Meine Damen und Herren!*

In the very first lecture, Freud has to address the essential problem of the whole enterprise: psychoanalysis cannot be publicly demonstrated in the way one expects during an anatomical lecture or a chemistry lesson (SE 15:16–18). In spite of Freud's deep personal conviction of being an empirical scientist, he cannot "perform his science" in the fashion that a medical faculty would demand. His great teacher Charcot had somewhat notoriously managed to get his patients to perform their symptomatology in his "theater of hysteria" and before the camera (Goetz et al. 1995). But there is no way to perform the talking cure in the space of a lecture or really to present it in any other sense before a third party: "The talk of which psychoanalytic treatment consists brooks no listener; it cannot be demonstrated" (SE 15:17). The highly personal nature of the analytic encounter, the very thing that guarantees the empirical basis of his psychological theories about the unconscious, precludes by its nature the performative scenario of a "public science," that hallmark of empirical culture in its classic pre-twentieth century form. Thus he states from the outset that his audience will simply have to take his word for the empirical events and evidence to which he can only allude.

In order to secure the good will of his audience, he then poses an analogy with a lecture on Alexander the Great (SE 15:18–19). An audience listening to a professional historian knows very well that he is not an eyewitness to the events he describes; they know as well that the evidence the historian cites must be subject to critical scrutiny and sifted through with care. But they will not therefore doubt that Alexander the Great ever existed. Why? Because they *trust* that the historian has no reason to lie about his topic, and they know that other history books will attest to these same events. The main gist of Freud's analogy seems to be: you may quibble about details, but you need not think I am trying to fool you; the unconscious truly exists. And the psychoanalyst is in a superior position to the historian, because he *is* an eyewitness to the events he describes in so far as they emerge from the analytic encounter.

Here we see how analogy addresses the problem of the evidentiary by establishing a relationship of *personal trust* between the audience and Freud himself. In a sense, he wants to claim that he *is* the body of evidence upon which his science stands. As an agent in the empirical romance, he has seen and conquered new realms for us, and these realms are in some ways terrible and very difficult to reach. He will bring us there only if we can submit to his (well grounded) authority and believe him. But Freud goes on to make a statement about the evidentiary that gives the audience some hope of understanding him and further reinforces the links between the evidentiary and the personal: "One learns psycho-analysis on oneself, by studying one's own personality" (SE 15:19). So once again, the truth of psychoanalysis is self-evident; your own person-ality is like a chemistry set with which to learn and demonstrate the new science. At the same time, his historical analogy subtly suggests at the very outset the greatest difficulty and yet the most intriguing promise that psychoanalysis provides for us: a confrontation with the *prehistory* and even *antiquity* of the self. By initiating his audience with an historical anal-ogy, he is already suggesting the affinity of psychoanalysis with the his-torical *Wissenschaften*, which, as will emerge in the lectures, it has a right to join.

The selection of Alexander the Great for his analogy is personally very significant, for it betrays the level of ambition that lurks behind the en-terprise. Alexander was the pattern of masculine achievement from Freud's earliest school days, when one of the very first Latin prose texts he read was an adaptation of Curtius Rufus' *Memorabilia Alexandri Magni* (Schmidt and Gehlen 1865).[1] He was reported to have had such enthu-siasm for the Macedonian conqueror as a child that he argued to have his younger brother named after him. His sister Anna recalled: "I remember how Sigmund enthusiastically chose Alexander, basing his selection on Alexander's generosity and prowess as a general, and how he recited the whole story of the Macedonian's triumph in support of his choice. His choice of name was accepted" (Bernays [1940] 1973, 142). This enthusi-asm for Alexander fits a pattern of martial heroism that seems to define his youthful identifications, which also included figures like Napoleon, Hannibal, Oliver Cromwell and Bismarck. The German estimation of Alexander was particularly high in the nineteenth century; Hegel termed him "the freest and finest individuality that the real world has ever pro-duced" ([1899] 1956, 224). For Freud he was "undoubtedly one of the most ambitious men that ever lived" (*Psychopathology of Everyday Life*, SE 6:108). The evocation of an ancient figure in a moment of discursive cri-sis also fits a pattern we have seen. As in the case of Oedipus, Artemi-dorus, Plato, and Empedocles, a figure of Hellenism comes to the fore; and yet this time there is a very great difference, for Alexander is a mili-tary figure, a conqueror, and an exponent of an *imperialist* Hellenism far more potent than the self-absorbed milieu of classical Athens. This opens up the question of what the cultural politics of Hellenism might be for Freud, which is worth a slight digression.

Imperialist Hellenism

Sander Gilman has suggested that Freud's adoption of Greek terms and cultural references was a reaction to the German Empire's neo-Roman pretensions and their anti-Semitic reverberations in the realm of science (1993a, 106–112). Freud's adoption of Greek culture was, in Gilman's account, at one and the same time a protest and an attempt to forge a new language of science devoid of the prejudices embedded in the dominant discourse of the age. Hellenism would thus be for Freud a kind of counterculture that creates a safe haven for the liberal Jewish *Bildungsbürgertum* from the hostile impulses of the emergent German Imperium. The problem with this reading is that it is not entirely accurate as to the German reception of either Rome or Greece. For while Germany, like all empires in modern Europe, displayed a degree of identification with the Roman Empire (and an historical connection to it through the Holy Roman Empire of the German Nation), it also had a profoundly anti-Roman sentiment at its heart during its reconstitution between the Napoleonic Wars and the Franco-Prussian War of 1870–71.[2] During this time, a veritable cult was created centered on the ancient Cheruscan prince Arminius (or "Hermann" as he was affectionately known), the *liberator Germaniae* who had engineered the ignominious defeat of Augustus' legions in the Teutoburg forest in 9 CE.[3] It is thus quite revealing that when the German Reich was reunified, a massive monument to Arminius (the *Hermannsdenkmal*, still standing outside of Detmold) begun after the Napoleonic Wars was finally completed in 1875. It was inaugurated in the presence of Kaiser Wilhelm I himself, though the doublethink of the new German Caesar invoking the ancient enemy of Augustus seems to have escaped notice.[4]

Just as Freud had a "Hannibal complex" that gave shape to his opposition to the Catholic anti-Semites of Austria, the whole of northern Germany seemed to suffer from an "Arminius complex" that stylized its resistance to the French Revolution, Napoleon I, Napoleon III (whose defeat in the Franco-Prussian War was seen by some not just as payback for the humiliations of Germany under Napoleon I, but also as a restoration of Arminius' legacy of political unity through military opposition to the *Welsche*), and to all of Catholic Europe during the *Kulturkampf* of the 1870s.[5] A major symptom of the essential schizophrenia of German classical education in the late nineteenth century was its devotion to Tacitus' *Germania*, where schoolboys could read in elegant Latin syntax about their barbaric ancestors who terrorized the Empire.[6] Freud read it during the school year 1871/1872, i.e., the year following the German victory over France. His history teacher that year, Victor von Kraus (1845–1905), had served during the fighting as a medical orderly just as Nietzsche had done, and was an ardent German nationalist (Knoepfmacher 1979, 293). Von Kraus began his fall lectures in 1871 with a recapitulation of "the battles of the Romans with the Germans," which no doubt were presented with a tendentious drift given his recent experiences (Pokorny 1872, 67). Freud got along well with von Kraus, who was probably responsible at least in part for the young Freud's flirtation with German nationalism, which continued on into his university years, when he joined the nationalist *Leseverein der deutschen Studenten Wiens* in 1873 and remained a member until its dissolution by the government in 1878.[7]

In addition to its fierce opposition to Rome and its *revenants*, German culture had long defined its essential difference from Latin Europe by affecting a unique affinity with ancient Greece. As Jacob Burckhardt put it, "From the time of Winckelmann and Lessing, and of Voss's translation of Homer, a feeling has grown up of the existence of a 'sacred marriage' (*hieros gamos*) between the spirit of Greece and the spirit of Germany, a special relationship and sympathy shared by no other Western people in modern times. Goethe and Schiller were classical in spirit" ([1898–1902] 1998, 11). This affinity did not change with the advent of German imperialism, since Prussia's greatest historian, Johann Gustav Droysen (1808–1884), was also the man who virtually invented the field of Hellenistic historiography and who had made it easy for Germans to see correlations between the Macedonian ascendancy and the rise of the German Reich. In fact, it is very likely that Freud had read as a boy Droysen's classic *Life of Alexander* ([1833] 1943), in which Macedon emerges as the clear predecessor to Prussia with the world-historical mission of unifying petty, bickering states into a massive empire.

This political vision could appeal readily to both the young Freud's German nationalism (a common sentiment among liberal Jews in Austria previous to the turn toward anti-Semitism which the Pan-German movement took only in the 1880s) and his sense of Jewishness, since after the Macedonian conquest, the Jews of the ancient world had readily manufactured their own rapprochement with the *Wunderkind* of world history (see chapter 11 below). It was Alexander, after all, who created Alexandria, the city that saw the birth of a unique Hellenic-Jewish culture that led, among other things, to the Septuagint, a translation of the Hebrew scriptures into Greek, the universal intellectual language of the time.[8] In sum, Alexander represented a figure of *inclusive* imperialist Hellenism, a culture imposed upon barbarians to be sure, but open to the co-optation of intelligent "wogs."[9] As Droysen put it, the Hellenistic culture brought about by Alexander provided the first true *Weltbildung* which in turn created the first world unity (*Welteinheit*) in human history, enlightened the Asiatic cultures, and set the stage for the world revolution of Christianity ([1833] 1943, 484–487). Thus, Greek culture did represent individual striving against entrenched power, as Gilman suggests, but equally conveyed the sense of a *universal* culture brought about by a truly exceptional, world-historical individual of a decidedly anti-democratic temper. Alexander, as a son who had overcome his father and was yet fulfilling a paternal mission (the conquest of Persia), conforms to Freud's pattern of both the hero and the Great Man of History.[10]

So Freud's use of Greek culture is not necessarily to be read as an evasion of either Jewishness or German nationalism; it could be seen as the opposite. It can be seen as a holdover from a time when his secular, assimilationist leanings made him sympathetic with the German appropriations of Hellenism that served a nationalist agenda before the advent of true political anti-Semitism. Moreover, his invocation of Alexander is part of a pattern of martial imagery that tinctures his language about the psychoanalytic movement. It has long been the consensus among the biographers that Freud's early political and military enthusiasms were sublimated into a career in science, hence the use of militant language in reference to his expanding *Wissenschaft*.[11] But Louis Breger has recently observed how this pattern, too pervasive to escape anyone's notice, has nonetheless rarely been commented on in relation to its historical setting (2000, 192). Freud's movement reflected the values and language of the great turn-of-the-century arms race that led to the catastrophic *sparagmos* of European culture during the First World War, which was raging right as Freud delivered his *Introductory Lectures*. Freud also repeatedly invoked the language of imperial conquest to signal psychoanalysis's expansion into other areas of research. To Jung he wrote, "I shall be very happy when you plant the flag of libido and repression in that field

[mythology] and return as a victorious conqueror to our medical moth-
erland" (McGuire 1974, 388). Such comments and language in his letters
are far from uncommon.

When Jung's behavior as crown prince of the movement troubled him,
he even cajoled the Swiss doctor in terms that bring us right back to the
analogy with which we began this section: "Just rest easy, my dear son
Alexander, I will leave you more to conquer than I myself have managed,
all psychiatry and the approval of the civilized world, which regards me
as a savage! That ought to lighten your heart" (McGuire 1974, 300).
Freud's characterization of Jung as his son Alexander in turn implies that
he is the uncouth Philip II (382–336 CE), the man the liberal tradition
held responsible for the destruction of the freedom of the Greek city
states. But this identification has deeply oedipal undertones, since it has
been suspected since ancient times that Alexander had a hand in Philip's
assassination.[12] Not only does this cast a dark side on what Freud is saying to Jung at this juncture about his father complex, it also calls into
question Freud's original desire to name his own brother Alexander in the
first place, as if to displace his own oedipal feelings toward his father.

It is also a further reminder of the oedipal cast of Freud's view of science, which we discussed above in reference to Thebes and Leonardo.
But we must see that the figure of Alexander compensates for the political implosion implicit in the Theban paradigm, and promises a world dominion to which only the most ambitious could aspire. Ferenczi firmly
thought that genuine political change would have to come about through
the triumph of psychoanalytic truth, though this would mean that the
analysts would form a guardian class reminiscent of Plato's *Republic*. Writing to Freud in 1910 he confessed, "I do not think that the ψα [psycho-
analytic] worldview leads to democratic egalitarianism; the *intellectual
elite of humanity* should maintain its hegemony; I believe Plato desired
something similar" (Brabant et al. 1993–2000, 1:130; original emphasis).
To this Freud replied in his letter of a few days later, "I myself, mean-
while, have surely already made the analogy with the Platonic rule of the
philosophers" (Brabant et al. 1993–2000, 1:133). This dream was still
alive in 1932, when Freud declared at the end of the *New Introductory Lectures* that "Our best hope for the future is that the intellect—the scientific spirit, reason—may in the process of time establish a *dictatorship in
the mental life of man*" (SE 22:171; my emphasis). As with Plato, the hegemony of reason is not only a psychological desideratum, but a political
goal as well, since "the common compulsion exercised by such a dominance of reason will prove to be the strongest uniting bond among men

and lead the way to further unions" (SE 22:171). And Alexander, as a student of Aristotle, was an intellectual grandson of Plato and therefore a convenient image of one whose strength bonded men in further unions.

To conclude: this particular analogy, which seems so off-handed in its context in the *Introductory Lectures*, has deep reverberations within the general contour of Freud's life and works. It suggests a will to domination that, upon consideration, will require us to think more deeply about other analogies Freud uses, such as archaeology, to which I will turn in a moment. But I wish to emphasize my initial point that recourse to analogy is in part a direct consequence of psychoanalysis's scientific double bind. Namely, that it is not just a theory or a philosophy but a discursive practice firmly rooted in the experience and rigor of analysis; yet because the personal and the evidentiary coincide so closely, its empirical moment is not conventionally demonstrable. Hence there is the turn toward discursive gestures like analogy, the use of composite or fictionalized narratives made to protect the identities of analysands, the deployment of myth, art, and literature, and the studied indiscretions drawn from the analyst's own life. As I shall argue now, the desire for an unequivocal, public demonstration of his "findings" forever feeds Freud's compulsion to deploy his master metaphor: the archaeological analogy.

Archaeology as Decipherment

Archaeology readily provided Freud with three key evidentiary paradigms: excavation (or material recovery), reconstruction, and decipherment. While we shall examine aspects of his use of archaeology further below in chapter 9, I wish to dwell here on the paradigm of decipherment as it appears in the *Introductory Lectures*, since this discloses not only a key function of his master metaphor, but also a model of public science to which he assimilates his growing *Wissenschaft*. Since the royal road to Freud's unconscious realm is dreaming, a major evidentiary concern throughout the *Lectures* is the validity of psychoanalytic dream interpretation. His fifteenth lecture, "Uncertainties and Criticisms" (SE 15:228–239), openly addresses the concern we traced earlier in reference to *The Interpretation of Dreams* and Artemidorus, namely, that psychoanalytic interpretation seems to rely too much on the personal skill of the interpreter, which suggests a disturbing degree of arbitrariness and a lack of scientific consensus.[13]

While Freud does not want to deny there are qualitative differences between analysts' abilities to interpret, he defends the lack of consensus in his lecture by first pointing out the inherent ambivalence and indefiniteness of dream symbolism. He grounds this observation by assuming that the "picture-language" of dreams is a primitive mode of expression like Egyptian hieroglyphics and other archaic scripts, and this linguistic analogy allows him to deflect attention *away* from a more rigorous characterization of dream content and the considerable elements of disanalogy, since dreaming is not a conventionalized "system" analogous to a language or a script (SE 15:180). The radical implications of the disanalogy have been unpacked in an exquisitely detailed essay by Jacques Derrida, "Freud and the Scene of Writing."[14] Instead of pursuing this radical line, Freud talks at length in the lectures about ancient scripts and their seemingly intolerable vagueness and indefiniteness, but stresses that the scripts *really functioned* as systems of meaning for the societies that invented them, and that indefiniteness does *not* imply contextual ambiguity at the level of utterance (SE 15:230–231). In Saussurean terms, one could say Freud stresses that, whatever the apparent ambiguities at the level of *langue*, real significance only emerges from *parole* and the competence of users (e.g., that *club* can mean a dance bar, sports equipment, or a cudgel is rarely a problem in real life, since there are adequate strategies of contextual selection).

The whole linguistic analogy is underwritten by the pervasive Freudian assumption that dreaming is a regressive or even archaic form of mentation, and that its archaism is of the same order as the archaism of hieroglyphic and cuneiform scripts. The relation between dreaming and hieroglyphics, in particular, seems troubled by the vacillation between the mode of similarity and the mode of cognate origin, just as Mut fluctuates between being analogous to Leonardo's vulture-fantasy and being commonly derived from the same infantile source. Freud can even conceal this vacillation under the curious language of "complete analogy," as when he said a few years before the *Lectures* that "In fact the interpretation of dreams is *completely analogous* [*durchaus analog*] to the decipherment of an ancient pictographic script such as Egyptian hieroglyphics" (SE 13:177; my emphasis).

But "complete analogy" threatens to cease being analogy and to become instead something approaching identity. Once again, the analogical in this argument is shading off into an evidentiary claim through recursive thinking: *since* the ancient scripts are of the same order of primitive thought as dream images, the intelligibility of scripts is therefore "proof" that dreams too are intelligible. Or at least, that dreams are in-

telligible to experts, for one convenient aspect of the deciphering metaphor is its implicit culture of expertise. He had already said in *The Interpretation of Dreams* (his "Egyptian dream book") that the productions of
dream-work "present no greater difficulties to their translators than do
the ancient hieroglyphic scripts to those who seek to read them" (SE
5:341). While this helps to give the Freudian interpreter a patina of re-
spectability, it also reminds us of that other latent peril in his characterization of psychoanalytic dream interpretation; namely, the emergence of
the ancient dream "expert" as the feared model for the analyst. Deciphering is the activity of the modern expert, the respected *Wissenschaftler*,
not the ancient soothsayer. One could say that "deciphering" thus becomes a way even to *deny* that interpretation is going on at all, since decipherment is less troubled by the subjective associations that plague the
ancient interpreter in Freud's reading. It is better to be seen as a Champollion than an Artemidorus in this regard.

However, the greatest difficulty with the linguistic analogy is that
Freud's fundamental interest is in *censorship*, or in not-saying as opposed
to saying. Thus he is forced in the *Lectures* to undo his own argument by
admitting flatly that "[a] dream does not want to say anything to anyone,"
which would *eo ipso* invalidate his previous analogy (SE 15:231). To him,
however, it merely shows how the dream problem is different in degree
of difficulty, not in kind, since the point of contact is again the archaic
Grundsprache "of which different pieces have survived in different fields"
(SE 15:166). That individual fragments of this language should seem
rather different in form or function does not disturb him. Ultimately, instead of admitting the unsuitability of his analogy, Freud makes a characteristic *further* analogy with cuneiform decipherment that shows just
how much these events in public science remain a paradigm for his own
desired success.

> The lay public, including the scientific lay public, are well known
> to enjoy making a parade of skepticism when faced by the difficul-
> ties and uncertainties of a scientific achievement. [. . .] There was
> a time when public opinion was very much inclined to regard the
> decipherers of cuneiform as visionaries and the whole of their re-
> searches as a "swindle." But in 1857 the Royal Asiatic Society made
> a decisive experiment. It requested four of the most highly re-
> spected experts in cuneiform, Rawlinson, Hincks, Fox Talbot and
> Oppert, to send it, in sealed envelopes, independent translations of
> a newly discovered inscription; and, after a comparison between the

four productions, it was able to announce that the agreement between these experts went far enough to justify a belief in what had
so far been achieved and confidence in further advances. The deri-
sion on the part of the learned lay world gradually diminished after
this, and since then certainty in the reading of cuneiform documents
has increased enormously. (SE 15:232)

The psychoanalytic movement did indeed try to create a kind of database
for dreams in order to generate a lexicon of dream symbols that would
lead to more uniformity in interpretation (the results of this were included in the later editions of *The Interpretation of Dreams* [Marinelli and
Mayer 2002]). But ultimately the desired consensus was never reached,
and one could even say that this analogy was a dangerous one for Freud
to make by this time, knowing as he did how very differently dreams can
be interpreted, and that interpretation is *not* synonymous with decipherment. He even has to warn the audience explicitly in his lectures *against*
the theories of his colleagues and erstwhile students Maeder, Stekel,
Adler, and Silberer, who in his estimation mislead their readers with their
fuzzy thinking (SE 15: 236–237).

   Yet the tenacity and unsuitability of the decipherment analogy make it
all the more illustrative for our purposes: in the course of his scientific
improvisation, Freud reveals the desired paradigm of an archive unlocked
and deciphered, releasing riches for historical understanding and public
knowledge. In fact, Freud's archaeology of desire can readily be understood as betraying *a desire for an archaeology:* i.e., the yearning for a clear
and distinct body of demonstrable evidence coupled with a decisive consensus of meaning, something which his new science seems to approach
yet inevitably fails to achieve. He appears to have suffered throughout
most of his professional life from a kind of "spade envy."

Archaeology as Triumph

As we have seen, archaeology provided not just a paradigm of procedure,
but also a paradigm of success. This is evident from the very beginning
of Freud's attempts to forge a new psychotherapy, as we see in his lecture
"On the Aetiology of Hysteria" of 1896. It is no coincidence that in the
forum of a public lecture (where the public consisted of first his colleagues in the *Verein für Psychiatrie und Neurologie* and later the readers of
the *Wiener klinische Rundschau*), the analogy comes into prominence here

as well. In this somewhat lengthy citation, the image of the archaeologist
is merged with that of the scientist through the word *Forscher*, "researcher,
explorer." His intrepid quest to make bold discoveries is rife with self-
assertive and romantic imagery.

> Imagine that an explorer [*Forscher*] arrives in a little-known region
> where his interest is aroused by an expanse of ruins, with remains of
> walls, fragments of columns, and tablets with half-effaced and un-
> readable inscriptions. He may content himself with inspecting what
> lies exposed to view, with questioning the inhabitants—perhaps
> semi-barbaric people—who live in the vicinity, about what tradition
> tells them of the history and meaning of these archaeological re-
> mains, and with noting down what they tell him—and he may then
> proceed on his journey. But he may act differently. He may have
> brought picks, shovels and spades with him, *and he may set the in-*
> *habitants to work with these implements. Together with them* he may start
> upon the ruins, clear away the rubbish, and, beginning from the vis-
> ible remains, uncover what is buried. *If his work is crowned with suc-*
> *cess, the discoveries are self-explanatory:* the ruined walls are part of the
> ramparts of a palace or a treasure-house; the fragments of columns
> can be filled out into a temple; the numerous inscriptions, which,
> by good luck, may be bilingual, reveal an alphabet and a language,
> and when they have been deciphered and translated, yield un-
> dreamed-of information about the events of the remote past, to
> commemorate which the monuments were built. *Saxa loquuntur!*
> (SE 3:192; my emphasis)

This long analogy shows Freud's emotional reliance at this very delicate
stage in his career on a paradigm of self-evident success; that is, the excavation of material remains whose proper reconstitution makes their
function self-explanatory, once all the pieces fit together and the deciphered inscriptions release the meaning and purpose of the structures.

This pattern of success reverberates throughout the personal dimension
as deeply as the Alexander analogy mentioned earlier. The citation above
should be read in the light of another statement he makes in the same lecture, when he declares that he has found at the bottom of every case of hysteria one or more instances of premature sexual experience: "I believe that
this is an important finding, the discovery of the *caput Nili* [source of the
Nile] in neuropathology" (SE 3:203). This second analogy conjures up the
romantic image of John Hanning Speke (1827–1864), the first European

to discover the source of the Nile at Lake Victoria in 1858, and it recalls as well Freud's own self-characterization to Wilhelm Fliess a few years later as "by temperament nothing but a conquistador—an adventurer, if you want it translated—with all the curiosity, daring, and tenacity characteristic of a man of this sort" (Masson 1985, 398). If Speke is behind the *caput Nili* metaphor, who is the model of the archaeological analogy?

It is fairly well established that Freud admired and even envied the success of the Homeric archaeologist Heinrich Schliemann (1822–1890), whose *Ilios* he read while he was drafting the *Interpretation of Dreams*. Schliemann's international fame as a discoverer, in spite of all the controversy surrounding him, would have inspired any ambitious researcher of the time. Freud keenly wanted to assert his new truth with the same decisive flourish as Schliemann did at the end of his first book on Troy: "In conclusion, I flatter myself with the hope that, as a reward for my enormous expenses and all my privations, annoyances, and sufferings in this wilderness, but above all for my important discoveries, the civilized world will acknowledge my right to re-christen this sacred locality; and in the name of the divine Homer I baptize it with that name of immortal renown, which fills the heart of everyone with joy and enthusiasm: I give it the name of 'Troy' and 'Ilium,' and I call the Acropolis, where I am writing these lines, by the name of the 'Pergamus of Troy'" ([1875] 1994, 211). Compare this to a comment Freud makes privately to Fliess in 1899, concerning a breakthrough with a patient.

> Buried deep beneath all his fantasies, we found a scene from his primal period (before twenty-two months) which meets all the requirements and in which all the remaining puzzles converge. It is everything at the same time—sexual, innocent, natural, and the rest. I scarcely dare believe it yet. It is as if Schliemann had once more excavated Troy, which had hitherto been deemed a fable. (Masson 1985, 391–392)

Schliemann's discovery of "Troy" not only was a paradigm of success for Freud's scientific imagination, it was also the model of adult happiness in general. In a letter to Fliess of May 28, 1899, Freud comments: "I gave myself a present, Schliemann's *Ilios*, and greatly enjoyed the account of his childhood. The man was happy when he found Priam's treasure, because happiness comes only with the fulfillment of a childhood wish" (Masson 1985, 353). Schliemann's money could not have made him happy, since money is not a childhood wish; so his whole biography made perfect sense to Freud as the pattern of a happy, successful life. As such, this pattern is worth considering in more detail.

It is quite revealing that Freud based his reading of Schliemann's life on the autobiographical narrative that the archaeologist had concocted for his *Ilios* at the end of his career, a text which peddled the myth that his earliest ambition was to prove the historicity of Homer ([1881] 1968, 1–17). Schliemann was himself a great improviser and cultivated the self-narrative that he was not at heart a businessman, but rather a man devoted to a great cultural cause, and his autobiography is constructed as an archaeological romance that could rival Jensen's *Gradiva*.

The romance begins with an oedipal rivalry as the young Heinrich debates with his father the reality of Troy. When his father tells him that the illustrations of Troy in a book he was reading were fanciful creations, the boy prophetically retorts: "'Father [. . .] if such walls once existed, they cannot possibly have been completely destroyed: vast ruins of them must still remain, but they are hidden away beneath the dusts of ages.' He maintained the contrary, whilst I remained firm in my opinion, and at last we both agreed that I should one day excavate Troy" ([1881] 1968, 3). This sets the young Heinrich up as the perfect hero in the paternal romance: he is on a mission defined in tension with his father, and carrying it out will lead him to overcome his father and yet also to win his approval. The fact that Schliemann's father's financial failure kept him from a proper education is also a note that would have resonated with Freud, who was clearly disappointed in his own father's lack of business acumen (though he was more fortunate in securing a *Gymnasium* education).

Schliemann's romance also has its erotic twist in the form of a childhood love at the age of nine for a girl in his village with whom he dreamed of excavating Troy. For those who like Peter Swales' narrative of illicit love between Freud and his sister-in-law, it is worth noting that Schliemann's sweetheart—his Zoe Bertgang—was named Minna. Tragically separated from her by his family's disgrace, Schliemann strikes an early note of foreshadowing in the narrative: "Thanks to God, my firm belief in the existence of that Troy has never forsaken me amid all the vicissitudes of my eventful career; but it was not destined for me to realize till in the autumn of my life, and then without Minna—nay, far from her— our sweet dreams of fifty years ago" ([1881] 1968, 5). The double narrative of desire, that is, the paternal romance and the young-love story, remains the red thread throughout as he recounts his business career in Europe and America. The telos of his life remains clear from beginning to end: "But in the midst of the bustle of business I never forgot Troy, or the agreement I had made with my father and Minna in 1830 to excavate it. I loved money indeed, but solely as the means of realizing this great idea in my life" ([1881] 1968, 17).

That the Schliemann myth found its public is quite evident from the preface the great polymath Rudolf Virchow wrote for *Ilios*, where the pattern of Schliemann's life is laid out for pious envy:

> And therefore thrice happy the man to whose lot it has fallen to re-
> alize in the maturity of manhood the dreams of his childhood, and
> to unveil the Burnt City. Whatever may be the acknowledgement
> of contemporaries, no one will be able to rob him of the conscious-
> ness that he has solved the great problem of thousands of years.
> [. . .] He had the courage to dig deeper and still deeper, to remove
> whole mountains of rubbish and *débris;* and at last he saw before him
> the treasure sought and dreamt of, in its full reality. [. . .] May the
> work which he has terminated become to many thousands a source
> of enjoyment and instruction, as it will be to himself an everlasting
> glory! ([1881] 1968, xvi)

This is a pattern that obviously appealed to the man who was trying to solve another great problem of thousands of years; namely, the interpre-tation of dreams, the "full reality" of which lies not in material remains, but can only be reached by means of the interpretive conquests of a novel theory of signification. In a note discovered by Ilse Grubrich-Simitis, we see the paradigms of decipherment and excavation are tied very neatly by Freud to two of their most famous representatives in relation to his own status: "Champollion very interesting. A real genius [,] not just through the favor of his disciples, as I am now becoming for a while. Confirms my idea that only the idée fixe makes a discoverer of one. 'Everywhere I see myself in Egypt.' Holding fast to the wishes of one's youth is the only way to lend strength to intention, i.e., as with Schliemann. One could initiate a collection: the importance of infantile wishes" ([1993] 1996, 126).

Thus Freud's modeling of his own scientific improvisation on Schlie-mann's biomythography reveals another part of the tenacious affinity that underwrites the archaeological analogy within psychoanalysis, apart from the procedural metaphors of excavation, reconstruction, and decipher-ment. As I will argue here in a moment, we can see how archaeology feeds not just a *descriptive analogy* — one merely used for momentary rhetorical effect—but a *transactional analogy,* one that helps to define the process of

analysis *as it is being undertaken,* one that is there *from its inception* as part
of the self-understanding of its founder and his co-workers (including, I
suggest, the analysand). As such, the analogy is not simply one more
rhetorical color to add to the palette of persuasion. Archaeology was the
alter ego that helped to give shape to the analytic enterprise as it came to
define itself; it was a role adopted in improvisation.

If we take the long view, the structural affinities in the lives of Schliemann and Freud are equally reflected in their legacies, given the great
amount of biographical excavation and debate surrounding both *Forscher.*
Just as we debate whether Freud really discovered anything with his delving into the "unconscious," Schliemann's site is also subject to constant
interrogation, for while there was undeniably an archaeological dig going on at Hisarlik in Turkey, it still is not clear that this place is Homer's
"Troy."[15] And current research in both instances does not stop at reconsideration of the two men's objects of study ("unconscious" and "Troy"),
but inevitably delves into the history of their own excavations and their
personalities.[16] The personal seems inextricably linked to the evidentiary
fields they marked out for conquest. The fact that this new millennium
began with two controversial exhibitions, *Freud: Conflict and Culture* (in
the USA, Brazil, and Austria, and worldwide at http://www.loc.gov/
exhibits/freud) and *Troia: Traum und Wirklichkeit* (in Germany and worldwide at http://www.troia.de) shows the degree to which we continue in a
sense to live the repercussions of the psycho-archaeological revolution.[17]
We are still disturbed enough to debate the reality of our primal scenes
a full century after they were said to have been excavated and recovered.

Freud's Alternative Ego

However, the references to Schliemann that we find in Freud's letters to
Fliess postdate the lecture on hysteria by three years. Who else could be
the model of Freud's *Forscher* in 1896? If we are concerned with the tenacity of the archaeological analogy—and its tenacity is *transactional,* as I
said, not just descriptive—we cannot neglect to ferret out the relevant
material in the personal dimension, even at the cost of a historical digression. Besides the influence of Schliemann, it is less well known that
Freud had an intimate friend who had lived something very much like the
scenario he describes in the analogy from the lecture. This man was
Emanuel Löwy (1857–1938), one of Freud's few *Dutzfreunde,* whom he
met in the 1870s when he first went to the University of Vienna. Löwy

was a sort of *éminence grise* throughout Freud's life and kept him intimately aware of the professional world of archaeology until his death a month before the Anschluss.[18]

Though Löwy was, like Freud, a Jew of modest parentage from Leopoldstadt, he rose to become the first Professor of Art and Archaeology at the University of Rome, inspiring his students to such an extent that he has been likened to Winckelmann for the scope of his erudition and passion for art.[19] A recent retrospective study of his work has termed him "a forgotten pioneer" in archaeology, though he was not quite the maverick Freud turned out to be in his respective field (Brein 1998). What Freud could admire in him was that, unlike Winckelmann, he did not have to convert to Roman Catholicism to succeed in the Eternal City. The very year (1901) Freud overcame his "Rome neurosis" and finally went there, Löwy was promoted to full professor, which makes one wonder about Freud's own decision in that same year to play the game and seek his appointment as *professor extraordinarius.* Particularly in the 1890s, Löwy's greater success in his career would have given Freud considerable cause for envy, and that Löwy achieved it in Rome over anti-Semitic opposition must have reverberated deeply against his own "Hannibal complex" and the grave political disappointments which he confronted in Vienna at the time.[20] While Löwy was never quite the *alter ego* that Wilhelm Fliess was for Freud, he could be seen as an *alternative ego*, a kind of fantasy-figure for an alternative life Freud could vicariously experience. The richness of the fantasy is clear in his letters to Fliess: "Otherwise I am reading Greek archaeology and reveling in journeys I shall never make and treasures I shall never possess" (Masson 1985, 427).

I dwell on this personal connection because the very activities Freud describes in his 1896 lecture's analogy are reminiscent of Löwy's work as an epigrapher and field archaeologist. Löwy had participated in the 1882 Austrian expedition to Asia Minor, where they made an extensive survey and study of remote ancient sites at Gölbashi/Trysa and Rhodiapolis (Benndorf and Niemann 1884, von Luschan 1889). He proved indispensable to the expedition with his fluency in modern Greek and Turkish which allowed him to palaver with the natives, with his expertise in copying inscriptions, and with his superb sketches (Wolf 1998, 32). He remained behind after the main work was completed to supervise the transport of the friezes from the *heroon* at Gölbashi/Trysa that were destined for the museums of Vienna. One can therefore imagine the influence of Löwy's friendship in the 1880s and '90s on the fertile imagination of a relatively under-traveled Freud.

Once Löwy moved to Rome, this influence hardly seems to have abated—quite the opposite. Writing to Fliess, Freud reported on November 5, 1897:

> Recently I was treated to a stimulating evening by my friend Emanuel Löwy, who is professor of archaeology in Rome. He is a scholar as solid as he is honest and a decent human being, who pays me a visit every year and usually keeps me up until three in the morning. He is spending his fall vacation here where his family lives. Of his Rome. . . . (Masson 1985, 277–278)

There has even been speculation as to whether Löwy's work on the genesis of the artistic impulse might be materially responsible for parts of Freud's early dream theory.[21] While I am somewhat skeptical about our ability to map out the causal relations between the two men's work, it is clear that they found enticing similarities between their fields. That Freud knew very well what Löwy was up to is clear from the fact that in his personal library he possessed copies of virtually all of Löwy's publications.[22] In the only extant letter from what must have been a considerable correspondence, Löwy makes plain that the excitement over interdisciplinary possibilities went both ways. Having just read Freud's *Jokes and Their Relation to the Unconscious* and *Three Essays on the Theory of Sexuality*, the busy professor writes back from Rome in 1905:

> I certainly don't have to tell you that I read both works with the greatest interest and was convinced in most cases by your interpretations. All these problems certainly interest everyone, they pertain to everyone, and everyone must have thought about them in some way. That this occurred in my case many times in the direction you pursued need not give you any satisfaction—though it does to me. In both cases [i.e., both books], there are for me in addition the special connections with my own area of research, and who knows whether we shall someday come into immediate contact? [. . .] As for the specific points about which I would gladly have further clarification, we'll talk—soon perhaps—in person [*mündlich*].[23]

In fact, there is rare silent film footage of the two men having just such a conversation in 1932, a testament to a friendship that was unique among Freud's intellectual bonds for its longevity. There is even one bit of evidence heretofore neglected that shows how Löwy's presence in the background of Freud's life *directly* stimulated the deployment of an archaeological analogy. In a letter to Stefan Zweig, Freud says:

> I had long struggled to find an analogy for your method of working; yesterday it occurred to me at last, conjured up by the visit of a friend who is an epigrapher and archaeologist. It is a procedure as when one makes a "squeeze" from an inscription. Namely, one puts a wet piece of paper on the stone and forces the softened material sink into the tiniest depression on the written surface. (Stefan Zweig 1989, 134)

There is little doubt that the friend in question is Löwy, and that this therefore represents a "smoking gun" of evidence about Löwy's capacity to ignite the analogical fireworks in Freud's mind. The very intimacy of this relationship—and it bears remembering that it was an exceptional intimacy for Freud in that he used the informal *du* with Löwy—reinforces the point that the analogy-formation goes beyond the descriptive, and impinges rather on a lived metaphor. And as we know, a lived metaphor often ceases to be lived as a metaphor, but rather soon slips into becoming a grounding *méconnaissance* at the heart of self-identity, with all the aggressivity that entails. If Freud lived the metaphors of *conquistador*, *Forscher*, explorer and archaeologist, what does this imply for the analytical situation? Who is conquered, researched, explored, and excavated?

The Right of Conquest

Freud's analogy clearly links his scientific enterprise with another aspect of archaeology that has less often been brought out, but which we can link directly to the Alexander analogy with which I began this chapter: the imperialist agenda. For the scenario Freud constructs is not the self-excavation of a nation (which certainly went on all over Europe), but the excavation of some exotic locale by a foreign interloper. From the way the analogy is written, it is clear that the "semi-barbaric" people the researcher encounters are useful "wogs" who can be enlisted in the grand adventure of historical *Wissenschaft*. But if one begins to unpack the analogy, it is obvious that the figure thus represented is the analysand, who is both the worksite and the laborer in the psychic excavation. Unlike the altruistic medical paradigm of curing and aiding, the archaeological paradigm enforces a pure regime of historical knowledge—quite often re-

stricted to centers of power and domination—and underwrites an economy of display that serves to bolster the fame of the discoverer. But what
Freud avoids in all his analogies is the serious and perennial question: to
whom does the past belong? For the final stage of the archaeological enterprise at the time he was writing is decidedly suppressed in his account
of "self-evident" success: the expropriation of ancient artifacts from their
find-sites and their removal to the great imperial museums of Europe and
America. So we must ask the impertinent question: to what extent does
the analysand lose her Elgin marbles in the course of Freud's scientific
expedition?

Archaeology at the turn of the century was in many ways a further expression of the imperial rivalries that characterized the age on other
fronts.[24] The ability to conduct archaeological research and to stuff one's
great museums with cultural riches were direct consequences of political
power, and in this regard the Austro-Hungarian Empire was trying hard
to keep up with the British, French, and especially the Germans. Exploration and excavation funds were raised with the promise that material
goods would be provided for public display, as occurred in the 1882 Austrian expedition, which was explicitly organized to acquire items for the
imperial collections (Benndorf 1884, 4). The year Freud first theorized
what was later to be called the Oedipus complex, 1897, saw the official
order for the incorporation of the Austrian Archaeological Institute by
the Emperor Franz Josef, with the express purpose of using this research
to bolster imperial prestige. For that reason, the Austrians worked dili-
gently on their excavations at Ephesus (begun in 1895 and continuing off
and on to this day in cooperation with the Turks), which were aimed at
gaining respect for the Empire's cultural achievements and adorning its
new museums. Freud was well aware of these Austrian excavations and
alludes to them in print ("'Great Is Diana of the Ephesians,'" SE 12:342).

So while Freud's analogy casts the *Forscher* as a lonely discoverer, the
reality behind him is that he is quite often an agent in an imperialist enterprise. I am not suggesting that the great empires always paid the tab
from imperial coffers, since most of the excavations were funded by private means, at least in their initial, pioneering phases. But this private
funding is in fact what links the civilian culture of grand capitalism to archaeology: whereas before only the aristocrat could afford to play the
antiquary, in the late nineteenth century a captain of industry like Schliemann or the son of an industrialist like Arthur Evans could pay for their
own adventures, thus converting their sudden wealth into "cultural capital." But it is always imperial Europe and America that form the *context*

of archaeological desire and that provide the audience for archaeological performance by ambitious individuals. For the stones are made to speak by those with the power to do so; that is, those who can erect temples, mausoleums, and triumphal arches, and those who can recover and reconstruct them.[25] In the nineteenth century at least, only empires excavated empires.

The implication of this for psychoanalysis is that Freud the adventuring *Forscher* may have harbored a kind of scientific imperialism toward the analysand and the possession of her past. This might seem at first a terribly "politically correct" objection, but when one considers some of the more disturbing comments Freud made to his colleagues, the suggestion begins to seem all too plausible. Late in his life, Sándor Ferenczi reflected on Freud's candid remarks to him about their patients: "'Patients are a rabble.' . . . Patients only serve to provide us with a livelihood and material to learn from. We certainly cannot help them" (Ferenczi 1988, 93). According to Ferenczi, Freud lost the ability to fully empathize and deal effectively with his patients the moment he discovered that hysterics lie; from that moment on, he ceased to love his patients. Instead he retreated "to the love of his well-ordered and cultivated superego (a further proof of this being his antipathy toward and deprecating remarks about psychotics, perverts, and everything in general that is 'too abnormal,' so even against Indian mythology)," a remark that clearly aligns the patients and their delusions with the "wogs" and their curious beliefs (Ferenczi 1988, 93). Given Freud's relentlessly global formulation of regression, the neurotic and the child have a demonstrable mental kinship with the primitive "savage," so the link between the consulting room and the colonial outpost is not fanciful. It was the crucial link that empowered the nerve specialist to pronounce on matters of cultural history.

The Jewish analyst listening patiently in his armchair may seem a far cry from the textbook image of the imperialist sahib, but Freud participated fervently for a time in the armchair imperialism characteristic of the age, when a vast influx of accounts about primitive peoples fed into the European imaginary at a time when the doctrine of uniform cultural evolution was in vogue. Non-industrial societies were thus "archived" and served to explain deep universal truths pertaining to all cultures (Kramer 1977). This was more than a matter of Freud's readings. On his desk in the 1930s was an ivory figure of Vishnu sent to him by the Indian Psychoanalytic Society; writing to Girindrasekhar Bose to give his thanks for the gift, Freud commented, "As long as I can enjoy life it will recall to my mind the progress of Psychoanalysis(,) the proud conquests it has made in foreign countries" (cited in Hartnack 2001, 1). Clearly the conquest of India could have played on his Alexander fantasy. Freud also showed sympathy for real colonial operatives like C. D. Daly, who was using psychoanalysis to understand the political unrest occurring in the Indian subcontinent, but in ways that betrayed considerable imperialist and racist points of view (see Hartnack 2001, chapter 2; also Nandy 1995).

The growing archive of primitive cultures created a very wide-ranging fad for comparative analysis, and here psychoanalysis is far from atypical in either its eclectic use of ethnography or its deep ambivalence about the "primitives" concerned. At the same time as Freud was forging the myth of the *Urvater* from accounts of totem meals, classical scholars like the Cambridge Ritualists used the "beastly devices of the heathen" to explicate the mysteries of Greek and Roman religion.[26] Jane Ellen Harrison, one of the most famous exponents of this school, freely confessed, "Savages, save for their reverent, totemistic attitude towards animals, weary and disgust me, though perforce I spend long hours in reading of their tedious doings. My good moments are when, through the study of things primitive, I come to the better understanding of some song of a Greek poet or some saying of a Greek philosopher" ([1927] 1962, 555). Devoted reader of Frazer's *Golden Bough* as he was during the years 1911–1913, Freud made a similar use of such accounts to serve his own ends in his conflict with Carl Jung, which formed the background to the writing of *Totem and Taboo*. Even those who left their armchairs under Freud's influence were not able to acquire a less imperialist attitude toward the primitives and their sexuality. Freud's fellow-Austrian subject Bronislaw Malinowski, author of *Sex and Repression in Savage Society*, could not help but express his contempt for those other neurotics, the savages, in 1915: "On the whole my feelings toward the natives are decidedly tending to 'Exterminate the brutes'" ([1967] 1989, 69). By 1923, this bad temper still had not changed: "The natives still irritate me, particularly Ginger, whom I could willingly beat to death. I understand all the German and Belgian colonial atrocities" ([1967] 1989, 279). Neurotics and natives only serve to provide a livelihood and material to learn from; this is the assumption we can link to the imperial adventure of archaeology in the matrix of Freud's analogizing, an adventure that helps both to express and to cleanse psychoanalysis of its own inherent aggressivity.

Let us conclude this chapter, then, by taking the lived, transactional analogy of imperial archaeology to one of Freud's clinical situations. In what remains his most notorious case history, the incomplete analysis of the young hysteric "Dora," Freud resorted to the archaeological analogy in the midst of a long apology for publishing a case study so replete with personal information, and yet so incomplete from the scientific standpoint.

> In face of the incompleteness of my analytic results, I had no choice but to follow the example of those discoverers whose good fortune it is to bring to the light of day after their long burial the priceless though mutilated relics of antiquity. I have restored what is missing, taking the best models known to me from other analyses; but, like a conscientious [*gewissenhafter*] archaeologist, I have not omitted to mention in each case where the authentic parts end and my constructions begin. ("Fragment of an Analysis of a Case of Hysteria," SE 7:12; my emphasis)

With such and other justifications, Freud moves to put this poor girl's Elgin marbles on display for the learned world, that is, the sordid circumstances of her father's liaisons and her mother's "housewife neurosis"; the sexual advances of a man her father's age; her crush on an older woman who turns out to be her father's lover, not to mention the myriad physical symptoms she displayed, such as her *tussis nervosa* and vaginal discharges. The conscientious psycho-excavator unpacks from her symptomatic cough the repressed fantasy of fellatio between her father and his lover (SE 7:47–48); and he reconstructs the physical sensation of her molester's erection from the very different feeling of pressure on her thorax (SE 7:29–30). These symptoms were the "stones" made to speak in the pages of the *Monatsschrift für Psychiatrie und Neurologie*. What Dora actually said herself is only glimpsed through the samplings Freud reports.[27]

This analysis ended with the "site" running off on the excavator, but that did not stop him from presenting his precious fragments to the learned world with all the fervor of Schliemann with "Priam's Treasure" (though Freud did delay publication for a few years). As even Hannah Decker, who has written the most balanced account of this analysis, comments: "His primary interest in her predicament lay in using her psychoanalysis to support his theories and his reputation; his interest in curing her, though real, was secondary" (1991, 199). Louis Breger, who is consistently more critical of Freud, has said, "It is clear that Freud's treatment of Dora was quite damaging, and it is painful to read the case today, to witness his unsympathetic and aggressive treatment of this young woman, already a pawn in the selfish games of her father and the other significant adults in her life" (2000, 158). The gain for psycho-

analysis, however, was that this case is a hallmark in the emergent awareness of both transference and counter-transference, and reading the
analysis's failure in the light of these two vital concepts allows many
thoughtful Freudians to salvage the text in heuristic terms.[28] But it is just
that very pair of concepts that shows the inadequacy—even the latent
therapeutic danger—of an overly-literal application of the archaeological analogy. Freud could well have benefited from a lesson Schliemann
learned all too late during his excavations at Troy: you can do a lot of dam-
age to the site if you go about it too aggressively.

PART II

Memory and History

To unmask: that was our sacred task, the task of us moderns. To reveal the true calculations underlying the false consciousnesses, or the true interests underlying the false calculations. Who is not still foaming slightly at the mouth with that particular rabies?

—Bruno Latour, *We Have Never Been Modern*

And lastly I cannot resist pointing out how often light is thrown by the interpretation of dreams on mythological themes in particular. Thus, for instance, the legend of the Labyrinth can be recognized as a representation of anal birth: the twisting paths are the bowels and Ariadne's thread is the umbilical cord.

—Freud, *New Introductory Lectures*

CHAPTER 7

■

Memory, Biography, History, Myth

> As for the biographers, let them worry, we have no desire to make it too easy for them. Each one of them will be right in his opinion of the "Development of the Hero," and I am already looking forward to seeing them go astray.
>
> —SIGMUND FREUD TO MARTHA BERNAYS (1885)

Thus far I have explicated a concept, Freud's "compulsion for antiquity," as it relates to his personal life and scientific ambitions. I have attempted to map it simultaneously in three dimensions in order to overcome more limited approaches that segment what cannot be segmented if we take Freud's thought seriously, that is to say, if we refuse categorically to divorce individual desire from intellectual abstractions. Previous approaches have often sought Freud's truth either solely in his biography—his trajectory as a Jew, his filial drama, his radical dishonesty—or in terms of the system of his psychoanalytic thought in the absence of its structuring subject, Freud himself. With respect to the Theban paradigm and its best internal challenge, the Leonardo study, I attempted to establish the principle that by triangulating the discursive maneuvers of the analogical and evidentiary domains with the personal dimension—by means of linking argument with desire—one could develop a richer reading of the Freudian invocation of the ancient archive, which in turn yields a richer reading of psychoanalysis itself. By means of examining Freud's "return to the past," I sought to characterize his peculiar vision of scientific revolution, one that, by his own admission in the Leonardo study, is ostensibly predicated on *forgetting* the authority of the past, yet inevitably seems to tie its truth to a repetition of it (i.e., ignoring "the ancients" just like the Greeks, yet rediscovering a *terra praecognita* among Sophocles, Artemidorus, Plato, and Empedocles). Finally, I have sought through the figure of Alexander and the spectacle of archaeology to expose the desire for dominion (the *libido dominandi*, as the Church Fathers would say) that lies at the heart of the enterprise and the man.

We know full well why we invest so much in the Freud scenario as opposed to those of Havelock Ellis or Richard von Krafft-Ebing, who are simply figures of history at this point, not figures of memory like Freud. As Foucault says, Freud founded a discursive practice and did not simply make a "contribution" to science, like so many obscure men and women whose personal self-effacement is essential to their credibility as workers in the field (1979, 154). According to Foucault, the feature that separates a new discursivity from its contemporary science is that "the work of initiators of discursivity is not situated in the space that science defines; rather, it is the science or the discursivity which refers back to their work as primary coordinates" (1979, 156). Thus Freud's initial state of mind, his ambitions and desires, give shape to how we view this discursive practice. By arguing as I have that Freud invests heavily in his relationship with the ancient archive, I am moving toward a thick description of psychoanalysis's initial self-understanding as *a historical science*, and as a form of knowledge that participates both in the *Naturwissenschaften* from which it grew, but more importantly, in the *Geisteswissenschaften* where it hopes to make its mark as the great decoder of millennial mysteries. I wish, in other words, to re-institute the initial horizon of psychoanalysis in order to trace its momentous connection to the ancient archive. This connection is momentous not just for aficionados of cultural reception like myself, but for anyone who cares to know how such a thing as psychoanalytic truth came to be.

Through my approach I am essentially challenging the confessional paradigm of Foucault's *The History of Sexuality* (vol. 1) which alleges that the development of the *scientia sexualis* is to be seen chiefly as the paradoxical marriage of the ancient practice of confession with the modern procedures of natural science. In a paradox of his own, Foucault stressed that the "history of sexuality—that is, the history of what functioned in the nineteenth century as a specific field of truth—must first be written from the viewpoint of a history of discourses." Yet the fundamental discursive relation he ignores is that between psychoanalysis and the discourses of historical *Wissenschaft* ([1976] 1980, 69). In other words, in his history of discourses, Foucault forgets to add the discourse of history. The memory work of the couch at Berggasse 19 was the invention of a secular Jew, enacted initially on mostly other secular Jews. To see this invention as the logical extension of the Catholic sacrament is therefore in itself ahistorical, though its reception as such by Christians is certainly plausible, hence its facile inroads among the *goyim* later on in the twentieth century.[1] But to ascribe the initial phenomenon to assimilationist mimicry will not adequately explain it.

Moreover, Foucault's reading of the history of *scientia sexualis* misinterprets the "truth of sex" that emerges from the Freudian context, confusing the formularity of sin and redemption with the radical implications of psychoanalytic investigation.[2] He confuses, in other words, the archaeologist with the papal inquisitor through his tendency to focus on juridical discourses.[3] But one cannot *confess* to a sexual trauma, since repression has made the experience *unthinkable* in the conventional sense. The Wolf Man did not confess to the primal scene that emerged from his analysis; he *agreed* to it as a historical hypothesis. Freud himself was very clear about the "great difference" which prevents the analyst from becoming "a secular father confessor." "What we want to hear from our patient is not only what he knows and conceals from other people; he is to tell us too what he does *not* know" (SE 23:174). As such, Freud said that "[c]onfession no doubt plays a part in analysis—*as an introduction to it*, we might say. But *it is very far from constituting the essence of analysis* or from explaining its effects" (SE 20:189; my emphasis). Obsessed as he is with the archive of the sayable, Foucault's inadequacy for dealing with Freud is primarily his resistance to the notion that the unconscious archives *that which speaks without being said*. In fact, we might say that the *scientia sexualis* plotted by Foucault is more akin to Anglo-American ego-psychology that Lacan saw as the utter *betrayal* of Freud's truth, particularly at the level of history. For if confession is the allocution of individual desire and error so as to effect a reconciliation with God the Father, the Body of Christ, the Mother Church, and society at large, then the adaptable "autonomous ego" of post-Freudian theorists is the real target for Foucault's "political economy" of the sexologist's will to knowledge.

As I shall argue in chapter 11, there is indeed a way in which Freud's specific project reflects an inversion of the Judeo-Christian tradition; but this is an inversion not of the discursive form of the confessional itself so much as of the claim that we shall find ourselves only in the true wisdom that is knowledge of the Father. Freud's greatest joke on the dominant culture was that he created a historical theology for the death of God, and not that he co-opted the authority of the priest and hijacked the care of souls. The real political economy of psychoanalysis is, as I have already suggested in the imperialist paradigm of chapter 6, rather to be sought in the aggressive move toward the take-over of history itself: the occupation of the archive, we might say, by the legionaries of psychoanalysis. The will to power of psychoanalysis was originally a will to history at heart, hence the importance of the figure of Gradiva in my view of the Freud scenario.

In this second part of the book, I shall therefore map more directly the *institutional* implications of Freud's compulsion for antiquity, in particular, the complex relationship with historical discourses that his peculiar form of memory work entails. This relationship is complex first and foremost because it requires understanding the interaction between the dynamic labor of memory work (which Freud likened to the archaeological dig) and the synthetic narratives that either emerge from it or implicitly direct it. Such narratives can be targeted as attempts at biography, at history in a grander sense, or at myth; therefore, we must also attend to differences in the level of articulation. But this discussion is further complicated by psychoanalysis's internal vacillation (an ambivalence perhaps, though it could also just be a strategic oscillation) between seeing history as *res gestae*, on the one hand, and *res digestae*, on the other.[4] That is, between characterizing history as an objective record of facts and deeds done, or as a digested, evolving narrative serving present needs and mapped exclusively from the present horizon. What is at stake for memory work is whether we shall employ it as: (1) a form of "orthomnemics," a *corrective* recollection of the facts, the institution of the past "as it essentially was" (von Ranke) in the historicist tradition; or rather (2) as a form of "autopoetics," the creative appropriation of a usable past, a self-narrative that integrates and synthesizes the residual *effects* — and not so much the "facts"—of experience in hopes of a clarified agency. The choice, when pushed to its extremes, is between absolute historicism and effective therapy. The strange position Freud adopts, as I will relate in this chapter, is essentially the proposition that historicism *is* the most effective therapy, which is precisely why certain of his greatest admirers broke with him.

We must be certain of one thing: no matter how radically psychoanalysis reworks historical narrative, it still clings to the notion of history, if not in the form of a final narrative, then at least as an on-going project of narrative renewal.[5] It clings to *historía* in the original Greek sense of "inquiry." Even as post-modern speculations in the wake of Freud undid the possibility of grand meta-narratives, psychoanalysis's initial promise of history continued to reassert itself. Jacques Lacan empowered no one to assert that history is bunk, even while he claimed that the unconscious is "neither primordial nor instinctual" but concerns merely "the elements of the signifier" ([1966] 1977, 170). On the contrary, in his report to the Rome Congress, "The Function and Field of Speech and Language in Psychoanalysis," Lacan vociferously reasserted the full panoply of the Freudian historical apparatus:

> The unconscious is that chapter of my history that is marked by a blank or occupied by a falsehood: it is the censored chapter. But the truth can be rediscovered; usually it has already been written down elsewhere. Namely:
> —in monuments: this is my body. That is to say, the hysterical nucleus of the neurosis in which the hysterical symptom reveals the structure of a language, and is deciphered like an inscription which, once recovered, can without serious loss be destroyed;
> —in archival documents: these are my childhood memories, just as impenetrable as are such documents when I do not know their provenance;
> —in semantic evolution: this corresponds to the stock of words and acceptations of my own particular vocabulary, as it does to my style of life and to my character;
> —in traditions, too, and even in the legends which, in a heroicized form, bear my history;
> —and, lastly, in the traces that are inevitably preserved by the distortions necessitated by the linking of the adulterated chapter to the chapters surrounding it, and whose meaning will be re-established by my exegesis. ([1966] 1977, 50)

And having trotted out this list of metaphors, Lacan asserts that "what I have just said has so little originality, even in its verve, that there appears in it not a single metaphor that Freud's works do not repeat with the frequency of a *leitmotiv* in which the very fabric of the work is revealed" ([1966] 1977, 51).

Ultimately even Lacan, who unsettles so many assumptions about self-knowledge and agency, firmly believed that the business at hand was a matter of historical consciousness. This is why, in "The Freudian Thing," he combated so strongly the "cultural ahistoricism" he saw emanating from the United States, and wished to remind psychoanalysts that theirs was the field "whose function presupposed history in its very principle, their discipline being that which had re-established the bridge linking modern man to the ancient myths" ([1966] 1977, 115). This is also why

in "Agency of the Letter in the Unconscious" he was unflinchingly loyal
to the Freudian worksite, the analysand's memory and body with its chain
of dead desire. "It is the truth of what this desire has been in his history
that the patient cries out through his symptom, as Christ said the stones
themselves would have cried out if the children of Israel had not lent them
their voice" ([1966] 1977, 167). For this reason, our investigation of the
discursive affinities between psychoanalysis and history retains its actual-
ity more than a century after Freud opened the *via regia* to Acheron (and
more than half a century after it was routed through Paris). The procedure
in this part of the book will be to focus in this chapter on the narrative
revolution Freud effected in respect to self-history, laying out some principles of organization and their implications for the grander narratives of
history and myth. In chapter 8, I shall trace a particular genealogy for the
critical historiography that his entire project rests upon, while also mapping out Freud's essential differences with it. In chapter 9, there is a return to the topic of archaeology, though not in the genealogical mode so
much. Rather that chapter looks more closely at archaeology's functioning as a transactional analogy in the light of what we have learned about
narrativization in the clinical context. And, finally, in chapter 10, I end
this section by considering more broadly how Freud's new science of the
mind was articulated in response to the greater cultural background of
historicism, and how it lays claim to a genuine historical consciousness
and not simply a critique of such consciousness. This will effectively return us to the *Gradiva* scenario with which I began my characterization
of the compulsion for antiquity in chapter 1.

Psychoanalysis and the Shape of Life

> Τοὺς ἀνθρώπους φησὶν Ἀλκμαίων διὰ τοῦτο ἀπόλλυσθαι,
>   ὅτι οὐ δύνανται τὴν ἀρχὴν τῷ τέλει προσάψαι.

> Alcmaeon says that human beings perish for this reason: they cannot join
> the beginning to the end.
>   —PSEUDO-ARISTOTLE, *Problemata*

To relate the past to the present, or vice versa, entails memory work that
encodes or implies some form of narrative.[6] Whether we are dealing with
biography, history, or myth, narrative orders time for us in such a way
that we clarify our relationship with the past and in a sense negotiate its
"pastness" and relevance to truth in the present. The first curious feature

of psychoanalysis is its seemingly *endless* negotiation with the past; that is, its general refusal to accept prefabricated narratives at face value and its openness to renegotiate the terms on which one lives with the past. Analysis is a process of breaking-up, excavating, and critiquing our standard view of the past, based on the assumption that this standard view occludes a living past we won't allow ourselves to see or talk about. Our first task is to understand the consequences of Freud's emphasis on the persistence of the past and how this affects the relationship with its narrativization in the conventional forms of biography, myth, and history.[7] We shall begin with the first of these terms.

We all know that the past is weighty in psychoanalysis. But the weight of the past is not like Marx's "tradition of all the dead generations," which "weighs like a nightmare on the brain of the living" ([1852] 1978, 595). It does not generally produce historical travesties, as Marx asserts, or the kind of crippling diglossia that grotesquely contorted the discourse of officialdom in modern Greece up to the 1970s. Rather, the weight of the past is felt through a process of *dynamic encryption:* the past, when subjected to repression, is dynamically submerged in the present to which it stands in an uncanny causal relation.[8] The trajectory of past to present is not one of discrete linear progress through the void of time, but one more like that of a self-transforming boomerang.[9] In fact, no metaphor of spatial movement can capture adequately the temporal vectors of the Freudian psyche, given the fundamental postulate of the unconscious's timelessness.[10] The past just will not play dead for us; there is no "over" over there. Only the costly energic investments of repression seem to support the apparent pastness of the past, and these investments by their nature are variable and mobile, calculating the profitability of pastness in relation to present interests.[11] Repression, to cite the central example, bribes the oedipal past to go away, but the oedipal past has the singular indiscretion of returning in drag if it is not constantly paid again and again to *stay* away, and in our nightly regressions it constantly slips over the wire.[12] To make matters worse, the Freudian psyche has much more than its own past to worry about, since as we have seen, the phylogenetic past also barges in at unexpected moments to disrupt our individual agency. It is not just a cheap pun to assert that there is an organic link between individual and collective history in Freud.

To engage the past, then, is necessarily a work of interpretation of both past and present, a delving into the *compresence* of the past in hopes of dealing with the present's unruly population of masquerading *revenants*. Needless to say, this works against the grain of coherent historical plot

lines and violates conventional notions of progressive temporality. It
amounts to assessing the cunning of *unreason* in history, to borrow Ernest
Gellner's apt phrase; and unreason's first and foremost stratagem of cunning is to deny the past its pastness ([1985] 1993). This is precisely the
drama played out in the analytic situation through the dynamics of transference, where the intersubjective space that opens between analyst and
analysand becomes effectively a breach in time through which unconscious elements of the past spill into the present.

> The unconscious impulses do not want to be remembered in the
> way the treatment desires them to be, but endeavor to reproduce
> themselves in accordance with the timelessness of the unconscious
> and its capacity for hallucination. Just as happens in dreams, the pa-
> tient regards the products of the awakening of his unconscious im-
> pulses as contemporaneous and real; he seeks to put his passions
> into action without taking any account of the real situation. The
> doctor tries to compel him to fit these emotional impulses into the
> nexus of the treatment *and of his life-history, to submit them to intel-
> lectual consideration and to understand them in the light of their psychical
> value.* ("The Dynamics of Transference," SE 12:108; my emphasis)

Coming to terms with the unconscious's pernicious influence thus involves both critical *and narrative* modes of understanding, putting the
buried past into a new cognitive framework based on the patient's life-
history. As the science of unreason, psychoanalysis is uniquely situated to
provide the memory work that extricates the past's uncanny presence and
hopefully reduces it to *mere* memory.[13] As Freud once put it succinctly in
a general presentation of his science, "You can, if you like, regard psychoanalytic treatment as no more than a prolongation of education for
the purposes of overcoming the residues of childhood" (*Five Lectures on
Psycho-Analysis*, SE 11:48).

But since psychoanalysis construes the past as compresent, it shatters
the mold of *conventional* life-narratives and throws into doubt the previous accounts of conscious agency. Accordingly, the problematization of
biographical discourse is a direct consequence of the analytical viewpoint,
and not just a quirk of Freud's personality (which it also was). Adam
Philips observes:

> "What Freud is aiming at," the French psychoanalyst Jean La-
> planche writes, "is a kind of history of the unconscious, or rather of

its genesis; a history with discontinuities, in which the moments of burial and resurgence are the most important of all." This burial and resurgence that one might track—as both Darwin and Freud did in species and individuals—made the whole notion of the discontinuity of lives neither the problem nor the solution. It was just the nature of a human life to be elusive as an object of knowledge. The idea of a life having a shape, or being a discernibly coherent story, could seem nonsensical. (Philips 2000, 75)

We can cite two good examples of post-Freudian autobiography to illustrate how he thus changed the narrative perspective of life-stories: Ernest Jones' *Free Associations* (1959) and the classical scholar E. R. Dodds' *Missing Persons* (1977), which from their very titles warn the reader not to expect a coherent narrative, but rather fragments that may not bear any relation to a whole. They reflect an autobiographical poetics of the demystified self.

One might argue, then, that the "archaeological" or excavating, analytical frame of mind ought to lead to the utter suspension of valid self-narrative; for if we conceive of memory work as an open site, we are left in a state of constant tension about the finality of any possible narrative based on recollected experience. It was also the persistent mendacity in one's own relation to oneself that led to Freud's notoriously dyspeptic condemnations of biography and autobiography. Writing to Arnold Zweig (who had suggested writing a biography of him), he said:

Anyone who writes a biography is committed to lies, concealments, hypocrisy, flattery, and even to hiding his own lack of understanding, for biographical truth does not exist, and if it did we could not use it.

Truth is unobtainable, mankind does not deserve it, and in any case is not our Prince Hamlet right when he asks who would escape whipping were he used after his desert? (Ernst Freud 1970, 127)

That these sentiments apply equally to *auto*biography in Freud's mind can be shown from an earlier letter to his nephew in which he rejected the offer of $5,000 from an American publisher for his life story: "What makes all autobiographies worthless is, after all, their mendacity" (Ernst Freud 1960, 391). This leads us to assume that Freud's archaeological view of the self is somehow post-narrative.[14]

And yet it is not the case in Freud's work that the self ceases to have a story, nor was it any part of the initial appeal of psychoanalysis that individuals were conceived of as vast, unknowable abysses. On the contrary, what attracted many to the Freudian project was precisely the new narrative web it cast. Hanns Sachs, a very important member of the early psychoanalytic movement, remembers in his memoirs what it was like to be one of the few aficionados of the new science in the early days. Attending Freud's lectures at the University of Vienna, Sachs "began to understand the unconscious as the presence of an inner destiny which decrees that the same pattern must be re-lived since the wheel of life turns around a fixed center, and that the oldest experiences repeat themselves over and over again under various disguises (repetition-compulsion)" (1946, 45). The sense of individual life-pattern and meaning, however, was not the only compelling aspect of the lectures: "the many new vistas opening before our eyes, the unexhausted possibilities for new fields, and new methods of explorations in almost every branch of science added a great deal to the absorbing interest of these hours" (1945, 44). Sachs himself would later be instrumental in the application of psychoanalysis to cultural studies, so the interplay in his interest between therapeutic and cultural applications is a crucial indicator of what drew him into the movement. What is most striking, however, is Sachs' memory of Freud's tone. He did not assume the dogmatic tone of a prophet nor the cynical snarl of the skeptic, but the witty, ironical voice of bourgeois expertise. And yet, behind the congenial tone lay unsettling certainties. "His conviction of the far reaching consequences of the new truth was too deep to stand in need of emphatic asseveration" (1945, 45).

We also need to see how the analysands themselves—who were both the co-workers and the sites of the psychoanalytic "dig"—felt about the process of self-excavation in relation to the narrativization of their past. The Wolf Man's experience was initially one of a grand adventure. He recalls in his memoirs that within the first months of his analysis, "a completely new world was opened to me, a world known only to a few people in those days" (Gardiner 1971, 83). The analysis as he remembered it was decidedly a joint effort; he felt like "the younger comrade of an experienced explorer setting out to study a new, recently discovered land. This new land is the realm of the unconscious, over which the neurotic has lost that mastery which he now seeks, through analysis, to regain" (1971, 140). In his case history, Freud made much of a primal scene thrice repeated in which the young Wolf Man allegedly saw his parents in a posture of *coitus a tergo* ("From the History of an Infantile Neurosis," SE

17:55; he later expresses revisionist misgivings, however, and allows it might have been the *fantasy* of such a scene; see SE 17:57–60).[15] This scene was by Freud's own admission a construction, not a memory, and he advanced its validity entirely on the notion of its *narrative fit* with the facts of the case. The Wolf Man assented to this new point of view in a way that was quite satisfactory to Freud. "Much that had been ununderstandable in my life before that time began to make sense, as relationships which were formerly hidden in darkness now emerged into my consciousness" (Gardiner 1971, 83). What emerged from the excavation, in other words, was an *unconventional* narrative that responded well to myriad details of the case and produced a general semantic coherence—a "narrative fit" as I have termed it—that had deep resonance with the analysand.

I would also argue that rather than working *against* the narrativization going on, the archaeological model enabled it in various ways. Sitting in Freud's consulting room—which he explicitly remembered very well as looking more like an archaeologist's study than a doctor's office—the Wolf Man willingly participated in his own self-excavation. The unexpected insertion of antiquity in that space constantly reinforced the metaphor of temporal depth. Freud explained to the Wolf Man that, "like the archaeologist in his excavations" the analyst "must uncover layer after layer of the patient's psyche, before coming to the deepest, most valuable treasures" (Gardiner 1971, 139). The physical presence of artifacts and images of antiquity thus aided and abetted the individual analysis, helping the analysand to assent to what could *not* be remembered but only inferred. Here we see the transactional effect of the archaeological analogy, which smacks so strongly of suggestion that we will have to return to it in more detail below. But for now we need only see the main point: the archaeological framework of analysis *enables* the new narratives, and does not disable them.

Moreover, there is a whole world of objects that gets caught up in the narrative web of both the analyses and the unfolding discursive practice, and these objects tend to take up residence at Berggasse 19. In fact, so deeply implicated was the archaeological analogy in his relationship with Freud that the Wolf Man's parting gift to him was an Egyptian figurine. This figure stayed on Freud's desk for decades afterward, symbolizing the analysis which itself had come to be an important part of the movement's own developing history.[16] From this example, we can see the fuller picture of the narrative praxis of psychoanalysis that I have termed the "em-

pirical romance." The bold new narrative about the Wolf Man's life that
was generated in the empirical analytic encounter is intricately woven together with the narrative of the treatment itself, and forms the same kind
of double narrative that we have seen in Freud's reading of *Gradiva*. As in
the Leonardo case study, Freud cannot find meaning in the life of another
without highlighting the story of psychoanalysis and advancing its claims
for truth. So not only is there a life-narrative in psychoanalysis, there is
also an ever-present meta-narrative too. The story of the life is framed
within the story of psychoanalysis's ferreting out the story of that life.

Thus it is best to describe Freud's investment in narrative not in terms
of conventional totalizations (such as the narratives of genius one would
usually find for a Goethe or a Leonardo, or the confessional narratives of
sin and error), but rather in terms of *backdoor totalizations*, often couched
in provisional terms, yet every bit as binding once they are clenched. The
narrative texture is reconstructive, argumentative, and somewhat open-
ended; but it *has* a definite form. In fact, Freud often has to acknowledge
with some misgiving the formal narrative properties of his own discourse,
which distance him from the native discourses of science from which he
diverges. Already in *Studies on Hysteria*, he admits: "Like other neuro-
pathologists, I was trained to employ local diagnoses and electro-prog-
nosis, and it still strikes me myself as strange that the case histories I write
should read like short stories and that, as one might say, they lack the serious stamp of science" (SE 2:160). In the Leonardo study, and later still
in his initial plan for *Moses and Monotheism*, the narrative specter that
emerges is the historical novel (*Leonardo da Vinci and a Memory of His
Childhood*, SE 11:134).

Moreover, since Freud adopts the rhetoric of nineteenth-century natural science, the life patterns that emerge often transcend the narrative
of the merely contingent and reoccupy the contours of traditional "fate"
through the extreme determinism of his causal notions.[17] This was his
strategy in the reading of Oedipus already in the *Interpretation of Dreams*:
to convert the coercion of the gods into the compulsive force of Nature.
Hence his reading of our oedipal feelings, in spite of its gratuitous "perhaps," is every bit as binding even though it is an accidental feature of
Nature. "His destiny moves us only because it might have been ours—
because the oracle laid the same curse upon us before our birth as upon
him. It is the fate of all of us, *perhaps*, to direct our first sexual impulse towards our mother and our first hatred and our first murderous wish
against our father" (SE 4:262; my emphasis). That this kind of language

did not change by the end of his life is clear from comments in *An Out-line of Psychoanalysis* (1938): "the coercive power of the oracle, which makes or should make the hero innocent, is a recognition of the *in-evitability of the fate* which has conducted *every son* to live through the Oedipus complex" (SE 23:192, my emphasis). A notorious consequence of his new universal narrative of oedipal fate is that every *daughter* is left to play the role of envious understudy to her brother, finding ways to make up for the fact that she did not get the right "part" from the begin-ning. For her, anatomy itself is destiny.

So we can see how in the oedipal scenario, the ancient archive was en-listed to achieve a backdoor totalization on the level of life narrative, one that forms the bridge to myth and macrohistory. The question arises, of course, as to whether such a narrativization need have the status of personal *history* in a factual sense. After all, to interpret one's own life in relation to a drama like *Oedipus Tyrannus* can produce meaning, but is "meaning" the same as veridical history?[18] Whether the past that emerges from the couch is *truly* historical or merely a narrative artifact produced in analysis is a question that continues to plague the whole en-terprise. Indeed, it has long been recognized that "narrative mastery of the past" in therapy and historical truth may not coincide, hence the precarious nature of conflating the experience of analysis with the methodology of the credentialed historian. The philosopher Ludwig Wittgenstein thought that Freud's lengthy explanations in his case histo-ries were not matters of scientific reasoning or "true histories," but rather acts of persuasion that had a soothing effect even if they seemed to dis-close terrible things (Bouveresse 1995, chapter 3). Thus the "discovery of the primal scene" that is at the heart of the Wolf Man case need not be accepted as a true event or even true fantasy to have its effect. In Rush Rhees' notes to conversations he had with Wittgenstein about Freud, Wittgenstein is reported to have said that:

> This often has the attractiveness of giving a sort of tragic pattern to one's life. It is all the repetition of the same pattern which was set-tled long ago. Like a tragic figure carrying out the decrees under which the fates had placed him at birth. Many people have, at some period, serious trouble in their lives—so serious as to lead to thoughts of suicide. This is likely to appear to one as something nasty, as a situation which is too foul to be a subject of a tragedy. And it may then be an immense relief if it can be shown that one's

life has the pattern rather of a tragedy—the tragic working out and
repetition of a pattern which was determined by the primal scene.
(1966, 51)

What Wittgenstein reportedly suggested is that *narrative relief* ought not
to be confused with a true account; hence the latent danger in Freud's deployment of staged myths in the process of investigating his patient's past.
By importing tragic myth into self-narrative, psychoanalysis itself becomes a "powerful mythology" that is effective without necessarily being
true (1966, 52).

We might even further Wittgenstein's critique and say that in Freud's
earliest work on hysteria there is a fundamental conflation of the archaeological and theatrical paradigms. For while the metaphor of excavation
was essential to enabling the therapy, the recovered "object" of this archaeology was a "scene" of memory, to which the patient would come to
react through *catharsis*—a distinctly theatrical concept.[19] So in a sense
Freud could be seen to have transferred the performative element from
the symptoms of hysteria (quite literally performed before the camera
and on stage for an audience in Charcot's "theater of hysteria") to their
removal in the "private theater" of the talking cure. But as we have seen
above in his view of the transference, Freud sees the patient's performance as effectively targeted for a different audience than the analyst,
since the reactions elicited in therapy represent the emergence of the
timeless past from its entombment in the unconscious. In other words,
the patient's transference represents the *objective* emergence of the past.
Otherwise, Freud would have to interpret it simply as cheap drama
cooked up on the couch for his benefit.

Even if we assume that the transference *is* the emerging past and nothing else (like simple infatuation or annoyance with the analyst), it does
not follow that knowledge of the past is sufficient for effective therapy,
even as one "works through it." Otto Rank, Freud's former follower,
found that Freud had created in the analytic situation an artificial relationship that he misread as a kind of museum of the self, where the professional analyst could observe from a distance the roiling currents of the
past that transference brings to light. "Freud's causal interpretation of the
analytic situation as repetition (chiefly in recollection) of the past—instead of an emphasis on it as a new experience in the present—amounts
to a denial of all personal autonomy in favor the strictest possible determinism, that is to say, to a negation of life itself. Such a detached attitude
may be justified in the realm of pure science, that is, of theoretical psy-

chology, but is certainly contrary to all therapeutic endeavors, which ought to aim towards life itself" ([1941] 1958, 278). Freud's insistence on the therapeutic value of historical understanding, Rank argues, is just another form of Socratic intellectualism, i.e., the belief that knowledge is sufficient to virtue. It offers us its own critique in the guiding myth of Oedipus, "on the interpretation of which Freud based the justification of his truth-therapy," since Oedipus "perishes [sic] as soon as he knows the truth about himself, revealed by the historical self-analysis of his past in true Freudian fashion" ([1941] 1958, 279). We see here how Rank tries yet again to undo Freud through a more incisive reading of Sophocles, even at the risk of producing his own misreading of the play.

Rank's Nietzschean bent took him back to the concept of the will, but others challenged Freud's radical fixation on the past through proposing a "psycho-synthesis" that would follow from analysis. The idea was again that the therapy ought to be oriented toward the *future*, not just the past. The Zurich school led by Carl Jung and others wanted there to be a synthetic view in dream analysis that looked toward the elucidation of future trends in the patient's character in order to create a teleological focus for therapy. This would effectively lead the patient out of the half-infantile relationship of transference and historical excavation into a freer, self-chosen life with a new direction (Marinelli and Mayer 2002, chapter 8). For Freud, this was clearly a way of dodging the ugly truth of analysis and of replacing its well-founded historical memory-work with high-minded but misguided ethical encouragement. He effectively accused the Swiss of operating a crypto-theological form of treatment that fled the "facts" of his new science and took refuge in moral niceties that ultimately had no therapeutic value ("On the History of the Psycho-Analytic Movement," SE 14:60–66).[20]

For Freud, there is no greater trap for the analyst than to suppose that his task is to lead the patient away from his past and toward sublimation and ethical improvement. Writing in 1914 to the Harvard neurologist James Putnam (who was pushing psychoanalysis into a more positive ethical role from yet another quarter), Freud argued that avoiding the analysand's past would only expose the personal timidity of the analyst.

> As soon as they [the analysts] are entrusted with the task of leading the patient toward sublimation, they hasten away from the arduous tasks of $\psi\alpha$ [psychoanalysis] as quickly as they can so that they can take up the much more comfortable and satisfactory duties of the teacher and the paragon of virtue. This is just what the people in

Zurich are now doing. Moreover, ψα [psychoanalysis] as a science itself is not even half complete; not to speak of the fact that it does not yet penetrate the individual deeply enough. *The great ethical element in ψα [psychoanalytic] work is truth and again truth and this should suffice for most people. Courage and truth are of what they are mostly deficient.* (Hale 1971, 171; last sentence in English in original)

Freud's patent tension with any idea that smacked of pastoral care is very important here, as it shows how historical truth and not confessional meliorism where at the heart of his views (*pace* Foucault). But it also shows how historical discourse paradoxically divided him from the deterministic natural science in which he was raised. For while he radically espoused the doctrine of strict causality in mental events (cf. *Introductory Lectures on Psycho-Analysis*, SE 15:28)—and the causal chain, after all, is what gives us the trail for reconstructing mental phenomena—at the same time he refused to assume these causes and effects could be predictable and therefore *verifiable* (i.e., that they would be approachable within the framework of empirical experimentation). But if the mind is truly the causal mechanism he supposes and is no different from other natural phenomena, then there is no good reason to think we cannot *foresee* the outcomes of at least some mental events, as signaled by certain parapraxes, for example. This would be to exploit the "natural laws" of the psyche for our benefit, instead of accepting them as an unalterable fate.[21] Yet for Freud this would suggest effectively that one could use psychoanalytic self-knowledge as a form of augury, something he rejects categorically. "As a rule we dare not do so; it would make us feel as though, after a detour through science, *we were becoming superstitious again*" (SE 15:59; my emphasis).

So once more we run up against Freud's *friction* with the ancient archive. Though he claims to be a "partisan of antiquity and superstition," he is very aware that his elaborate mapping of the mind could lose the status of serious *Wissenschaft* if it is over-extended to popularizing appropriations (*Delusions and Dreams in Jensen's Gradiva*, SE 9:7). All future-oriented interpretation seems to have troubled him as moralizing mischief, even when it was far from incompatible with analytic presuppositions. This represents a decisive rupture with the mentality of the ancient world vis-à-vis self-interpretation and the "technologies of the self," since divination of the future through dream interpretation in particular was a dominant form of self-analysis in antiquity (cf. Artemidorus' *Oneirocritica*). Even in the underworld, the dimension of futurity is never absent; on the contrary, the dead often lay out the shape of the future for the living in ancient epic. Odysseus goes to Hades to learn his future from Tiresias, not his past (*Odyssey* 11.90–151); and Aeneas is given a sublime vision that extends many generations into the future by his dead father, Anchises (*Aeneid* 6.756–892). But already in the conclusion to *The Interpretation of Dreams*, Freud made his difference with antiquity quite explicit, and was so bold as to conceive the whole future import of dreams as merely *copied* from the past. "By picturing our wishes as fulfilled, dreams are after all leading us into the future. But this future, which the dreamer pictures as the present, has been molded by his indestructible wish into a perfect likeness of the past" (SE 5:621). *Forward into the Past!* seems again to be his motto, one forged with a sense that hope in a radical future is a kind of superstition—and here the great fissure opens not just between Freud and antiquity, but also between him and scientific socialism. For Karl Marx, all hope in the *past* is a pernicious superstition that must be eradicated.[22]

This major difference with antiquity in relation to the future should give us cause to reassess Freud's appropriation of the underworld as a trope for the unconscious, something apparent already from the title page of *The Interpretation of Dreams*, on which he promises in a pilfered Vergilian verse, *Acheronta movebo* ("I shall raise up Acheron"). The appropriation of the underworld continues in the same work when he says our dream wishes are certainly not always present-day wishes, but rather "wishes of the past which have been abandoned, overlaid and repressed" and yet that have some kind of continued existence in dreaming. "They are not dead in our sense of the word but only like the shades in the *Odyssey*, which awoke to some sort of life as soon as they had tasted blood" (SE 4:249; cf. 5:553, note 1). By the end of the book, these unconscious wishes are no longer the wraiths of Hades, but rather the Titans of Tartarus who drive the whole dream process: "These wishes in our unconscious, ever on the alert and, so to say, immortal, remind one of the legendary Titans, weighed down since primaeval ages by the massive bulk of the mountains which were once hurled upon them by the victorious gods and which are still shaken from time to time by the convulsion of their limbs" (SE 5:553).[23] That Freud even took a proprietary attitude toward his new worksite in the underworld is clear when he invoked this trope years later in refuting his dissenting colleagues, who wished to shift their focus away from a relentlessly historical approach. "I can only express a wish that fortune may grant an agreeable upward journey to all those who have found their stay in the underworld of psychoanalysis too uncomfortable for their taste. The rest of us, I hope, will be permitted without hindrance to carry through to their conclusion our labors in the depths" ("On the History of the Psycho-Analytic Movement," SE 14:66).

But the depth of his depth-psychology is radical in being situated *only* in the past. There is no depth to the future for Freud; for that, one has to have the imagination of a Vergil, whom Freud invokes yet cannot follow. Though he calls the unconscious "timeless," it is really just a realm of temporal phenomena drained of their "pastness." It is a world of stopped calendars, not eternal Platonic forms. Hence it seemed perfectly natural to him to cast the analytic praxis in mythological terms as an underworld journey (though on some days it seemed no doubt more like the labors of Sisyphus) rather than a mystical ascent or some form of transcendence. For the "powerful mythology" he was professing, as Wittgenstein noted, was a promise that there *is* meaning in life, no matter how tragic it might be, but it lies in interpreting the past correctly, just as Oedipus sought the meaning of the Delphic oracle only to find that it did not concern his future at all, but only what he had already done. Freud offered a transfiguration of all the contingent *minutiae* of selfhood through the will to history, not the will to a future. And for treating the future as an illusion, the most ambitious of his "sons" would never forgive him; they include the socialist Adler, the mystical Jung, and "little Rank," the irrepressible Nietzschean.

Mythic Analysis

To refer to psychoanalysis itself as a mythology as Wittgenstein does is of course witty, but misleading. The real point is that psychoanalysis is not *merely* a body of myth (i.e., falsehood) trussed up as science. I do not invoke "myth" as synonymous with falsehood, but in terms of a shared orientation—*a common narrative configuration of the past*—which remains *productive* of meaning.[24] A myth is not a final narrative, but one that thrives in retelling; it is not a static repository of truth so much as a way of processing truth in narrative form. This is why Wittgenstein termed psychoanalysis a *powerful* mythology; it is highly effective at transfiguring the squalor of the past into tragic grandeur, which is to say, it provides a powerful narrative matrix for configuring experience within an emergent worldview that speaks of instincts and repressions instead of moral laws and ethical responsibilities. Freud himself was aware that his recourse to the broad language of instinct had something mythological about it, grand in narrative effect yet vague in reference (*New Introduc-*

tory Lectures on Psycho-Analysis, SE 22:95).[25] As he said to Einstein in relation to his dual instinct theory, "does not every science come in the end to a kind of mythology like this? Cannot the same be said today of your own physics?" ("Why War?" SE 22:211). And if we look at some of the weirder products of psychoanalysis, like Ferenczi's *Thalassa* ([1924] 1989), Fritz Wittels' *Alles um Liebe* (1912), or Freud's own unpublished "phylogenetic fantasy," which traces the origins of the neuroses back to human experience in the Ice Age (Grubrich-Simitis 1987), we can see how far the new narrative matrix was able to bring its devotees—for good or ill.[26]

However, in the case of psychoanalysis we are dealing with a "scientific mythology" that *embeds* ancient myth on the analogical and evidentiary planes, and that finds a certain historical truth to myth that inhabits the personal dimension. Perhaps more than any other modern discourse, psychoanalysis (and its derivatives, like Jungian analytic psychology) is strongly tied to its "work on myth"—as Hans Blumenberg calls it; that is, its need to explicate its own burgeoning discursive practice vis-à-vis ancient mythology in order to service the need for *significance*, a need that is created by the "findings" of the new science ([1979] 1985, 95). For once one discovers such unpleasant "facts" about oneself as incestuous desire or patricidal urges, what does that all *mean* in relation to who we are? Here again, the mere confession of such desires is no therapy in itself if such allocution fails to connect with a greater discursive web; hence Freud's replacement of the discourse of God's mercy and justice with the language of tragic Necessity and the blind workings of physical forces.

Psychoanalysis's dependence on the ancient archive in this regard seems the best example of the "dialectic of enlightenment" mapped out by Max Horkheimer and Theodor Adorno in their famous book of that name ([1944] 1972). In fact, Freud's reinsertion of the rule of Necessity (Ἀνάγκη) as a quasi-mythic principle in the Leonardo study reveals all too well the pattern laid out by the Frankfurt School:

> The principle of fatal necessity, which brings low the heroes of myth and derives as a logical consequence from the pronouncement of the oracle, does not merely, when refined to the stringency of formal logic, rule in every rationalistic system of Western philosophy, but itself dominates the series of systems which begins with the hierarchy of the gods and, in a permanent twilight of the idols, hands down an identical content: anger against insufficient righteousness. Just as the myths already realize enlightenment, so enlightenment

with every step becomes more deeply engulfed in mythology. It receives all its matter from the myths, in order to destroy them; and even as a judge it comes under the mythic curse. It wishes to extricate itself from the process of fate and retribution, while exercising retribution in that process. ([1944] 1972, 11–12)

Thus Leonardo's successful escape from the clutches of the Christian religion—as Freud describes it—only serves to thrust him into the new plot woven by Freud's Necessity, which tragically casts him as a homosexual by leaving him in the care of Caterina/Mut. Similarly we trade the old mythological reading of the vulture portent for a new one, where it does not augur the future achievements of Leonardo at all, but rather reveals the essence of his past. The forward teleology of destiny is replaced with the rearward determinations of childhood experience.

One could even go so far as to say that the secret affinities between psychoanalytic narrative and ancient myths betray a cultural nostalgia for such common narratives on the part of the analysts. The work of mythic analysis—that is, the *story* of an enlightened reading of the past, as couched in terms like "we now see that the Oedipus myth is based on childhood fantasy," and "we now know that Moses was an Egyptian"—becomes itself the saving myth that reconstitutes the panicking modern who no longer knows what to believe. This is, in fact, the thesis of one of the most profound socio-psychological readings of psychoanalysis, Peter Homans' *The Ability to Mourn* (1989). In its appropriation of the cultural past, Homans argues, psychoanalysis attempts to recreate a relation to a lost common culture through the process of de-idealization, providing a secular coin of vantage that allows for the bourgeois subject to confront the loss inherent in modern industrial individualization.[27] As Homans maintains at length (in admirable historical detail), "[a]s a theory of culture, analysis authorizes mourning for the abandoned ideals, often unconscious, of the ancient and archaic cultural heritage. [...] Without mourning, there can be no growth, no historical advance, no value change, no hope—the most valuable of all historical acquisitions, for hopelessness is little more than mourning gone awry" (1989, 104). Psychoanalysis thus represents a unique response to the *personal* crisis of losing one's place in an organic cultural past, or of falling out of the traditional narrative configurations that gave life a clearer meaning and agenda. In this sense, psychoanalytic therapy serves as the recovery of a cultural narrative as well as an individual life-history, which would explain its appeal to those secular intellectuals who had lost their religious and cultural moorings (Homans bases this argument on the life histories of Carl Jung, Otto Rank, and Ernest Jones, in particular).

Whence came the perennial danger in the movement of an *idealization* not only of psychoanalysis as a powerful new mythology, but also of Freud as its creator. The young Otto Rank, for example, was taken from despair to extreme elation by his adherence to psychoanalytic truth, writing in his diary, "Now I see everything clearly; the world process is no longer a riddle; I can explain the whole culture, yes I can explain everything" (cited in Homans 1989, 163). Such is the heady wine of backdoor totalization as taken up by a poor Viennese Jew in search of a purpose in his life. The Welshman Jones, an apostate Christian, was taken in by the new sense of order in the cultural landscape of psychoanalysis. "It is *beautiful* to trace the connections between different legends in the same and different countries, and in getting further and further back to see how inevitably we get back to the source of life, the old grand theme" (Paskauskas 1985, 6; my emphasis).

For this reason, so many of the works by the original members of the psychoanalytic movement manage, even many years hence, to recount not simply the latest decodings offered by the science, but also the tale of Freud himself as the Founding Father. Witness, for example, the recollections of Theodor Reik, another major figure in the early movement who focused on cultural applications. Reik's account in the introduction of *Myth and Guilt* (1957) first of all tells "the story of this book," inscribing the analysis of myths in a metanarrative that shows us in some detail another kind of originary myth. Reik provides a genealogy for his own text that goes back not only to *Totem and Taboo* (the work that in many ways authorized Reik's entry into religious and ethnographic studies), but to the awesome presence of Freud himself:

> It is difficult to describe what impression Freud's *Totem and Taboo* made upon us, his Vienna circle. I still vividly remember the meeting of our Analytic Association in 1913 in which Freud presented to us the last and most important part of the work about the return of totemism in childhood. We were enthusiastic and we immediately understood that here was an intellectual challenge for generations of psychologists and historians of civilization. Privileged to speak with the author of the great book, we discussed with him the overflow of ideas it had stimulated in most of us. (1957, ix)

As he delves into the genesis of his own book on lapsarian myth, Reik paints a revealing picture of the movement's self-ritualized gathering which links scenes of childhood, authority, and discipleship all around the theme of Freud's successful decoding of primitive and ancient cultures.

> On June 30, 1913 we celebrated *Totem and Taboo* by a dinner we gave on the Konstantinhügel in the Prater (a nice restaurant on a little hill overlooking the chestnut trees of the old park in which we had played as children). We jokingly spoke of that dinner as of a totemistic meal. Freud was in a very good mood. He sometimes looked thoughtfully at an ancient Egyptian animal figure, which an ex-patient had given him on that occasion. We were, I am sure, more than twelve at the table, but something must have reminded me of Christ and His apostles at the last Supper. (1957, x)

It is remarkable that Freud becomes a Christ-figure here in Reik's account: a revolutionary Jew who fulfills the enigmatic promises of the past and reveals the true meaning of past utterances. The powerful sense of mission which Freud inspired in the young Reik—including his sense of historical irony—shows that he had not imparted an aporetic or skeptical mentality to his circle at all, but rather one of a privileged truth-quest.

> I already knew that I would devote my life to psychologic [*sic*] research, especially to the trail that Freud had blazed, and I passionately felt that "holy curiosity" of which Einstein often spoke. With the conceit of a young man, I daydreamed that I had discovered something valuable and imagined that it would have revolutionary effects in the field of comparative religion. I have never since known the urge and grip of the creative impulse as intensely. (1957, x)

To understand the mythic import of psychoanalysis, then, one has to see it as doubly configured. On the one hand, psychoanalysis firmly implants itself in a project of deciphering ancient culture, such as Reik's book on myths of the Fall. This gives it a highly appealing quality of explaining the incomprehensible elements of tradition, particularly those elements that come from the "childhood" and prehistory of the species. Thus psychoanalysis *revivifies* ancient myth on a constant basis through insisting on its continuing relevance as psychic evidence, and these psychoanalytical appropriations might even be seen themselves as crystallizations and applications of the traditional mythic material, just as a given

Greek tragedy would be (Burkert 1979, 1–34). Yet psychoanalysis reviv-ifies ancient myth not just through repetition, but *through analysis*, which rewrites the real reference and import of the myth according to a new master-narrative, the metanarrative of rational understanding, of over-coming the opacity of tradition through the application of *Wissenschaft*. This synergistic relationship is thus both mytho-centric and mytho-clas-tic, relying heavily on a cultural matrix it is trying to transform.[28]

For this reason, it is not merely a snide remark to point out how the analysis of myth and the myth of analysis coincide; it is a fact of the in-stitution inscribed in the communications, both official and unofficial, that pass between the players. "We mustn't quarrel when we are besieg-ing Troy," Freud wrote to Jung in 1908. "Do you remember the lines from the *Philoctetes* [of Sophocles, line 113]: αἱρεῖ τὰ τόξα ταῦτα τὴν Τροίαν μόνα (These arrows alone will take Troy)?[29] My self-confidence has so increased that I am thinking of taking this line as a motto for a new edition of the *Collected Papers on the Theory of the Neuroses*"—which in fact he did (McGuire 1974, 146). The mythic tones invoked by Freud's disci-ples further underscore the point, and even show in their recurrent pat-ricidal themes the oedipal, conflictual reality that made mythology reverberate so powerfully for his followers. Jung writes, "like Herakles of old, you are a human hero and demi-god, wherefore your dicta unfortu-nately carry with them a sempiternal value. All the weaker ones who come after you must of necessity adopt your nomenclature [. . .]" (McGuire 1974, 275). Already in 1909, we find the future renegade son disclosing the tensions that would lead to the break in 1912–13 (a break effected through a work that is itself a veritable flurry of mythological references). "It is a hard lot to have to work alongside the father creator" (McGuire 1974, 279).[30] It is no wonder, then, that once Jung, Alfred Adler, and Wil-helm Stekel had left the movement, Freud presided over his Secret Com-mittee bearing the ring of Jupiter. And was it mere coincidence that there were seven rings in that committee—one for every gate of Thebes?

Total History

Freud's great conflict with Jung in the years 1912–1913 is also a turning point for the psychoanalytic appropriation of history, not just myth.[31] For part of the outcome of his rivalry with Jung involved returning the myth of Oedipus to the space of real events instead of the "psychic reality" it had initially represented to Freud. As is well known, Freud's initial espousal of the Oedipus complex was in order to avoid an unpleasant historical thesis: that hysteria has its ultimate etiology in *real, historical* occurrences of sexual abuse. More precisely, he had come to the improbable conclusion "that in all cases, the *father*, not excluding my own, had to be accused of being perverse" (Masson 1985, 264). By converting these acts of molestation into events of fantasy, Freud had effectively switched the import of his mythic material to a different register altogether from the hurly-burly of "material truth." Which is why it seems like hypocrisy when he chides Carl Jung for turning the oedipal narrative into something of merely symbolic value, particularly when we consider how much his reading relies on the idea that such notions as "fate" within the Sophoclean drama are symbolizations of other phenomena (in this case, the inevitability of real oedipal conflict).

The tension with Jung also seems odd when one considers how much they had in common concerning the appropriation of mythology and cultural history into the psychoanalytic evidentiary domain. For Jung, this was an imperative based entirely upon the compelling validity of analogical reasoning—a reasoning Freud did not reject by any means. Jung expressed blatant methodological imperialism during their honeymoon period in 1909, when he cast the co-optation of history into psychoanalysis *not* as desirable but rather as purely necessary. "It has become quite clear to me that we shall not solve the ultimate secrets of neurosis and psychosis without mythology and the history of civilization, for *embryology* goes hand in hand with *comparative anatomy*, and without the latter the former is but a freak of nature whose depths remain uncomprehended" (McGuire 1974, 279; original emphasis). In the dire need to find *significance* in the clinical facts, history is thus commandeered by psychoanalysis, which in turn will now make sense of the whole sweep of human existence: "For this reason," writes Jung, "antiquity now appears to me in a new and significant light. What we now find in the individual psyche—in compressed, stunted, or one-sidedly differentiated form—may be seen spread out in all its fullness in times past. Happy the man who can read these signs!" (McGuire 1974, 269). And it is Father Freud who orchestrates this methodological imperialism from the Berggasse: "Our colonists in foreign fields [. . .] should also speak up," he writes to Jung; "I long for mythologists, linguists, and historians of religions; if they won't come to our help, we shall have to do all that ourselves" (McGuire 1974, 276). This is effectively the rationale for psychoanalysis's militant dilettantism in cultural history, to which I shall return in the next chapter.

Yet Freud began to panic at the prospect of deploying the cultural past in terms that were *too* symbolic and not based on notions of an existential past, a past of *real, lived events.* Hence he became critical of Jung's invocation of phylogenetic explanation on two fronts: first, in the precipitous recourse to phylogenetic factors before the ontogenetic ones were exhausted in an individual's analysis ("From the History of an Infantile Neurosis," SE 17:97); and second, in the deployment of myths as cultural archetypes without regard for their genesis in real historical experience and their subsequent transformation by the processes of repression. In reference to the latter, Freud effectively drew a line in the sand with *Totem and Taboo,* a book written in response to the ongoing composition of Jung's *Transformations and Symbols of the Libido* ([1912] 1956). Here Freud reopened the hypothesis of an *historical* event that would essentially explain the father complex at the heart of all culture, and this is given in a narrative form with the added sanction of the words of "father" Goethe in the book's dramatic conclusion: *Im Anfang war die Tat* ("In the beginning was the deed").

Freud's historical hypothesis is simple: the original human "family" was a horde or primate troop ruled by a dominant male, who chased away the other males in the horde as they matured and thus effected a sexual monopoly on the females. Eventually the exiled "sons" banded together and killed this primal father, eating him afterward. The psychological Oedipus complex developed from the unconscious repercussions of this event; namely, the guilt and need for atonement with the murdered father that led to the development of religion, social order, and art. Though initially it was couched in terms of a discrete event, Freud later modified his characterization of the hypothesis as a condensed narrative (*Geschichte,* which conveniently means both "story" and "history"). "The story is told [i.e., in *Totem and Taboo*] in an enormously condensed form, as though it had happened on a single occasion, while in fact [*in Wirklichkeit*] it covered thousands of years and was repeated countless times during that long period" (*Moses and Monotheism,* SE 23:81). Freud later referred to this narrative as a "scientific myth" (*Group Psychology and the Analysis of the Ego,* SE 18:135) and even as his "vision" ("An Autobiographical Study," SE 20:68), but one should be cautious about assuming that this meant he was not serious about its status as a historical hypothesis. He was serious enough that it dominated his later thinking on social psychology and religion, and as we just saw, his only real modification of it was to multiply the scenario "countless times" in *reality.*

Nor was he the only one to entertain the historicity of oedipal conflict.

Ernest Jones reacted quite favorably to *Totem and Taboo* in part because it confirmed his own convictions. "I have for years believed that the Oedipus situation originated in *actual* conflicts between the pretensions of the sons and the jealousy of the sire, these being later converted into inner conflicts, and that we have there the central problem of the development of civilization [. . .]. That being so, I can see no possible solution to the problems of totemism other than the one you offer" (Paskauskas 1995, 206). Thus, although there was always an assumed commonality between the modern audience and the ancient myth of Oedipus in relation to the personal experience of oedipal conflict (that is, on the ontogenetic plane), what changed with *Totem and Taboo* was the formal introduction of an "archaic heritage" of *historical* oedipal conflict that would forever supplement the nature of individual experience. The specter of the real, historical father who haunted the seduction hypothesis was let in the backdoor as the *Urvater* at the heart of cultural memory. The stone rejected became the corner stone.

This led Freud, in spite of his famous dislike of epistemology, into a theory of knowledge that usurped philosophical terms and converted them into historical precipitates; namely, phylogenetic "schemata" of thought "which, like the categories of philosophy, are concerned with the business of 'placing' the impressions derived from actual experience" ("From the History of an Infantile Neurosis," SE 17:119). Thus the situation can arise that the experience of the individual is eclipsed in retrospect by these "inherited" interpretive pathways, and an individual analysis can easily butt up against the antiquity of the entire human species. Of these phylogenetic schemata, which are "precipitates from the history of human civilization," the Oedipus complex is "the best known member of the class" (SE 17:119). It is important to note again that Freud wants to invoke this phylogenetic patterning as *supplementary* to individual experience instead of guiding it completely, in part to stave off the full blown implications of a collective unconscious as theorized by Jung, and in part to keep the empirical work of individual analysis in the forefront of his narrative. This is effectively an attempt to save the phenomena of the empirical romance.

He once described an individual's hereditary disposition not as a single unity but rather "an infinite number of dispositions which are developed and fixed by an accidental fate. The disposition is so to speak polymorphous" (Ernst Freud 1960, 284). Thus each individual is shaped by δαίμων καὶ τύχη (fate and chance), he said, citing the first two stanzas of Goethe's *Urworte. Orphisch*. These cannot be seen as an antithesis, "since constitution after all is nothing but the sediment of experiences from a long line of ancestors; and why should the *individual* experience not be granted a share alongside the experience of ancestors?" (Ernst Freud 1960, 284).

As a consequence, ancient history thus bleeds through biography only at particular junctures: "All that we find in the prehistory of neuroses is that a child catches hold of this phylogenetic experience where his own experience fails him. He fills in the gaps in individual truth with prehistoric truth; he replaces occurrences in his own life by occurrences in the life of his ancestors" (SE 17:97). Freud uses this explanation to take the Wolf Man's experiences of castration threats from the *women* in his life and to reconfigure them in a manner that buttresses the *father* complex in the case history. Though the Wolf Man had no experience of such threats from his father, "in man's prehistory it was unquestionably the father who practiced castration as a punishment and who later softened it down into circumcision," and so "heredity triumphed over accidental experience" in this case and the young Wolf Man came to fear this penalty from his father all the same (SE 17:86). This is one of the more blatant instances of Freud's application of narrative adjustments to the "facts" of a case. But it yields the interesting result that the hapless boy is not just caught in a squalid personal drama, ridiculed by the women in his life. He is living the history of his species in the form of a masculine rivalry, becoming a kind of Everyboy through the persistence of phylogenetic memory. This is precisely the powerful mythology Wittgenstein admired and dreaded in psychoanalytic explanation.

It is thus that Freud, the supposed founder of discontinuous and ruptured history, became instead the author of a backdoor "total history." In Foucault's view, total history is a project that "seeks to reconstitute the overall form of a civilization, the principle—material or spiritual—of a society, the significance common to all the phenomena of a period, the law that accounts for their cohesion" ([1969] 1972, 9). The master plots of *Totem and Taboo* and *Moses and Monotheism* conform very well to Foucault's idea of total description that "draws all phenomena around a single center" ([1969] 1972, 10). Both works attempt to tie complex historical phenomena to a single narrative thread of patricide and the transgenerational precipitates of filial guilt. Psychological repression itself is the great center at the heart of the Freudian web of history, concealing and yet preserving the past in a process much like entombment.[32] Hanns Sachs attests well in his memoirs to this tendentious drift in Freud's fascination with history. "In all of Freud's historical interests, down to the minute details of the things in his collection, the 'red thread' of psychoanalysis was present. In the strata of extinct civilizations on which our own was built, he studied the diversity of the methods of cultural repression and its results" (1946, 102–103).

And I hasten to add that this was no mere quirk of an archaeological hobbyist, but a serious part of the psychoanalytic movement. In a 1923 encyclopedia article, Freud paints a picture of the developing movement that shows how central the disturbing acropolis of oedipal theory was for the expanding psychoanalytic domain:

> The significance of the Oedipus complex began to grow to gigantic proportions and it looked as though social order, morals, justice and religion had arisen together in the primeval ages of mankind as reaction-formations against the Oedipus complex. Otto Rank threw a brilliant light upon mythology and the history of literature by the application of psychoanalytic views, as did Theodor Reik upon the history of morals and religions, while Dr. Pfister, of Zurich, aroused the interest of religious and secular teachers and demonstrated the importance of the psychoanalytic standpoint for education. Further discussion of these applications of psychoanalysis would be out of place here, *and it is enough to say that the limits of their influence are not yet in sight.* ("Psycho-Analysis," SE 18:253; my emphasis)

The declaration of this brave new world of oedipal truth in 1923 was simply a further confirmation of Freud's firm belief that psychoanalysis is not just *analogous* to cultural history, but ought to be deployed as a proper form of it. While he was effectively doing this already in his early analysis of *Oedipus Tyrannus* in the *Interpretation of Dreams*, he made this agenda explicit in a telltale addition to that text in 1919, after he had reformulated the oedipal scenario as not just a Greek myth, but a Darwinian scenario of origins.

> Behind this childhood of the individual [traceable in dreams] we are promised a picture of a phylogenetic childhood—a picture of the development of the human race, of which the individual's development is in fact an abbreviated recapitulation influenced by the chance circumstances of life. We can guess how much to the point is Nietzsche's assertion that in dreams "some primaeval relic of humanity is at work which we can now scarcely reach any longer by a direct path"; and we may expect that the analysis of dreams will lead

us to a knowledge of man's archaic heritage, what is psychically in-
nate in him. Dreams and neuroses seem to have preserved more
mental antiquities than we could have imagined possible; so that
psychoanalysis may claim a high place among the sciences [*einen
hohen Rang unter den Wissenschaften*] which are concerned with the
reconstruction of the earliest and most obscure periods of the beginnings of the human race. (SE 5:548–549)

Though based on the evidentiary claim that certain individual psychical
features may be historical precipitates, the statement shows the extent of
Freud's desire to "claim a high place" in the scientific hierarchy, and it is
most notably a position for historical reconstruction. Though from the
start Freud had entertained interesting parallels in history with his clinical work, this passage shows his *revision* of the founding text of psychoanalysis to include history as an integral part of the mission. Its status is
therefore something more like a constitutional amendment than a mere
updating of his text.

   In the light of this claim, we should also see the final positioning of
psychoanalysis itself as a *scientia mediatrix* between the traditionally separate domains of the *Geistes-* and *Naturwissenschaften*.[33] As a *Wissenschaft*
that concerns itself with the *Natur* of *Geist*, or the interface between the
cultural and the natural in the mind, psychoanalysis holds the position of
an interstitial science that ideally mediates between fields.

   Any estimate of psychoanalysis would be incomplete if it failed to
   make clear that, *alone* among the medical disciplines, it has *the most
   extensive relations* with the mental sciences [*Geisteswissenschaften*],
   and that it is in a position to play a part of the same importance in
   the studies of religious and cultural history and in the sciences of
   mythology and literature as it is in psychiatry. (SE 18: 252; my emphasis)

History itself is the link between *Natur* and *Geist*, since Freud's point of
view typically compels him to blend natural and cultural history; that is,
the evolution of the mind's structures with the evolution of their place in
cultural history. As he conceived of his new *Wissenschaft*, it was something
well beyond the medical profession in which it originated. Freud's later
formula for an analyst's education stressed "the history of civilization,
mythology, the psychology of religion and the science of literature,"
without which "an analyst can make nothing of a large amount of his ma-

terial" (*The Question of Lay Analysis*, SE 20:246). In contrast, "the great mass of what is taught in medical schools is of no use to him for his purposes" save for basic biology, sexology, and "*familiarity* with the symptomatology of psychiatry" (SE 20:246; my emphasis).[34]

It behooves us then to consider for a moment the product of Freudian *paideia:* a person deeply versed in cultural history and literature, but with only a passing familiarity with psychiatry, biology, and sexology. The long-term danger of this arrangement was to make the psychoanalyst too much a dilettante in science, and yet a most peculiar product vis-à-vis the humanities. Was psychoanalysis to be applied science or applied humanities?

CHAPTER 8

■

Critique and Divination

Freylich ist das Wahre nicht immer das Wahrscheinliche.

Certainly what is true isn't always what seems true.
—R. G. Niebuhr [1811–32] 1853, 360

I have argued that we must see the novelty of Freud's *scientia sexualis* in its reconfiguration of historical discourses, and this is a claim that bears further illustration if it is not simply to remain a bland critique of Michel Foucault's brilliant work on the history of sexuality. In the next three chapters, therefore, I shall draw out the lines of filiation a bit more clearly, contributing from my quarter of cultural history some insight into the subtle (and not so subtle) ways in which the great emergence of professional history in the nineteenth century contributed to the formation of the discursive domain of psychoanalysis. The diachronic frame of mind was so vastly ensconced in intellectual circles of the time that it would be easier to find where it is *not* rather than where it is amid the projects of that age. The cultural historian Jacob Burckhardt (1818–1897) formulated the historical approach as nothing short of a categorical imperative for the intelligentsia. We can see that Freud took note of this remark while reading Burckhardt from the exact underlining in his own copy of the book:

It is self-evidently the special duty of the educated to perfect and complete, as well as they can, the picture of the continuity of the world's development. This marks off conscious beings from the un-

conscious barbarian. The vision of both past and future is what distinguishes human beings from the animals; and for us the past may
have its reproaches, and the future its anxieties, of which the animals know nothing. ([1898–1902] 1998, 12; translation slightly
modified to reflect original; the underlining mimics Freud's own)

This underlining in Freud's copy points again to the great value of the *literal* Freud archive vis-à-vis the archive of antiquity, since it reveals the
physical trace of a reading and suggests a moment of synergy.[1] It shows
us rather directly how psychoanalysis was born in dialogue with the larger
considerations of historical consciousness from the nineteenth century
that concern us here.

However, the exact filiation that concerns me in this chapter is more
precisely that between psychoanalysis and two distinct branches of historical discourse.[2] The first is the critical historiography that began right
around the turn of the nineteenth century in the field of Roman studies,
and the second is the cultural history (*Kulturgeschichte*) propounded by
Burckhardt himself. The first branch effected such a major change in
horizon that by Freud's day its suppositions were simply truisms to all educated people; thus, its presence in his work is as a diffused set of self-
evident axioms more than as a particular textual engagement with a given
historian's work. The second branch, however, can be clearly pinned
down to Freud's reading of Burckhardt's *Griechische Kulturgeschichte* in
1899. As in his reading of Schliemann, we shall have cause to return to the
scene of Freud's reading of Burckhardt in some specificity because of
the exact timing of the events, since this coincidence shows yet again how
the ancient archive was quite present at the birth of psychoanalysis. But
through Burckhardt we shall also see the particular opening toward total
history that Freud exploited for the positioning of his interstitial science.

The Science of Self-Criticism

The analysand's memory is the worksite of psychoanalysis. From it
emerges the material which, in the dialogic space of the analytic hour,
must be worked over, sifted, evaluated, interpreted, and set out in new relations. Individual memory with all its byways and quirks thus reaches a
kind of apotheosis in the analytic situation and acquires a scientific importance that is unique from a historical perspective. But memory's importance lies rooted in its own faultiness and essential unreliability, since

for psychoanalysis to be on track *there must be the constant evidence of repression*, which entails occlusions, gaps, and distortions in the "record" of memory. Freud must explain the validity of dealing with such untrustworthy material, and this leads him to search for legitimating analogies of the kind we have come to expect.

On more than one occasion, Freud described the complex nature of individual memory with recourse to an analogy with ancient historiography. In his study of Leonardo da Vinci (1910), he comes to discuss the nature of childhood memories, which for psychoanalysis are at the highest possible premium while at the same time they are all suspected of being utterly counterfeit. The analogy here is so full blown that it is worth citing at length:

This is often the way in which childhood memories originate. Quite unlike conscious memories from the time of maturity, they are not fixed at the moment of being experienced and afterwards repeated, but are only elicited at a later age when childhood is already past; in the process they are altered and falsified, and are put into the service of later trends so that generally speaking they cannot be sharply distinguished from phantasies. *Their nature is perhaps best illustrated by a comparison with the way in which the writing of history originated among the peoples of antiquity.* As long as a nation was small and weak it gave no thought to the writing of its history. [. . .] It was an age of heroes, not of historians. Then came another age, an age of reflection: men felt themselves to be rich and powerful, and now felt a need to learn where they had come from and how they had developed. Historical writing, which had begun to keep a continuous record of the present, now also cast a glance back to the past, gathered traditions and legends, interpreted the traces of antiquity that survived in customs and usages, and in this way created a history of the past. It was inevitable that this early history should have been an expression of present beliefs and wishes rather than a true picture of the past; for many things had been dropped from the nation's memory, while others were distorted, and some remains of the past were given a wrong interpretation in order to fit in with contemporary ideas. Moreover, people's motive for writing history was not objective curiosity but a desire to influence their contemporaries, to encourage and inspire them, or to hold a mirror up before them. A man's conscious memory of the events of his maturity is in every way comparable to the first kind of historical writing [which was a chronicle of current events]; while the memories that he has of his childhood correspond, as far as their origins and reliability are concerned, to the history of a nation's earliest days, which was compiled later and for tendentious reasons. (SE 11:83–84; my emphasis)

It is hard not to see the early books of Livy's history of Rome, the *Ab urbe condita*, as Freud's model for mature memory of childhood. Livy wrote his thrilling and romantic history of Roman character at a moment of deep constitutional transformation during the reign of Augustus (27 BCE–14 CE), when republican traditions were being subtly overturned by a new political order that at base was the antithesis of a self-determining people. The good old Roman values that distinguish the figures in his dramatic narrative were meant very much to be a "mirror" to his contemporaries, and so strong is the ethical characterization in the work that Livy's history retained its value as moral discourse well into the nineteenth century (one need only look at the work of Neoclassical painters like Jacques Louis David [1748–1825] to see this).[3]

However, a great hallmark of nineteenth-century German historiography was the critical analysis of the Livian narratives of early Rome by Barthold Georg Niebuhr (1776–1831) in his *Römische Geschichte* (1811–32), in which he proclaimed these hallowed accounts to be poetical fictions responding to national *psychological* needs, not historical truth. This type of source criticism became the model for the critical history that was to dominate German thought well into the twentieth century.[4] So it is not surprising that *both* the spell of Livian narrative and its dispelling could stand behind an account of childhood memory in Freud's work. On the personal plane, Livian narrative was a part of Freud's own childhood, as we know very well from his fixation on Hannibal.[5] But on the analogical plane, it is understandable that Freud would be drawn to the paradigm of critical historiography, which decodes pseudo-history as psychic truth, since he clings to the paradigm of psychoanalysis as a way to decode myth as psychic truth. If myth is analogous to the dream, then legendary history becomes the analogue to the "screen memories" and fantasies of childhood. Freud makes the comparison with screen memories explicit in the *Psychopathology of Everyday Life* (1901, though this passage was only added in 1907): "Thus the 'childhood memories' of individuals come in general to acquire the significance of 'screen memories' and in doing so offer a remarkable analogy with the childhood memories that a nation preserves in its store of legends and myths" (SE 6: 48).[6] We can also see here why in the Leonardo study Freud would have moved so quickly from a childhood screen memory to an ancient Egyptian mythical figure (Mut) in a zealous over-deployment of the analogy.

My suspicion of a Livian model behind this 1910 analogy is confirmed by comments Freud makes fifteen years later in the *Selbstdarstellung* (1925) precisely on the topic of his discovery that the seduction theory— i.e., that the neuroses have their ultimate etiology in actual sexual molestation—was wrong, and that the tales of abuse he was recovering where in fact his patients' fantasies. The fantasies had a "psychical reality" that did not correspond to a "material reality." In analogizing his own error, the Livian model is quite explicit.

> It will be seen, then, that my mistake was of the same kind as would be made by someone who believed that the legendary story of the early kings of Rome (as told by Livy) was historical truth instead of what it is in fact—a reaction against the memory of times and circumstances that were insignificant and occasionally, perhaps, inglorious. (SE 20:35)

The story of the early kings of Rome is definitely the territory traversed by Niebuhr, who had quite shockingly applied critical analysis to Livy's history of this particular epoch and debunked it, even though it had long served as a source of indelible moral *exempla* to people on all parts of the political spectrum.

Let us examine briefly one such case in point from Livy's history and Niebuhr's view of it. For centuries, readers of Livy's first book had shuddered at the monstrous ambition of Tullia, daughter of the sixth-century BCE Roman king Servius Tullius. Tullia conspired against her own husband and sister in order to marry Tarquin, her brother-in-law, whom she incited to overthrow her father the king. When their plan was achieved, she was first to hail Tarquin as the new king and gruesomely trampled over her father's mutilated corpse in her carriage, spattering gore on herself and her train. Thus defiled by paternal blood, she rode right to their home, openly offending her own *penates* or household gods (*Ab urbe condita* 1.46–48). For Livy, such a beginning to the reign explains its end in violent revolution, and his account attests that the very place where the sacrilegious trampling occurred was still known as the *Sceleratus vicus*, or the Street of Crime.[7] This is an example of what Freud meant by "traces of antiquity that remain in customs and usages" which are reinterpreted in line with the evolving narrative.[8]

To the Roman mind, the tale of Tarquin and Tullia was intelligible as a historical reality, since it described quite credibly the degradation of Roman kingship from the good old days of Romulus and Numa Pompilius to the final days of tyranny under Tarquin the Proud, a degradation which justified the foundation of a republic under the leadership of Lucius Junius Brutus, "the Liberator."[9] And Livy's Augustan readers could quickly see in Tullia a reflection of the devouring ambition of Cleopatra, who—according to the Augustan propaganda—incited Mark Antony to attempt the mad project of an oriental empire at the expense of Rome in Livy's own time. Against the type of Tullia arises the noble Lucretia, the good Roman wife who, having been raped by Tarquin's son Sextus, provides the precipitating cause for the rebellion. Lucretia dutifully informs her father and husband of the crime, then kills herself lest she provide a precedent for any future "unchaste woman" (*Ab urbe condita* 1.58). Brutus and the men of her family swear on her blood to avenge her, and thus is born the republican revolution that will transform Roman society. The symmetry of the cunning, virtuous Brutus vs. the haughty, uxorious Tarquin on the one hand, and the monstrous Tullia vs. the chaste Lucretia on the other, is all too perfect.

In the face of such a compelling narrative, Niebuhr dared to suggest that "Tullia's crimes may have an existence as unreal as those of Lady Macbeth" (1853, 218). The highly personalized tragedy of the royal family is at root just one instance of a whole world of popular ballads circulating in times long after and quite different from those they claim to describe. According to Niebuhr's theory, these ballads, far from relating the past, conceal its true events.[10] And the motivation for such confabulations was equally clear to Niebuhr. "A people that has been subject to a foreign yoke tries to destroy *even the memory* that it has sighed in bondage"; it is a motive that Niebuhr adduces as evident in other national traditions as well (1853, 218).[11] Niebuhr was suggesting that the narrative of the Tarquins concealed the primal reality that early Rome was either for a time under Etruscan domination or was in fact originally a colony of Etruscan Caere.[12] The thesis of "Etruscan Rome" was to prove a very durable one in the long run, and for some scholars was dogmatic truth well into the 1960s.[13]

The story of Tarquin and Tullia is thus seen in psychological terms as a tale of heroic self-assertion against impious tyranny. It serves the function of depicting in high relief the moral foundations of republican government in the place of the sacred kingship which had formed the *original* legitimating narrative of Rome. Brutus and Lucretia, Tarquin and Tullia thus serve as a kind of screen memory for a reality that is more complex and far less flattering. To the author who late in life would resurrect Moses as an Egyptian, and whose Moses would in fact be a trigger for the memory of the *Urvater* of the primal horde, an Etruscan Rome could serve as a compelling paradigm for memory's legerdemain through the mechanics of repression, one that obtains even at the individual level.

When it comes to origins, we remember what we want to remember—this was the troubling assertion that Niebuhr raised to a methodological principle.[14] By the time Freud was writing, this was citable as a matter of dogma: "It is *universally acknowledged* that where the origin of a people's traditions and legendary history are concerned, a motive of this kind, whose aim is to wipe from memory whatever is distressing to national feeling, must be taken into consideration" (*Psychopathology of Everyday Life*, SE 6:148; my emphasis). This principle from the ancient archive had filtered into the approach to individual memory undertaken at Berggasse 19.

The Need for a Past

Thus far I have merely pointed out the relevant background to one of Freud's analogies concerning childhood memories and legendary history; but Niebuhr's relevance here goes beyond mere historical footnoting, since this analogy is a tenacious one in Freud's mind and has far-reaching consequences in the trajectory of his thought. Later comments he makes in *Moses and Monotheism* (written in 1934–1938) show that the connection between legendary history and childhood memory remained highly suggestive for him well into his old age.

> Long-past ages have a great and often puzzling attraction for men's imagination. Whenever they are dissatisfied with their present surroundings—and this happens often enough—they turn back to the past and hope that they will now be able to prove the truth of a golden age. They are probably still under the spell of their childhood [*unter dem Zauber ihrer Kindheit*], which is presented to them by their not impartial memory as a time of uninterrupted bliss. (SE 23:71)

This remark echoes to a degree Livy's preface to his history of Rome, in which he proclaims:

I do not doubt but that for most readers there is less pleasure in the history of the very beginnings [of Rome] and of things close to that time, since they are in a hurry to get to more recent events through which the great strength of this long-since imperial people nearly brought upon its own destruction [i.e., the late republican civil wars]. I on the other hand will seek just this benefit from my work, namely that while I give my full attention to investigating these ancient affairs for a time, I shall avert my gaze from the sight of the evils that our age has witnessed for so many years and be freed from that anxiety that can trouble a writer's mind, even if it cannot make it wander from the truth. (*Ab urbe condita*, praefatio 4–5)

Freud's connection to Livy is actually documented here, though only indirectly, since the textual model to which he explicitly refers in a footnote in *Moses and Monotheism* is Macaulay's *Lays of Ancient Rome* (1842). This work is a series of English ballads constructed on stories from the first books of Livy and directly inspired by Niebuhr's historical criticism.[15] They are the imagined reconstructions of those early lays that Niebuhr saw as the basis for Livy's later narrative.

Freud's use of Macaulay's text in this instance is highly suggestive. By drawing attention to the imagination, Freud underscores the role of *creative fantasy* about the past as a form of adaptation to unsatisfying present circumstances, as a refuge or preserve from the pressures of the reality principle.[16] In this particular instance, we might suspect that this is the confession, hidden in plain view, of the cancer-ridden Freud who was investigating Jewish origins as the long dark night of Nazi Europe was settling in around him. As he writes about the great Jewish "progress in intellectuality" that came from the adoption of monotheism, he counters Nazi accusations of Jewish degeneracy and takes comfort in the long history of spiritual resilience among his own people. But the remark also underscores more generally the *need for a past* in the psychic economy, a past that extends beyond the individual and places him or her in a broader narrative context. Like the dream or the symptom, the writing of history is itself another compromise formation, a means of expressing the self's frustrated desire, which is in part the desire for a secure relation to the past.

Freud's remark reflects the other consequence of Niebuhr's critical assessment, one that is quite evident in Macaulay's work: the sudden *aesthetic and psychological* appreciation for what the English historian George Grote called "a past that was never present." Far from causing the wholesale rejection of Livy's text, Niebuhr's critical reassessment suddenly made the dreary Roman *Volk* into a poetic people on a par with the Homeric Greeks and the Germans of the *Nibelungenlied*.[17] Niebuhr undermined Livy's historical credibility, but increased the awareness of the Roman poetic *passion* for the past. Goethe wrote to Niebuhr saying, "Your discrimination of the poetical from the historical element is of inestimable worth, since by it *neither is destroyed*, but rather for the first time fully confirmed in its true value and dignity; and there is an inexhaustible interest in seeing how the two again coalesce, and exert a mutual influence."[18] With Niebuhr we find the thesis that the falsification of the past and the need for an imaginary history are characteristic of the Romans, a people well known for adaptation and success in the struggle for survival. To put it in a later idiom: lying to yourself might well have evolutionary advantages, and may even be at the heart of civilization. Goethe sensed the basic antinomy between successful living and critical research into origins when he commented to Niebuhr that "[i]t is devoutly to be wished by everyone who wants to return to a primitive view [*Uranschauen*] that there be a critique which smashes through everything secondary and which—if it cannot reconstruct the original condition—at least orders it into fragments and lets the whole be inferred. However, worldly people [*Lebe-Menschen*] don't want that, and rightly so" (Goethe 1985–, 34:118–119). Having a usable past may thus be a necessity, but having the *historical truth* may well not be.

The stories we tell of ourselves, as products of human fantasy, have their intrinsic qualities and functions which bear a complicated relation to historical truth. Caught between self-censorship and the genuine need to account for the past, narratives of origin are always compromises responding to complex psychological requirements. The critical perspective in historiography that was inaugurated by Niebuhr was clearly an inspiration to Freud, but for reasons he would find even more compelling than Niebuhr and his intellectual descendants. Those reasons lie in the analytic situation with its interrogation of "living memory" and in the evolving characterization of repression, which for Freud is simultaneously an agency of distortion *and* conservation. Repression is the main cause of the problems in the "record" of historical memory, though also the source of their solution, something Niebuhr could not claim for his song traditions. I will return to this, since it forms the core distinction between the posture of psychoanalysis and the available positions of the era. But first we must continue to draw out the implications of Freud's deployment of critical historiography to see how it serves his expansive agenda.

Treating the record of the past as a compromise formation requires a heightened awareness of methodology and a newfound respect for the intrinsic features of the evidence. Freud showed this working principle most thoroughly in reference to dreams, and in one particular instance he drew a parallel to the study of Livy that serves our discussion directly. According to Freud, dream interpretation consists of two phases: one in which the analyst "translates" the dream, and another in which he or she assesses its value; it is important to insulate oneself in the first instance from influences stemming from the second. "It is as though one had before one a chapter from some work in a foreign language—by Livy, for instance. The first thing one wants to know is what Livy says in the chapter; and it is only after this that the discussion arises of whether what one has read is a historical narrative or a legend or a digression on the part of the author" ("Remarks on the Theory and Practice of Dream-Interpretation," SE 19:112). Like historical texts, dreams have their own surface rhetoric and inherent strategies requiring an intrinsic analysis quite apart from assessing the dream text's overall value as a source of "information" about past events.

By deploying such analogies with critical historiography, however, Freud does not simply grasp for the authoritative status of Niebuhr's style of history in order to illustrate his own critical procedures. He also begins to encompass history within psychoanalysis's own area of competence, thus blurring the boundary between them by means of what I have termed *recursive analogy*. This is evident in the shift that takes place in the analogy's role between the time of the Leonardo study in 1910 and the citation above from *Moses and Monotheism* from the period 1934–1938, to which I now return.

In the Leonardo study, childhood memory is explained by analogy to ancient historiography and its romantic distortions; in this way, the critical historical studies of the nineteenth century seem to shed light on how an emergent psychological theory of memory might find a suitable model for its most difficult period—the period closest to ontogenetic origins. In the Moses analogy, however, the historian's very turn to the past is *causally* linked, at least by tentative suggestion, to the "spell" of childhood, seen through the propaganda of individual memory as a time of bliss. Which is to say, the psychologist now explains why people become historians. So in a sense Freud comes full circle in his deployment of the analogy: the Livian paradigm explains the dynamics of childhood memory (*Leonardo*), and childhood memory in turn explains the motivation of a Livy (*Moses*). The recourse to history is thus to be understood recursively. Psychoanalysis needs historical methods to illuminate and clarify the analytic task, but history is itself a psychological need that psychoanalysis can best explain. If psychoanalysis can thus explain the writing of history, does it not become itself a method of historiographical analysis?

In fact, Freud merely returned in *Moses* to a point he had made over three decades before in his earliest flirtation with this analogy, in the *Psychopathology of Everyday Life* (1901, but in parts added only in 1907). "Closer investigation would perhaps reveal *a complete analogy* [*eine vollständige Analogie*] between the ways in which the traditions of a people and the childhood memories of the individual come to be formed" (SE 6:148; my emphasis).[19] In many ways, *Moses* is an attempt to make just such a "complete analogy" from the opposite direction by turning ontogenetic development into a master pattern for cultural history. "The only satisfying analogy to the remarkable course of events that we have found in the history of the Jewish religion lies in an apparently remote field; *but it is very complete, and approaches identity [aber sie ist vollständig, sie kommt der Identität nahe]*" (SE 23:72). It is resting on this "near identical" designation that Freud will elaborate a theory of cultural trauma that ties the compulsions of Judaism to the historical murder of the Egyptian Moses, yielding a view of cultural repression that is psychologically more dynamic and complex than anything heretofore theorized in critical historiography.

The explanatory yield of such an approach is striking, if we step back for a moment from its substantive claims. If we compare Freud's *Moses and Monotheism* with the work of a contemporary scholar who inspired him, we can see how much farther Freud's historical reconstruction reaches than the previous critical approach. Robert Eisler's reconstruction of the life of Jesus (1929–1930) provides a ready comparison with Freud's *Moses*, not just because both were works of contemporary Viennese Jews who ended their lives in exile in England.[20] Just as Freud sought the *man* Moses—the historical individual behind the legendary figure—Eisler (1882–1949) had made a vast investigation into the man Jesus, working from the hypothesis that a massive cultural repression of the contemporary pagan and Jewish evidence was undertaken by later Christendom. Eisler's own historical effort was "nothing less than an attempt to recall into consciousness [*wieder ins Bewußtsein zu rufen*] for the historical memory of humanity all that which a wide-ranging and effective censorship since the time of Constantine the Great has attempted systematically to blot out from the tradition and has in fact nearly erased" (Eisler 1929, v). Eisler's evidentiary field was especially enriched by the text of Josephus' *Jewish Antiquities*, which he alleged had been thoroughly revised at a crucial point in the account of Jesus' life (18.63–64, the so called *Testimonium Flavianum*); and with an ingenuity Freud could not help but admire, Eisler provided a *textus restitutus* that better reflects what one imagines a Pharisee's opinion of Jesus would have been.[21] Freud so liked Eisler's conspiracy theory, in reference to the textual tradition of Josephus, that he later used it as an analogy for psychological repression ("Analysis Terminable and Interminable," SE 23: 236).

But Eisler, like Niebuhr, was working with a purely *documentary* hypothesis. To claim that the record of the past is falsified is easy enough, and to suggest an alternative history is, as we shall see, a natural enough obligation to thrust upon anyone who would undo the conventional narratives. But this entails mostly just some reshuffling in the ancient archive; the claims for contemporary impact are slight, and are mostly implicit in reworking the traditional bases of textual authority. In contrast, Freud's theory of *psychological* repression differed significantly with the past as construed by Niebuhr and Eisler, precisely in that the past is not over for Freud. Had Freud's hypothesis in *Moses* really been just the exposure of Judaism as the outgrowth of an Egyptian cult, he would have rested safely within the nineteenth-century paradigm of critical historiography—though "safe" in no other sense, for it is a daring and even offensive hypothesis, given the times. But at heart, Freud's investigation was rather aimed at a social-psychological *pathology*, namely German anti-Semitism, a historical precipitate of the age-old events he reconstructs through his own critical reading of scripture and history.[22]

So in this, his greatest deployment of a recursive analogy, Freud comes full circle in linking individual psychology with cultural history. Having begun his use of critical historiography to explain the dynamics of living memory among his patients, he reversed the analogy to use the theory of individual trauma to explain the dynamics of living historical memory among whole nations. The main difference between individual and social psychology in this light seems to be that for the latter *there is no hope of a cure*.

From Critique to Divination

There is a further aspect to these discursive relations that merits our attention: the way in which nineteenth-century historiography made *reconstruction* and not just critique part of a "scientific" or *wissenschaftlich* approach to the past. Mere critique by itself would of course lead us to dismiss the archive and to say with Henry Ford that "history is bunk." Any counter-narrative put in the place of traditional accounts would obviously succumb to the same scrutiny unless it is couched in different terms. Thus Niebuhr himself called for the counter-narrative to carry with it an evidentiary armature. Only such a *positive* work could make someone a true historian and not just a critic of sources.

> The historian [...] requires something positive [*bedarf Positives*]: he must at least disclose with verisimilitude a certain coherence [*Zusammenhang*] and a more believable story [*Erzählung*] in the place of the one he has sacrificed to his [critical] conviction. If he separates from his work the researches through which he believes to have summoned up the shadows of bygone times, he must then either renounce the use of their results or he runs the risk of seeming to put forth confidently and boldly as historical truth what is only hypothesis or vague possibility—a high price to pay for greater concinnity in the overall composition. (Niebuhr 1853, x)

The call is thus for a historical narrative that moves by argument and evidence, not the naked narration of events. This draws history into the rhetoric of empirical demonstration, as a disclosure of "researches," a move that, as we shall see, is not without its problems.

Niebuhr's critical approach gave further impetus for the nineteenth century's interest in expanding the evidentiary domain of antiquity. For Roman history in particular (a bellwether for the development of historical method at the time), this led to a focus on Roman law, institutional history, archaeology, and inscriptional evidence in place of the previous "literary" historiography based on ancient authors. In a way, then, the whole archaeological model might be said to rest upon the paradigm shift begun in Niebuhr's day, whose hermeneutics of suspicion increased the value of even ordinary material evidence. Whereas the previous antiquarian archaeology looked mostly for "treasure" and works of immortal art, the archaeology of the late nineteenth century took a broader view of material culture, particularly in the wake of the Darwinian revolution, which established the value of original and transitional forms and not just the finished products of cultural evolution. The growing institutions of the national university and the museum supported the accumulation and study of a larger amount of historical archives and material artifacts, and the rising industrial might of Western Europe and America helped to finance these endeavors.[23] So significant shifts in the organization of society favored the development of history as a *Wissenschaft* formally organized around an ever-expanding archive and following a model of professional, ever-progressing research.

It is also important to note that excavation had already been metaphorized in historical studies long before Freud's psychoanalysis, and that it was held to be the pattern of modern historical research. The telling difference in the analogy, however, is that before the advent of systematic archaeological digs, the metaphor was based on the activity most familiar to Europe in its earlier phase of industrialization: mining. In the *Outline of the Principles of History* by Johann Gustav Droysen (1808–1884)—one of the greatest historians of nineteenth-century Germany—the science of historical research is called heuristics. "Heuristics puts us in possession of the materials for historical work. It is the *miner's art*, that of finding and bringing to the light, 'the underground work' (Niebuhr)" ([1881] 1967, 18; my emphasis). It is also important to note that the systematic mining of philological sources preceded the wholesale incorporation of material evidence, which was more difficult to achieve in a systematic way. However, during Freud's student years at the University of Vienna (1873–1881) a fuller integration of the sciences of the archive was finally being achieved there. Alexander Conze (1831–1914) had just come to the first chair in archaeology at the University of Vienna in 1869, and together with Otto Hirschfeld (1843–1922), Conze founded the Archaeological and Epigraphical Seminar in 1876, which became a powerhouse of interdisciplinary training and research, integrating philological approaches with archaeological and epigraphical study. Freud's lifelong friend Emanuel Löwy was in fact among the first graduates of the Seminar, and Löwy's later career was itself proof of the outstanding preparation the Seminar gave its students.

In spite of all the rhetoric of *Wissenschaft*, however, throughout the nineteenth century the profession of history had to struggle with the inherently subjective nature of its craft. In fact, long before psychoanalysis, sociology, and anthropology, German historicism wrestled with the concept of a "science" that worked through the psychological faculty of subjective understanding (*Verstehen*) and intuition, yet which simultaneously laid claim to the domain of objective *Wissenschaft*. As John Hind has written, "the distinguishing feature of nineteenth-century historiography was not that historicists had discovered a 'science' of history; rather it was the general emergence, not just in Germany but throughout Europe, of a new language of historical representation based upon the privileging and legitimizing rhetoric of science. Historians could now proclaim that it was possible to arrive at absolute Truth and certainty through historical knowledge" (2000, 146). And what is most telling in moments of history's self-assertion is the recourse to the very empirical romance we have already seen at work in Freud's presentation of psychoanalysis.

We can see this empirical romance clearly etched in the work of Niebuhr. In one of his central methodological analogies, he tries to explain how the professional historian's version of history emerges from a more powerful gaze than that given most non-historians. The researcher who has spent many years studying the past with a "constantly renewed, objective gaze [*Beschauung*]" causes "the history of unknown, hidden, vanished events" to win "existence and form [*Bildung*] out of the fog and night" ([1811–1831] 1853, 360). He likens this to the process by which "the barely visible, airy form of the nymph in Slavic folktale becomes embodied in the form of an earthly maiden through the desirous gaze [*Hinschauen*] of love" ([1811–1831] 1853, 360). The researcher's tireless gaze and constant testing bring it about that this new history obtains "a more complete coherence and that immediate revelation of reality that stems from genuine existence," but this new reality is not openly available. "Such a researcher may assume that another person, who merely chances by and throws his glance where he lives and dwells, will not agree to the correctness of his observations, because he does not see them" ([1811–1831] 1853, 360). This gnostic characterization of his method shows that the realm of the evidentiary is not just an array of "things," but a whole new way of "seeing things." Niebuhr's invocation of erotic ogling seems to betray the element of subjective desire inherent in such "objective gazing," and lends further justification for my use of the term empirical *romance* to describe such accounts of methodology. The empirical romance comprises not simply a series of serendipitous discoveries, but an *askesis* of technique, the development of a gaze that transforms through its *desire* to see things. In this sense, Niebuhr's method shares psychoanalysis's curious coupling of gnosis and empirical rhetoric, asserting simultaneously the commonality of the evidence and the rarity of the capacity to really see it. This presupposes an epistemology of what Ernest Gellner calls "conditional realism," which is the assumption that the mind can know reality *provided* that it removes the inner veils that prevent us all from seeing what is simply there ([1985] 1993, 82–85).

Even under the pressure of professional criticism, Niebuhr continued to stress that his approach entailed a whole gnostic quality of mind that was far from common.

> I am as certain of the correctness of my views as I am of my own existence, and that I have discovered the solution of the enigma. It is not the love of conjecture that has impelled me, but the necessity of understanding, *and the faculty of guessing and divining.* For many points, still more numerous and express proofs might be produced than those I have brought forward. He who presumes to pronounce a judgment on this subject without knowing more than the current opinions on it has really no voice at all in the matter. Further, it is not to be expected that everyone, or even that many, should have *that faculty of immediate intuition* which would enable them to partake in my immovable conviction, for which I should be ready to die. [. . .] This I may say without arrogance, that he who refuses respect to my *History* deserves none himself. (Bunsen et al. 1852, 330; my emphasis)

The fuller characterization of this method is in fact not historical critique, but rather *critique and divination*, a designation that at the time was worn like a badge of honor.[24] Just how this hermeneutics of guesswork laid claim to being a genuine historical consciousness is a matter we shall revisit below in chapter 10.

From Freud's perspective on ancient history, the *positive* outcomes of the critical method guarantee and underwrite his own branch of *Wissenschaft*. He tells us in the Leonardo study that it would be an injustice to reject the body of legends, traditions, and interpretations from a nation's early history, since:

> In spite of all the distortions and misunderstandings, *they still represent the reality of the past:* they are what a people forms out of the experience of its early days [*Urzeit*] and under the dominance of motives that were once powerful *and still operate today;* and if it were only possible, by a knowledge of all the forces at work, *to undo these distortions,* there would be *no difficulty in disclosing the historical truth* lying behind the legendary material. The same holds good for childhood memories or fantasies of an individual. What someone thinks he remembers from his childhood is not a matter of indifference; as a rule the residual memories—which he himself does not under-

stand—cloak priceless pieces of evidence about the most important features in his mental development. (SE 11:84; my emphasis)

Already implicit in Freud's use of this analogy is a different view of the historical distortions of culture, which he clearly sees as ongoing repressions begun long ago and still remaining in force. One can see, in other words, that this analogy is recursive from the start, transforming both terms in the process of comparison. But it still works at this point from the cultural toward the individual: *if* one can apply a critical understanding to legendary history, *then* one should be able to do the same for individual memories. The memory work of "undoing distortions" will yield historical truth in both cases, giving us "priceless pieces of evidence," as in the way that Leonardo's bird fantasy, once decoded, reveals the "facts" of his early life with Caterina.

The very fact that the ancient archive provided transactional analogies and methodological cues for Freud gives the lie to his own version of the empirical romance, as when he claimed in the wake of the early secessions that he had in fact been influenced by no one in his great days of "splendid isolation," when he was like Robinson Crusoe alone on his island.

I did not have to read any publications, nor listen to any ill-informed opponents; I was not subject to influence from any quarter; there was nothing to hustle me. I learnt to restrain speculative tendencies and to follow the unforgotten advice of my master, Charcot: *to look at the same things again and again until they themselves begin to speak.* ("On the History of the Psycho-Analytic Movement," SE 14:22)

As we saw in his lecture of 1896, "Aetiology of Hysteria," the paradigm of things "speaking for themselves" comes from the *saxa loquuntur* of archaeology, which is precisely the quarter from which key influence came in his days of isolation. We shall revisit that scenario in the next chapter, but we must first finish the discussion of historiography, since archaeology was not alone in suggesting parallels to psychoanalytic work during its crucial formative period of the 1890s.

From *Quellenforschung* to *Kulturgeschichte*

By 1872, when Jacob Burckhardt delivered his first lectures on Greek culture to a general audience in Basel, the noise of historicism's expanding archive had drowned out the message of history. The cult of factuality had so complicated the approaches to the ancient archive that Burckhardt could proclaim a state of crisis in historical study which paradoxically conferred great freedom, since it allowed one to find one's own way ([1898–1902] 1998, 5). His own way was "cultural history" (*Kultur-geschichte*), which he thought to be on a firmer footing than the standard narrative history that Niebuhr had thrown into confusion through his critical evaluation of the sources.

> One great advantage of studying cultural history is the *certainty* of its more important facts, compared with those of history in the ordinary sense of narrated events: these are frequently uncertain, controversial, colored, or, given the Greek talent for lying, entirely the invention of imagination or self-interest. Cultural history by contrast possesses a primary degree of certainty, as it consists for the most part of material conveyed in an unintentional, disinterested, or even involuntary way by sources and monuments; they betray their secrets unconsciously and even, paradoxically, through ficti-tious elaborations, quite apart from the material details they may set out to record and glorify, and are thus doubly instructive for the cul-tural historian. ([1898–1902] 1998, 5)

The distinction Burckhardt makes here is precisely the one Freud main-tained to the end of his life between "material truth" or the brute factu-ality of events and a "psychic truth" which is itself historical. The historical value of fiction and fantasy was what emerged from the great crisis in his research on neurosis in 1897, when he came to doubt the sim-plistic premise that sexual molestation was the invariable cause of hyste-ria (the *caput Nili* of neuropathology, as he had put it so proudly in his 1896 lecture).

Just as Niebuhr's critical approach to legendary history suggested par-allels with individual memory, Burckhardt's *Kulturgeschichte* showed the clear outline of a historical method whereby fantasy plays as much a role as do actual deeds in revealing the "essence" of a whole culture or the per-sonality of an individual. Thus we must read carefully Freud's remark to Fliess in early 1899. "For relaxation I am reading Burckhardt's *History of Greek Civilization*, which is providing me with unexpected parallels. My predilection for the prehistoric in all its human forms has remained the same" (Masson 1985, 342). In this same letter, he is happy to report that "bits of insight are dawning now here, now there—a genuine reinvigoration by comparison with the desolation of last year. What is rising out of the chaos this time is the connection to the psychology contained in the *Studies on Hysteria* — the relation to conflict, to life [. . .]. Puberty is becoming ever more central; *fantasy as the key holds fast*" (Masson 1985, 342; my emphasis). A week later Freud reports, "I am deep in Burckhardt's *History of Greek Civilization*"; this is borne out by the evidence of his underlining throughout his copy (Masson 1985, 344). A week later still, he remarks at length about the direction of his new approach to mental phenomena.

> My last generalization has held good and seems inclined to grow to an unpredictable extent. Not only dreams are wish fulfillments, so are hysterical attacks. This is true of hysterical symptoms, but probably applies to every product of neurosis, for I recognized it long ago in acute delusional insanity. Reality—wish fulfillment— it is from these opposites that our mental life springs. (Masson 1985, 345)

It cannot be mere coincidence that the two aspects of Greek civilization Burckhardt elicits for constant analysis are its *agonal* or conflictual nature and its susceptibility to fantasy, particularly through myth.

Mythology was in fact one of the first topics in the lectures that were later published after Burckhardt's death as the *Griechische Kulturgeschichte*. Since all accounts of origin are linked to myth in the Hellenic world, it is inevitably where one must begin to assess the Greek sense of self. Commenting on how much historical information is confused in the mythic accounts of migrations and genealogies, Burckhardt comments (and Freud underlines his words here):

> For myth has swathed all this in its fine shimmering veil, embracing the terrestrial and the cosmic, religion and poetry, unconscious observation of the world, and experience distilled. The images that arose from it all were accepted as having a bearing upon the remotest times, but in a very free and flexible way. The wildest variations and contradictions, inevitable when the origins of the things recounted were so different, were not found at all disturbing. In addition, free invention was used to help out, particularly in genealogical matters. Authors of every period, even when they appear to lay claim to exactitude, always served an apprenticeship to myth, and saw everything in a mythical way; but apart from this they in-

vented and elaborated in a manner completely alien to the modern world. ([1898–1902] 1998, 15)

Burckhardt's words remind us how a long tradition before Freud had read myth in terms of "unconscious observation of the world" (*unbewußte Weltbetrachtung*), and in a sense his recourse to myth as the dream-language of humanity was a mere shift in the definition of "unconscious": from simply "pre-rational, naïve, unreflective" to "repressed, not-consciously thinkable."

Burckhardt's approach to cultural history was furthermore psychological in the sense that he was not concerned with establishing a record of facts so much as an account of "Greek habits of thought and mental attitudes." His desire was "to establish the vital *forces*, both constructive and destructive, that were active in Greek life" ([1898–1902] 1998, 4). As such, it was as much a history of desire as of achievement, as interested in tragic failures as in great deeds and noble accomplishments.

> This kind of history aims at the inner core of bygone humanity, and at describing what manner of people these were, what they wished for, thought, perceived and were capable of. In the process it arrives at what is constant, and finally this constant comes to seem greater and more important than the ephemeral, and qualities greater and more instructive than actions; for actions are only particular expressions of the relevant inner capacity, which can always reproduce such acts. Desires and assumptions are, then, as important as events, the attitude as important as anything done; for at a given moment this attitude will be expressed in action:

> > The man whose inmost heart I have once probed,
> > Is known to me in all his will and deeds.
> > [Schiller, *Wallensteins Tod* 2.3]
> > ([1898–1902] 1998, 5)

This "inner core of bygone humanity" as Burckhardt envisages it creates the opening to what Foucault termed "total history": "Perhaps indeed the constant that emerges from these typical statements is the truest 'real content' of antiquity, even more than the antiquities themselves. Through it we learn to know the *eternal* Greek, the whole structure instead of an individual factor" ([1898–1902] 1998, 5–6). The desire, in other words, is to effect a "total description" of the Greeks, one that "draws all phenomena around a single center" (Foucault [1969] 1972, 10).

There are further peculiarities in Burckhardt's methodology we should take note of. He deliberately ignored the professional apparatus of scholarship in favor of a personalized contact with the primary sources, and this was justifiable in part because of the special nature of cultural history, and in part because this responded to his ideal of *Bildung*.[25] Unlike the antiquarian and critical histories he rejects, Burckhardt felt the value of cultural history was its ability to place stress on the "*proportional* importance of facts" instead of cultivating facts for their own sake. To create the necessary *Gestalt*, however, implies an intersubjective link that is the key to understanding. "This kind of history draws attention to those facts that can form a link with our own way of thinking, and awaken a genuine response, either by their affinity with us or by the contrast of their remoteness. The rubble of history is left on one side" ([1898–1902] 1998, 6). But the subtle methodology this requires is not to be underestimated as to its difficulty. It is here that Burckhardt advocates a way of working that struck a chord with Freud from the perspective of his clinical work, for which he later formulated the principle of "evenly suspended attention" and careful listening ("Recommendations to Physicians Practicing Psycho-Analysis," SE 12:111–112). Here again it is revealing to see in this passage just what Freud underlined.

Only long and varied reading can give assurance; in the meantime much will be overlooked that was of profound significance, and importance attributed to what was merely fortuitous. In the course of reading every word the researcher happens upon may seem either insignificant or vitally interesting, and this will depend on current mood and state of alertness or fatigue, and especially on the degree of maturity that the research has arrived at. All this will adjust itself only after long reading of the various genres and types of Greek literature. Strenuous effort at this stage <u>is precisely the wrong way to achieve the desired result; an attentive ear and a steady pace of work</u> will succeed better. ([1898–1902] 1998, 6; underlining reflects Freud's own)

We have more than Freud's underlining to go on in this case, since an undated note in the Freud Archives labeled "Quotations and Analogies" makes his understanding of this passage quite explicit: "For the proper

attitude to the work of interpretation: <u>Burckhardt</u>. Hist. Greek Civilization p 5, intense effort is actually least likely to secure the desired result
here; quietly attentive listening with steady diligence takes one further"
(cited in Grubrich-Simitis [1993] 1996, 100; see also 266).

In another passage stressing the commitment to primary sources, we see
Freud again taking note of the importance of individual understanding.

> <u>What should impel us to read the **whole** of an author's work is the</u>
> <u>perception</u> that only *we* can find what is of importance to *us*. No
> work of reference can possibly produce by means of excerpts that
> chemical reaction <u>between a piece of information we have discov-</u>
> <u>ered for ourselves, and our own dim foreknowledge of it, that makes</u>
> <u>it our intellectual property</u> [*so daß sich ein wirklich geistiges Eigentum*
> *bildet*]. ([1898–1902] 1998, 10; underlining reflects Freud's own)

This last reference to the formation of real intellectual property reveals
how Burckhardt's *Griechische Kulturgeschichte* is a great expression of the
cultural ideals of the *Bildungsbürgertum*, the educated middle class. By deliberately refusing to deliver his lectures to a coterie of professional ap-
prentices, Burckhardt returned to the humanistic principles of classical
education, which he felt were lost in the excessive professionalization of
history, particularly as it was being played out in Germany.[26] (A consequence of this was that when his *Griechische Kulturgeschichte* was posthu-
mously published, it was universally panned by professors in Germany,
though widely read by the middle class.) Contrary to academic professionalism in his field, he proposed a kind of militant dilettantism that
served not the profession of history but the ideal of self-cultivation, of
Bildung, upon which the *Gymnasium's* system of education had originally
been founded.

> This course offers a particular academic prospect for non-classi-
> cists; since the mere wholesale communication of antiquities is to
> be avoided, it makes classical studies immediately accessible. Any
> interested person can become a fellow researcher by reading the
> sources, which in this case are unusually open to the non-specialist.
> [...] [T]he discipline of cultural history as here understood can
> bring direct enrichment to any humanist; and if only for this reason
> it seems proper to pay respect to a shared humanistic education.
> ([1898–1902] 1998, 8)

The openness described here, of course, is really much less than Burckhardt lets on, for he is talking about the relatively elite group of bourgeois professionals who have had a proper *Gymnasium* education. But the fact that Freud was reading this course of lectures for "relaxation" (*Erholung*) is an indication of the *habitus* instilled in the mandarin culture of the *Gymnasium's* graduates. Moreover, the clear license given to non-specialists to become fellow researchers by this method would be of great encouragement to the many doctors and alienists in the psychoanalytic movement who would feel that history is too important to be left to the historians, especially now that a potent new form of cultural "listening" had arisen. They could follow with conviction Burckhardt's historical imperative that Freud had literally underscored: "It is self-evidently the special duty of the educated to perfect and complete, as well as they can, the picture of the continuity of the world's development" ([1898–1902] 1998, 12).

Lastly, it must be noted again that Freud came upon Burckhardt's work on Greek culture less than two years after his initial intimation of oedipal conflict, which led him from despairing of his etiology of the neuroses to a whole new line of thought about the universal place of fantasy in individual psychic history. Burckhardt's passion for antiquity was predicated on the assumption that the Greeks have an *exceptional* relationship to modernity. The very crisis of modernity, in his view, can only be addressed by realizing a relationship with antiquity, a relationship that already exists, though it may remain unconscious. "All human knowledge is accompanied by the history of the ancient world as music is by a basechord heard again and again; the history, that is, of all those peoples whose life has flowed together into our own" ([1898–1902] 1998, 364). It is a mistake to assume that the modern mastery of nature through the sciences will give us the knowledge we need as human beings. "The contemplation of nature does not suffice, nor console, nor teach us enough" ([1898–1902] 1998, 364). To ignore the task of historical understanding is to fall into utter barbarism. But the exceptional place antiquity holds for Burckhardt is again the place of a chosen childhood, a family romance that gives a tragic grandeur to the early days of European civilization, even for those peoples whose "childhood" was rather steeped in the anonymous squalor of the Germanic forests and marshlands.

It is perhaps enough to say that, for us, antiquity is only the first act of the human drama, and indeed, in our eyes, a tragedy complete in itself, one of incalculable efforts, transgressions and suffering.

Though we are also the offspring of peoples who were still wrapped in the sleep of childhood at the time of the great civilizations of antiquity, it is from these that we feel we are truly descended, because they transmitted their soul to us, and their work, their path, and their destiny live on in us. ([1898–1902] 1998, 365)

We shall return by way of conclusion to the implications inherent in Freud's adoption of this family romance, and what it meant for a Jew to assert from his own corner of the world that the tragic grandeur of ancient culture lives on in the oedipal destiny of modernity's scattered millions.

CHAPTER 9

■

The Archaeology of Freedom

> We are all buried alive.
> —H.D., *Tribute to Freud*

Niebuhr and the critical historians understood distortion and repression as products of a long cultural and political tradition, but never dealt with actual ancient Romans (though Niebuhr lived in Rome among their descendants). Their approach was entirely textual, epigraphic, and archaeological. In contrast, Freud had to contend with actual human beings, which entails the complicating fact that most people consider themselves authorities on their own experience, eyewitnesses (and I-witnesses) who are in possession of an accurate "tradition" of memory and self-narrative. Given his belief in repressed memory, however, Freud had to work out *together* with the analysand nothing short of an alternative history of the self, one in which mere conjecture rarely achieved anything of value. Although we looked in chapter 6 at the broader implications of the archaeological analogy in terms of its links to imperialism and Freud's own ambition toward the past, I now wish to focus on archaeology as the transactional analogy that *enabled* him to work directly with the analysand.[1] We must ask ourselves in all seriousness just how it was possible for a relationship to function wherein the analyst works *with* the patient to create a whole new view of the past, despite the fact that the analyst may assume the attitude, as Freud rightly put it, of "Heads I win, tails you lose." In other words, "if the patient agrees with us, then the interpretation is right; but if he contradicts us, that is only a sign of his resistance, which again shows that we are right" ("Constructions in Analysis," SE 23:257). Clearly the peculiar quality of this relationship is too jarring to dismiss as a mere detail.

The point once more is to stress that Freud did not invoke the paradigm of the confessional with his patients, in part because the nature of the material was not something one *can* confess, and, in part, because Freud's desire to create a value-free climate of mere *study* of the past required a radically different "technology of the self" (see Freud's explicit directive in *An Outline of Psycho-Analysis*, SE 23:174). In fact, we might say psychoanalysis only begins by *deconstructing* the confessional, by refusing to believe that a complete confession is really even possible. Moreover, the physical digging of excavation was a far more adequate metaphor to describe Freud's dynamic of memory, whereby repression and resistance are the vital forces that the analyst must learn to overcome. I have come to the conclusion, however, that while his new transactional analogy served his needs very well, it ultimately laid him open to the gravest accusation of all, the one that haunted him from beginning to end in his psychoanalytic career, namely, that psychoanalytic memory work is really just an elaborate form of suggestion.

The Archaeology of Freud's Archaeology

Though the archaeological analogy is often linked to Freud's personal hobby of collecting antiquities, it is very important to note that its transactional status significantly precedes his collecting activities by several years. It is generally agreed that Freud's collection was begun only after his father's death in 1896, but already in *Studies on Hysteria* (1893–1895), we find the archaeological analogy in place (Gamwell 1989). Therefore, I shall begin with a look at these key early deployments, which reinforce the notion that the ancient archive was already implicated in the enterprise well before the publication of Freud's seminal *Interpretation of Dreams*. As Breuer and Freud improvised their way into a new "talking cure" for the neuroses, the need for a definable methodology was clear, and not just for their colleagues, to whom they would report their findings and successes, but for the patients themselves, who could only be served by them to the extent that they cooperated. Psychoanalysis, as Stanley Fish has suggested following in the steps of Wittgenstein, is a scene of persuasion ([1986] 1998). For this reason, then, the use of analogies *in analysis* requires attention, for their deployment in the course of treatment moves them from description to, as I have said, a transactional status, one defining the game and the roles to be played in it by both patient and analyst.

A good definition of the roles is quite crucial considering that repression, which is the first basic premise of Freudian memory work, requires that the analyst subvert the patient's authority over the view of events in her past. Initially the analyst is up against a wall since the patient most often presents a perfectly reasonable account.

> We cannot expect that the free communications made by the patient, the material from the most superficial strata, will make it easy for the analyst to recognize at what points the path leads into the depths or where he is to find the starting-points of the connections of thought of which he is in search. On the contrary. This is precisely what is carefully concealed; the account given by the patient sounds as if it were complete and self-contained. It is at first as though we were standing before a wall which shuts out every prospect and prevents us from having any idea whether there is anything behind it, and if so, what. (*Studies in Hysteria*, SE 2: 293)

But the trained analyst learns to examine the account "with a critical eye" (note again the *visual* metaphor inherent in the empirical romance, as in the case of Niebuhr) and will infallibly find gaps and imperfections. Rather than simply treating the patient's account as a lie, the metaphor of stratigraphy instead allows for a more neutral characterization of surface over depth, freeing the patient from the apprehension of coming into conflict with a moral or juridical authority. In the curious transformation of a Christian practice, Freud resorted in an earlier phase of his therapy literally to the laying on of hands in order to *empower* the patient to work against the grain of her own memory. The following remark describes this "pressure technique," which makes use of manual pressure on the forehead. "We say to the patient: 'You are mistaken; what you are putting forward can have nothing to do with the present subject. We must expect to come upon something else here, and this will occur to you under the pressure of my hand'" (SE 2:293).

The transactional value of the analogy emerged in particular once Freud realized the limitations of hypnosis, which he would eventually abandon entirely. His first full analysis of an hysteric, "Fräulein Elisabeth von R," shows in fact just this emergence of the analogy vis-à-vis the technique of therapy:

> Thus it came about that in this, the first full-length analysis of a hysteria undertaken by me, I arrived at a procedure which I later developed into a regular method and employed deliberately. This procedure was one of clearing away the pathogenic psychical material layer by layer, and we liked to compare it with the technique of excavating a buried city. (SE 2:139)

In this excavating analogy, it is clear that the image of stratigraphy helps bring a real sense of order to the strange procedure, since the hypothesis of "buried strata" behind the narrative of the patient gave shape to what could otherwise seem like the tendentious challenging—or even badgering—of the informant.

> I would begin by getting the patient to tell me what was known to her and I would carefully note the points at which some train of thought remained obscure or some link in the causal chain seemed to be missing. And afterwards I would penetrate into deeper layers of her memories at these points by carrying out an investigation under hypnosis or by the use of some similar technique. (SE 2:139)

The necessity for seeing temporal depth in the model was tied to Freud's deterministic assumptions of mental causation, about which he was quite open from the outset. "The whole work was, of course, based on the expectation that it would be possible to establish a *completely adequate set of determinants for the events concerned*" (SE 2:139; my emphasis).

As I mentioned before in chapter 6, the key features of the archaeological analogy that Freud deploys are excavation, reconstruction, and decipherment, and we shall consider reconstruction separately toward the end of this chapter, since it is most closely tied to the problem of suggestion. But we can see already how much the excavating analogy gave shape to his early therapeutic improvisation by suggesting the comfortingly neutral model of stratigraphic technique. This technique is collaborative, which implies that it is as much a matter of timely forbearance as intervention in the memory work of the patient. Thus the collaborative worksite as Freud would like us to envision it requires a concerted coordination of effort.

> If we interfere with the patient in his reproduction of the ideas that pour in on him, we may "bury" things that have to be freed later with a great deal of trouble. On the other hand we must not over-

estimate the patient's unconscious "intelligence" and leave the direction of the whole work to it. If I wanted to give a diagrammatic
picture of our mode of operation, I might perhaps say that we ourselves undertake the opening up of inner strata, advancing *radially*,
whereas the patient looks after the *peripheral* extension of the work.
(SE 2:292; original emphasis)

By forcing the analysand to confront the walls of resistance, the analyst
effectively says "dig here" to his coworker and sits back to watch (or
rather, hear) what comes out of it. This procedure in fact replicates the
power relations of the archaeologist directing his plucky native assistant.

But besides the work of excavation, there is already in place in the *Studies* the equally vital metaphor of decipherment, which would leap to the
fore as Freud put dream analysis to the center of the analytic endeavor.
Using the Rosetta-stone paradigm, Freud co-implicates the semiotic
properties of symptoms into the stratigraphic layout of the past, assuming again that distortions of memory bear some relation to the enigmatic
utterances of the body. In the following passage, the editors of the Standard Edition assume that the "we" of this scene of interpretation means
Breuer and Freud, and this is not impossible; but what I would prefer to
stress here is how the "we" of the analysis could imply the patients as well.
In this regard, the analogy of decipherment is clearly a valuable persuasive tool in working toward the discovery of meaning in physical symptoms, a meaning that is supposedly *confirmed* by the sudden recollection
of new material for excavation.

> We [Breuer and I] had often compared the symptomatology of hys-
> teria with a pictographic script which has become intelligible after
> the discovery of a few bilingual inscriptions. In that alphabet being
> sick means disgust. So I said: "If you were sick three days later, I be-
> lieve that means that when you looked into the room you felt dis-
> gusted."
>
> "Yes, I'm sure I felt disgusted," she said reflectively, "but dis-
> gusted at what?"
>
> "Perhaps you saw something naked?" (SE 2:129)

The suggestion Freud makes here to the young Katharina is obviously a
blatant and leading one, though it initially leads to a blind alley. All the
same, Freud's account of decipherment is very telling in part because of
his highly positivistic assumption that all the pieces were there and only

needed to be uncovered, reconfigured, and/or translated. "But I told her to go on and tell me whatever occurred to her, in the confident expectation that she would think of precisely what I needed to explain the case" (SE 2:129). In this regard, the transactional nature of their interchange is clear in his final "decipherment" of her disgust, which he links to her previous experiences of being accosted by her uncle late at night. Specifically, her disgust is tied to the feeling she had when she woke up and felt her uncle's naked body.

> "It may well be," she replied, "that that was what I was disgusted at and that that was what I thought."
> "Tell me just one thing more. You're a grown-up girl now and know all sorts of things . . ."
> "Yes, now I am."
> "Tell me just one thing. What part of his body was it that you felt that night?"
> But she gave me no more definite answer. She smiled in an embarrassed way, as though she had been found out, like someone who is obliged to admit that a fundamental position [*auf den Grund der Dinge*] has been reached where there is not much more to be said. I could imagine what the tactile sensation was which she had later learnt to interpret. Her facial expression seemed to me to be saying that she supposed that I was right in my conjecture. But I could not penetrate further [*ich kann nicht weiter in sie dringen*], and in any case I owed her a debt of gratitude for having made it so much easier for me to talk to her than to the prudish ladies of my city practice, who regard whatever is natural as shameful. (SE 2:131–132)

What is curious here is that Freud seems almost to replicate the advances of her uncle in his drive to get to the phallic artifact of memory, to "penetrate" the strata of her memory in order to find the meaning of her disgust. He presses on beyond the mere sexual situation that lay confused in her memory in order to get at the physical intrusion of the penis itself, which assumes the status of a "fundamental position," *der Grund der Dinge*. But the final moment of truth is a moment without speaking, in which we have his *interpretation* of her expression and nothing more. The triumph of his decipherment is itself a decipherment. In a footnote added in 1924 [SE 2:134, note 2], Freud admits that the sexual assault was not attempted by her uncle, but rather by her *father*, a fact he had himself concealed for reasons of discretion. So we might even say the decipherment is not even complete for the reader until the 1924 edition—assuming that the reader sees the footnote!

On the surface, this scene of interpretation might seem to be just that confessional paradigm Foucault suggests behind the operations of psychoanalysis, but that would be to ignore the clear transactional nature of the dialogue *from Freud's* point of view. He is "grateful" for the girl's openness, for the ease with which he can penetrate her memory, since it serves his scientific interest and confirms his current theories of the sexual etiology of neurosis. She successfully served up just those elements of memory he needed to make a nice case for the deferred action of traumatic memories; her narrative serves *his* narrative well. This particular tale is in fact not even the tale of a cure—the *cura animarum* was not the objective of the Dr. Freud who was at the time of his "analysis" of Katharina on vacation in Hohe Tauern. This casual contact was simply a good occasion to do some recreational psycho-archaeology. "I hope this girl, whose sexual sensibility had been injured at such an early age, derived some benefit from our conversation. I have not seen her since" (SE 2:133).

Freud's final generalizations on the procedure of psychotherapy in the *Studies* stress first and foremost the importance of the analysand's intellectual co-optation in working on the site of memory. "By explaining things to him, by giving him information about the marvelous world of psychical processes into which we ourselves only gained insight by such analyses, we make him himself into a collaborator, induce him to regard himself with the objective interest of an investigator, and thus push back his resistance, resting as it does on an affective basis" (SE 2:282). Only when the motives for resistance have been discovered can the emotional drama of transference, as it would later be known, be played out in the improvisation of multiple roles on the part of the analyst.

> This no doubt is where it ceases to be possible to state psychotherapeutic activity in formulas. One works to the best of one's power, as an elucidator [*Aufklärer*] (where ignorance has given rise to fear), as a teacher, as the representative of a freer or superior view of the world, as a father confessor [*Beichthörer*] who gives absolution, as it were, by a continuance of his sympathy and respect after the confession has been made. (SE 2:282)

Here it is true that confession is an option in the analytical game, but only one of various possibilities in a shifting series of roles the analyst might have to play (confession would no doubt resonate with a Christian, but not with a Jew).[2] Moreover, such role playing can only be adopted *after* the archaeological investigation has made its most important inroads. "It is an essential precondition for such psychical activity that we should have more or less divined the nature of the case and the motives of the defense operating in it, and fortunately the technique of insistence and pressure takes us as far as this. The more such riddles we have already solved, the easier we may find it to guess a new one and the sooner we shall be able to start on the truly curative psychical work" (SE 2:282). Once more we see, then, how much the archaeological procedure still operates by means of critique and divination.

The Hypotheses of Freud's Method of Hypothesis

Clearly the deeply intersubjective nature of the analytic encounter required some transactional guidelines in order to succeed in the days long before it had itself become a cliché and an identifiable social practice. Operating as it did in the interstices of moral laws, legal obligations, and medical cures, psychoanalysis was a discursive innovation that sought its alliances with the secular *Wissenschaften* that probed the past in an objective spirit of critique, but with the intuitive finesse of the detective. Moreover, the realm of archaeology, in particular, summoned a solid world of objects whose very materiality underscored the notion of the past's unassailable reality.

But it is a fallacy to assume that solid objects lead to solid theories. Martin Bernal has termed this attitude "archaeological positivism," which is "the fallacy that dealing with 'objects' makes one 'objective'; the belief that interpretations of archaeological evidence are as solid as the archaeological finds themselves" (1987, 1:9). This was an attitude characteristic of the first generations to apply archaeology seriously to historical problems, and is not therefore a peculiar sin of Freud's way of thinking. Freud's *need* for this analogy, however, is peculiar in that by dealing with his own living historical sources, he had always to defend himself against the accusation that his patients were influenced by suggestion and were not actually "remembering" repressed desires or experiences, but were merely *responding* to a more compelling explanation.

Thus the recourse to the object-world (*Dingwelt*) of ancient artifacts was a way of deflecting criticisms concerning psychoanalysis's persuasive operation on the patient. If we look to certain features of the analogy over time, we can see that the threat of suggestion haunted Freud from the

early studies of hysterics from the 1890s well into the 1930s, when he
wrote the paper "Constructions in Analysis" (1937) in order to set down
his final views on the matter. In *Studies on Hysteria* (1893–1895), he prints
with typographical emphasis that "*we are not in a position to force anything
on the patient about the things of which he is ostensibly ignorant or to influence
the products of the analysis by arousing an expectation*" (SE 2:295). He assures
us that some "contradiction in the material" would inevitably be detected
if he had elicited a memory through some kind of suggestion or "fore-
telling" (SE 2:295). The model is again that of the historical hypothesis,
for which a narrative fit must be found that concords with the emergent
"facts" of memory.

> Things that are brought to light from these deeper strata are also
> recognized and acknowledged, but often only after considerable
> hesitations and doubts. Visual memory-images are of course more
> difficult to disavow than the memory-traces of mere trains of
> thought. Not at all infrequently the patient begins by saying, "It's
> possible that I thought this, but I can't remember having done
> so." *And it is not until he has been familiar with the hypothesis for some
> time that he comes to recognize it as well;* he remembers—and confirms
> the fact, too, by subsidiary links—that he really did once have the
> thought. (SE 2:299; my emphasis)

The psycho-archaeological "dig" becomes more and more difficult the
deeper it goes, and this, according to the theory of repression, is only to
be expected. This allows Freud to be quite unconcerned that the *insistence*
of the hypothesis seems to produce positive results; his redefinition of the
patient as a "site" effects this startling immunity.

However, the problem is that, following Freud's metaphor, the deepest strata effectively go *beyond* memory. This means there is a point (the
most crucial point) when the analysand can no longer produce corroboratory evidence through recollection. Freud is disarmingly candid about
this moment in the excavation.

> The ideas which are derived from the greatest depth and *which form
> the nucleus of the pathogenic organization* are also those which are ac-
> knowledged as memories by the patient *with the greatest difficulty.*
> Even when everything is finished and the patients have been *over-
> borne by the force of logic* and have been *convinced by the therapeutic ef-
> fect accompanying the emergence of precisely these ideas*—when, I say, the

patients themselves *accept the fact that they thought this or that*, they
often add: "But I can't *remember* having thought it." *It is easy to come
to terms with them by telling them that the thoughts were unconscious.*
(SE 2:300; my emphasis)

Freud continued to be candid about this aspect of technique well up to
1937, when he writes that when a construction of the past does not elicit
any recollections in the patient, "we produce in him an *assured conviction
of the truth of the construction* which achieves the same therapeutic result
as a recaptured memory" ("Constructions in Analysis," SE 23:266; my
emphasis). This is effectively saying: psychoanalysis is after historical
truth *or its functional equivalent.*[3] The faulty record of memory can be
patched, as long as the patch provides the desired results, which is tanta-
mount to espousing a usable past over a veridical one, in spite of all the
enormous effort employed in the course of excavation.

Thus despite the pretensions to veridical history that permeate his approach, we find that an emphasis on the therapeutic efficacy comes to the
fore at the end, though Freud does not concede that he is peddling curative fictions. On the contrary, the successful removal of symptoms is assumed to corroborate the historical explanation, no matter what the
analysand says about it. What is clearly at stake is that the metaphor of
depth—the archaeological metaphor in its essence—subverts the analysand's authority over her own memory of the past to such a degree that
eventually the analyst's hypothesis can simply override it, though this is
done gradually and not arbitrarily, relying very much on the analyst's own
convictions. This is fed by the assumption that what is earliest is most influential in determining the nature and dynamic of the illness, and such
a prioritizing of the "lowest strata" disarms the patient from making objections the further he has surrendered to the method and its historical
"hypotheses." Once the patient is *used* to being wrong about his past,
whole new narrative syntheses are possible.

The transactional analogy works not just on the analysand, of course,
but also on the analyst. Freud's early explanation of his methods shows
him embracing the discipline of accepting whatever the troubled "site"
of memory produces. This requires, in part, turning a deaf ear to whatever the analysand professes about the emergent memories.

I make it a rule, however, during the analysis to keep my estimate
of the reminiscence that comes up independent of the patient's acknowledgment of it. *I shall never be tired of repeating that we are bound*

to accept whatever our procedure brings to light. If there is anything in it that is not genuine or correct, the context will later on tell us to reject it. But I may say in passing that I have scarcely ever had occasion to disavow subsequently a reminiscence that has been provisionally accepted. *Whatever has emerged has, in spite of the most deceptive appearance of being a glaring contradiction, nevertheless turned out to be quite correct.* (SE 2:299–300; my emphasis)

Here again the memories are clearly modeled on emergent objects of excavation, not on mental responses to the artificial situation of analysis itself. While "archaeological positivism" does require a certain discipline of mind—the accommodation of whatever emerges—it also privileges the practitioner of the technique over the patient's claim to self-exegetical authority. By not being swayed by the analysand's opinions about the "evidence," the analyst appears to be an "objective" observer. In this way, the analyst's *coercion* of the analysand in persuading him to accept a given hypothesis is made to look like a logical necessity drawn from the evidence. But since the analyst does not feel he can control what emerges, he can rest assured that suggestion has not occurred, only good intuitive excavating, like Schliemann's burrowing into the mound of Hisarlik.

Here we see, then, how the archive of antiquity played a major role in the development of this discourse, which uses an *analogy* to enable an unusual *personal* relationship that effectively structures a whole *evidentiary* protocol toward the self's evidence. This analogy was as important in articulating the role of the analyst and his expectations of success as it was in allaying the fears of the analysand and in preparing her for a long and arduous process of treatment. Though Freud clearly relied on existing discursive practices to effect this novel approach, he so thoroughly reshuffled them that psychoanalysis has all the appearance of a startlingly new coin of vantage on the human soul. We have never really thought of ourselves the same way ever since.

A Suggestive Milieu

Since archaeology was the analogy invoked to insulate Freud from charges of suggestion, it is the ultimate irony that this same topic came to be deployed quite overtly in the space of the analytic hour to suggest the reality of the unconscious to the analysand. We just saw how easy Freud felt it was to "come to terms" with the analysands by convincing them of the reality of unconscious thoughts (SE 2:300); after 1897, the heavy presence of artifacts and images of antiquity in the consulting room served just this conviction. While Freud was initiating the Rat Man into treatment, for example, he openly called these props into action.

> I then made some short observations upon *the psychological differences between the conscious and the unconscious*, and upon the fact that everything conscious was subject to a process of wearing away, while what was unconscious was relatively unchangeable; and I illustrated my remarks by pointing to the antiques standing about in my room. They were, in fact, I said, only objects found in a tomb, and their burial had been their preservation: the destruction of Pompeii was only beginning now that it had been dug up. ("Notes upon a Case of Obsessional Neurosis," SE 10:176; original italics)

Earlier we saw how points about the process of excavation were similarly made with the Wolf Man, and how he felt Freud's consulting room was more the office of an archaeologist than a doctor. While the full extent of such suggestion is not known, it seems clear that with particular analysands it could be quite intense. Research into memory since Freud's time has taught us to be highly attentive to the very environment in which recollections are made. As Prager reports on the basis of empirical studies, "the environment in which memories are retrieved has a significant effect on the memory process, and often generates a conviction of accuracy that empirical study does not support" (1998, 185).

It seems the most intense case of archaeological suggestion in Freud's practice was with H.D. (the American poet, Hilda Doolittle) who was initially quite shocked to find the famous doctor standing "like a curator in a museum, surrounded by his priceless collection" ([1956] 1974, 116). H.D.'s case is far from representative, however, since her own enthusiasm for archaeology was such that her analysis exhibited what we might term an instance of *archaeological transference and counter-transference*. But since it forms the most elaborate example, it still merits some attention here. There was a clear mutuality in the interchange of ideas and objects in her record of the analysis.

> We talked of Crete. [. . .] We spoke of Sir Arthur Evans and his work there. The Professor said that we two met in our love of antiquity. He said his little statues and images helped stabilize the

evanescent idea, or keep it from escaping altogether. I asked if he had a Cretan serpent-goddess. He said, "No." I said that I had known people in London who had had some connection with Crete at one time, and that I might move heaven and earth, and get him a serpent-goddess. He said, "I doubt if even *you* could do that." ([1956] 1974, 175)

H.D. depicts Freud as a Janus figure on the threshold of the present and the past, at home amid the treasures of antiquity. His Jewishness suggested further continuity with remote ages. "He has his family, the tradition of an unbroken family, reaching back through this old heart of the Roman Empire, further into the Holy Land. [. . .] He is the infinitely old symbol, weighing the soul, Psyche, in the Balance" ([1956] 1974, 97). By surrounding himself with artifacts, Freud became to her "part and parcel of these treasures" and seemed in his advanced age to wield a mysterious power over time, as if he were an emissary from eternity. "I knew the things in his room were symbols of Eternity and contained him then, as Eternity contains him now" ([1956] 1974, 102). (In point of fact, Freud's ashes are contained now in one of the Greek vases from his collection.) In the depths of her transference, she fantasizes about playing the role of Alcestis, giving the aged Freud her years to go on living as the Greek heroine did for her husband, Admetus; yet Freud is not just Admetus in her view, but also Herakles, triumphantly conquering Thanatos itself ([1956] 1974, 74).

At the time of her analysis, H.D. was also suspicious of Freud's use of his collection. "I did not always know if the Professor's excursions with me into the other room [his office adjoining the consulting room] were by way of distraction, actual social occasions, or part of his plan. Did he want to find out how I would react to certain ideas embodied in these little statues, or how deeply I felt the dynamic *idea* still implicit in spite of the fact that ages or aeons of time had flown over many of them?" ([1956] 1974, 68). On one occasion, he appears to have made a rather pointed suggestion about penis envy to her, something we might think inevitable in his analysis of an ambitious female writer.[4] This suggestion was made by showing her his beloved statuette of Athena, which always rested on his desk.

"*This* is my favorite," he said. He held the object toward me. I took it in my hand. It was a little bronze statue, helmeted, clothed to the

foot in carved robe with the upper incised chiton or peplum. One
hand was extended as if holding a staff or rod. "She is perfect," he
said, "*only she has lost her spear.*" I did not say anything. ([1956] 1974,
69; original emphasis)

Her interpretation of this comment shows to what extent she understands
the principle of masculine domination implicit in the symbol, and to what
extent she allows herself to be co-opted by that principle. Freud meant,
she says, "that the little bronze statue was a perfect symbol, *made in man's
image (in woman's, as it happened)*, to be venerated as a projection of abstract thought, Pallas Athené, born without human or even without divine mother, sprung full-armed from the head of her father, *our-father,*
Zeus, Theus, or God" ([1956] 1974, 70; my emphasis). One can certainly
read the spearless little image as a "projection of abstract thought,"
namely the Freudian conception of femininity as both castrated and re-
pellent (like the *gorgoneion* inscribed on her front or on her shield). But I
wish to stress that this scene poignantly illustrates how a physical artifact
of Greek antiquity mediated the inevitable resistances arising between
the male doctor and the female patient, the Jewish patriarch and the
Christian single mother. As he held it out to her, she says, "like a Jew, he
was assessing its worth"; but this Jew was also weighing *her* like the female figure in his hand. "He knew his material pound, his pound of flesh,
if you will, but this pound of flesh was a *pound of spirit* between us, something tangible, to be weighed and measured, to be weighed in the balance
and—pray God—not to be found wanting!" ([1956] 1974, 70; original
emphasis).

H.D.'s portrait of Freud shows us quite clearly that analytic memory
work and the object-world of the site cannot be separated. In fact, there
is an outright *artifactual economy* that links the business of analysis with
the growing collection of objects. Freud jokingly referred to his fees from
single consultations as the *Nationalgeschenk* ("national donation"), reserv-
ing this amount for his collection. The acquisition of artifacts was mixed
in with many of the same relationships that formed the analytic enterprise.[5] For example, Freud wrote constantly to Ferenczi during 1910
concerning their joint effort to underwrite excavations in Duna Pentele,
the site of a former Roman legionary camp.[6] Sprinkled in among their
scientific discussions and professional gossip are references to payments
to be made, items to be seen and procured. More importantly, Freud's patients would offer him antiquities as gifts, and so would his eager col-

leagues, some of whom, like Marie Bonaparte (Princess George of Greece), were in a position to acquire things from the best European dealers. H.D., as we have just seen, clearly promised extraordinary efforts to find a pleasing artifact for Freud, and was made to feel that she had in some sense to perform her analysis in relation to Freud's collection. So although the collecting activity might at first appear like a stalwart bourgeois passion—a mere hobby and not a *habitus*—it was unusually implicated in the network of analysis. So much so that Freud's successful relocation to London at the end of his life required the symbolic transfer of *both* the collection *and* the couch, which still go on tour together to this day.

My major point here is that while the archaeological analogy was an enduring means of countering the accusation of suggestion, at the same time Freud's insistence on the topic *with the analysands* could very well be labeled as a form of that very thing. His visual deployment of the historical and archaeological in the inner sanctum of analysis—that allegedly "private" space closed off from the world in order to protect the delicate nature of "self-evidence"—imposed a sense of historical time on the analysand, constantly suggested a model of depth and surface, and enabled a serious engagement with the fragmentary and enigmatic character of "self-evidence." The Wolf Man's parting gift of an Egyptian figurine could therefore bear the sinister allegorical reading of an analysand "producing" the required artifact for his analyst in order to play the game. The Wolf Man was, after all, obedient enough later to produce paintings of his wolf dream that corresponded better to Freud's interpretation than his original drawing (Whitney Davis, 1996, 293). Martin Bergmann has even gone so far as to suggest that Freud's obsessive lining of his own writing desk with an audience of ancient figurines was a deliberate means of convincing *himself* of the reality of the unconscious, since doubt about the existence of that mysterious realm is a regular part of the analytic process (1989, 177). As Freud admitted to H.D., "his little statues and images helped stabilize the evanescent idea, or keep it from escaping altogether" ([1956] 1974, 175). It is hard, then, not to judge Freud's own choice of décor as an instance of the return of the repressed, i.e., the recurrence of suggestibility through the means he used to dispel it. To cite Freud's own words against him: "This is also a good example of the rule that in time the thing which is meant to be warded off invariably finds its way into the very means which is being used for warding it off" ("Notes upon a Case of Obsessional Neurosis," SE 10:225).

Recursive Analogy Once More

It is clear that part of the excavating analogy rested on the assurance that there are "strata" of memory that the proper method can access, and the link from the site to the mind was in part Freud's own physiological notions of neurological stratification in the brain.[7] One could say, however, that as Freud's dogmatic insistence on the "timelessness" of the unconscious increased, he undermined the validity of his own stratigraphic analogy. For if the items of the unconscious are all like dateless artifacts from a succession of entombments, then how does one establish relative chronologies with any reliability? After all, memories and associations cannot be carbon dated. Freud's later analogy of the mind with the site of Rome with all its historical structures coexisting in the same place illustrates the very absurdity created by trying to uphold *both* the timelessness and stratification of the unconscious's contents (*Civilization and Its Discontents*, SE 21:20). By 1937, Freud conceded that relative chronology is a problem, but simply countered that it is equally a problem for the archaeologist, without taking stock of the *vastly* different way material objects age compared to mental items ("Constructions in Analysis," SE 23:259). As in the case of decipherment, Freud seems to raise the right objections to his analogy, but then simply ignores them.

One could further object that Freud's views on memory as the reworking of experience (explicit in the analogy with legendary history) further problematize the facile model of buried objects. However, by the 1930s he was still confident enough to assert instead that the radical difference of mental artifacts from their archaeological analogs is their chief *strength* in historical analysis, not their weakness.

> Here we are regularly met by a situation which with the archaeological object occurs only in such rare circumstances as those of Pompeii or of the tomb of Tut'ankhamun. All of the essentials are preserved; even things that seem completely forgotten are present somehow and somewhere, and have merely been buried and made inaccessible to the subject. Indeed, it may, as we know, be doubted whether any psychical structure can really be the victim of total destruction. *It depends only upon analytic technique whether we shall succeed in bringing what is concealed completely to light.* (SE 23:260, my emphasis)

As John Forrester notes, this represents a curious reversal of the sciences in that the "subjective" psychological realm is held to be more permanent

THE ARCHAEOLOGY OF FREEDOM

than the "objective" material realm (1980, 209). It is clear that Freud sought to put his memory work in a privileged position by continuing to cite dogmatically the principle that "it is rather the rule than the exception that the past is preserved in mental life" (*Civilization and Its Discontents*, SE 21:72).

And so we have another instance of recursive analogy: the archaeologist initially helped to order the psychoanalytic domain's evidence and procedures, but now psychoanalysis can lay claim to being a *superior* form of archaeology because the contents of the mind are a much better site than what lies beneath the earth. "The two processes [of archaeology and analysis] are in fact identical, except that the analyst works under better conditions and has more material at his command to assist him, since what he is dealing with is not something destroyed but something that is still alive [. . .]" (SE 23:259). The wealth of the analytic site is its own drawback, however, in that it is far more complex and full of "so much that is still mysterious" ("Constructions in Analysis," SE 23:260). Moreover, the metaphors of entombment and accidental burial cannot convey adequately the essential paradox that gives the analyst the upper hand in finding historical truth: the *truth-avoiding* powers of repression and resistance are what underwrite the untold riches of the psychoanalytic dig. Repression guarantees the conservation of the contents, and resistance clues the analyst in as to where the spade must bite into the endless heap of mental detritus.

Repression and resistance are dynamic concepts that greatly empowered not only Freud's historical methodology vis-à-vis the analogous *Wissenschaften*, but the very concept of professionalism which guided him. Whereas other scientific *conquistadores* could quietly await the vindication of their hypotheses (like the surly Niebuhr, who simply despised his reviewers and kept working), Freud could derive great satisfaction from the fact that attempts to refute and ridicule him would be inevitably stronger than in other cases due to the very nature of the site he worked on: the nuclear complex of civilization's own repressive regime. Thus he not only decoded neurotic symptoms, but could see in the vociferous attacks on his work further symptoms of the same neurotic processes at work. It is as if Darwin accused his opponents of not accepting the theory of evolution because they were in fact *less evolved* and therefore could not understand it. Freud thus made a potential public failure the backdoor to success, one of the greatest rhetorical triumphs in modern history, even at the risk of giving psychoanalysis the appearance of what John Farrell has called a "paranoid quest" (1996). Sándor Ferenczi once wrote jokingly to Freud, "If psychoanalysis is a paranoia, then I have already been successful in overcoming the stage of persecution mania and replacing it with megalomania" (Brabant et al. 1993–2000, 1:187). Was that the necessary condition of all the true believers, to have sufficient megalomania to uphold a delusional system in the face of scathing criticism?

The final question we must address concerning Freud's indebtedness to the historical *Wissenschaften* is how this deeply historical method avoids the accusation of being itself just a paranoid delusion. By his own admission, "the delusions of patients appear [. . .] to be the equivalents of the constructions which we build up in the course of an analytic treatment— attempts at explanation and cure [. . .]" ("Constructions in Analysis," SE 23:268). And yet, he says that "the way in which a conjecture of ours is transformed into the patient's conviction" is "hardly worth describing" (SE 23:265). This raises again the ugly specter of Wittgenstein's "powerful mythology." How do we know that psychoanalysis is a manifestation of genuine historical consciousness and not just a new myth—or as the great sexologist Krafft-Ebing remarked at the first public performance of Freud's archaeological analogy in 1896, a "scientific fairy tale" [*ein wissenschaftliches Märchen*]? (the editor's note to "The Aetiology of Hysteria," SE 3:189)

CHAPTER 10

∎

Uncanny Understanding and a Grave Philosophy

Mercutio: Ask for me tomorrow, and you shall find me a grave man.
— *Romeo and Juliet*

Freud's teacher of history at the *Gymnasium* that he attended in Vienna was Viktor von Kraus (1845–1905), a Pan-German nationalist who had been the student of the greatest figures in nineteenth-century German historicism: Leopold von Ranke (1795–1886), Johann Gustav Droysen (1808–1884), and Theodor Mommsen (1817–1903).[1] On the surface, it would thus seem an easy enough inference to draw that Freud's view of historical consciousness is a mere product of the "climate" of historicist thinking, a *habitus* so pervasive in the academic setting of his time that there simply was no thinking beyond it. To answer the question I just raised in the previous chapter, we must consider the subsidiary questions that come along with it. Does psychoanalysis in its historical aspirations *merely reflect* or *emerge from* the historicist framework? Is psychoanalysis's struggle for domination in historical *Wissenschaft* to be seen as a genuine revolution in thought, or an epigone of the earlier historical revolution content to hop on the bandwagon?

It bears repeating here that these questions of filiation are not merely academic, since psychoanalysis depends so heavily on analogies with the historical *Wissenschaften* for the legitimation of its curious techniques. This speaks to the heart of Freud's enterprise, because its association with historical science would by implication ensure our acceptance of it as a legitimate manifestation of modern historical consciousness. I have been arguing that recapitulation, repression (as *Freud* understands it in psychological, not political terms), resistance, and regression would make the historical aspirations of psychoanalysis quite distinct from the garden-variety historicist practice of Freud's time. But what if we look to how Freud reconfigured the notion of historical consciousness overall and how he sees the *total* direction of human history? In other words: is there a more comprehensive philosophy of history in Freud, and how does it relate to those of the nineteenth-century cultural matrix?

This would obviously require a book-length treatment in itself, but we can trace psychoanalysis's relationship with historicism in broad strokes for our immediate purposes. Droysen made it dogmatically clear in the *Outline of the Principles of History* that history is itself a kind of collective consciousness or transcendental self-awareness.

> History is humanity becoming and being conscious [*das Bewußtwerden und Bewußtsein*] concerning itself. The epochs of history are not the life periods of this "I" of humanity—empirically we do not know whether this racial "I" is growing old or renewing its youth, only that it does not continue to be what it was or is—but they are stages in that ego's self-knowledge, its knowledge of the world and of God. ([1881] 1967, 48)

This disciplinary definition certainly raises the stakes for the historical enterprise, endowing it with a serious Delphic edge. "History is humanity's knowledge of itself, its certainty about itself [*Selbstgewißheit*]"; "History is the γνῶθι σαυτόν [know thyself] of humanity, its conscience [*Gewissen*]" ([1881] 1967, 48 and 44). But Freud's great historical insult to humanity, as he liked to claim, was in pointing out that this ego or "I" was not master in its own house and did not, in fact, *know itself.* His characterization of the ego's self-ignorance is itself tellingly reminiscent of the historical situation in which he wrote—that is, a tottering imperial monarchy with myriad dimensions of interethnic and social intrigue that would soon break it to pieces. In "A Difficulty in the Path of Psychoanalysis" (1917, SE 17:137–144), he apostrophizes the ego in terms of a Delphic exhortation:

> You behave like an absolute ruler who is content with the information supplied him by his highest officials and never goes among the people to hear their voice. Turn your eyes inward, look into your own depths, learn first to know yourself! Then you will understand

why you were bound to fall ill; and perhaps, you will avoid falling
ill in the future. (SE 17:143)

It would be tempting to take this as a great reversal of Droysen's view of
history, as if to say that once the inherent fictions of the ego have been
exposed (including the fiction of God), ego-centric histories would simply fall apart in the face of analytic rigor.

Ego-centric histories like to stress the conscious determinations that
shape historical events, even when the general pattern is only detectable
through the hindsight that exposes the "cunning of reason" in history (as
Hegel put it). After all, it is the tragic reality of human hindsight (and lack
of foresight) that *empowers* the practice of history and makes it necessary
to the politicians (Droysen himself became the greatest historian of the
Prussian state during the period of German unification). Even Burckhardt's pessimistic views—quite untimely as they were for the 1870s and
1880s—did not undermine his sense of the historical imperative. On the
contrary, doubt and confusion about the present and future are precisely
what necessitate "the empirical perception of humanity as we encounter
it in life and as it is revealed in history," even when history shows us "a
tragedy complete in itself," as in the case of ancient Greece ([1898–1902]
1998, 364–365). Peddlers of ego-centric history can thus lay claim to being themselves the agency of human consciousness, the I of humanity.
Droysen makes it very clear that "the many" caught up in their own concerns work for history unawares, "without choice or will, unfree, as a
mass" ["*ohne Wahl und Willen, unfrei, als Masse*"]. They are the noisy thyr-
sus-bearers in the god's festal procession, but the real Bacchants are few
(βάκχοι δέ τε παῦροι = Plato, *Phaedo* 69c) ([1881] 1967, 46). Such theories of "absolute spirit" or of a greater "I" can thus be traced to the historian's own delusions of mystical gnosis: "I am more I than thou."

But is not the whole objective of psychoanalysis to point out instead
the cunning of *unreason* in history, and to expose historical rationality as
mere rationalization written over darker, unconscious motives? By the
1930s, the whole world was painfully aware that the nineteenth-century
apotheosis of the German State (by Droysen, in particular) was a delusion persisting like a disease in the German mind. At this very moment,
Freud attacked the systematic delusions of history, but did so *still in the
name of historical reasoning*.

If we consider mankind as a whole and substitute it for the single
human individual, we discover that it too has developed delusions

which are inaccessible to logical criticism and which contradict reality. If, in spite of this, they are able to exert an extraordinary power
over men, investigation leads us to the same explanation as in the
case of the single individual. They owe their power to the element
of *historical truth* which they have brought up from the repression
of the forgotten and primeval past. ("Constructions in Analysis," SE
23:269; my emphasis)

The power of such delusions (and here his unspoken target was German
anti-Semitism) lies not merely in their cogent serving of present needs,
but in their conveyance of uncanny historical truths, in the essential unpastness of the past that roils beneath them. Here again is where the
memory work of analysis comes into play, and in this particular case that
work took the form of *Moses and Monotheism*, Freud's most extended historical investigation.

As we can see, Freud's historical attitude was far from an ateleological
critique of historical narratives; for history, alas, is not merely bunk.
Quite the opposite: human history has an uncanny, irrational persistence
beyond the surface of its narratives. But it also has a definite shape, an
evolutionary contour. Freud subscribed to a progressive directionality in
historical consciousness that was in some ways much more rigidly formulated than Droysen's. Freud's view of history is a passage through successive *Weltanschauungen*, from animism to religion and thence to science
(*Totem and Taboo*, SE 13:77). This is in fact an echo of Auguste Comte's
three ages of religion, metaphysics, and positivism, though it shows modification under the influence of James Frazer (whose *Golden Bough* Freud
ransacked while writing *Totem and Taboo*).[2]

Freud's particular scheme, however, is not a naively optimistic "triumph of the human spirit," but something more akin to a progressive
resignation of the human spirit—a progress, we might even say, in disillusionment.

> At the animistic stage men ascribe omnipotence to *themselves.* At the
> religious stage they transfer it to the gods but do not seriously aban-
> don it themselves, for they reserve the power of influencing the gods
> in a variety of ways according to their wishes. The scientific view of
> the universe no longer affords any room for human omnipotence;
> men have acknowledged their smallness and submitted resignedly
> to death and to the other necessities of nature. None the less some
> of the primitive belief in omnipotence still survives in men's faith in

the power of the human mind, taking account, as it does, of the laws of reality. (*Totem and Taboo*, SE 13:88)

Though the scheme is not a joyous one—one need only recall the highly guarded cheerleading for the secular "god" Logos which he attempts in his polemics with religion (*The Future of an Illusion*, SE 21:54–56)—it is clearly articulated as a shift toward an epistemological advantage; i.e., knowledge of the "laws of reality" in place of the purely narcissistic "omnipotence of thoughts." Since the resignation of instinct and accommodation to the dreary reality principle are what drive the civilizing process, it is not entirely clear what the *psychological* value of this firmer self-consciousness would be beyond a more efficient adaptation to the environment. Are not the narcissistic primitives *happier* in their delusions?

A first hint at the scheme's value comes from the associations that accrue around each stage. The scheme is itself an analogy, mimicking a developmental psychology and consisting of the infantile narcissism of animism, the adolescent inhibitions of religion, and the mature adult assessment of one's place in the world through science.[3] In contrast, Droysen, as we saw, refused to age the periods of the I of humanity (partly because the German nationalists of his era liked to think of the newly unified Germany as enjoying a second youth). Here Freud's view of historical consciousness is mediated by a different post-Hegelian, the philosopher Ludwig Feuerbach (1804–1872), whom the young Freud read and admired above all other philosophers and whose formative influence on him is quite often forgotten.[4] Feuerbach was relentless in his insistence that "in religion, man is a child" ([1848] 1967, 209), and held that though religion once fostered civilization, now it holds it back. In his *Lectures on the Essence of Religion*, Feuerbach declared outright that "In all other fields man progresses; in religious matters he remains stone-blind, stone-deaf, and rooted to the spot" ([1848] 1967, 216). But the way Feuerbach chose to combat the stifling effect of religion was "on the basis of concrete historical material, namely, nature religion," a move that privileges the primal truths of paganism over the pernicious abstractions of transcendental monotheism, which posits a great God standing above all the workings of nature ([1848] 1967, 216). Hence for Feuerbach, the return to the historical perspective of the mythologies of antiquity is fundamentally a return to man's childhood conceptualizations of nature, which form a kind of primary psychological truth.

For Feuerbach as for Freud, then, the return to the "reality" of nature entails freeing oneself from a condition of intellectual immaturity and in-

hibition, but it requires an historical perspective that draws *strength* from
the formative "experiences of childhood" that led to the current psychological horizon. The exclusive focus on nature is what links the primitive
to the modern, as opposed to theism, or at least the transcendental,
monotheistic perspective, for which God is too good and too great for
this world.[5] But the recourse to nature is both internal and external; that
is, it is both a matter of physics or biology *and* a matter of psychology. In
fact, it is the *psychological* derivation of worldviews that marks the movement of history, and here Feuerbach anticipated Freud by half a century
at least, in saying that "The ultimate secret of religion is the *relationship*
between the *conscious* and *unconscious*, the *voluntary* and *involuntary in one
and the same individual*" ([1848] 1967, 311; original emphasis). By locat-
ing the task of modernity in the expansion of humanity's consciousness
of itself, Feuerbach made historical understanding simultaneously a tool
of social change as well as academic reflection. It took courage, after all,
to assert in 1848 that "in nature [. . .] there is only one regime, and that
regime is republican," even if Feuerbach's humanistic idealism failed to
impress dialectical materialists like Marx and Engels ([1848] 1967, 139).

   Which is to say, then, that the product of advancing historical consciousness is freedom itself—a point on which Hegel, Droysen, Feuerbach, and Freud would all be in agreement. Freedom is the life-pulse of
history for Droysen ([1881] 1967, 44–45), while for Hegel "the final
cause of the world at large" is Spirit's consciousness of its own freedom
([1899] 1956, 19). That Freud's own historical work centers mostly
around religious psychology itself shows his indebtedness to Feuerbach,
whose self-appointed task was "to illumine the obscure essence of religion with the torch of reason, in order that man may at least cease to be
the victim, the plaything, of all those hostile powers which from time im-
memorial have employed and are still employing the darkness of religion
for the oppression of mankind" ([1848] 1967, 22). The goal of Feuerbach's historical investigation of religion as the product of wish-fulfill-
ment was quite simply to reveal divine authority as merely humanity
itself, "so that man, who is always unconsciously governed and determined by his own essence alone, may in future consciously take his own,
human essence as the law and determining ground, the aim and measure,
of his ethical and political life" ([1848] 1967, 22–23). The past thus reinterpreted creates freedom *from* a history of obfuscation and oppression.

   For the individual in Freud's consulting room, freedom *from* but
through history is in essence the most optimistic goal the analytic encounter could have, and the analyst as *Aufklärer* finds himself conse-

quently in the role of proselytizing for a "freer or superior view of the world" on a daily basis (SE 2:282).[6] In this regard it is hard not to see Freud as the "last *philosophe*," embracing the Enlightenment's promise of happiness in a progressive frame of mind and embodying the ideals of historical demystification (Gay 1987, chapter 1). "But surely infantilism is destined to be surmounted," he pleads in *The Future of an Illusion* (SE 21:49). "Men cannot remain children forever [. . .]."

Tartuffery or Enlightenment?

However, Freud's novel psychological views on "repression" greatly complicate this progressive historical scheme. As human society becomes more civilized, it also represses more and increases the unconscious content of the mind, finding various other ways to reinvest the primary instinctual energies, only some of which are healthy sublimations. So a characteristic feature of civilization is progressive self-alienation in the face of ethical, technological, and scientific advancement. (It is robbing peter to pay Paul, so to speak.) Since the motor force of the civilizing process is the repression of instinct, this could imply that the whole Comtean scheme is now contradictory: repression, the great force of self-alienation in history, is what makes civilization possible. Yet civilization brings us science and the self-reflexive epiphanies of psychoanalysis, which presuppose a heightened consciousness that takes in the "laws of reality," including the laws governing the reality of the mind. How can one reconcile the seemingly opposite trends of tartuffery and enlightenment in civilization? How can the growth of the *unconscious* lead to progressive *expansion* of consciousness?

Freud made a candid assessment of this paradox early on during a meeting of the Vienna Psychoanalytic Society in 1909. It is certainly worth noting that this assessment was in response to a presentation by Alfred Adler on Marx's contribution to the understanding of historical consciousness (and in this presentation, Adler's personal relationship with Trotsky shows clear influence on his ideas [Nunberg and Federn 1967, 172–178]). In his response, Freud outlined both the paradox of historical consciousness and its solution. As reported in the minutes, Freud said:

> The entire development of humanity could also be characterized, from the psychological point of view, by a formula in which two elements stood out: on the one hand, it is a question of an enlarge-

ment of the consciousness of mankind (analogous to the coming
into consciousness of instincts and forces hitherto operating unconsciously); on the other hand, progress can be described as a repression that progresses over the centuries. Our culture consists in
this: that more and more of our instincts become subject to repression, for which there are beautiful illustrations, particularly in poetic productions [...].

When placed next to each other, these two characteristics seem
to be entirely contradictory to each other, for with the progress of
repression, more and more should become unconscious, and not the
other way around. *But then comes the liberating thought* that these two
processes are the condition for each other: *the enlargement of consciousness is what enables mankind to cope with life in the face of the steady
progress of repression.* [...] That would be the introduction of psychology into historical studies. (Nunberg and Federn 1967, 174; my
emphasis)

In essence, this "liberating thought" allows Freud to have it both ways:
to maintain the "repressive hypothesis" that allows psychoanalysis to remain the definitive method of unmasking—the master discourse for finding out the truth of the human mind through its processes of decoding
the cunning of unreason—while still participating in the organic, progressive concept of civilization. Civilization contains not just science but
also the consoling cultural capital of literature and art, all of which support the particular coin of vantage on humanity that psychoanalysis values and presents. Psychoanalysis is thus not a fluke or an inexplicable
grace in the historical movement of the psyche, but a logical consequence
of human history, or rather, an evolutionary event. It is itself an *"education to reality,"* and the most advanced form of coping in the struggle for
existence (*Future of an Illusion*, SE 21:49). It represents the adult consciousness of humankind in a state now able to understand its own childhood (which would again promise a perspective of *total history*). But
how, exactly, do we understand our primitive ancestors from our civilized
perspective?

Uncanny Understanding

Historical consciousness implies a historical hermeneutics, to which I
now turn because this matter reveals Freud's dependence upon the con-

ceptual framework of historicism, but also reveals how he expands it. In Droysen's formulation, history is the human ego (the "I of humanity") talking to itself through a process of "researching to understand" (*forschend zu Verstehen*); in Freud's view, this is also true, but not true in the same way. For Droysen, the very possibility of historical consciousness (and therefore, for the *Wissenschaft* of history) lies in the psychological ground of empathetic human understanding (*Verstehen*). One cannot assimilate human history to natural history, because fundamentally human history is "a second creation, not of new material but of forms, of thoughts, of societies with their virtues and duties, in a word, the Moral World [*die sittliche Welt*]" ([1881] 1967, 77). Unlike the extra-human world of nature, we have a profound mental affinity with this second creation, which we can understand through immediate intuition [*unmittelbare Intuition*].[7]

> In this realm of the moral world everything is accessible to our understanding, from the most insignificant love-story to great state transactions, from the solitary mental work of the poet or the thinker to the immeasurable combinations of the world's commerce, or poverty's struggle so beset with temptation. *Whatever exists we may understand, inasmuch as we can apprehend it as something that has developed from beginnings.* ([1881] 1967, 77; my emphasis).

These remarks by Droysen come from a very important review he wrote of Henry Buckle's *History of Civilization in England* (1857), a book that greatly inspired Freud as a young *Gymnasium* student. In his review essay, Droysen pointedly attacks the notion that the *Wissenschaft* of history is of the same kind as the *Wissenschaft* of the natural sciences, a notion that Buckle had naively advanced in full positivistic fervor.[8] This particular debate, then, should interest us precisely because it seems to point out the stress inherent in Freud's conflation of natural and human history, a conflation powered by the evolutionary paradigm of the day with its promising dialectic of phylogeny and ontogeny.

Freud invoked a unitary view of the *Weltanschauung* of *Wissenschaft*, even when it is clear he was often more deeply indebted for the modeling of his science to the *Geisteswissenschaften* than those of *Natur*.[9] He insists that it is psychoanalysis itself that essentially *unifies* the scientific *Weltanschauung*, since it assumes that "the intellect and the mind are objects for scientific research in *exactly the same way as any non-human things*"

(*New Introductory Lectures on Psychoanalysis*, SE 22:159; my emphasis).
Thus psychoanalysis "has a special right to speak for the scientific *Weltanschauung*" in that it naturalizes mental phenomena (SE 22:159). It was
more specifically his phylogenetic assumptions which made it possible
for him to lay claim to a genuine methodology of human history via natural history, through a kind of biohermeneutics.[10] To press this claim,
however, required something even more mystical than historicism's soul-
blending "understanding" (*Verstehen*); it required an uncanny understanding, an *unconscious understanding*. Thus to the "moral world," which
Droysen posited as the second creation that understanding can access, is
added a further co-creation (for it is consubstantial with that outward
"moral world" of ego-history), the mental underworld that is only acces-
sible through unconscious processes. While this is implicit in Freud's earliest exegesis of *Oedipus Tyrannus*, it is quite explicit in *Totem and Taboo*.

In arguing for intergenerational awareness of the primal patricide,
Freud found himself in need of a more robust historical unconscious, and
therefore, of an unconscious understanding to mediate its contents. The
fundamental assumption behind this is biophysical in nature: mental impulses which are suppressed cannot entirely disappear.

> Even the most ruthless suppression must leave room for distorted
> surrogate impulses and for reactions resulting from them. If so,
> however, we may safely assume that no generation is able to conceal
> any of its more important mental processes from its successor. For
> psychoanalysis has shown us that everyone possesses in his uncon-
> scious mental activity *an apparatus* which enables him to interpret
> other people's reactions, that is, *to undo the distortions* which other
> people have imposed on the expression of their feelings. *An uncon-
> scious understanding such as this of all the customs, ceremonies and dog-
> mas left behind by the original relation to the father may have made it
> possible for later generations to take over their heritage of emotion.* (SE
> 13:159; my emphasis)

No matter what culture says, we know what it really means, in other
words. This notion of unconscious understanding, or of a dialogic encounter between unconsciousnesses, first grew from the analytic encounter. It finds its technical expression in the later formula that "[the
analyst] must turn his own unconscious like a receptive organ towards the
transmitting unconscious of the patient" (SE 12:115). In *Totem and Taboo*,
it is generalized into a principle not only of unconscious traditions, but

also of a critical understanding of those traditions that could be divined through the very kind of psychohistory Freud undertakes in that work. In other words, Freud the historian relies on *critique and divination* to arrive at the conclusion that the primal horde murdered and devoured its father; but unlike Niebuhr, he had a wealth of experience in the dialogic encounter of the couch to deepen his conviction toward his historical hypothesis.[11]

The Historical Individual

Thus psychoanalysis's ultimate license to write cultural history is granted by a particular *dilation* of the historicists' hermeneutical understanding, and not the unqualified invocation of it nor its utter dismantling by the rhetoric of natural-science objectification. It is important, however, not to make light of the frictions that arise on a constant basis between psychoanalysis and the German philosophies of history. The developing *muthos* of organic life and the instincts empowered psychoanalysis's inversion of human motives in the historical process, an inversion akin to Marx's materialist inversion of Hegel. The unconscious realm that psychoanalysis has discovered reveals the dirty secrets of a humanity that would otherwise prefer to see itself as an ethereal "absolute spirit" fulfilling purely rational aims in its world-historical progress. For this reason, Freud regularly dismissed the systematic views of philosophers ("metaphysicians" of the likes of Hegel most especially) as delusions.[12] Metaphysics, he boldly proclaimed, was now to be replaced by metapsychology (*The Psychopathology of Everyday Life*, SE 6:259).

As a Jew and former German nationalist, he would especially have had to reject Hegel's rosy views of "reconciliation" between the human spirit and the world in the form of the German state, in which "Freedom has found the means of realizing its Ideal—its true existence" ([1899] 1956, 109–110). To be Jewish in Freud's day meant to become painfully, *historically* aware that the promised "freedom" to be enjoyed at the end of history in the German state was just another philosophical mirage; political and psychological realities had stripped such "reconciliations" of any meaning. So there could easily be a political dimension behind Freud's private tantrums against philosophy. "I believe that one day metaphysics will be condemned as a nuisance, as an abuse of thinking, as a survival from the period of the religious *Weltanschauung*. I know well to what extent this way of thinking *estranges me from German cultural life*" (Ernst

Freud 1960, 375; my emphasis).[13] All one needs to be cured of the metaphysics of history is a good dose of Darwin, which is effectively what Freud delivers in *Totem and Taboo*. This certainly was the basis for the Nazis' tantrums against Freud, as was announced at the book-burnings in Berlin in 1933. "Against overestimating base instincts to the detriment of the spirit and in the name of the noble human soul, I deliver to the flames the writings of Sigmund Freud" (cited in Elon 2002, 396).

Freud's constant dismissal of philosophy became itself a kind of ritual in his work, a need to denounce the purveyors of bogus Baedekers of the mind in order to mark out the discursive space of analytic truth (*Inhibitions, Symptoms, and Anxiety*, SE 20:96). The delusional cabal of modern philosophers thus functions as the shadow of psychoanalysis, the way the sophists did for Plato's delineation of a purely truth-loving activity known as *philo-sophia*. The empirical romance of psychoanalysis—the story of factual discovery that sets it off from all fuzzy thinking and the totalizing impulses of philosophy—grows out of the daily clinical confrontation with living memory; that is to say, it grows from the *experience* of the past which emerges from transference as unpast, unsettled, and wildly unpredictable. Transference, by revealing the unpastness of the past, reveals the truth of the historical in the present, and empirically grounds the whole venture of analysis on a case-by-case basis. Thus the piecemeal truths of analysis claim a greater validity through their accumulation than all the wholesale theorizing performed by philosophers. Or so the argument runs.[14]

But the totalizing impulse of the nineteenth century dies hard, because it promises to make sense of individual misery through the consolations of historical consciousness. Here I wish to stress again that Freud's investment in the ancient archive bears the twin hallmarks of *refuge and synergy*. The great consolation of historicism, in Droysen's formulation at least, is the historian's participation in the mystical vision provided by the I of humanity instead of his own wretchedly limited field of vision. The soul-blending, sexually characterized act of "immediate intuition" of the past is what also gives those who think historically their reconciliation with the moral world of human beings as it continues to emerge, since "the knowledge of history is history itself" ([1881] 1967, 16). By contrast, one might assume that the intersubjective space of analysis would only provide insight through so many little portholes of wretchedness, those eccentric perspectives provided by neurotics. But Freud was keenly convinced, up to the end of his life, that the historical consciousness created by the analytic encounter cannot be bounded by the biography of the empirical individual, since every individual comprises the "organic past" of the id and the cultural past of the super-ego. These agents of the past exert pressure on the ego in addition to the external world, which "represents the power of the present," and put it in a position of constantly needing to come to terms with a past that extends well beyond the ego's immediate experience (*An Outline of Psycho-Analysis*, SE 23:206–207). Since this point is so commonly ignored in socio-historical critiques of Freud's work, I will spell it out one last time.

First, the human need to acquire culture—and therefore the historical consciousness embedded in it—creates the situation whereby the child recapitulates the cultural past through education as an "after experience." This sense of recapitulation was, of course, reinforced in Freud's day by sending the child to a *Gymnasium*, where he studied Latin, Greek, and Hebrew, filling his own childhood with the contents of humanity's salad days. Second, true to his phylogenetic principles, Freud asserts that in addition to what is consciously imparted, the child awakens in himself "precipitates" of cultural acquisitions that were *physically* inherited, "left behind in the id" (SE 23:206). This yields the result that "not a few of the child's new experiences will be intensified because they are repetitions of some primeval phylogenetic experience" (SE 23:206–207). Every developing mind is thus a theater of world history—a theater, we might add, in which *Oedipus Tyrannus* is always playing. But it is world history in constant conscious and unconscious interaction with the pressures of an immediate environment, a particular family, and a specific trajectory of experience. In the terms of Goethe's poem *Urworte. Orphisch*, one moves under the dual influence of δαίμων καὶ τύχη (destiny and chance) toward the kindling flame of eros, but we find in our apparently free choices later in life we are still under the rule of Ἀνάγκη (Necessity): "*So sind wir schein-frei denn, nach manchen Jahren / Nur enger dran, als wir am Anfang waren* [Thus we have an illusory freedom, after many years / only faster bound than we were at the start]."

So when Freud still values consciousness as "the one light which illuminates our path and leads us through the darkness of mental life," he is referring to a darkness of the ages and a light that can only be a fully *macro*-historical awareness ("Some Elementary Lessons in Psycho-Analysis," SE 23:286). For otherwise psychoanalysis would be very far from understanding all that goes on in the bizarre microcosm of the human mind. The failure to understand the historical origins and nature of the unconscious, after all, is in Freud's view what leads to religions, philosophies, and other abuses of thinking. If the pressures of the analytical situation are macrohistorical, so too by implication are its empirical benefits—for it gives us the proof we need that at last we understand what is going on in the world of the human mind. Thus the analytic encounter, for all its connotations of privacy, uniqueness, and isolation, still brings us to the brink of total history and seduces us with seemingly limitless possibilities of extension. In his 1935 postscript to "An Autobiographical Study" (*Selbstdarstellung*), Freud admitted as much: "I perceived ever more clearly that the events of human history, the interactions between human nature, cultural development and the precipitates of primaeval experiences (the most prominent example of which is religion) are *no more than a reflection* of the dynamic conflicts between the ego, the id, and the super-ego, which psychoanalysis studies in the individual—*are the very same processes repeated upon a wider stage*" (SE 20:72; my emphasis).

I will conclude with a remarkable image of historical totality that comes right from the analytic situation. Lou Andreas-Salomé, one of the first female analysts, once described analysis in a vivid simile that conveys the expansive nature of the experience for many of Freud's early followers.

> The way in which one beholds a person in psychoanalysis is something that goes beyond all affect toward him; somewhere in the depths both aversion and love become only differences of degree.
> A relationship is achieved beyond one's own fidelity or infidelity.
> Approximately this way: if hitherto one had so swiftly and so forcefully penetrated the partner that he too soon and to one's own disappointment was left behind, one now would turn quietly, strangely, and see him following and be close to him. And yet not close to him, but to all. Close anew to all, and in it, to oneself. And all the vanished persons of the past arise anew, whom one has sinned against by letting them go; they are there as from all eternity, marked by eternity—peaceful, monumental, and one with being itself, as the rock figures of Abu Simbel are one with the Egyptian rock and yet, in the form of men, sit enthroned over the water and the landscape. (1987, 192–193)

The reference to the temple at Abu Simbel is more than just a free association here, because a colored engraving of it hung *right above Freud's couch*. The vision of a monumental, human totality is thus again mediated through the specific archaeological setting of Berggasse 19, but here the unity is not just with the human, but with all of being itself, over which the human sits "enthroned."

Yet what is also striking in Lou's evocation of Freud's personal space is that it seems to convey a peaceful unity with the world that Freud never promised and seems rarely to have felt. Her words are redolent of the "oceanic feeling" that had become the secular interpretation of religious sentiment, particularly through the influence of Freud's friend, Romain Rolland. For Lou, freedom from the forces that lie smoldering in the past leads to a reconciliation with the past and with the whole of Being and Time. But Freud never promises that a freedom *from* history will lead to a freedom *in* history—only the most optimistic of European Jews could have assumed such a thing, and Freud was no optimist. Harold Bloom has written that "Freedom, for Freud, had to be freedom from the past, but never from time, the Jewish (and Freudian) reality principle. Pragmatically, Jewish freedom is freedom of interpretation, though Jewish (and Freudian) memory results in all meaning being overdetermined. What *is* freedom where everything is overdetermined, where character is fate, and there are, after all, no accidents?" (1989, 154).

The extension of historical understanding down into the underworld of unconscious motives increases knowledge, but does not promise reconciliation. The freedom that stands at the end of analysis cannot reconcile the patient to a world of blind Darwinian struggle; it merely releases him from hysterical misery into common, historically determined unhappiness (*Studies on Hysteria*, SE 2:305). The Rat Man, after all, went from his analytic cure to the battlefields of World War I, where he died. Thus we can see how Herbert Marcuse was right to insist that "Freud actually reveals the negativity of freedom," though we cannot all agree that Freud thus paradoxically points the way to "another possible freedom in which the repression of the instincts would be abolished along with political repression" (1970, 24). Freud seems temperamentally distanced from the utopian reveries of the Freudian Left. The reason for Freud's anti-utopian sentiment is clear: the revelation of Unreason in History puts us forever in a state of siege, knowing—as Freud reminded his readers during World War I—that where there is progress there can also be regression and a return of the repressed.[15]

Perhaps for this reason the only entity in Goethe's orphic poem that Freud did *not* invoke is Hope, whose power of flight effects the *annihilation* of the past:

Ein Wesen regt sich leicht und ungezügelt:
Aus Wolkendecke, Nebel, Regenschauer
Erhebt sie uns, mit ihr, durch sie beflügelt,
Ihr kennt sie wohl, sie schwärmt durch alle Zonen—
Ein Flügelschlag—und hinter uns Äonen!

A Being rises lightly and unrestrained:
From cloudy skies, fog, and driving rain
She lifts us up with her, giving us wings,
You know her well, she roams through every zone—
One beat of her wings—and eons lie behind us!

To stay true to Freud's historical attitude, then, one has to accept psychoanalysis ultimately as the "disenchanting product of the disenchantment of the world" (Bourdieu [1972] 1977, 92). Thus the true tenor of Freud's historical consciousness is *not* a form of nirvana or sublime vision, nor the gnostic use of history in order to master time, nor the springboard for a utopian reverie. It is rather something approaching a kind of gallows humor, an ironic insight similar to Mercutio's dying gests. As Freud confessed to H.D., "My discoveries are primarily not a heal-all. My discoveries are a basis for a very grave philosophy. There are few who understand this, *there are very few who are capable of understanding this*" (H.D. [1956] 1974, 18; original emphasis).

CONCLUSION

The Myth of Ur

Moses sent messengers from Kadesh to the king of Edom, "Thus says your brother Israel: You know all the adversity that has befallen us: how our ancestors went down to Egypt, and we lived in Egypt a long time; and the Egyptians oppressed us and our ancestors; and when we cried to the LORD, he heard our voice, and sent an angel and brought us out of Egypt; and here we are in Kadesh, a town on the edge of your territory. Now let us pass through your land. We will not pass through field or vine-yard, or drink water from any well; we will go along the King's Highway, not turning aside to the right hand or to the left until we have passed through your territory."

But Edom said to him, "You shall not pass through, or we will come out with the sword against you." The Israelites said to him, "We will stay on the highway; and if we drink of your water, we and our livestock, then we will pay for it. It is only a small matter; just let us pass through on foot." But he said, "You shall not pass through." And Edom came out against them with a large force, heavily armed. Thus Edom re-fused to give Israel passage through their territory; so Israel turned away from them.

—NUMBERS 20:14–21

[T]his royal road, which we have stated to be true and genuine philosophy, the Law calls the word and reason of God; for it is written, "Thou shalt not turn aside from the word which I command thee this day, to the right hand nor to the left." So that it is shown most manifestly that the word of God is identical with the royal road, since Moses' words are not to depart either from the royal road, or from this word, as if the two were synonymous, but to proceed with an upright mind along the middle and level road, which leads one aright.

—PHILO OF ALEXANDRIA, *The Posterity and Exile of Cain*

The interpretation of dreams is the royal road [*via regia*] to knowledge of the uncon-scious activities of the mind.

—FREUD, SENTENCE ADDED TO *Die Traumdeutung* IN 1909

CHAPTER 11

■

The Myth of Ur

Do not lose heart. Our ancient Jewish toughness
will prove itself in the end.
—Freud to Karl Abraham (December 26, 1908)

Is psychoanalysis a Jewish science? This question has haunted Freud's
Wissenschaft since his own time, when the term "Jewish science" appears
to have been disparagingly coined by analogy with Mary Baker Eddy's
"Christian Science" (Friedell [1931] 1954, 3:582). It is certainly true that
the Jewish predominance in the early movement worried Freud enough
that he tried to engineer a diplomatic Aryanization of its leadership structure, a plan that failed because of Jung's rebellion.[1] But from what I have
argued so far in relation to the archival sciences of antiquity, there is little that is specifically Jewish in the general historical armature of Freud's
method.[2] His method finds its inspiration in a historical outlook that
dominated Western Europe, and which came predominantly from either
devout or apostate Christian sources and was at the forefront of secular
thought. Although the historical, philological, and archaeological *Wissenschaften* did not inevitably lead one to utter atheism, they were cata-
lysts for a general turmoil in the religious sphere, particularly among
radical Christian theologians and religious scholars like David Strauss
and Ludwig Feuerbach. The influence of these *Wissenschaften* upon European Jews was in the formation of the *Wissenschaft des Judentums*, a "science" of Judaism that would lead to a whole new Jewish historical
perspective that diverged from rabbinical authority and ended the paradoxical neglect of historiography among the Jewish people (Yerushalmi

1982). Add to these currents the scientific materialism and evolutionary fervor of Freud's adolescence (along with Feuerbach and Buckle, he was reading Büchner's materialist gospel *Kraft und Stoff* in his rebellious teenage years), and one can see why an assimilating Jew would feel an affinity with the emergent secular culture's historicizing and materialist apparatus.

But while I think it is unprofitable to look always for something "essentially Jewish" about Freud's method, at the same time it would be completely ahistorical to ignore the Jewish *trajectory* of psychoanalysis; that is, its genesis through a vector of Jewish experience that was quite distinct. After all, the characteristics of a given socio-historical group cannot be simply ignored because one cannot find an appropriately essentializing cultural, textual, or ethnic genealogy for them. It was in Freud's day *very* Jewish in a sense to be highly devoted to Goethe, Schiller, and Wagner (whose music was played at the opening of the second Zionist congress). That is to say, it was a characteristic of the German-speaking Jewish *Bildungsbürgertum* to place a high value on *Kultur,* part of which included a particular placement of the archive of antiquity that was quite different from the historical vision of Jewish tradition. I would not care to reduce such cultural mandarinism to a mere "overzealous fulfillment of the norm," as if the Jews merely meant to out-German the Germans, though there might be an element of truth in that. It would rather appear to be the result of a variety of factors not unique to the Jewish bourgeoisie, and yet which had unique effects on that very group through the peculiar constellation of circumstances, characters, and opportunities.

One factor shaping the nature of the Jewish *Bildungsbürgertum* would be the particular route of social advancement opened to Jews through the *Gymnasium* system and the liberal professions, where scientific achievement became a dignified means of finding (or trying to find) one's place in society at a time when other avenues were closed. As statistics show, Viennese Jews were quick to make extraordinary use of this non-Jewish institution as a way of bettering the lives of their sons (Beller 1990, [1989] 1993; Cohen 1996, 199–201). By the time Freud graduated from his *Gymnasium,* the numerical majority of students in the school was Jewish (102 Catholic versus 300 Jewish students overall; Pokorny 1874, 44). Another factor that shaped this class was the common desire of all bourgeois smarting under the stigma of their mundane business backgrounds to turn their wealth into "cultural capital." This was as true of Heinrich Schliemann and the Evans family as of any Jewish parvenu patron of the arts, though the Jews had far worse historical stereotypes to overcome. A third (and for my purposes, crucial) factor was enlightened Europe's refurbishing of Greek antiquity as the suitably non-Christian source of a centralized European tradition and identity, a vital maneuver for giving purchase to secular culture in the face of religious authority, whether Jewish or Christian. As we have seen in cases such as that of Feuerbach, the emergent secular culture developed an affinity with pagan antiquity that can be linked to various shifts in aesthetic and sexual norms, psychological and biological ideas, and seismic political developments. As Yaacov Shavit (1999) has shown in ample detail, the rapprochement with Greece was just as important to the formation of modern secular Jewish identity as it was for gentiles, even though its resonances were quite different. So the Helleno-centric bias of the *Gymnasium* created a common ground for gentiles and Jews, even if they approached it from very different perspectives.

In many ways, Freud's compulsion for antiquity is a symptom of his being a European intellectual, not a specifically "Jewish" intellectual; the common ground Freud and Jung found initially in their mythological excursions and analogical assumptions is proof enough of that. And yet, as I shall trace by way of concluding this study, there is a discernibly Jewish trajectory to key aspects of Freud's compulsion that makes it unique and worth discussing in relation to his sense of Jewishness. My ultimate objective is not to attempt another disclosure of the secret Jewish essence of psychoanalysis, but rather to illustrate that psychoanalysis was the unique product of an age when the multiple marginality of European Jewry helped to create a distinct coin of vantage on human experience, which in turn resonated with non-Jews and perhaps in ways that were not intended, for example, by replacing the confessional with the analytic hour.[3] Therefore I shall stress the heterogeneity of this trajectory, even as I return to some familiar themes in the vociferous debate on Freud's Jewish identity.[4]

By "multiple marginality" I refer in particular to the Jewish psychoanalysts' exclusion from three distinct value spheres: the devout Judaism they rejected with varying degrees of vehemence; the dominant Catholic culture of Austria which most of them did not care to enter through conversion; and the competing European nationalisms into which the Austro-Hungarian Empire dissolved, and which often made a point of excluding Jews as they constituted themselves.[5] In a sense, psychoanalysis is, as Rank observed, a symptom of the crisis of patriarchy, since its early adherents were operating without God the Father and without a Father-land—but this is to anticipate our discussion (1931, 191–192). We can see Freud's unique trajectory best by beginning with the scene of education.

From Hannibal to Oedipus

One of the most poignant and pathetic stories from Freud's youth involves a fateful walk with his father, Jakob. Freud's father recounted how long ago on the streets of Freiberg in Moravia he had been forced off the sidewalk by a gentile on a Sabbath when he was well dressed with a new fur cap, which his assailant knocked into the mud (*The Interpretation of Dreams*, SE 4:197). He was trying to express to his son that things were much better for Jews now than in those days, and in the late 1860s, when the conversation occurred, there were real reasons to be optimistic about the changing civil status of Jews, and particularly in Vienna (full civil equality had come to the Jews in 1867—on paper). But the young Freud experienced a great moment of disappointment when his father told him all he did on that day long ago was to pick his cap up out of the mud. "This struck me as unheroic conduct on the part of the big, strong man who was holding the little boy by the hand. I contrasted this situation with another which fitted my feelings better: the scene in which Hannibal's father, Hamilcar Barca, made his boy swear before the household altar to take vengeance on the Romans. Ever since that time Hannibal had had a place in my phantasies" (SE 4:197).

This scene of memory is quite revealing as it connects Freud's personal life to the themes of the family romance and the hero, which both figure recurrently in his deployment of the ancient archive. Having lost respect for his father, the boy seeks an alternative; from the mandarin's gallery of historical worthies, he finds the *filial* hero Hannibal. The shift from father to son is important, for it shows us the key element of paternal romance: Hannibal is not to replace Jakob Freud, but rather the young Sigmund Freud; the father's failure is retained in that it must be rectified by filial agency, giving room for the son to be and be rid of the Father. In other words, young Sigmund does not re-imagine the scene in Freiberg, but rather the scene in Vienna, wishing his father had imparted to him the sacred task of revenge. He nowhere states that his wish was for his father to have slain the offending *goy* of yore. The failure of the Jewish father in this tale is a failure to impart a proper pattern of masculine agency to his son; he failed to give his son the proper mission.

As Daniel Boyarin has discussed, this is a painful moment in masculine self-definition in that Freud failed to appreciate his father's quality of *Edelkayt* (literally, "nobility"), the traditional Jewish trait of long-suffering patience and personal dignity that had developed over the centuries of pariah status (1997, 33–38). Under the influence of his *Gymnasium* curriculum, which placed great stock in reading the lives of illustrious men (*viri illustres*) such as Hannibal and Alexander, Freud saw Jakob's Jewish strategy of dignified survival as simply a failure to act like a man— that is, like a violent gentile hero. Fritz Wittels once said in his polemical work *Der Taufjude*, "I wish the Jews had fewer martyrs and more Maccabees" (1904, 11). The rationale was clear: "the free man strikes back when he is openly attacked, and if his attackers are in the majority, then he will perish" (1904, 11). Thus the very fact of Jewish survival is not a cause for pride, as Wittels argued; the great intellectual achievements of modern Jews (including the baptized ones) "mean nothing, if honor has thereby been damaged" (1904, 11).

So here we see how the archive of antiquity intervenes in a specifically Jewish life in a rather complex manner. Freud knew, of course, that it was all too common for any schoolboy to identify with the underdog (SE 4:196); this is why he described his attachment to Hannibal ironically as a *Gymnasialschwärmerei* or "high school infatuation" (Masson 1985, 285). Yet the Semitic Hannibal was in a sense more attractive as a model for Freud for the very distance that differentiated him from his own family identity: Hannibal was in every important way *not* a Jew (not the stereotypical *Ostjude* Hasid who gets his *shtreimel* knocked off and does nothing about it), but a pugnacious Semite of a different order. Thus while Freud was doing something very typical for a *Gymnasium* student in admiring Hannibal, he did it for atypical reasons. Hannibal is therefore the focus of a *double* resistance: a resistance to traditional Jewish *Edelkayt* in the face of oppression, and a resistance to Roman Catholic anti-Semitism represented by the specter of a monolithic Rome. The Hannibal scenario thus shows the hallmarks of multiple marginality to which I referred above. It is a position of opposition, an anti-anti-Semitism, and it is significant that Freud defined his Jewish identity in part as an oppositional self-awareness: "as a Jew I was prepared to be in the opposition and to renounce agreement with the 'compact majority'" (Ernst Freud 1960, 367). Also through Hannibal, the theme of national resistance is reduced to a kind of family *jihad* against hereditary enemies and does not resonate with any *Blut und Boden* populism, as might an Italian, Czech, or Magyar act of defiance against the Germano-Austrian elite. Hannibal is the avenger who brings the war home to the enemy's *patria*, after all, something that might well resonate with a father-landless Jew.

But strategies of pure opposition do not suffice. Freud reinvented his father as the upwardly mobile are wont to do in any age, but he was less free to reinvent his fatherland, though, to be sure, his flirtation with German nationalism while at university points in this direction. But in these youthful negotiations of identity which define his personal trajectory, it is important to see how they fail as much as how they succeed, for Freud's attempt to become a German nationalist—to secure himself a fatherland to bequeath to his sons (cf. *The Interpretation of Dreams*, SE 5:442)—was foiled by the emergent anti-Semitism of German nationalism itself. His feeling of Germanness became something "which I long ago decided to suppress" (Ernst Freud 1960, 203). "Whenever I have experienced feelings of national exaltation," he confessed to the B'nai B'rith Lodge in Vienna, "I have tried to suppress them as disastrous and unfair, frightened by the warning example of those nations among which we Jews live" (Ernst Freud 1960, 366–367). He remained in a sense a canceled German, a ~~German~~ Jew.[6]

Thus far, then, the distinctly Jewish trajectory we are tracing involves the self-awareness of belonging "to an alien race" (SE 4:196), a certain crisis in the transmission of masculine ideals, and a failure to achieve a nationalist solution to the problem of secular identity. In what follows below, we shall see how the historical alienation of the Jews, the need for an aggressive male life plan, and a critical appraisal of nationalist ideologies are woven into the tapestry of Freud's engagement with antiquity, an engagement deeply implicated in his scientific improvisation of psychoanalysis.

Freud's predicament over masculine agency vis-à-vis the ancient archive was no idiosyncrasy, but was symptomatic of his age and even caused a shift in Jewish historical consciousness. At least, such a judgment is to be derived from the textbooks used in Freud's mandatory religion classes at the *Gymnasium*. Leopold Breuer clearly saw that just as the Greeks and Romans "found in the history of their great men the most appropriate means for the *Bildung* and upbringing of their young," so too the Jews "should certainly not scorn and reject such an educational means in a time of decline [*Gesunkenheit*]" (1860, v). In order to stave off the decline in Jewish historical consciousness (*Selbstbewußtsein*) in the age of assimilation, the presentation of Jewish history must show Jewish figures as independent agents (*selbstthätig*) acting under their own power. This poses a certain friction between Jewish history as it ought to be written and Jewish tradition:

> The failure to recognize this [heroic, individualist] view has weakened, even undermined the Jews' sense of their own history from time immemorial. One thought it was an injury to Divine Power to also let a human being perform his very own feat in God's kingdom, and so, for example, one made do at Hanukkah with the prayer of thanksgiving על הנסים and במי מתתיהו and with the saga of the little jug of oil by way of historical explanation, while even the very names of the Maccabees remained unknown to most of the *Volk*. (Breuer 1860, vi)

The emergence of a pugnacious Jewish male identity has been traced along with the history of Zionism and the refurbishing of the Maccabees as proper national heroes, but the important thing to note in relation to Freud is that he nowhere seems to have fallen into a "separate but equal" sense of history grounded in a recovered Jewish heroic tradition.[7] On the contrary, the integrative figures from his youth are martial *goyim* like Napoleon, Alexander, and Oliver Cromwell. His one reputedly Jewish war hero from youth, Napoleon's Marshal Masséna, was far more a scion of the French Revolution than a son of the covenant (and as Freud himself later realized, he may not even have been Jewish [SE 4:197–198]).

Alexander represents a particularly important figure of integration in Freud's life, one that takes us away from the dead-end oppositional strategies of Hannibal and into the more complex phenomena of cultural assimilation as configured through Hellenism. As we have seen, the cult of Alexander in the nineteenth century was linked to German aspirations of political unity and cultural ambition. Freud's preference for Alexander over the Maccabees betrays a very distinct kind of Hellenism: not the particularist Hellenism of the classical *polis*, nor a Hellenism defined dichotomously against Jewish tradition as in the Maccabean narratives, but rather a universalizing Hellenism seen through the hindsight of the later Hellenistic era. In this regard, it is important to note how Freud's own schoolbooks sought to link both the Jewish and German communities historically to the figure of Alexander. Breuer's Jewish history book relates a tale from the Babylonian Talmud (Yoma 69a—also related by Josephus, *Jewish Antiquities* 11.8.4–5) which describes how Alexander came to punish the recalcitrant Jews of Palestine. Surprisingly, when Alexander confronted the High Priest Yaddua, he suddenly did him deep reverence, recognizing the name of God on the priest's diadem (Breuer 1860, 170–171). A dream vision had assured Alexander he would prosper on his Persian campaign, and he had suddenly realized the vision came to him from the God of the Jews. In gratitude, he personally honored the God of the Jews and gave them special concessions and privileges. This was an apocryphal tale, but one that clearly was meant to legitimate Judaism within the power relations of the Hellenistic world.[8] Breuer relays it without qualification in his history textbook, passing it on as historical truth.[9]

The Austrian Christian editors of Freud's Latin text of the *Memorabilia Alexandri Magni* were perhaps even more dishonest in that they deliberately changed an anecdote about Adriatic Celts (Arrian, *Anabasis* 1.4.6–8; Strabo, *Geography* 7.3.8 [c 302]) to be one concerning Danubian Germans, as if to make the story to be about the ancestors of the Viennese *Gymnasium* students (Schmidt and Gehlen 1865, 9.17–30). The story goes that Alexander asked the physically imposing Germanic envoys what they feared most in the world, expecting that his own power held them in awe. Instead, they replied they feared nothing, save that the sky might fall down upon them, but that they greatly esteemed the friendship of brave men. Alexander was dumbstruck by the Germans' arrogance, but made an alliance with them all the same. In both of these apocryphal tales, Alexander is a figure of memory who becomes "remembered" as a way of inscribing elements of group identity (the piety of the Jews, the bravery of the Germans) into a universal past. Both groups are able to negotiate a better footing with the flow of inevitable power through a show of resistance which in turn earns them respect; we might term this "cooptation with dignity." This pattern of universalizing Hellenism does not require the radical renunciations inherent in the paradigm of Christian conversion, and it is not hard to see its existential relevance to assimilating Jews.[10]

In light of such a universalizing Hellenism, then, it is also not surprising that the paradigm of Oedipus came to the fore as a model that solved various tensions arising in relation to male identity and integrative aspirations. It is significant first of all that the oedipal model was conditioned and mediated by the great bourgeois institution of the theater. The theater in Vienna, especially the Burgtheater, where Adolf Wildbrandt's production of *König Ödipus* was performed in the 1880s and '90s, was itself an organ of German culture in an age when German cultural nationalism was a matter of embarrassment for the Habsburg regime (Armstrong 1999b). As Fritz Wittels recalled many years later, the Viennese theater of the 1880s and '90s was an institution where Jews could see themselves as very much a part of that culture (1931, 14–16). They could see the great Jewish actor Adolf Sonnenthal in the quintessentially German role of Faust, without hint of contradiction or irony. They could also see him in the role of Hamlet, a figure quite crucial to Freud's oedipal truth from its conception.[11] Theodor Herzl, later the founder of modern Zionism, realized his ambition to have his plays performed in the Burgtheater long before turning to politics. Freud's own *Doppelgänger* on the stage was the Jewish playwright Arthur Schnitzler, a doctor turned anatomist of the modern soul.[12] Jews could therefore feel a very real link to the cultural sphere of the theater, which since the age of Lessing had a strong role in articulating the imaginary of national consciousness. "When the Germans were not yet hated by the world, Jews might frequently contribute to the renown of the German idea" (Wittels 1931, 15).

The institution of spectacle gives a specular unity to culture, and Freud uses the *theatrical* success of *Oedipus Tyrannus* to claim the universality of the eponymous complex. So in a sense, the theatrical paradigm itself responds to the need to feel both a strong unity with the national culture and a profound link to heroic individualism as manifested on the stage. The Hellenism of Freud's Oedipus is thus inclusive (versus Philo's exclusive view of it), and the play even subsumes the patriarchal conflict of Freud's earlier "Hannibal complex." For the oedipal hero definitely will *not* let himself be thrown off his path, even by one who clearly has a superior social status. We could even entertain the idea that there is a symbolic condensation in Oedipus for Freud, such that through the Theban's patricidal encounter Freud kills off both his father's *goy* adversary *and* his unheroic father, asserting through this filial hero the proper role of the male. In point of fact, Freud acted out such aggression quite memorably before his own sons in the summer of 1901, dispersing an entire crowd of anti-Semitic hecklers with nothing but his walking stick to wield at them (Martin Freud [1958] 1983, 70–71). And yet, as Madelon Sprengnether observes, Freud's shift of the oedipal paradigm to a *complex* rather than a pattern of action disables the very conflict he set out to highlight. "The father's authority will prevent the son from enacting his incestuous desire, hence instilling in him the habit of renunciation necessary for participation in culture. If the mother is unavailable, moreover, it is not because of any wayward desire of her own, but rather because of the son's deference to his father's authority" (2000, 26). As such, the notorious patricidal theme of psychoanalysis can be seen as much to construct a view of patriarchy as to deconstruct it.

It might seem historically relevant to link Freud's obsession with patricide to a loss of paternal authority, and to assume for the Jewish *Bildungsbürgertum* that this means the erosion of the kind of patriarchal structure that typified the Jewish communities of the *Judengasse* and *shtetl*. Freud's Acropolis letter might even be read in such a way as to expose the guilt of the "Hellenizing" sons over the memory of their more traditional father. But the Viennese Jewish community was not at all structured in a traditionally patriarchal fashion, and Freud's free-thinking father was as unsuitable a model for the angry Moses as he was for the cyclopean *Urvater*.[13] Here we must see that the historical dimensions of patriarchy Freud deploys and deconstructs go well beyond the sphere of his Jewish experience. The cultural configuration of the Father's authority in Freud's writing seems hardly Jewish at all: the *patria potestas* of Roman Law (SE 4:257), the transparently Latin concept embedded in the very term "father *imago*," the castrating antics of Hesiodic gods (SE 4:256), the "refined hypocrisy" of Greek tragedy (*Totem and Taboo*, SE 13:156), the Nietzschean Superman (*Group Psychology and the Analysis of the Ego*, SE 18:123) and the mysterious transgressions of totemic sacrifice have little or nothing to do with Jewish authority or Jewish consciousness.[14] Harold Bloom has even said that "Freud's grandest heresy, from a Judaic perspective, is his transfer of the Hebraic trope of the fatherhood of Yahweh to the hideous totemic ancestor god of the primal horde" (1989, 154). The primal patricide is more able to be seen as a perverse genealogy for the Christian sacrament of communion than any Jewish ritual or idea. The Father that looms over the Freudian scenario is thus not Jakob Freud, but a symbolic amalgam that, as Freud's theory itself explains, cannot be reduced to *one's* father.

Freud situates his patriarchal de/construction within *Wissenschaft* and a naturalizing discourse of human sexuality, and here the gambit of Hellenism is doubly implicated in the improvisation of a universal scientific language. On the one hand, the Greeks as the spectral fathers of empirical science maintain their constant presence in his work, as we have seen in the cases of Sophocles, Artemidorus, Empedocles, and Plato. The spiritual fatherland of science is the realm of Logos, the secular god with the Greek name, as he proclaims in his anti-religious polemic (*The Future of an Illusion*, SE 21:54). But the voice that makes such a proclamation has not ceased to be a Jewish voice, if we carefully listen to the choir of which it is a member. The philosopher and theologian Hermann Cohen staked the Jewish affinity with the grand cause of German *Kultur* precisely on the common Hellenism that links the two cultures, and more precisely on the Logos linking the Alexandria of Philo to the Berlin of the German philosophers and theologians ([1915–1916] 1924). This appeal to a tradition of Jewish Hellenism may indeed have its frictions with rabbinical Judaism and have suspicious affinities with Christianity, but it still remains an historically identifiable ground for a Jew to stand on.[15]

How this gambit of Hellenism can serve a Jewish perspective deserves illustration. I wish to put the case that in Freud's great moment of stress and disappointment with the "Aryan" Christian Jung, what emerged from his sense of alienation was not any return to the Judaism of his fathers, but to a Hellenistic Judaism of his own improvising. I refer here to his first Moses study, "The Moses of Michelangelo" (1914; SE 13:211–238). First, it is telling that the center of this study is not the man Moses as it would later be for Freud, but rather a sculpted statue very much in the Greek figural tradition and sitting in a church in Rome. This insistent object draws him into the Greco-Roman economy of the gaze; yet, its theme at the same time draws him into a drama of Jewish guilt, such that the disturbance is created not through obsessive seeing but rather through obsessively being seen. "How often have I mounted the steep steps from the unlovely Corso Cavour to the lonely piazza where the deserted church stands, and have essayed to support the angry scorn of the hero's glance! Sometimes I have crept cautiously out of the half-gloom of the interior as though I myself belonged to the mob upon whom his eye is turned—the mob which can hold fast no conviction, which has neither faith nor patience, and which rejoices when it has regained its illusory idols" (SE 13:213). Like the enigma of Gradiva's gait, Moses' curious posture stimulates in Freud a narrative renewal of the scene, but one that leads to a very different interpretation from the traditional view of the angry lawgiver. In arguing that Michelangelo created a Moses "superior to the historical or traditional Moses," Freud effectively recreates this Moses as the Philonic philosophical hero (SE 13:233).

In Freud's narrative reconstruction of Moses' posture, he explains that the figure represents not the oncoming wrath and destruction of the Tables of the Law, but rather the calming self-mastery of a man in control of himself. "In this way he has added something new and more than human to the figure of Moses; so that the giant frame with its tremendous physical power becomes only a concrete expression of the highest mental achievement that is possible in a man, that of struggling successfully against an inward passion for the sake of a cause to which he has devoted himself" (SE 13:233). This recalls the more than human figure of Philo's *On the Life of Moses*, which recounts Moses' extraordinary education as a child in all the wisdom of the Egyptians, Greeks, and Chaldaeans. Through his unusual preparation, this Moses becomes the Platonic master of himself through the hegemony of reason:

> And he tamed, and appeased, and brought under due command every one of the other passions which are naturally and as far as they are themselves concerned frantic, and violent, and unmanageable. And if any one of them at all excited itself and endeavored to get free from restraint he administered severe punishment to it, reproving it with severity of language; and in short, he repressed all the principal impulses and most violent affections of the soul, and kept guard over them as over a restive horse, fearing lest they might break all bounds and get beyond the power of reason which ought to be their guide to restrain them, and so throw everything everywhere into confusion. For these passions are the causes of all good and of all evil; of good when they submit to the authority of dominant reason (ἡγεμόνι λόγῳ), and of evil when they break out of bounds and scorn all government and restraint. (*De vita Mosis* 1.25 = Philo 1993, 461)

So rather than representing some sort of retreat to Jewish authority, I would argue this "return to Moses" is a reinvention along the lines of what we have to term a kind of improvised Jewish Hellenism, one that puts a premium on rational self-mastery and the subjugation of the irrational within (through even a kind of self-admonitory "talking cure"). Moses was undoubtedly a figure from Freud's Jewish past, one to which he returned with ambivalence; but the Moses he refashioned for himself, like the reinvented Punic father, conforms to a heroic tradition that better responds to the trajectory of his experience, especially at the time he was feeling like the embittered patriarch whose foolish sons would not guard the patrimony of his Truth. Freud's Moses is a pointed departure from the wrathful patriarch, created through a sympathetic reading aided (as he expressly claims) by psychoanalytic insight (SE 13:212). One need not tack on a textual genealogy going from Moses Mendelssohn, Salomon Maimon, Spinoza, all the way back to Maimonides and Philo in order to appreciate here how Freud forges a Judeo-Hellenism for his own purposes. It was his own synaesthesis responding to his peculiar needs, yet it reverberates within an identifiable tradition of Jewish thought.[16]

But if Hellenism offered a common ground upon which to build a universal *Wissenschaft* through the Logos, it was a ground that provided a giddy footing on account of the return of the repressed which it enabled. I began this study by situating Freud's compulsion for antiquity in relation to the ancient archive's precarious placement in modern European thought, and I here return to Hellenism's second form of implication in the Freudian project. As sanitized and bedecked with fig-leaves as it was, the ancient archive always retained its explosive potential for mischief, and in 1889 it let out another one of its minor tremors with the publication of Nietzsche's *Twilight of the Idols*. This text clearly showed a pointedly different deployment of Hellenism, one Nietzsche had delivered in installments since *The Birth of Tragedy* (1872) and that was increasingly rooted in the Foucauldian "truth of sex," rather than the humanistic pieties of the Logos.

> We are affected quite differently when we probe the concept of "Greek" which Winckelmann and Goethe constructed for themselves and find it incompatible with that element out of which Dionysian art evolved—the orgy. [...] For it is only in the Dionysian mysteries, in the psychology of the Dionysian condition, that the *fundamental fact* of the Hellenic instinct expresses itself— its "will to life." *What* did the Hellene guarantee to himself with these mysteries? *Eternal* life, the eternal recurrence of life; the future promised and consecrated in the past; the triumphant Yes to life beyond death and change; *true* life as collective continuation of life through procreation, through the mysteries of sexuality. It was for this reason that the *sexual* symbol was to the Greeks the symbol venerable as such, the intrinsic profound meaning of all antique piety. ([1889] 1968, 109; original emphasis)

In this Nietzschean polemic of the "sacred road" of sex, Christianity emerges as the great enemy "with *ressentiment against* life in its foundations, which made of sexuality something impure: it threw *filth* on the beginning, on the prerequisite of our life ..." ([1889] 1968, 110; original emphasis).

The value of this naughty Hellenism for a Jew like Freud was that it declared a common enemy in Christianity.[17] Though there were secular types who would blame Judaism for marring the primal truths of Hellenism in Western culture and bearing the bastard child of Christianity, a secular Jew could join forces with post-Nietzschean Hellenism and ignore the accusation in favor of a shared opposition.[18] It is the tartuffery of the Christian dominant culture that Freud targets, for example, in the Leonardo study with words that echo Nietzsche's. "If one makes a broad survey of the sexual life of our time and in particular of the classes who sustain civilization, one is tempted to declare that it is only with reluctance that the majority of people alive today obey the command to propagate their kind; they feel that their dignity as human beings suffers and is degraded in the process" (SE 11:96–97). In earlier times, it was different, "the genitals were the pride and hope of living beings; they were worshipped as gods and transmitted the divine nature of their functions to all newly learned activities" (SE 11:97). Thus the apostate sons of pastors and Hasids can intone together the elegy of lost vitality. Thus also derives the clear affinity between the psychoanalyst and the creative artist, since psychoanalysis "is forever striking upon the vital pleasure principle which irradiates all psychic events; and this granting of a meaning to what is only apparently meaningless, *Eros sive Natura* [a play on Spinoza's *Deus sive Natura*], must delight every artist" (Wittels 1931, 25).

Freud's curious Judeo-Hellenism can thus be credited with suturing together the Logos of scientific emancipation (which Nietzsche held at arm's length) with that instinctual Dionysian undercurrent hawked as the necessary antidote to the *niaiserie allemande* of Winckelmannian classicism and Christian prudery. Freud strategically linked the "sacred road" of sexuality with the royal road of the unconscious, allowing for ample access to attack his old foe, the Church Militant, in the process. It was a tenet of Freud's "psychological Judaism" that Jews could readily understand him since they had so much less repression to overcome, whereas Aryan Christians encountered more layers of resistance.[19] Hence his "co-irreligionists" like Ferenczi could readily participate in a psycho-excavation of the hidden Greek within the European, an act in which the very Jewish psychoanalytic movement had the upper hand. Ferenczi wrote to Freud in 1908 (May 9):

> In the April issue of the *Neuer Rundschau* I read the following lines by Gerhart Hauptmann in a description of his travels in Greece:
> And it becomes strangely vivid to me, how Greek culture is

buried, but still not dead. It is buried very deeply, but only in the souls of living men; and only when one knows all the layers of marl and slag under which the Greek soul lies buried, as one knows the layers over the Mycenaean, Trojan, or Olympian sites of old cultural remains, of stone and ore, then perhaps the great hour of excavation will also come for the living heritage of Greece.

I would like to call Hauptmann's attention to the extent to which the excavations have already progressed. (Brabant et al. 1993–2000, 1:9)

From Oedipus to Mithras

Our story could end here were it not for the fact that Freud's archival maneuvers vis-à-vis Christianity went well beyond the strategic alignment of Apollonian and Dionysian Judeo-Hellenisms. Freud's conflict with Jung was overdetermined by many factors, rooted as it was in the explicitly paternal-filial dynamic of their personal relationship and the touchy political relations between the Viennese Jews and their Swiss Christian colleagues. But the particular idiom of their final conflict—brought out in the pages of *Totem and Taboo* and *Transformations and Symbols of the Libido*—was a Walpurgisnacht of ancient and primitive cultures in which, as they both felt, the central truth of psychoanalysis was at stake. At this decisive moment Freud's oppositional *habitus*—in part, the heritage of his Jewish experience—deployed no simple originary Hellenism or Hebraism, but resorted rather to the Myth of Ur. This was not Ur of the Chaldees, the home of Abraham, but the Ur of the *Urzeit*, the *Urhorde*, and the *Urvater*, the realm, that is to say, of Darwinian prehistory. Fritz Wittels remarked that this work was an attempt to follow Jung into the domain of folk-psychology and to annihilate him "on his own vantage ground" ([1924] 1971, 191). As Freud himself commented to Karl Abraham, the work would "serve to cut us off cleanly from all Aryan religiousness" (Abraham and Freud 1965, 139). Written as a tale of patricide, it is a work with decidedly filicidal intentions—annihilating the errant Jung's revisionism and the "Aryan" penchant for evading the ugly truth.

Totem and Taboo distills very carefully Freud's anti-Christian polemic of the time, while remaining rather reticent about Judaism. What seems clear from Freud's personal remarks is that the conflict appeared to him as the failure of Christians to live up to the challenge of science in the case of psychoanalysis, a challenge that Jews seemed more predisposed to meet. Writing to Ferenczi (June 8, 1913), Freud said,

> On the matter of Semitism: there are certainly great differences from the Aryan spirit. We can become convinced of that every day. Hence, there will surely be different world views and art here and there. But there should not be a particular Aryan or Jewish science. The results may be identical, and only their presentation may vary. [. . .] If these differences occur in conceptualizing objective relations in science, then something is wrong. It was our desire not to interfere with their more distant worldview and religion, *but we considered ours to be quite favorable for conducting science.* You had heard that Jung had declared in America that ψα [psychoanalysis] was not a science but a religion. That would certainly illuminate the whole difference. *But there the Jewish spirit regretted not being able to join in.* (Brabant et al. 1993, 1:490–491; my emphasis)

He ends this letter with a remark that suggests his pleasure at striking the Aryan *Geist* in its religious heart: "It couldn't hurt to be somewhat derisive.—Since knocking off the work on totem I have been light and gay."

However, Freud's sense of Jewish identity is tied up with the self-discipline of science here, not with the content of Jewish culture. In *Totem and Taboo* he strikes back once again with an archival reconstruction that is careful to avoid the contents of Jewish tradition, save for a passing reference to circumcision which serves to underwrite the validity of the castration complex (SE 13:153, note 1). Instead, the book bristles with the names of British ethnologists, scholars, and scientists like E. B. Tylor, William Robertson Smith, James Frazer, Andrew Lang, J. J. Atkinson, and Charles Darwin, who are joined by an equally august crowd of prominent secular Jews: Franz Boas, Émile Durkheim, Marcel Mauss, and Salomon Reinach.[20] Freud makes a point of merely echoing the scandalous equation of the Christian Eucharist with the primitive totem meal, something suggested long before him by Frazer among others.[21] His main contribution is simply to suture the ritual structure of totems and taboos to the narrative of Darwin's primal horde and Atkinson's "cyclopean family," all in the light of the psychoanalytic theory of trauma and the father complex (SE 13:140–143). Ultimately his most radical shift is to deploy the vast evidentiary array of comparative ethnography at the service of analogical argument, based on the idea of a "return of totemism in childhood." Once again, it is analogy that transforms the possibilities of the evidentiary within the psychoanalytic domain.

The result is a complete reversal of the structure of Abrahamic religion, something that touches traditional Judaism as much as it does Christianity. Instead of the filicidal thematics of the Akedah—the Binding of Isaac, central to the religious imaginary of the Jews—or of the economy of salvation (the Christian God's gracious counterpoint to the Akedah, the sacrifice of *His* only begotten Son), Freud's oedipal truth insists upon a patricidal thematics which, as Ferenczi duly noted, makes the Oedipus complex the fulcrum "supported on which one can unravel all the secrets of the soul" (Brabant et al. 1993, 1:494).[22] As mentioned in chapter 7, this represents a curious backtracking from the original fantasy status of the Oedipus complex, one that now insists on the literal murder and cannibalization of the primal father. Though this returns the crimes of Oedipus to their rigorously *non-symbolic* literality (*pace* Jung and his quasi-Pauline "ceremony of atonement") in line with the insistent literalism of Freud's reading of Sophocles, the historical existence of the primal father is later couched in terms that are an obvious mockery of the Incarnation: "God the Father once walked upon the earth in bodily form and exercised his sovereignty as chieftain of the primal human horde until his sons united to slay him" ("Preface to Reik's *Ritual: Psycho-Analytic Studies*," SE 17:262).[23]

Freud's gothic Myth of Ur certainly engages in the scandal of prehistory, and it is remarkable for its peculiar construal of totemism, a reigning vogue in religious studies at the time.[24] Where the Jewish socialist Émile Durkheim saw the collective intellectual power operating in religion, even in its totemic forms, Freud saw collective neurosis and his dread "historical" truth.[25] From the time of *Totem and Taboo* onward, Freud's social theory would continue to reenact the scenario of the Myth of Ur, using it as the convenient explanation for everything from Greek tragedy and the transference neuroses to the cult of personality in nationalist movements, the mystique of authority in the army, and the place of God in religion. He continued to mull over the implications of this primal reality for heroic culture, which seems locked in a cycle of regressive traumatic mummery. Greek tragedy, for example, is now in its form clearly just a "refined hypocrisy," a restaging of the primal patricide in the beguiling disguise of a sympathetic chorus lamenting a suffering hero (*Totem and Taboo*, SE 13:155–157). Thus the genre of tragedy as a whole is now officially co-opted into the explanatory system of psychoanalysis (and one wonders if this is Freud's response to Nietzsche's *Birth of Tragedy*); Freud even refers to his own myth as "the tragic drama of the primal father" (*Urvatertragödie — Moses and Monotheism*, SE 23:135). By 1921, heroic epic is also co-opted and becomes the clever means of depicting the historical emergence of individual psychology through an identification with the Son who kills the Father, who evolves in turn from the role of heroic patricide into becoming the Father God himself through apotheosis (*Group Psychology*, SE 18:135–137). This shows us very clearly the complicity between patriarchy and hyoarchy (i.e., the rule of the sons) in the paternal romance. Later still, the heroic figure of Moses becomes another stand in for the primal father and is murdered by the Hebrews (SE 23:129); the same relates to Jesus Christ (SE 23:135–136), who previously had been seen as just another patricidal son (*Totem and Taboo*, SE 13:154). This Freudian monomyth attains all the simplifying beauty of a paranoid construction, for as Wilhelm Stekel wryly commented, Freud had a "primal horde complex"—"He is the Old Man, afraid of his disciples" (Wittels [1924] 1971, 192). Freud's "archive fever" is very much a patriarchal malaise, an *Unbehagen* (uneasiness) as his theory of civilization diagnoses it (*Civilization and Its Discontents*, SE 21:131–132).

What is most revealing of this new Myth of Ur within the culture of psychoanalysis is that it became firmly attached to the mythical status of Freud himself as the man with the courage to declare such truths in the first place. Though he finished writing it with a sense of elation, he later had severe misgivings about it. But his good son Sándor (i.e., the Magyar "Alexander") Ferenczi quickly explained Freud's own feelings in the light of the pattern of his discoveries:

> I am thinking after all that your subsequent vacillation is actually a displaced *retrospective obedience* with respect to the fathers (and your own father), who in this work are depriving you of the last remnants of your power over the soul of man. Your work is namely also a totem meal; you are the priest of *Mithras*, who singlehandedly kills the father—your students are the audience to this "holy" action.— You yourself compared the significance of the Totem paper with that of the *Interpretation of Dreams.*—But the latter was the "reaction to [your] father's death"! In the *Interpretation of Dreams* you carried out the struggle against your own father, in the work on Totem, against the ghostly, religious father imagoes.—Hence, the *festive joy* at the work's coming into being (at the sacrificial act), which was then followed by subsequent *scruples*.

I am firmly convinced the work on Totem will one day become the nodal point of the study of the history of civilization. (Brabant et al. 1993–2000, 1:494; original emphasis)

With his reference to Mithraism, Ferenczi picked up on a point in *Totem and Taboo* where he had contrasted the cult of Mithras with Christianity. The two religions were in a competition in the ancient world, and "for a time it was doubtful which of the two deities would gain the victory" (SE 13:153).[26] In Freud's view, the sculptural motif of Mithras slaying the cosmic bull "represented a son who was alone in sacrificing his father and thus redeemed his brothers from their burden of complicity in the deed" (SE 13:153). In the Christian myth it is rather Christ who "sacrificed his own life and so redeemed the company of brothers from original sin" (SE 13:153).

Ferenczi thus obligingly cast Freud in the role of redeemer-patricide (a perfectly oedipal role!), overtly tying Freud's heroic self-analysis to his slaying of the cosmic bull of religion.[27] This sets psychoanalytic truth up as a heroic act which replicates the earlier rivalry with Christianity that Mithraism allegedly posed, and it bears remembering in reference to the psychoanalysts' corporate identity that Mithraism was particularly strong in the Roman army. *Totem and Taboo* is thus a bold declaration for the manly intellectual elite that God not only is dead, but was always dead. How this relates to Freud's polemic with Christianity is revealed by another loyal son, Ernest Jones, who made the same association as Ferenczi in reference to Freud's historical role:

That the son wishes to murder his father and to marry his mother you showed thirteen years ago; *but while Jung devalues this discovery by calling the wish "merely symbolic," you on the contrary go on to point out that it is dread reality.* Probably this progress on your part indicates a still further personal development in an even more absolute conviction of the unqualified truth of the discovery (*wahr; aber so wahr!*). Hence the impression the present work makes on you. At all events that is my own opinion, and if there is any truth in it I sincerely trust you will not weaken what you have written, but will stand by every word. *You have chosen the part of Mithras, and must play it out with his courage, as you always have.* (Paskauskas 1993, 207; my emphasis)

Jones earlier had provided a thorough diagnosis of Jung's "Christ complex" that sheds light on his characterization of Freud as Mithras. "Jung is going to save the world, another Christ (with certainly Anti-semitism combined). The world is trembling with fear because the *böse Vater* [evil father] has found out their secret thoughts, their incest wishes and infantile sexuality. But the gallant St. George steps forward and reassures the world: 'continue with your infantile sexuality, which is not sexual, and your incest wishes, which are not incestuous. Such things are quite innocent and harmless, and now that I have saved you you need no longer fear'" (Paskauskas 1993, 180). Freud agreed with the diagnosis, replying that Jung "behaves like a perfect fool, he seems to be Christ himself" (Paskauskas 1993, 182).

It is remarkable how deftly the Aryan Jones deployed the charge of anti-Semitism above and showed his own repudiation of his Christian origins through his mockery of Jung. It seems clear that he identified the Jewish trajectory of Freud's truth as a source of resistance, but not the source of the truth itself. Like Ferenczi, Jones—the movement's faithful *Shabbesgoy*—quickly closed ranks in the corporate identity by heroicizing the founder's narrative of grappling with ugly cosmic truths.[28] It is no coincidence that, at this time, the idea of the Secret Committee was hatched, "designed, like the Paladins of Charlemagne, to guard the kingdom and policy of their master" as Jones put it privately (Paskauskas 1993, 82). The shrinking community of the faithful even ritualized Freud's reduction of religion to neurotic ritual. "On June 30, 1913, we celebrated the occasion [of *Totem and Taboo*] by giving Freud a dinner, which we called a totemic festival, on the Konstantinhügel in the Prater. Loe Kann [a former analysand and Jones's wife] presented him with an Egyptian figurine which he adopted as his totem" (Jones [1953–1957] 1981, 2:355).

So far we see that Freud's oppositional fantasy shifted from the Hannibalic avenger, to the oedipal self-analyst, and finally to the role of cosmic redeemer who was decidedly not Christ, but rather that *other* cosmic redeemer who was worshiped among the brother bands of the Roman legions. This trajectory reveals a consistent oppositional theme, more open in its negative engagement with Christianity than its asymptotic relationship with Judaism and Jewish tradition.[29] At the same time, it shows remarkable integrative aspirations that it realizes through ancient associations shot through the evolving drama of the scientific quest. It seems no small coincidence that Freud wrote the original preface for *Totem and Taboo* while in the city of Rome, declaring his scandalous truth *urbi et orbi* ("to the City and the world") and feeling quite at home inside the "head of the world" (*caput mundi*). Hannibal had entered Rome, Moses was no longer angry, God was dead, and all was right with the world.

The Juno Principle

For Freud, to be Jewish clearly meant identifying strongly with the Other of history. To side with Hannibal, after all, was to choose the *losing* side, for Carthage was erased by Roman power, just as Jerusalem was destroyed by Roman armies. It might seem that psychoanalysis, being born among a Jewish community and being a profession that found its genesis through listening to hysterical women, would be in an ideal position for understanding the Other of history. That much is implicit in Freud's famous motto of the *Interpretation of Dreams: Flectere si nequeo superos, Acheronta movebo*, "if I cannot bend the gods above, I'll rouse the gods below" (*Aeneid* 7.312). This is the voice of Juno, who—in representing Carthaginian interests against the master-plot of Roman history in Vergil's *Aeneid*—seems a perfect symbol of the historical repressed. The fact that Freud purloined the verse from the writings of the Jewish socialist Ferdinand Lassalle further underscores this association.[30] The verse explicitly refers to Juno's desire to slow the forward trajectory of history—the Trojan foundation of what will become Rome—by bringing up the past. Angry at Aeneas's success in arriving at long last in Italy, she raises up the fury Allecto in order to revisit the Trojan War upon the hapless survivors of that long and bloody conflict. By inciting a war between the Trojan refugees and the native Latin peoples, Juno tries to cast Aeneas in the role of Paris (*Paris alter*) and make his wooing of Lavinia the equivalent of Paris' abduction of Helen. The result will be a blood wedding with Bellona (Goddess of War) as the bridesmaid, and with the wedding torch as the equivalent of the funeral torch for a Troy reborn through violent repetition (7.322).[31]

Freud liked the *Acheronta movebo* verse because it seemed to express very well that "*what is suppressed continues to exist in normal people as well as abnormal, and remains capable of psychic functioning*" (*The Interpretation of Dreams*, SE 5:608; original italics). In the economy of epic psychology, the fury Allecto indeed represents a psychic agency, the burning bloodlust that leads the Rutulian hero Turnus to oppose Aeneas in open conflict over the hand of Lavinia. The losing side in Vergil's poem is often represented by striking female characters: the angry Goddess Juno, the fury Allecto, Dido the Queen of Carthage, and Camilla the warrior princess. We must reflect here on how the Other of history in Vergil's poem, being set against the inevitable course of Roman *virtus* ("manliness"), is quite often associated with the female gender, for it has relevance to a discussion of Freud's deployment of the Other(s) of Roman history in the figuration of his concept of the unconscious.

Besides Juno's purloined verse, one could read Freud's citation of Dido's words in the *Psychopathology of Everyday Life* as a clear indication that the historical Other comprises not just the female side of history, but the other "losers" as well. In the *Psychopathology's* most famous vignette, Freud alleges that he and a fellow Jew were traveling together, and the latter expressed deep bitterness at belonging to a marooned social group, the educated Jewish middle class. In his anguish, Freud's companion attempts to cite the Vergilian verse: *Exoriare aliquis nostris ex ossibus ultor,* a rather complicated line that can be literally translated as: "May you arise as the avenger, whoever you are, from our bones" (*Aeneid* 4.625).[32] That an angry Jew should cite such a verse is highly significant to Freud's personal trajectory, since the line is said by the Semitic Queen Dido and refers indirectly to Hannibal, the avenger (*ultor*) who, in Vergil's historical vision, will make the Romans of a later century pay for the enmity fomented by their *Urvater,* Aeneas. But the young man falters over the verse in Freud's vignette, and Freud ferrets out that his real problem is not an ignorance of Latin or a faulty memory, but rather a psychological disturbance based on his anxiety over getting a young woman pregnant (SE 6:9–10). Freud's clinical ear, in other words, listens to this voice of the exasperated Jew, and finds behind his political rantings the universal ground of sexuality, the figure of a pregnant female whose body is bearing the unfinished business of the past. The pregnant lover, after all, is the perfect symbol of the unpastness of the past, the entrapping snare of woman for whom "anatomy is destiny" while the phallic hero hopes to move on to achieve other things ("The Dissolution of the Oedipus Complex," SE 19:178).

Jews, Carthaginians, wronged and wounded women, Mithraists, Aten-worshippers, totemistic savages—Freud's ancient gallery seems to highlight a history that could be seen Other-wise, as if to challenge the dominant culture's views of the past, the tales told by the winners. So far I have argued that the course of secular Jewish alienation seems clearly linked to his masculine aspirations and oppositional strategies, and I would now like to turn the discussion toward the implications of this approach for his deployment of gender within the grander contours of psychoanalysis. For while Freud is willing like a good Vergilian narrator to give a sympathetic voice to the Other of history, he settles the issue of power in the end through a patriarchal teleology that returns herstory to the neverland of Acheron.[33] What this has to do with Freud's deployment of Jewish history will emerge as a consequence of his struggle with femininity.

Much work has been done since the 1990s on the complex link between femininity and Judaism in Freud's thought, but I wish first to link femininity to non-Jewish sources in relation to science.[34] From what we have already seen in the Leonardo study, it is clear that science was a means of oedipal self-assertion, a way of escaping the dangerous implications of feminization—emasculation, passivity, sensuality—through a masculine rivalry over the knowledge of Mother Nature. Freud's views of femininity might well represent a "Penelope principle" that threatens to unravel his work (as Madelon Sprengnether suggests [1990, 119]), or form part of a "counter-thesis" with which to reverse the psychoanalytic project and reweave it along feminist lines (Jonte-Pace 2001). But I wish to argue instead that like the Vergilian *Aeneid*, what seems to operate in the Freudian historical epic is the Juno principle. The voice of the Other may be heard through the Freudian text, but the patriarchal closure of history remains poised to strike down feminine agency in the fullness of time. The power of femininity has its brief day in the sun, just as Juno is able to work her schemes of delay, but ultimately the task of civilization will require femininity to cede to masculine authority, just as we know from the very beginning of the *Aeneid* that Juno will reconcile herself to Jupiter's plan for Roman dominion. In the brotherhood of the rings, the Secret Committee, Freud wore the ring of Jupiter, and it is Jupiter who stops Juno directly from unraveling the skein of history in the *Aeneid* by his simple declaration that she is forbidden to continue messing up the grand narrative of the world (*ulterius temptare veto*, "I forbid you to try further"—12.418). The quest for scientific *imperium*, tied as it is quite vitally for Freud to the cause of civilization, remains masculine in character, even if it is not entirely undertaken by men. And in Freud's personal trajectory, it is this masculine task that leads the Jew out of the troublesome category of the feminine and the historically defeated and into the narrative of conquest, the *Fortschritt in der Geistigkeit* or "progress in intellectuality" (see comments by Bernstein 1998, 86–89).

I will first adduce as evidence Freud's clear discomfort with something lurking in the very same archive of prehistory that generated the Myth of Ur: matriarchy and gynaecocracy. Freud's myth clearly stakes *both* the social origin and the final state of human civilization on a vision of patriarchy, first the primal patriarchy of the *Urvater* who ruled like a Nietzschean Superman (*Group Psychology*, SE 18:123), and second the filial patriarchy that restored the role of the Father, but on the basis of a cohesive social network of the sons as *patresfamilias* (*Totem and Taboo*, SE 13:149).[35] The intervening era was matriarchy, which Freud seems compelled to admit in the wake of the *Urvater's* death (and particularly given the influence of Bachofen's *Mutterrecht* [1861] 1948), though it is also something he clearly cannot use. As he pondered the problem, he admitted to Jones, "I know of the obstacle or the complication offered by the matter of Matriarchy and have not yet found my way out of it. But I hope it will be cleared [a]way" (Paskauskas 1993, 148). It seems clear from his references to it that it was mostly something that needed "to be cleared away" and not taken seriously. In *Totem and Taboo*, he casts the historical possibility of matriarchy as a consequence of the *sons'* voluntary renunciation of the women of the horde through the law against incest. Here the civilizing act is the self-mastery of the sons who accommodate themselves to the reality principle by renouncing the object of their desires (SE 13:144). This is clearly an historical vignette created according to the pattern of the Oedipus complex, which relies on the son's renunciation of his own desire. Thus masculine deference to a homosocial order and *not* female agency creates "the germ of the institution of matriarchy, described by Bachofen" which, he hastens to add, "was in turn replaced by the patriarchal organization of the family" (SE 13:144). He no sooner mentions the possibility of matriarchy in *Totem and Taboo* than he reminds us of its historical demise.

A similar gesture is made later in reference to the genesis of heroic epic in *Group Psychology and the Analysis of the Ego* (1921, SE 18:135–137). The heroic myth represents the emergence of individual psychology—the kind of psychology that truly matters to the free-thinking intellectual, after all, who rebels like Leonardo against conventional authority. Yet in Freud's account of it, he goes out of his way to deny any significant agency to women in the course of the myth's development.

> Just as the father had been the boy's first ideal, so in the hero who aspires to the father's place the poet now created the first ego ideal. The transition to the hero was probably afforded by the youngest son, the mother's favorite, whom she had protected from paternal jealousy, and who, in the era of the primal horde, had been the father's successor. *In the lying poetic fancies of prehistoric times, the woman, who had been the prize of battle and the temptation to murder, was probably turned into the active seducer and instigator to the crime.* (SE 18:136; my emphasis)

It is remarkable here that a moment of significant agency, the mother's power to choose and protect the father's successor, is quickly deflated by the assumption that any more active role, such as incestuous seduction or incitement to patricide, must simply be the result of tendentious distortion in the mythic tradition, not historical fact. The possibility that the horde might have undergone an insurrection organized by women in which the sons were simply subordinates is whisked away in favor of the homosocial "brother band" scenario. The heroic sons kill their enemy and renounce their pleasures; the women are simply prizes and pretexts for slaughter. Thus the period of matriarchy always falls under the shadow of the sons, since it is really just the product of "fraternal alliance" (*Moses and Monotheism*, SE 23:82).

The Myth of Ur thus shows us a great failure of imagination, since it seems so very clear on the matter of the homosocial contract, yet professes great doubt concerning the possibility of knowing anything about the role of women in prehistory.[36] "The vicissitudes of women in these primeval times are especially obscure to us," he demurs at the end of one of his most outrageous phylogenetic excursions (Grubrich-Simitis 1987, 20). "Under the influence of external factors into which we need not enter here and which are also in part insufficiently known, it came about that the matriarchal social order was succeeded by the patriarchal one," he flatly states in *Moses and Monotheism* (SE 23:113). Moreover, the figure of the great Mother Goddess, which as we saw seems to raise all the ambivalences toward feminine power that stem from the pre-oedipal mother, becomes in Freud's later work yet another problem to be "cleared away." In *Moses and Monotheism*, he alleges that patriarchal gods represent the true conditions of the patriarchal age, yet he hastens to deny the same possibility for the mother goddesses. "It is likely that the mother-goddesses originated at the time of the curtailment of the matriarchy, as a compensation for the slight upon the mothers" (SE 23:83). Thus while patriarchal religion is always founded on the perennial longing for the lost Father and the need for his protection, but also on objective social relations, mother cult is simply a booby prize for the always already passé matriarchy, *not* a manifestation of genuine social power. It is telling that Freud even resorts to materialistic speculation on the demise of the mother goddesses *in a footnote* to his patriarchal history of religion (SE 23:46). Noting Arthur Evans's speculation on the destruction of Minoan Knossos by an earthquake, Freud remarks:

> In Crete at that period (as probably in the Aegean world in general) the great mother-goddess was worshipped. The realization that she was not able to protect her house against the assaults of a stronger

power may have contributed to her having to give place to a male deity, and, if so, the volcano god had the first claim to take her place. After all, Zeus always remains the "earth-shaker." There is little doubt that it was during those obscure ages that the mother-goddesses were replaced by male gods (who may originally have been sons). (SE 23:46, note 2 continued)

Though all is murky about women in prehistory, the one thing about which there is "little doubt" is the inevitability of their displacement from social power. As Nicole Loraux has said in relation to Greek myth, "Basically, origins are never so carefully constructed as when it is important to build on them, no matter what the cost. One has the advantage of being in the position of *telos* and assigning a prehistoric place to whatever should not be in the history" (1995, 192).

Where does the Jew fit into this narrative of matriarchy manqué? First of all, it is the whole undercurrent of Freud's view of the sacred that it represents "originally nothing other than the prolongation of the will of the primal father," and the Jews, in their exceptional history of a singular Father cult, would seem to be a pure instance of the return of the repressed Ur-patriarchy. But the Hebrews were not regressive in their religion. Quite the opposite, they took on the enlightened rational religion of Akhenaten, which Freud depicts following Breasted as the product of "the first individual in human history" (SE 23:21, note 1). By worshiping the sun as the creator and preserver of all things, Akhenaten is credited with an "astonishing anticipation of the scientific discovery of the effect of solar radiation" (SE 23:22). By rejecting other cults, he introduces a powerful exclusion of "myths, magic and sorcery" from religion, a decisive step toward a more rational theology based on an abstract concept of divinity (SE 23:24).[37] Though his innovations were hated by the polytheistic, superstitious Egyptians, it seems clear that Freud identifies with this remarkable pioneer, who in Karl Abraham's earlier study (1912) was depicted as a clear-cut case of oedipal revolt.[38]

Freud's Moses furthers the rational trajectory of civilization in turn by insisting on a total prohibition against making images of God, thereby bringing it about that "a sensory perception was given second place to what may be called an abstract idea—a triumph of intellectuality over sensuality or, strictly speaking, an instinctual renunciation, with all its necessary psychological consequences" (SE 23:113). It seems clear that matriarchy is implicated in sensuality from a remark he makes on the next page concerning the historical passage to patriarchy. "But this turning from the mother to the father points in addition to a victory of intellectuality over sensuality—that is, an advance in civilization, since maternity is proved by the evidence of the senses while paternity is a hypothesis, based on an inference and a premise. Taking sides in this way with a thought-process in preference to a sense perception has proved to be a momentous step" (SE 23:114). Thus the shift to patriarchy underwrites an intellectual progress that is further abetted by the Mosaic prohibition on graven images, and "the Jews retained their inclination to intellectual interests" which has held them together as a people for centuries (SE 23:115). In the wake of our discussion above concerning Freud's assumptions about the Jewish affinity with science, it seems clear he is providing a genealogy for the masculine Jewish *Wissenschaftler* who, like Akhenaten, is quite suited to being a heretic in his own time for the sake of civilization. This seems to be corroborated by another one of Freud's telltale analogies. This time he compares the gradual acceptance of Mosaic monotheism with the victory of Darwinism in his own day, which though violently disputed at first "took no longer than a generation" to be seen as "a great step forward towards truth" (SE 23:66–67).

This shift from maternal sensuality to paternal abstraction also marks a very important change in the scientific dynamic: the move from the empirical romance to the paternal romance. Reliance upon the senses in the context of this ancient scenario is backward, not revolutionary. Christianity with its wide use of images and Mother of God cult is clearly a *regression* in a sense, a return to maternal sensuality and a failure to live up to the abstract (masculine) rigor of Judaic monotheism. Above all, Christianity did not "exclude the entry of superstitious, magical and mystical elements, which were to prove a severe inhibition upon the intellectual development of the next two thousand years" (SE 23:88). Christianity was more advanced in only one aspect: the covert admission of patricide that is latent in its filicidal myth, which is the basis for the Christian justification of anti-Semitism. Christianity blames the Jews for *not admitting* that they have killed God; in Freud's reading of the Christian subtext, the Christians are really saying, "We did the same thing, to be sure, but we have *admitted* it and since then we have been absolved" (SE 23:90). But this supposed advance in the history of religions is, of course, *Freud's* truth, not Christianity's, since he long ago subverted the Christian reoccupation of the Akedah in order to bring it in line with his patricidal Myth of Ur. Thus Christianity's only historical advantage over Judaism is based on its uncanny conveyance of the Freudian myth; the rest of its content is intellectually retarding. Though the Jew is always in danger of association with femininity for being circumcised (nearly castrated), here Freud turns the tables on Christianity by feminizing it through the reliance on sensuous images and casting it back into the maw of the Mother Goddess. This brings us back to the topic of femininity and civilization.

In the Leonardo study, we saw how Leonardo's scientific interests were related to his desire for his mother as symbolized in nature, and how the figure of the great mother goddess Mut represented the mother's awesome generative and destructive powers. And yet scientific achievement was, in Freud's reading of Leonardo's life, the result of a homosocial masculine rivalry. It is clear from Freud's very notions of *Kultur* (what is regularly translated as "civilization") that it is a homosocial contract which pits men against both women at large and mother nature. The "better path" in life is to become "a member of the human community, and, with the help of a technique guided by science, *going over to the attack against nature and subjecting her to human will*" (*Civilization and Its Discontents*, SE 21:77; my emphasis). The quest for knowledge of the Law of the Mother has now become an outright attack, which triggers in turn the need for defensive thinking. "Civilization" or *Kultur* describes "the whole sum of the achievements and the regulations which distinguish our lives from those of our animal ancestors and which serve two purposes—namely *to protect men against nature* and to adjust their mutual relations" (SE 21:89; my emphasis). Women, on the other hand, by representing "the interests of the family and of sexual life" soon "come into opposition to civilization and display their retarding and restraining influence" (SE 21:103). We are told that the work of civilization has become the business of men, and that it requires instinctual sublimations "of which women are little capable" (SE 21:103). Once more, the instinctual self-mastery of the males creates the homosocial bond that lasts.

Since civilization at this point is clearly allied with science, and since the modern secular Jew seems so well suited for (psychoanalytic) science, the trajectory seems clear enough: the Jew is released from historical humiliation through the "progress in intellectuality" with which *he* (and the pronoun is indelibly masculine here) is associated. Freud states that the political misfortune of the Jewish nation in Palestine "taught it to value at its true worth the one possession that remained to it—its literature" (SE 23:115). Since Rabbi Jochanan ben Zakkai asked permission to open the first Torah school in Jabneh only *after* the destruction of the Temple, this is proof that the Jews have triumphed over the humiliations of history through intellectual persistence. Thus while the trajectory of Jewish history is distorted by outside interference, the essential core of Jewish integrity remains intact, in a way that comes to represent Freud's only real break with Hellenism.

> The pre-eminence given to intellectual labors throughout some two thousand years in the life of the Jewish people has, of course, had its effect. It has helped to check the brutality and the tendency to violence which are apt to appear where the development of muscular strength is the popular ideal. Harmony in the cultivation of intellectual and physical activity, such as was achieved by the Greek people, was denied to the Jews. In this dichotomy their decision was at least in favor of the worthier alternative. (SE 23:115)

On the one hand, harmony between mind and body was "denied" to the Jews [*blieb den Juden versagt*], on the other it was the basis of "their decision" [*die Entscheidung*]. This very slip shows Freud's difficult negotiation of Jewish identity through the pressures of external history and the triumph of internal choice, the very triumph, after all, embodied in his Judeo-Hellenistic reading of Michelangelo's Moses. If by the late thirties we find Freud parting ways with the Greek ideal, it is in no small measure due to the *German* appropriation of classical culture, which under Hitler became the fascist cult of Olympian athleticism. This vulgar new Hellenism would prove all too well that "brutality and the tendency to violence" are "apt to appear where the development of muscular strength is the popular ideal."[39]

At this point the integrating gesture of Hellenism fails, and the Jew is finally content to remain a Jew, as long as he can be a Jewish psychoanalyst, unafraid to expose even the origins of Judaism itself on the eve of the Shoah. Though his entire scientific enterprise relied on the archival sciences of antiquity, his "first appearance as a historian" was made only at the end of his life, and this was a genealogy of anti-Semitism that showed him still maintaining his asymptotic relationship with Judaism. "Jewry will be very offended," he told his son in reference to *Moses and Monotheism* (Ernst Freud 1960, 440). But at the same time, he said that "It is typically Jewish not to renounce anything and to replace what has been lost. Moses, who in my opinion left a lasting imprint on the Jewish character, was the first to set an example" (Ernst Freud 1960, 440). Through his patriarchal Myth of Ur, Freud replaced the missing tradition of his fathers with a new tradition which still prized the manly efforts of reason. Writing to Charles Singer in 1938, he said that "I have spent my whole life standing up for what I have considered to be the scientific truth, even when it was uncomfortable and unpleasant for my fellow men. I cannot end up with an act of disavowal" (Ernst Freud 1960, 453). Though Singer had told Freud everything he wrote was bound to cause misunderstanding, Freud replied:

> Well, we Jews have been reproached for growing cowardly in the course of the centuries. (Once upon a time we were a valiant nation.) In this transformation I had no share, so I must risk it. (Ernst Freud 1960, 454

Thus in the guise of Hannibal-Oedipus-Mithras-Moses he made not an unworthy exit and stoically died through assisted suicide. Hannibal too had taken poison to deprive his hereditary enemies of their prey.

In this condensed narrative, I have traced the highly heterogeneous nature of Freud's archival improvisation, showing its shifting tactics of opposition, integration, genealogy, archaeology, and critique. While he made ample use of the tools and topics of his time (such as the vogue of totemism, the topicality of tragedy in performance, or the matriarchal hypothesis), the end result was something unique to Freud and his followers, something re-centered, re-stitched, and re-configured around oedipal conflict and the dynamics of the unconscious. Some see in Freud's late-life interest in Jewish history a clear pattern of departure and return (e.g., Rice 1990), and while I agree with this characterization generally, I would like to qualify just how one is to understand "return." For it seems brutally clear that Freud's "return" to Jewish tradition in *Moses and Monotheism* is no facile reconciliation, nor a death-bed lapse into some suitably modified form of piety. Rather than a returning apostate, I would say Freud was a returning asymptote, one whose trajectory in life and in thought was constantly defined *in relation to* Jewishness, without being dictated by it or identical to it. One looks in vain for a viable "Jewish" explanation for the great myth of *Totem and Taboo*. All the same, the narrative of psychoanalysis's development is *enriched* by the consideration of Freud's status as a Jewish subject, one thinking his way out of Judaism and around the imposing edifice of Christianity, one who dodges the dangerous currents of secular nationalism and socialism, and seeks refuge in the rigors of science. Perhaps most importantly and most damningly, he is also a Jewish subject who felt his own historical crisis distinctly as a cri-

THE MYTH OF UR

sis of masculinity, and who ended his life still failing to consider how re-configuring the history of masculinity in the hopes of healing can still replicate a certain pernicious logic of domination in relation to women.

Coda: Via Regia

For me, the final lesson to be gleaned from Freud's compulsion for an-tiquity would be how much the allegedly radical epistemic breaks of mod-ernism still channel the cultures of antiquity, still echo the voices of ancient piety even as they promise a final overcoming of the past and the twilight of the idols of humanity.[40] I see such a gesture in Freud's curious use of the phrase *via regia* in something he added in 1909 to the later edi-tions of *The Interpretation of Dreams*. When Freud declared that "The in-terpretation of dreams is the royal road [*via regia*] to knowledge of the unconscious activities of the mind," he coined a memorable slogan that vindicated the seemingly archaic art of dream interpretation for the pur-poses of modern *Wissenschaft* (SE 5:608). The dictum promises a wide road down to the Acheron of human experience, bringing us to a fright-ening underworld which, if we are brave enough (if we are *men* enough), will teach us about "the untamed, indestructible elements in the human soul, the *daemonic* powers that produce the dream-wish and that we re-discover in our Unconscious" (Freud [1900] 1999, 406). The processes and the contents of the unconscious make up Freud's scandalous gospel, and a cultural excavation of the term *via regia* will show just how he stands in relation to the ancient traditions he (under)mines, deploys, and over-comes—and also how they mediate his revolutionary truths.

Via regia is originally the ecclesiastical Latin translation of a Hebrew expression, the *derek hammelek* or King's Road of Numbers 20:14–21 (the expression refers to the old commercial road between Damascus and Aqaba). This passage describes an historical situation still all too familiar to Jews in Freud's own day: the attempt by the ancient Israelites to pass through Edom, keeping to the royal road and not bothering the Edomites or eating up their resources. But Edom refuses Israel any passage, and comes out in all hostility against the wandering people of Moses. Because of this passage, "Edom" became associated with the hostile gentile world that forever seems to menace the Jews, to knock them off the road. As Freud says, the Jew does not renounce anything, but replaces what has been lost. Though the royal road was not granted to Moses by the

Edomites, it became in the works of Philo the way of the Logos, the *basilikē hodos* (the Greek translation of the Hebrew phrase) that leads to knowledge of the Father. In Philo's Platonizing theosophy, those who hold to this rational, spiritual road are the true children of Israel, while those caught in the material and the sensual are earthly Edomites who will never have access to the royal road of Truth. "The royal road is that of which there is no private individual in the world who is master, but He alone who is also the only true king" (Philo 1993, 171).[41]

Philo's *basilikē hodos* became among the Greek Fathers of the Church not just the way of Truth, but the way of orthodoxy. As they hammered out the complex synthesis of Jewish and Hellenic culture that we know today as Christianity, it became essential for the holy fathers to stick to the royal road of Truth on such cosmically absurd and vital matters as the Incarnation and the Resurrection. It required vigilance in the synods and councils of the early Church to sort through the discordant claims of Jewish scripture and Greek philosophy, and to find the "one royal road" that avoided the myriad pitfalls of heresy. This royal road became the way of Faith, the doctrinal Truth that, by the world's standards, was riven with incredible illogicalities. It thus became synonymous with the Church itself, and deviation from Her Truth led to the darkness of heretical ignorance.[42] From Philo's improvised Judeo-Hellenistic philosophy, it had become the imperial road of the Church Militant.

I do not know if Freud was aware that the term *via regia* had this particular genealogy; I am in a sense excavating the cultural unconscious of a set phrase. It came to him as part of the stock of Latinity, an item from the educated person's armory of gallant phrases, which were all mediated through many centuries of Christian culture and classical scholarship. Freud entered that world when he matriculated at the Leopoldstadt *Gymnasium* as an Israelite to whom Edom had finally allowed passage. But Freud's deployment of the phrase seems to conform all too perfectly to his view of the Jew as one who does not renounce anything, but who replaces what has been lost. The Hellenistic Jew's theosophical fancy of turning the blocked royal road into the intellectual way of Truth resonates very powerfully against the Viennese Jew's desire to open new paths of *Wissenschaft* through hysteria, dreams, jokes, and parapraxes. Where the ancient Judeo-Hellenist sought through the Logos the knowledge of the Father as a living presence in the Law, where the Christians sought to make the Logos a filial aspect of the triune Godhead, Freud turned this Logos against all religion by inviting us to consider without flinching the underworld of our desires. Psychoanalysis still professed

through its *via regia* to lead us to the knowledge of the Father—knowledge of the Father's death, of the eternal desire to be and be rid of the Father; this is the deep wisdom that decodes the symptoms we call culture.
Psychoanalysis is, in a way, a new literacy for a very ancient text; its historical vision is the figural allegory of the death of God.

NOTES

1. Disturbing Acropolis

1. Freud's letters from the journey to Greece in 1904 have been newly edited in a volume of *Reisebriefe;* see Tögel 2002, 175–193.

2. The essay, "A Disturbance of Memory on the Acropolis," is in the form of an open letter to Romain Rolland, theorist of the "oceanic feeling" (SE 22:238–248). William Parsons argues convincingly that Freud's reading of his own experience is in part a means of dispelling the threat of Rolland's mystical experience (1999, 80–85). Vermorel and Vermorel 1993 studies the Rolland-Freud relationship in great detail, and reads the Acropolis letter as an act of self-analysis, which they then trace to Freud's last burst of creativity at the end of his life. Sugarman (1998) attempts an analysis of derealization using Freud's experience as a typical example, a premise which is highly questionable; see my review of all three (Armstrong 2001b).

3. On the physical reconstruction of Athens, see Bastéa 2000; for the Bavarian monarchy in Greece, see especially Seidl 1981. Gourgouris' *Dream Nation* (1996) is a sophisticated critical essay on the modern Greek nationalist imaginary. He analyzes Freud's Acropolis derealization as a paradigm of Philhellenic desire, "a social-imaginary institution, replete with all the realities that constitute the operation of ideological fantasy, the destructions and punishments of the sublimated object" (128).

4. At present, it seems the concept of mnemohistory (Assmann) is still not clearly articulated in reference to the various conceptualizations of "the archive" (Foucault, Derrida). I address my own interpretation of the "archive of antiquity" or "ancient archive" below in note 5, but I should mention here that I see the archive as a site of memory work, which in turn feeds into the maintenance or creation of further archives. So while mnemohistory and archival analysis are not synonymous, they are not in my mind incompatible.

5. By ancient archive I mean not just the physical archives of antiquity (the sites, artifacts, inscriptions, and textual remains), but also the powers and principles that order them into monuments, evidence, and information, or that deploy them to mediate historical consciousness. As such, physical archives exist because of a particular context of archaeological or archival desire, and they reflect the cognitive style informing their construction and establishment. As Derrida put it in *Archive Fever,* "the technical structure of the *archiv-*

ing archive also determines the structure of the *archivable* content even in its very coming into existence and in its relationship to the future. The archivization produces as much as it records the event" (1995, 17; original emphasis).

Relevant are the archiving processes in antiquity responsible for what could be archived: ancient editions and anthologies that led to textual survival via canon formation; treatises on heresies and philosophical errors that preserved the very ideas they refuted through their citations; political acts of commemoration that led to inscriptions, as well as acts of vengeance or barbarism that erased previous commemorations; sumptuous burials in well-hidden tombs that preserved grave goods; and even accidental interventions, such as volcanic eruptions, palimpsests preserving what was erased, or the use of "scrap" paper in mummy-case *cartonnage* which led to textual immortality when the papier-mâché was dissolved to reveal the text written on the "scrap" paper.

The modern energies and institutions that create the archive include the *Gymnasium* curriculum, the museum, the antiquities market (including petty collecting for hobbyists), imperial as well as amateur archaeology, textual recension, the profession of history, neoclassical architectural citation, and even popular fiction (e.g., Jensen's *Gradiva*). While mediated through language and professional discursive practices, "the ancient archive" is not a thing possessed by university hierophants but is a creative orientation to the past in dialogue with traces of antiquity. However, this is *not* a dialogue in which everyone carefully listens, hence the inevitable misprisions that arise. Thus my own conception is closer to Derrida's notion of an "archive fever" than that of a museum or computer database full of true information and self-evident evidence about the past.

Mine is not exclusively an archaeology of the *sayable*, an excavation of utterances. Rather, it is often concerned with the impinging objects that challenge or outpace the sayable, posing problems and enigmas to the networks of the sayable (in this sense, I am following lines similar to those laid out by Leonard Barkan [1999]). Throughout this study I have tried to think hard about the consequences of the site of analysis as not just a context of saying, of speaking, but also of a *Dingwelt*, a site of things, artifacts, and images that mediate, facilitate, or at times inhibit the sayable, against the background of a scientific materialism that, while faded and no longer the exclusive paradigm, still colors the terrain considerably.

6. This class has been the subject of excellent, detailed studies such as Josef Fraenkel 1963, Rozenblit 1983, Berger 1987, Wistrich 1989, McCagg 1989, Don and Karady 1990, Beller [1989] 1993, and Gary Cohen 1996 (who deals with the Austrian educational system overall), among many others. One of its most famous contemporary portraits is Stefan Zweig's *Die Welt von Gestern* ([1944] 1997). To understand its political plight, see especially Boyer 1981 and 1994.

7. Such police work can be found in Sir Hugh Lloyd-Jones' "Psychoanalysis and the Study of the Ancient World" (1990, chapter 23); Robert Eisner's *The Road to Daulis* (1987); G. S. Kirk's *Myth: Its Meaning and Functions in Ancient & Other Cultures* (1970, chapter 6); Sebastiano Timpanaro's *The Freudian Slip* ([1976] 1985); and in Jean Pierre Vernant's classic "Oedipus without the Complex" (Vernant and Vidal-Naquet, 1990, chapter 4). A more nuanced approach to Freud's reading of classical literature and philology can be found in Mitchell-Boyask 1994.

8. To my surprise and delight, I found after I had completed the manuscript of this book that Lawrence Johnson also approaches Freud's work in terms of an improvisation (2001, 4–5).

9. Psychotherapy itself is in danger of decline in the age of Prozac, as has been eloquently argued by Elio Frattaroli in *Healing the Soul in the Age of the Brain* (2001).

10. This link is the Egyptian priest Manetho's account of Osarsiph/Moses, which Ass-

mann takes to be a reemergence of an oral tradition concerning Akhenaten's religious revolution (1997, 29–36).

11. I am especially influenced by the type of immanent critique produced by feminist scholars, of whom Mitchell (1974), Sprengnether (1990), and Jonte-Pace (2001) have stood out most in my mind at this writing. Brenkman (1993), Gilman (1993b) and Daniel Boyarin (1997), male authors writing from the perspective of gender studies, have provided me with a similar inspiration.

12. In this regard I would say that my reading of Freud is similar in tone to the new biography by Louis Breger (2000), whose influence will be seen in parts of this book. My main divergence from Breger's views is that I am less inclined to use the term "trauma" in reference to the experiences of his youth (see the review by Robert Holt [2001]).

13. See for example Janet Malcolm's journalistic account of the skullduggery in the Freud archives (1984), or Frederick Crews' polemic on recovered memory (1995) and his anthology of critical essays that represent an "unauthorized Freud" (1998), itself a product of the controversy surrounding the 1998 *Conflict and Culture* exhibition at the Library of Congress. The very fact that in the 1990s two books could still be written with the titles *Freud's Answer* (Wain 1998) and *Why Freud Was Wrong* (Webster 1995) is proof of Freud's continuing disturbance of the twentieth century. That this disturbance will continue on into the twenty-first century seems evident in the recent pages of the *PMLA* (Marshall 2002; Crews 2003).

14. At this writing, the new, "literary" Freud translations in the *New Penguin Freud*, edited by Adam Phillips, have not yet supplanted the *Standard Edition*, so I have not cited them. On the philological complexities of the German Freud editions, see Grubrich-Simitis [1993] 1996.

2. Compulsive Situations

1. Suzanne Cassirer Bernfeld used this very thesis to explain Freud's fascination with archaeology; mixing up her analogy a bit, she stated boldly that "This simple geographic change was a catastrophe for Freud and he spent the next forty years of his life trying to undo it. Freiberg became Pompeii and he became its Schliemann" (1951, 113).

2. One should note, however, that Freud seems to be caught in a contradiction in his analysis of Leonardo, whom he takes initially to be a model instance of the "third type" of personality that avoids neurotic inhibition and compulsive thinking (*Leonardo da Vinci and a Memory of His Childhood*, SE 11:80), only later to declare him "close to the type" of the obsessional neurotic who engages in compulsive brooding (SE 11:131). In this way, Freud shows the ambivalence he feels toward his object of analysis, who is both idealized and pathologized in the course of the study.

3. As Michael Rohrwasser points out, Freud's idealization of Hanold's archaeological vocation represses constant references to archaeological forgeries made in Jensen's text (Rohrwasser et al. 1996, 27–29). Forgeries are a fact of archaeological research, which Freud regularly ignores for the obvious reason that they provide a clear paradigm for tendentious products of interpretation "manufactured" for a gullible audience—that is, they provide an all too ready example for enemies of psychoanalytic interpretation who wish to attack Freud's "archaeology" of the mind. See chapter 10 below.

4. In other words, I am talking about a particular reading of ancient culture common in the eighteenth through the twentieth centuries. Foucault, for one, challenges the "repressive hypothesis" throughout the first volume of his *History of Sexuality*, and seeks the themes of self-mastery in ancient Greek sexuality in his later volumes.

5. On the development of aesthetics as an ideology, see especially Eagleton 1990. The best example of how aesthetic discourse can contain hedonic mischief is Winckelmann's assertion that the genuine appreciation of male beauty is essential for the cultivation of a feeling for the beauties of art in a lively and universal form. This effectively makes homoeroticism grounds for superior taste. See Potts 1994, 118–132. Freud for his part felt that the field of aesthetics had the character of an evasion, since it yielded no satisfactory explanation of beauty and "as usually happens, lack of success is concealed beneath a flood of resounding and empty words" (*Civilization and Its Discontents*, SE 21:83). While he does not claim that psychoanalysis can explain beauty any better, he still asserts that the love of beauty is a perfect example of an aim-inhibited impulse with attributes that originally belong to the sexual object.

6. On the aesthetic ideal of Greece in Hegel, Schiller, and Marx, see Kain 1982. It is important not to underestimate the lifespan of this ideal. In one of the first "modern" histories of ancient sexuality by Paul Brandt (alias Hans Licht), we see it clearly inscribed in his conclusions (Licht 1924, 1926). The characterization of Greek art in terms of psychological individuation is restated in psychoanalytic terms by Otto Rank in *The Trauma of Birth* ([1924] 1993, 146–147).

7. One citation will have to suffice to convey the physicalism of Winckelmann's view. In his introduction, he states that the Greeks' imagination "was not extravagant as it was among those nations [i.e., the Oriental peoples of antiquity], and their senses, which worked upon a fine-tuned brain through swift and perceptive nerves, discovered all at once the various properties of an object and concerned themselves above all with the contemplation of the Beautiful in itself" ([1764], 1993, 42).

8. Wilhelm von Humboldt, for example, defined the fourfold *Genuß des Altertums* ("enjoyment of antiquity") as: reading the ancient writers, looking at ancient art, studying ancient history, and living on classical ground (cited in Sichtermann 1996, 155). For him the pleasure principle organizes the archive, one could say.

9. *The Ego and the Id*, SE 19:26: "The ego is first and foremost a bodily ego; it is not merely a surface entity, but is itself the projection of a surface. If we wish to find an anatomical analogy for it we can best identify it with the 'cortical homunculus' of the anatomists, which stands on its head in the cortex, sticks up its heels, faces backwards and, as we know, has its speech-area on the left-hand side."

10. I cannot adequately address the complexity of the interface between the verbal and the visual here, but it bears remembering that the moment of the gaze throughout Winckelmann's own work is a moment *described*, a seeing *displaced* through ekphrasis and engravings in place of statues.

11. The "colonization" of Greece includes the literal intervention in modern Greek affairs, as is discussed brilliantly by Stathis Gourgouris in terms of the "colonization of the ideal" (1996).

12. Cf. Freud's comments on the national epic, *Moses and Monotheism*, SE 23:70–72.

13. In fact, the obscenity of these artifacts caused their modern collection and study to be quite an odyssey; on the famous collection of phallic artifacts from Naples, see Carabelli 1996.

14. There is some debate as to the nature and function of phallic and other seemingly obscene artifacts and images from antiquity. See Johns 1982.

15. These are the words of Richard Payne Knight, whom Freud later praises in his study of Leonardo (SE 11:97).

16. One might even find it ironic that here the phallus, which is so often seen as the most common *signified* in reductive Freudian readings, when it appears as a *signifier* itself

seems to be haunted by the trace of impotence. The phallus thus already signifies by virtue of its lability, its possibility of absence, as in the later castration complex.

17. For example, Larmour and Miller 1998 is a pointed response to Foucault's *History of Sexuality*, as is Goldhill 1995. Works inspired by Foucault include Halperin 1990, Winkler 1990, Hallett and Skinner 1997, and Craig Williams 1999, while James Davidson 1998 bucks the trend and openly challenges the Foucauldian dynamic of power=penetration. But the interest in ancient sexuality as a professional topic stems from Freud's own day, as we see in the work of Paul Brandt (alias "Hans Licht" 1924, 1926), the English version of whose *Sexual Life in Ancient Greece* was recently reissued without any historical contextualization (1930 [2000]). Non-Foucauldian approaches initiated by feminists include Keuls 1985, Lerner 1986, and Richlin [1983] 1993; Dover 1978 is a classic work on Greek homosexuality undertaken before the explosion of gender studies.

18. In the final paragraph of the story, Norbert asks Zoe to go on ahead so he can watch her cross the street. The final sentence reads, "A merry, comprehending, laughing expression lurked around his companion's mouth, and, raising her dress slightly with her left hand, Gradiva *rediviva* Zoe Bertgang, viewed by him with dreamily observing eyes, crossed with her calmly buoyant walk, through the sunlight, over the steppingstones, to the other side of the street" (Jensen [1903] 1956, 235).

19. The relief fragments form what is thought to be a depiction of the three daughters of Cecrops—Aglauros (Jensen's "Gradiva"), Pandrosos, and Herse—who were worshipped as the Dew Sisters in Attica. This is inventory no. 1284 in the Vatican Museum (Rohrwasser et al. 1996, 7), which Freud saw the same year he finished his study of *Gradiva* (see his letter to Martha of Sept. 24, 1907; Ernst Freud 1960, 267). An uncanny but unmade connection in Jensen's story would be that Aglauros herself was changed to stone by Hermes when through her sexual jealousy she refused him access to her sister's room (see Ovid, *Metamorphoses* 2.737–832). Her transformation from a girl into a stone artifact not only echoes Jensen's Pompeiian theme, but also conveys the petrification symbolizing repression of sexual desire, which haunts Norbert.

20. The double-narrative aspect of Freud's essay on *Gradiva* has made it so that the essay effectively displaced Jensen's original story, which few people read these days. See especially Peter Rudnytsky's "Freud's Pompeian Fantasy" (1994) on the question of the doubled text.

21. This work originally appeared in fact in 1907 as the first volume of a series titled *Schriften zur angewandten Seelenkunde*, and was meant for a general public of non-initiates. Hence the rhetoric of the entire study is effectively a kind of narrative seduction, and in this sense is worthy of extended stylistic analysis.

22. In addition to Rudnytsky 1994, Rohrwasser et al. 1996 is a collection of essays on the topic of Freud and Pompeii taken from a variety of historical perspectives. It represents the best collection of work so far on this text, which has been relatively neglected in spite of its seminal importance for understanding Freud's transition to cultural analysis.

23. Freud thus orchestrates a clever détente between the positions of the Knower and the Artificer, which represent the twin currents of Modernism in David Hollinger's formulation ([1986] 1994). That he does so, however, through a comparatively conservative writer shows his predilection for more nineteenth-century norms of literary representation.

24. The traditional story as told by Ernest Jones is that Carl Jung suggested *Gradiva* to Freud, but there is no clear evidence of this in their correspondence and the chronology of their personal relations does not match up to the production of Freud's work. Rudnytsky argues convincingly that it was rather Stekel who introduced the work to Freud (1994,

228–229). Freud sent a copy of his *Gradiva* essay to Jung, however, as a clear gesture of further enticing him into the psychoanalytic enterprise.

25. Winter herself does *not* assume that the content of the curriculum forms a simple causal nexus; she rather looks to the *Gymnasium* as a system of socialization that suggests norms of professionalization and self-discipline (*Bildung*) that later impinge upon Freud's ordering of psychoanalytic knowledge. Though I have deferred my own work on Freud's *Gymnasium* experience for the time being, it is important to note that detailed knowledge of its curriculum is available to all in the yearly reports published by his school (Pokorny 1864–1874), as well as in the reminiscences of schoolmates (Knoepfmacher 1979). General comments on it are made by Trosman (1976) in terms of Freud's cultural background.

26. For such synthetic studies, see (for German humanism) Butler [1935] 1958, Ephraim [1936] 1970, Rehm 1969, Trevelyan [1941] 1972; (for English Romantic Hellenism) Levin 1931, Stern [1940] 1969, Jennifer Wallace 1997, Ferris 2000; for the Victorian era, Turner 1981 and 1989, Jenkyns 1980, Lloyd-Jones 1982. The definitive work on modern Jewish Hellenism is Shavit 1999, which sadly neglects psychoanalysis as an instance of it; see my review (Armstrong 2001a). A crucial work on myth in particular is Lincoln 1999. The most comprehensive study so far that includes the later period 1890–1939 is Martin Bernal's indictment of European scholarship, *Black Athena* (1987); I concur with Jan Assmann's opinion that the first volume shows Bernal to be a brilliant historian of memory, while in the second he slips into trying to write a proper alternative history in which he suddenly fails to observe the very biases of cultural memory that made the first volume valuable (1997, 12–13). There are, however, some very good disciplinary studies of archaeology that take into account social and cultural factors; for example, see Hudson 1981, Trigger 1989, Sichtermann 1996, and Marchand 1996.

27. In a letter to Jung (December 17, 1911), Freud openly admits that in writing *Totem and Taboo* he is "already in possession of the truths I am seeking to prove" (McGuire 1974, 472). He then adds that he was not cut out for inductive investigation, that his whole makeup is intuitive, and that by setting out to establish psychoanalysis as an empirical science he had subjected himself to "an extraordinary discipline" (McGuire 1974, 472). For an extensive discussion of Freud's working methods based on his extant notes, see Grubrich-Simitis [1993] 1996, chapter 6.

28. The timing of the Darwinian revolution in Austria coincided with Freud's childhood and early adulthood, and provided for him a paradigm of "public science" that he used in modeling the psychoanalytic movement. See especially Michler 1999 and Ritvo 1990. On the narrative implications, see Beer 2000.

29. The most concrete example of this is his "phylogenetic fantasy," an unpublished metapsychological essay that traces the development of the neuroses to events that occurred in the species during the Ice Age (Grubrich-Simitis, 1987).

3. Compulsive Anatomy

1. This is, of course, the *exhibitable* Freud today, the Freud one encounters in the London and Vienna Freud Museums. For exhibit catalogues that include valuable essays on his collecting and his archaeological interests, see Gamwell and Wells 1989; Gubel n.d.; and Marinelli 1998 (with my review, Armstrong 1999a). The disposition of his rooms was thoroughly documented in photographs taken by Edmund Engelman (1993) which reveal the exact placement of his antiquities before his departure for London in 1938. For further essays, see especially Barker 1996 and Forrester 1994. Michael Molnar's edition of Freud's diary (1992) reveals in detail the acquisitions he made in the last decade of his life.

2. Christfried Tögel has recently published Freud's correspondence with his family during this journey in his edition of Freud's travel letters. See Tögel 2002, 333–362.

3. Although Swales' initial disclosure of this thesis caused considerable consternation in the 1980s, it has won over a certain number of scholars and has yet to be put to rest. Rudnytsky (1987, 69) accepts the identification of Freud as Herr Aliquis as "indisputable," though Hirschmüller (2002) makes the argument that it was in fact his brother Alexander. A recent article by Richard Skues (2001) upholds Swales' thesis against the rival claim that Freud's slip was caused by concern over his *wife's* pregnancy (as asserted by Kuhn 1999). I wish to thank Peter Swales for generously supplying me with copies of his various publications, unpublished correspondence, and manuscripts, as well as for discussing his views with me personally by telephone. I should also state that I am inclined to agree with Swales, though I shall not argue the point here, as my own project does not depend on it.

4. To be sure, there are those who see Wittgenstein's philosophical trajectory as deeply connected to the trajectory of his private life. See Janik and Toulmin 1973.

5. Jürgen Habermas discusses Freud's science of the personal in terms of an attempt to create a "science of self-reflection," which at base constitutes his "scientistic self-misunderstanding" ([1968] 1971, chapters 10–11). I myself use the terms "science" and *Wissenschaft* here in an entirely neutral sense; science is what Freud claims to be doing, and whether this meets our normative criteria for science today is not really an issue for me. One can defend his use of the term *Wissenschaft* with reference to the German and Austrian milieu, where it had broader application than the Anglo-American "science," being perhaps closer to our word "discipline." The fact remains that Freud was trained in what we still call the medical and biological sciences, and that this training greatly informed the disciplinary ideal to which he assimilated psychoanalysis.

6. The pervasive *formal* use of analogy in Freud's works forces me to declare Jacques Lacan to be openly dishonest when he claims that "Nothing is more repugnant to the spirit of our discipline [i.e., than analogy], and it was by deliberately avoiding analogy that Freud opened up the right way to the interpretation of dreams, and so to the notion of analytic symbolism. Analytic symbolism, I insist, is strictly opposed to analogical thinking" ([1966] 1977, 53). This was not true for Carl Jung, and part of Lacan's tirade here is linked to the narcissism of small differences among the epigones of Freud, as well as his desire to save Freud from his own abuses of phylogenetic analogies.

7. The characterization of Haeckel as St. Paul was made by the cultural historian Egon Friedell ([1931] 1954 3:225).

8. For a thorough critique and analysis of this doctrine, see Gould 1977.

9. In this regard, Freudian analogy often shows itself unable to handle this mode with sufficient respect for difference, or the fundamental postulate that analogy *per definitionem* cannot express a relation of identity (Schleifer 2000a, 11; 2000b). Another aspect of analogy, which Jung developed much more elaborately than Freud, was the connection with symbolism. See for example Jung [1912] 1956, 141: "It is evident that this tendency to invent analogies deriving from feeling-toned contents has been of enormous significance for the development of the human mind. We are in thorough agreement with Steinthal when he says that a positively overwhelming importance attaches to the little word 'like' in the history of human thought. One can easily imagine that the canalization of libido into analogy-making was responsible for some of the most important discoveries ever made by primitive man." Since this touches upon a religious, mystical vein of thinking with which Jung is quite at home, it is quite possible that Freud avoided developing it more fully in his own work for that reason, though he has to touch upon it briefly at times (*Introductory Lectures on Psycho-Analysis*, SE 15:152). See Kerr 1993, 272–279.

10. For an examination of psychoanalysis as a "pseudo-science," see Cioffi 1998.

11. See Freud's letter to Emil Fluß (May 1, 1873), where he announces his intention to become a *Naturforscher:* "Ich werde Einsicht nehmen in die jahrtausendealten Akten der Natur, vielleicht selbst ihren ewigen Prozeß belauschen und meinen Gewinst mit jedermann teilen, der lernen will" (Grubrich-Simitis 1971, 116).

4. The Theban Paradigm

1. Rudnytsky (1987, pt. 1) provides extensive biographical data on Freud's relation to Oedipus, to which one can add Freud's experience of the play *Oedipus Tyrannus* in Paris and Vienna (Armstrong 1999b, 1999c). A recent analysis of Freud's turn to the Oedipus complex as a compromise between his personal experiences and his scientific ambitions can be found in Louis Breger's new biography (2000, chapter 10), though this is a central theme in the appraisal of Freud's work, variously treated by Balmary [1979] 1982; Krüll [1979] 1986; Schorske 1981, chapter 4; Masson 1984; Spence 1994, chapter 1; Boyarin 1997, chapter 5; Sprengnether 1990 and 2000—just to mention a few diverse examples.

2. Freud to Fliess, Oct. 15, 1897 (Masson 1985, 272; my emphasis): "I have found, in my own case too, [the phenomenon of] being in love with my mother and jealous of my father, and *I now consider it a universal event in early childhood,* even if not so early as in children who have been made hysterical."

3. For the emergence of the Oedipus complex as the "core complex," see Forrester 1980, 84–96; and Kerr 1993, 247–261. It is important to note, however, that the Oedipus situation is clearly seen as universal as early as 1897; what changes is the gradual unification by 1912–1913 of neurotic phenomena via the "core complex" and the historical basis for culture stemming from the real oedipal rebellion of the sons in the primal horde. I am thus in agreement with Rudnytsky (1992) that the trajectory of the Oedipus complex is one of "deferred action" more than unexpected elaboration.

4. The German text here is quite forceful: "Ich hoffe, viele von Ihnen haben die erschütternde Wirkung der Tragödie, in welcher Sophokles diesen Stoff behandelt, *an sich selbst erlebt*" (Studienausgabe 1: 324; my emphasis).

5. For a detailed analysis of this argument, see Armstrong 1999b; and for an excellent argument that shows how Freud deploys the genre of tragedy to assert the tragic "necessity" of psychoanalytic knowledge, see Winter 1999, chapter 2.

6. Freud is not alone in this shift, however. For a view of the nineteenth century as an "Age of Oedipus" which took the figure of Oedipus to be a universal figure, see Rudnytsky 1987, pt. 2. There is a minority argument forwarded by Goodhart (1978) and Ahl (1991) that claims Oedipus *mistakenly* convicts himself; all subsequent identification with Oedipus would be thus a catastrophic error.

7. Robert (1915), for example, traces the origin of the Oedipus saga to a *Naturmythos* wherein Oedipus is a *daimôn* of fertility. Constans (1881) traces the story instead to a solar myth where Oedipus represents light struggling against darkness. In both these examples, Oedipus' moral conflict is considered a later elaboration of a primeval natural allegory. On the very problematic issue of Sophocles' religiosity, see the concise statement by Robert Parker (1999).

8. *Introductory Lectures on Psycho-Analysis,* SE 15:208: "It is my unaltered conviction that there is nothing in this [sc. the literal interpretation of the Oedipus legend] to be disavowed or glossed over. We must reconcile ourselves to the fact [*Tatsache*] which was recognized by the Greek legend itself as an inevitable fate."

9. The history of the press is recounted in the catalog essays from the 1995 exhibition

in Vienna (Sigmund Freud-Museum Wien 1995). For versions of the logo, see especially page 8. The 1910 bookplate is a lithograph produced by Bertold Löffler, based, it seems, on the medallion presented to Freud in 1906, itself a somewhat altered depiction of the encounter seen in Ingres' painting of 1808.

10. *Three Essays on the Theory of Sexuality*, SE 7:195; "The Sexual Enlightenment of Children," SE 9:135; "Analysis of a Phobia in a Five-Year-Old Boy," SE 10:133; *Introductory Lectures on Psycho-Analysis*, SE 16:318; and "An Autobiographical Study," SE 20:37.

11. It is interesting to note the great difference between Ingres' version and the more ambiguous paintings by Gustave Moreau ("Oedipus and the Sphinx," 1864) and Fernand Khnopff ("Art, the Sphinx, or the Caresses," 1896) where Oedipus is physically touched by the Sphinx, violently in the former and lovingly in the latter. Either case invites a Freudian reading much more overtly than Ingres' version, which seems rather to reflect the professional distance of the analyst.

12. Egon Flaig (1998, chapter 4) points out that Oedipus conceives of power purely in terms of *turannis* or tyranny, instead of the legitimate kingship (*basileia*) established at Thebes since the times of Cadmus. The irony is, of course, that the "tyrant" Oedipus is actually Laius' legitimate heir (and also a Semite by descent from the Phoenician Cadmus), and therefore rules as *basileus*.

13. Highly relevant here is François Roustang's observation that the movement refused to relinquish the transference to Freud which is scheduled to be overcome in the analyses of patients ([1976] 1982, 34).

14. Jacques Lacan remarks, "Thus Freud's words to Jung—I have it from Jung's own mouth—when, on an invitation from Clark University, they arrived in New York harbor and caught their first glimpse of the famous statue illuminating the universe, 'They don't realize we're bringing them the plague,' are attributed to him as confirmation of a hubris whose antiphrasis and gloom do not extinguish their troubled brightness" ([1966] 1977, 116).

15. Goux (1993) terms this the "monomyth of royal investiture." Goux's reading is too complex to relate here, but fundamentally he assumes that the myth of Oedipus is aberrant in being patricidal, not matricidal; for Goux, however, the Sphinx is central to the myth in representing the feminine-maternal.

16. Goux (1993) not only attempts to undo Freud through Freud's reading of Oedipus, but also the whole tradition of western philosophy to boot.

17. On the concept of "oedipal textuality," see Chase [1986] 1994.

18. Freud, however, preferred to map his oedipal rivalry onto the Sphinx episode by claiming that the Sphinx represented *the father*, not the mother ("Dostoevsky and Parricide," SE 21:188). "The hero commits the deed unintentionally and apparently uninfluenced by the woman; this latter element is however taken into account in the circumstance that the hero can only obtain possession of the queen mother after he has repeated his deed upon the monster who symbolizes the father." But this was written in 1927, which suggests that he was reacting to Rank's maternal reading of the Sphinx. I return to this below in chapter 4.

19. For discussions of Rank's biography in relation to the movement, see especially Klein 1981, chapter 4, and Homans 1989, 152–171.

20. For the mythic background, see Gantz 1993, 488–492, and especially the scholia to Euripides, *Phoenissae* 1760. On the theme of the curse, see West 1999. Euripides wrote an entire tragedy on the plight of this young man, Chrysippus, for which the extant fragments and testimonia can be found in Nauck 1964, 632–635 (nos. 839–844). On the notion of a "Laius complex," see Devereux [1953] 1988 and John Munder Ross [1982] 1988.

21. One of the many dramatic ironies early in the play is that Oedipus says he will pursue Laius' murderer as if Laius were his own father (264), and then proceeds to recite Laius' genealogy going back to old Agenor the Phoenician (267–268) without knowing that he has his place in this same line of descent.

4. Leonardo's Gay Science

1. This study has been thoroughly discredited for its historical reasoning by Stannard (1980, chapter 1), and as an art-historical study by Schapiro (1956). However, it was staunchly defended by Kurt Eissler (1961), and recently upheld as a psychological challenge to art history by Herding (2000). For a thorough review of Freud's work and the responses to it, see Bradley Collins 1997.

2. The Leonardo study was originally published in *Schriften zur angewandten Seelenkunde*, the same series where the *Gradiva* study appeared. While it was not the first psychoanalytic pathography to be written, it was Freud's first such endeavor (and, it turns out, his last).

3. In fact, Mut was *not* generally depicted as vulture-headed (as the goddess Nekhbet was), nor was she "usually represented" with a phallus. Mut's cult evolved over a considerable time and showed a great deal of variety in her manifestations, which ranged from casting her as a daughter, to a wife, to a matronly mother or crone. Lesko (1999, chapter 6) traces the cult in good detail.

4. Freud was certainly not alone in suggesting the infantile or childlike nature of ancient thought. Stanley Hall, for example, threads such phylogenetic comparisons throughout his work *Adolescence*; e.g., "In the souls of early races, which are only those of children magnified, the culture period begins with the domestication of fire, or subjecting Agni, or the yet wilder Loki, to the rule of Hestia" ([1904] 1969, 2:189).

5. For an extended argument that Freud's use of isolated "specimens" is a devolution to Aristotelian science, see Spence 1994.

6. We still lack an adequate study of the *exact* difference between Jung's and Freud's invocations of phylogeny and recapitulation, particularly as it emerged from their initial *agreement* on the validity of this approach.

7. There is the additional incestuous tinge to "Philippsohn," in that Freud's half-brother Philipp was only one year younger than his mother Amalie, and as a boy Freud seems to have suspected that somehow his brother was responsible for getting his mother pregnant (*The Psychopathology of Everyday Life*, SE 6:51–52, note 2; see also McGrath 1986, 34–39). Freud notes that he learned the word *vögeln* from a playmate whose name was also Philipp (*The Interpretation of Dreams*, SE 5:583).

8. On Freud's use of an expanded concept of translation, see Mahony 1980.

9. For the analogical role of the Egyptian pantheon, see also the Wolf Man case: "So it was that his mental life impressed one in much the same way as the religion of Ancient Egypt, which is so unintelligible to us because it preserves the earlier stages of its development side by side with the end-products, retains the most ancient gods and their attributes along with the most modern ones, and thus, as it were, spreads out upon a two-dimensional surface what other instances of evolution show in the solid" (SE 17:119).

10. The ferocity of Mut pales in comparison to the Hindu mother goddess Kali, still worshiped in India today (and for whose cult there are still illegal instances of human sacrifice). The British psychoanalyst C. D. Daly (1884–1950) was very interested in the figure of Kali in Hindu society, and even discussed his ideas with Freud, who found them an

important confirmation of psychoanalytic theory. See Daly's article on Kali in *Imago* (1927), and Hartnack 2001, 69–77, on Daly, his theories, and British colonialism in India.

11. The view of the mother-son bond put forward in the Leonardo study should also be read in the light of Freud's biographical experience, which was quite the opposite of isolated doting. Breger (2000) goes so far as to characterize his infancy as "traumatic" based upon his loss of intimacy with his mother (due to illness, death, and grief) and the disappearance of his nursemaid (17).

12. I find it hard to believe that so careful a scholar as John Kerr should claim that the Leonardo study has no oedipal themes (1993, 261). As I argue here, the oedipal dynamic (though it is not called a "complex") is central to understanding Freud's psychological configuration of empirical science.

13. Freud's reading of Leonardo's untimely scientific status forms part of a nineteenth-century tradition of casting the Italian master as the "Harbinger of Modernity," as A. Richard Turner argues (1993, chapter 7). Freud's awareness of this tradition was mediated through the novel by D. Merezhkovsky, *The Romance of Leonardo da Vinci* (English edition: London, 1903; German edition: Leipzig, 1903).

14. Freud's concept of passivity is complex and is the subject of an entire monograph by Russell Davis (1993). While he claims not to equate femininity with passivity on occasion (e.g., *New Introductory Lectures on Psycho-Analysis*, SE 22:115), Freud very often assumes that very equation.

15. It is important to note the personal connection between the discussion of the Moirai and Freud's dream of the Three Fates (*Interpretation of Dreams*, SE 4:204–205); see the discussion by Jonte-Pace (2001, 54–61).

16. For further reflection on femininity, Jewishness, and the "counter-thesis" of Freud's texts, again see Jonte-Pace 2001, which builds significantly on Sprengnether's influential book.

17. The term "paternal romance" I take from Robert Con Davis' excellent book by that name (1993). As I hope to show in a second book on classical education in Freud's day, the paradigms of illustrious virility encoded in the study of the *viri illustres* of antiquity amount to just such a paternal romance on a wide scale. This paternal romance greatly affected the young Jewish students in the *Gymnasien*, as we see in Freud's identification with Hannibal (see my discussion below in chapter 11).

5. The Cunning of Tradition

1. Again, I use the terms "science" and *Wissenschaft* in a neutral sense in Freud's case, since this is what *he* says he is doing.

2. Since I am interested in reproducing the horizon of the first edition of the *Interpretation of Dreams*, I cite throughout this section from the Joyce Crick translation (Freud [1900] 1999) which attempts to reproduce *only* the first edition. The later elaboration of this text reflects many conflicting trends in the development of psychoanalysis, for which see Marinelli and Mayer 2002.

3. Freud in fact is responsible for greatly improving the interest in Artemidorus' *Oneiro-critica* and had a material impact on the fate of that text in translation. Initially he had consulted the German translation by Friedrich Krauss (1881), but he complains in a footnote in *The Interpretation of Dreams* that Krauss had omitted certain crucial chapters that dealt with sexuality in dreams (SE 5:606, note 2). Krauss took the criticism to heart, it seems, for he later published in his own periodical *Anthropophyteia* a translation of the missing ma-

terial by Paul Brandt (alias Hans Licht), who explicitly mentions "the highly important work of the well known Viennese psychoanalyst Professor Freud and his students" as the reason why such a translation is now appropriate (Artemidorus n.d., 317). The later editions of *The Interpretation of Dreams* cite both translations. In an English translation published in 1975, we find the translator echoing Brandt's convictions about the importance of Freud. "The current interest in dreams and their meaning for man is one of the hallmarks of the intellectual life of this century. Freud's revolutionary theories of dream interpretation were doubtless initially responsible for this interest" (Artemidorus 1975, vii). Note, however, that Roger Pack in his 1963 edition of the Greek text shows no interest in Freud, but rather claims a historical interest in how the *homines proletarii* lived, what they hoped for, feared and believed (Artemidorus 1963, v).

4. On the inherent contradictions of this later trend with the initial enterprise of *The Interpretation of Dreams*, see the excellent study by Marinelli and Mayer (2002). Ilse Grubrich-Simitis has discovered notes that show Freud's assembling of material on universal symbols, wherein he makes the comment: "It goes much further than I thought" ([1993] 1996, 104).

5. This is the basis for a fairly standard critique of Freud on the part of classicists interested in ancient dream books and sexuality in general; namely, that in antiquity there is no isolatable "sexuality" that stands apart from the intricate mesh of social relations, honor, pleasure, and wealth. For studies of Artemidorus from a non-Freudian perspective, see Winkler 1990, chapter 1; Nussbaum 1994.

6. Alfred Adler was profoundly concerned with aggression and the will-to-power in the formation of personality themes, and Wilhelm Stekel, according to Fritz Wittels, "had discovered death instincts decades before [Freud] in dreams, and had recognized them to be the bipolar counterpart to the ferment of life" (Wittels [1924] 1971, 252).

7. For an excellent discussion of Freud and Empedocles, see Kofman [1974] 1991, chapter 2.

8. A concise introduction to the most important fragments of Empedocles' work can be found in Kirk, Raven and Schofield 1983, chapter 10. More extensive fragments and discussion can be found in Inwood 2001 (which includes recently discovered material), or in Wright [1981] 1995. Relevant to Freud's background is the chapter by his friend, the scholar Theodor Gomperz, in *Greek Thinkers* ([1905] 1931, 1: chapter 5).

9. As I discuss below, *Beyond the Pleasure Principle* culminates in a deployment of the myth of the three sexes from Plato's *Symposium* (SE 18: 57–58).

10. What I describe in terms of *habitus*, Derrida (1995, 91) approaches as *mal d'archive* or "archive fever." "It is to burn with a passion. It is never to rest, interminably, from searching for the archive right where it slips away. It is to run after the archive, even if there's too much of it, right where something in it anarchives itself. It is to have a compulsive, repetitive, and nostalgic desire for the archive, an irrepressible desire to return to the origin, a homesickness, a nostalgia for the return to the most archaic place of absolute commencement."

11. Masson (1984), for example, suggests Freud's seduction hypothesis was abandoned to save Fliess from accusations of molestation; Krüll ([1979] 1986) among others suggests it was to protect his father, Jakob. In a very convincing account by Louis Breger (2000, chapter 10), oedipal theory masks Freud's sense of trauma and loss particularly in reference to his mother Amalie.

12. For Hitler's discussion of the Parliament building, see *Mein Kampf* ([1925] 1999, 75–77). The building was designed by the Danish architect Theophilus Hansen, who had

also designed a number of the most famous neo-classical buildings in Athens. He built the first story in rough masonry to give the building the appearance of resting on a natural rock formation like the Acropolis of Athens. To underscore the Athenian connection, a massive statue of Pallas Athena stands right in front of the building, which Freud would pass on his daily walk along the *Ringstrasse*. On the *Ringstrasse* architecture in general, see Schorske's classic essay in 1981, chapter 1.

13. On the complex relationship between Orientalism and anti-Semitism, see Hess 2002, chapter 2.

14. Edward Said in *Freud and the Non-European* says quite flatly, "I believe it is true that Freud's was a Eurocentric view of culture—and why should it not be? His world had not yet been touched by the globalization, or rapid travel, or decolonialization, that were to make many formerly unknown or repressed cultures available to metropolitan Europe" (2003, 16). This discounts, however, all too easily Freud's awareness of Indian realities, both on the cultural level through Romain Rolland and the political level through C. D. Daly and others (see Hartnack 2001). One could also argue that if Moses Mendelssohn could be highly tolerant of Indian religion, then we need not lightly excuse Freud (see Hess 2002, 126–127).

15. Freud was counseled to read Buckle, among other things, by his classmate and friend, the future socialist leader Heinrich Braun. See Knoepfmacher 1979, 296.

6. Conquest and Interpretation

1. William Boven published an early psychoanalytic study of Alexander in *Imago* (1922), which has been utterly ignored by classical scholars. It is not known what Freud thought of this study.

2. On the general reception of Roman culture, see Edwards 1999.

3. The elaboration of this "political myth" has been very well studied by Belgum 1998; Callies 1975; Dörner 1993, 1997; Engelbert 1975; Gössmann 1977; Schama 1996; Seeba 1993; and Tacke 1992. Arminius had an important literary prehistory in the eighteenth century, which is discussed in Krebs 1992, Herrmann 1995, and Schumann 1997. For the historical Arminius, see the monograph by Dieter Timpe (1970) and the new book by Peter Wells (2003), which reflects the new perspective on the battle since the discovery of the battlefield itself in 1987 (a discovery Freud would have much enjoyed!). In some *Gymnasien* after the unification of Germany, it was customary to perform Arminius plays on the Kaiser's birthday (see Kraenkel 1893). The bitter post–World War I invocation of Arminius can be found in "Hermann der Cherusker" (1925), Ruperti 1925, and Paul Albrecht's terrible novel, *Arminius-Sigurfrid, Der Roman des deutschen Volkes* (1920). The Nazi invocation can be found in Groh 1934, and is discussed in Seeba 1993. The first indictment of the "Arminius complex" can be found in Thion 1877, a French edition of Ulrich von Hutten's *Arminius* published in the wake of the Franco-Prussian War.

4. The official *Hermannsdenkmal* website is currently at URL www.hermannsdenkmal.de. Veddeler (1975) examines in detail several national festivals that were held there. Hans Schmidt's monograph (n.d.) argues that the monument must be understood as representing a popular movement led by a private individual in the interest of national unity, and not an imposition from above. The post-1870 excesses of aggressive nationalism which centered on the monument are not a part of its true conception. There is a *Bruderdenkmal* in New Ulm, Minnesota, which reflects the activities of the Sons of Hermann lodges once very prevalent in American regions heavily settled by Germans. Many of

these lodges still exist as benevolent organizations no longer strictly tied to German ancestry, and currently the Texas Sons of Hermann organization claims 78,000 members (www.texashermannsons.org).

5. Much of what the Germans make of Arminius cannot be understood without first examining the neo-Roman pretensions of the contemporary French. On the French Revolution's complex invocations of antiquity, see Parker [1937] 1965 and Vidal-Naquet 1990, especially 161–264. For the Enlightenment background, see especially Gay 1975. On Napoleon III, see Baguley 2000.

6. Such nationalistic uses of the *Germania* have a long history. See Krapf 1979.

7. Freud describes his relationship with von Kraus as "indifferent, even comfortable" to Fliess on Oct. 15, 1897 (Masson 1985, 271). A recurrent dream concerning von Kraus's role in his *Matura* is discussed in SE 4:275; from a comment at SE 4:17, it seems Freud still met von Kraus from time to time in the 1890s, when he was a prominent member of the German National Party. For the political background, see especially McGrath 1974 and 1986.

8. As recently as 1998, we find Martha Himmelfarb commenting: "Alexander the Great could not have realized that from the point of view of later generations the most momentous result of his campaign of world conquest was neither the unification of all Greece nor the fall of the Persian empire, but rather the exposure of the Jews—a small and unimportant people—to the culture of their new rulers" (199).

9. The strongest statement of this ideology can be found in Plutarch's essays "On the Fortune or the Virtue of Alexander" (*Moralia* 326d–345b). At 328e, in particular, Plutarch holds the imperialist line that the barbarians conquered by Alexander were happier than those who escaped his hand, for they were led out of their native savagery to civilization. Green argues that these works were written by a very young Plutarch, who had changed his attitude considerably when writing his *Life of Alexander* (1991, 445–446).

10. It was common psychoanalytic dogma that the hero is the man who overcomes his father, but in *Moses and Monotheism* Freud goes to greater lengths to place the Great Man of History in the position of the Father. Since the oedipal impulse is to be and be rid of the Father, there is no real contradiction in the two positions.

11. The classic studies of Freud's retreat into science from politics are Schorske 1981, chapter 8, and McGrath 1986. A first serious blow to his "German" identity came already in 1875, when Theodor Billroth ignited anti-Semitic disturbances at the university with a report on the medical student body that showed strident prejudice, particularly against Eastern European Jews. See Klein 1985, 51; Emanuel Rice, 1990, 194–196.

12. Scholars who are willing to entertain this view are Badian 1963; Green 1991, 109–110; and especially Milns 1968, 31, who declares: "There can be little doubt that Alexander became King by becoming a parricide." On the other hand, W. W. Tarn, who prefers not to see Alexander's dark side, pronounces him "absolutely" acquitted of complicity, preferring the idea of a Persian plot (1948, 1:3); and N. G. L. Hammond, a very eminent historian of Greece, has recently asserted that Alexander was not only innocent, but surely another target of the plot (1997, 29). Hammond's Alexander is thus traumatized by being a witness to his father's murder, which "must have haunted [him] for the rest of his life" (1997, 27).

13. This is the gist of Donald Spence's critique of Freud's scientific approach (1994): he devolves psychoanalysis into an Aristotelian science based on the masterful interpretation of a few choice specimens which he controls almost exclusively.

14. Derrida, "Freud and the Scene of Writing" ([1967] 1978, chapter 7); he makes the disanalogy quite clear: "But [Freud] makes of psychical writing so originary a production

that the writing we believe to be designated by the proper sense of the word—a script which is coded and visible 'in the world'—would only be a metaphor of psychical writing. This writing, for example, the kind we find in dreams that 'follow the old facilitations,' a simple moment in regression toward a 'primary' writing, cannot be read in terms of any code. It works, no doubt, with a mass of elements which have been codified in the course of an individual or collective history. But in its operations, lexicon, and syntax a purely idiomatic residue is irreducible and is made to bear the burden of interpretation in the communication between unconsciousnesses" (209).

15. Just as Freud has his true believers, so does Schliemann, particularly in German-speaking Europe, where Manfred Korfmann and Joachim Lactacz have renewed the fight to secure Schliemann's site as the Homeric Troy. See Korfmann and Mannsperger 1998, and Latacz 2001.

16. On the very problematic nature of Schliemann's personality and his discoveries, see especially Traill 1995 and Allen 1999. A general view of the significance of his finds is given by Fitton 1996. D'Agata (1994) gives a precise discussion of the Mycenean material in Freud's collection. The psychoanalyst William Niederland undertook an extensive psychoanalytic study of Schliemann, part of which appeared in professional journals (1965a, 1965b). To my knowledge, this remains completely ignored by Schliemann scholars, at least to judge by their bibliographies.

17. Objections to the content of the Freud exhibit at the Library of Congress delayed its presentation for some time. In contrast, the controversy over the German Troy exhibit seems to have developed in retrospect, when the ancient historian Frank Kolb, Manfred Korfmann's colleague in Tübingen, expressed severe criticism of Korfmann's elaborate "reconstruction" of Homeric Troy. This archaeological debate was widely reported in leading newspapers in Germany, where Schliemann remains a powerful figure of memory, as well as in more popular archaeological journals abroad. The controversy is still monitored on Korfmann's *Projekt Troia* website at http://www.uni-tuebingen.de/troia/.

18. My point is that Löwy was a living *connection* to archaeology, not that he was himself the great excavator that Schliemann was. In point of fact, Löwy did not excavate much, but was chiefly concerned with matters of art history and epigraphy. However, he was well aware of the whole field of archaeology and could have certainly kept Freud up to date on the excavations in Italy in addition to his own experience in Asia Minor.

19. For Löwy's relations with the Italian royal couple (Victor Emmanuel III and Elena di Montenegro Petrovich-Njegos), see Freud's letter to Ferenczi of October 27, 1910 (Brabant et al., 2:229). Bianchi Bandinelli (1978, 117) stresses the importance of Löwy's attempt to reconnect the study of archaeology to the question of the essence of art, which is precisely where Winckelmann's own great achievement lay. Löwy returned to Vienna in 1915 after Italy's entry into WWI. Among Löwy's Viennese students were the famous art critic Ernst Gombrich and Ernst Kris, a curator at the Kunsthistorisches Museum in Vienna who became an adherent of psychoanalysis and wrote important works on the art of the insane and other topics in the psychology of the arts.

20. This may be responsible for Freud's casting of his desire to make a Rome journey as a choice between Hannibal and Winckelmann based on a misquotation of Jean Paul Richter (*Interpretation of Dreams*, SE 4:196). In a memorable chapter, William McGrath (1986, 209–213) discussed this "choice" as characterizing Freud's dilemma either to concede to Catholic Rome and enter it compromised like Winckelmann, or to continue his struggle with the *Erbfeind* in the manner of Hannibal. But Löwy showed Freud a way to enter Rome as a Jew without compromising with Catholicism. The citation in question is from Jean Paul's *Siebenkäs*, chapter 3, in which he discusses the protagonist's agitation at

drafting a text: "Ich kenne keinen größern geistigen Tumult—kaum einen süßern—in einem jungen Menschen, als wenn er in der Stube auf- und abgeht und den kühnen Entschluß fasset, ein Buch Konzeptpapier zu nehmen und ein Manuskript daraus zu machen—ja man kann darüber disputieren, ob der Konrektor Winckelmann *und* der Feldherr Hannibal hurtiger die Stube auf- und abliefen, als *beide* des ebenso kühnen Sinnes wurden, nach Rom zu gehen" (my emphasis).

21. Jack Spector (1972, 84–85) argues for some influence on Freud from Löwy's *The Rendering of Nature in Greek Art*, which appeared the same year as *The Interpretation of Dreams* (1900). The thesis of Löwy's book is that there are basic visual patterns in early Greek art which represent primitive images residual in the collective memory, and he engages in the kind of comparative analysis between the thinking processes of children, primitives, and early Greeks in which Freud himself was wont to engage (as in *Totem and Taboo*). Löwy holds that a schematic memory develops in the form of a "memory-picture," which bears resemblance to the Platonic Idea, and that art produced from this takes on a highly stylized—even unnatural—appearance. Spector argues that "Not only would Freud have been receptive to his friend's use of the Platonic theory of reminiscence, but to his linking of early stages of artistic realization to processes that parallel those of the dream-work and of regression in their removal from realistic perception to a more 'primitive' condition of mental work" (1972, 215 note 12). It seems unlikely that we can settle the question of influence (that is, of Freud on Löwy or vice versa), and the problem with Spector's suggestion is that he does not take into account how prevalent the recourse to such arguments was at the time. The parallel does, however, show the natural affinity between the two men's fields, regardless of the discrete lines of direct communication. At this writing Dr. Knut Ebeling of the Humboldt Universität of Berlin is undertaking a detailed examination of the correspondences between Löwy and Freud's works. This is part of a larger multi-person research project titled *Archive der Vergangenheit: Wissenstransfers zwischen Archäologie, Philosophie und Künsten*. I thank Dr. Ebeling for advance copies of his texts. For an analysis of Löwy's later work on the origin of artistic creation ("Ursprünge der bildenden Kunst" 1930), see the short essay by Michael Weissl (1998).

22. For a list of Löwy's books in Freud's library, see Botting and Davies 1989, 190.

23. Unpublished letter from Emanuel Löwy to Sigmund Freud, Rome August 21, 1905. I gratefully acknowledge my debt to Michael Molnar and Christfried Tögel for their timely transcription of this letter.

24. For the history of archaeological thought, see Trigger 1989. For current debates on archaeology and interpretation, see Bapty and Yates 1990; Hodder 1995; Tilley 1999; Andrew Jones 2002; and Joyce 2002. For the social and cultural history of archaeology, see Hudson 1981; Sichtermann 1996; and especially Marchand 1996. On the Austrian excavations in Ephesus in particular, see Wiplinger and Wlach 1996. Freud would no doubt have been pleased to see the new work in the "archaeology of sexuality," for which see Schmidt and Voss 2000.

25. In this connection, it is important to note that *saxa loquuntur* is an architectural motto as well as an archaeological one, used in connection to the historicist smorgasbord along the Viennese *Ringstrasse*.

26. On the Cambridge Ritualists in general, see Ackerman 1991.

27. For a procedure so devoted to the verbal interchange between analyst and analysand, it is odd, Donald Spence notes, that there is no archive of analyses that would allow one to see *verbatim* what is brought to the analytic surface (1994).

28. McCaffrey (1984) explains very well what was at stake for Freud's dream theory in

the Dora analysis, and uses the account instead to offer a fuller view of the dream phenomenon.

7. Memory, Biography, History, Myth

1. This is not to say that Foucault's paradigm is entirely wrong. It works better for the anecdotal collations of evidence one finds in the works of Ellis and Krafft-Ebing, and is even more forcefully suggested by the latter's translation of the affidavits of sexual deviants into Latin.

2. It seems Foucault's target is rather a *banalization* of psychoanalysis, as when he comments wryly, "Ours is, after all, the only civilization in which officials are paid to listen to all and sundry impart the secrets of their sex: as if the urge to talk about it, and the interest one hopes to arouse by doing so, have far surpassed the possibilities of being heard, so that some individuals have even offered their ears for hire" ([1976] 1980, 7).

3. Foucault's blindness toward the crucial Freudian metaphor of archaeology stems from his desire to co-opt it for his own "archaeology of knowledge." Thus he can state that "The history of the deployment of sexuality, as it has evolved since the classical age, can serve as an *archaeology of psychoanalysis*," without however discussing Freud's own deployment of archaeology itself ([1976] 1980, 130; my emphasis).

4. Thinking of the past as *res digestae* is in fact essential to Augustine's view of memory as the "belly of the mind" (*venter animi*); cf. *Confessions* 10.14.

5. I read psychoanalysis obviously from the standpoint of its cultural applications and published case histories. There is, however, a serious debate about narrative in relation to memory in the clinical setting, and the reader should beware that analysts lay claim to doing much more than telling stories in their work. On the role of narrative versus history in the clinical setting, see especially Spence 1982, Wallace 1985, Prager 1998, and Cotti 2004. For the broader issue of the "past" as it intersects with clinical needs, see Modell 1990 and Lamm 1993.

6. By "memory work" I mean broadly any process of elaborating an account, archive, or relationship to the past. This comprises not only the analytic endeavor to recollect and reconstruct, but also the historian's scholarly work and even ritual enactments such as commemorations. Some might object that I make no distinction between the distorting dynamics of tradition and the scholarly principles of historiography, but for my purposes it makes more sense to view the similarities of these operations, since they are organically linked. I can clarify this with an analogy. Freud's "dream work" represents the process of distortion in dreams, not the process of analytical understanding. However, to arrive at the latter, he had to first *posit* the processes of distortion that allow him then to retrace the movement from the manifest dream content to the latent dream thoughts. So Freud's "dream work" we might say, as a product of his theorizing, is just the other side of his dream analysis, not a natural process independent of it. Thus critical historiography, by offering explanations for traditional distortion and subsequent cures for it, similarly represents a more complex form of memory work and not something utterly different in kind.

7. For a different approach to narrative based on Freud's metapsychology, see Brooks 1984.

8. In his 1915 paper "Repression" Freud makes the clearest statement that this concept concerns both a primary act of repression as well as an ongoing one, a kind of "after-pressure" (SE 14:148).

9. Freud uses the image of the boomerang (or rather, the adverb *bumerangartig*

[boomerang-like]) to describe the trajectory of monotheism among the Jews in *Moses and Monotheism* (SE 23:110).

10. In "The Unconscious" (1915) Freud defines timelessness for the unconscious processes thus: "they are not ordered temporally, are not altered by the passage of time; they have no reference to time at all. Reference to time is bound up [. . .] with the work of the system Cs. [consciousness]" (SE 14:187). This does then raise the question of how there can be any analogy with stratigraphy for the excavation of the unconscious.

11. On the "mobility" of interest, see "Repression," SE 14:151. The economic metaphor is thoroughly Freudian, functioning at times in reference to the expenditure of libidinal "energy" and at times as an analogy with financial ventures (e.g., the ego is an *entrepreneur*, the id a capitalist). For the characterization that the contemporary European society is psychologically "living beyond its means," see "'Civilized' Sexual Morality and Modern Nervous Illness," SE 9:181–204.

12. In Lecture 21 of the *Introductory Lectures*, Freud discusses the origin of "evil impulses" in dreams from the Oedipus complex: "They are allocations of the libido and object-cathexes which date from early infancy and have long since been abandoned as far as conscious life is concerned, but which prove still to be present at night-time and to be capable of functioning in a certain sense" (SE 16:338). This largely corresponds to the conclusion of *The Interpretation of Dreams*, though more emphasis is put particularly on the Oedipus complex in the *Lectures*.

13. Such is the formulation in "Remembering, Repeating, and Working Through" (1914; SE 12: 146–156).

14. One could argue that these negative judgments on biography from Freud's later life stem from his own experience by that time of being the victim of biographers. His biographical "deflowering" as he termed it was at the pen of Fritz Wittels, a follower who parted ways with him for a time and who wrote a critical biography of him during their separation ([1924] 1971). Wittels later atoned for this book when he rejoined the Freudian fold and wrote another study (1931). Worse still was the biographical attack on Freud by the anti-Semitic Charles Maylan, *Freuds tragischer Komplex: eine Analyse der Psychoanalyse* (1929). Thus the difference in Freud's attitude from the days of the Leonardo study of 1910 may stem from his bitter personal experience, something Adam Phillips fails to consider in his otherwise fine essay on Freud and biography (2000). On the theory and practice of early psychoanalytic biography, see especially Sadger 1909 and 1912.

15. The Latin phrase *coitus a tergo* means "intercourse from behind," i.e. "doggy-style" or *more ferarum* as Freud prefers to gloss it ("in the manner of beasts"). It does not imply *anal* intercourse (*per anum*), as is mistakenly asserted by Whitney Davis (1996, chapter 11).

16. Gardiner 1971 details the Wolf Man's later experiences and his becoming a virtual ward of the movement after WWI. For a complex and clever view of the Wolf Man's case, see Johnson 2001.

17. The constitutive paradox of psychoanalysis is that it is predicated on a world of mere chance, utterly without divine providence or inherent teleology, and yet it is a radically determined world where even mental events have their definite and definable causes.

18. Donald Spence, for one, separates entirely the "narrative truth" of analysis from the search for "historical truth," blaming Freud for confusing the issues (1982).

19. In the later nineteenth century, the most authoritative interpretation of catharsis, which appears for the first time as a literary concept somewhat enigmatically in Aristotle's *Poetics*, was in fact by Jacob Bernays, the uncle of Freud's wife Martha and a distinguished classical scholar in Germany ([1858] 1970; see also Fraenkel 1932). Josef Breuer was himself in direct contact with the classical scholar Theodor Gomperz on the topic of cathar-

sis, which leads us to suspect that there is a direct connection to be made between cathartic therapy and the theatrical concept. See the very thorough article by Volker Langholf (1990) and Hirschmüller 1989, 158–159. For Freud's own expression of visual memory in theatrical terms, see SE 6:47.

20. Freud's most cogent response to this synthetic proposition is in "Lines of Advance in Psychoanalytic Therapy" (SE 17:159–168), where he simply asserts that the ego does the work of integration inherently as the analysis overcomes the resistances. "The psychosynthesis is thus achieved during analytic treatment *without our intervention, automatically and inevitably*" (SE 17:161; my emphasis).

21. Wittgenstein in fact saw fate and natural law as incompatible concepts. "Fate is the antithesis of natural law. A natural law is something you try to fathom and make use of, but not fate" ([1977] 1984, 61e).

22. Marx [1852] 1978, 597: "The social revolution of the nineteenth century cannot draw its poetry from the past, but only from the future. It cannot begin with itself, before it has *stripped off all superstition in regard to the past*. Earlier revolutions required world-historical recollections in order to drug themselves concerning their own content. In order to arrive at its content, the revolution of the nineteenth century must let the dead bury their dead" (my emphasis).

23. It seems Josef Breuer was the first to use this metaphor in *Studies on Hysteria* for describing the unconscious in general: "This half of a mind is therefore quite complete and conscious in itself. In our cases the part of the mind which is split off is 'thrust into darkness' [*Faust* Part I, iv], as the Titans are imprisoned in the crater of Etna, and can shake the earth but can never emerge into the light of day" (SE 2:229).

24. I should point out that my definition of myth is narratological, yet accommodates ritual and other observances that work by allusion rather than full recitation of the tale. For example, the use of mythical subjects on vases in the ancient world is a comprehensible practice *only* because the static image of, say, Oedipus before the Sphinx, is readable as a moment in the story, not as a static image per se. The tradition of mythical illustrations could thus be considered as a series of snapshots, or stills from a longer movie. In a more precise sense, the "narrative matrix" is the body of narrative versions to which the latest retelling or allusion refers. One should note that it is feasible in the ancient world to allude to a myth *by deviating* from it in some essential detail, as occurs with figures like Helen and Iphigenia.

25. Josef Breuer states clearly in the *Studies on Hysteria* that a scientific mythology is the result of reifying operant metaphors. "It is only too easy to fall into a habit of thought which assumes that every substantive has a substance behind it—which gradually comes to regard 'consciousness' as standing for some actual thing; and when we have become accustomed to make use metaphorically of spatial relations, as in the term 'sub-consciousness,' we find as time goes on that we have actually formed an idea which has lost its metaphorical nature and which we can manipulate easily as though it was real. Our mythology is then complete" (SE 2:227–228).

26. Recently, the new paradigm of String Theory in physics has returned us to this problem of how a new narrativity can radically reorient thought well in advance of any definitive proof. Physicists are currently wondering if String Theory functions as a hypothesis, or whether it is more a speculative "philosophy" or even mythology.

27. I employ the somewhat archaic architectural term "coin of vantage" because it contains a useful pun. On the one hand there is the notion of perspective, the view or "vantage" offered by the deliberate design of a corner lookout ("coin" in the less common sense of "corner"). But there is also in this the echo of the economic "coin" and "*ad*vantage," re-

ferring to the economic interests of the new profession. This term serves to address both the epistemological and sociological features of the psychoanalytic movement.

28. This is precisely why psychoanalysis profoundly irritates professional classicists. On the one hand, it makes much of ancient mythology (producing a vogue for it, in fact) and yet lays reductive claims to presenting its true meaning, ignoring the historical specificity which is the stock-in-trade of the Classics profession. It is therefore virtually a ritual for someone in Classics to take on psychoanalysis and defeat it as a rival to the throne. For examples, see Vernant and Vidal-Naquet 1990, chapter 4; and Eisner 1987.

29. More accurately, the line reads, "This *bow* alone will take Troy."

30. The work in question is Jung's *Transformations and Symbols of the Libido* (1911–1912). In a letter to Freud (September 4, 1912), Jones referred to the galleys of this work, "It is a most rambling and disconnected shoveling in of mythology with occasional remarks of his own" (Paskauskas 1995, 154).

31. For a thorough examination of Freud's deployment of anthropology, see Edwin Wallace 1983.

32. It is worth recalling that Freud himself declared that "The theory of repression is the corner-stone on which the whole structure of psychoanalysis rests" ("On the History of the Psycho-Analytic Movement," SE 14:16).

33. In our own day, archaeology still struggles with the problem of being an interstitial discipline, stuck between the hermeneutic demands of historical interpretation and the physical, scientific demands imposed by the artifacts as objects. See the thoughtful discussion in Andrew Jones 2002.

34. Note too that Lacan, in restructuring what an analyst should know, still keeps history very clearly in the curriculum. "It is with an initiation into the methods of the linguist, the historian and, I would say, the mathematician that we should now be concerned if a new generation of practitioners and researchers is to recover the meaning and the motive force of Freudian experience" ([1966] 1977, 144).

8. Critique and Divination

1. Ilse Grubrich-Simitis has written an eloquent plea for the joys and complications of the physical archive of Freud's writings, including a vast amount of unpublished notes and other material ([1993] 1996).

2. For general background on German historical thought in the nineteenth and twentieth centuries, see Guilland [1915] 1970, Iggers 1968, Krieger 1977, Bambach 1995, and Stuchtey and Wende 2000. For a discussion of the Victorian thirst for a "usable past," see Gay 1995, chapter 3.

3. Livy himself characterizes the moral valence of history in his preface: "This is the healthy and fruitful thing about historical knowledge, namely that you can inspect the records of every kind of [moral] example deposited in a glorious monument, from which you can grasp for yourself and your country what you should imitate and whatever, foul in its inception and foul in its end, you should avoid" (*praefatio* 10).

4. Freud possessed the entire *Römische Geschichte* by Theodor Mommsen (1817–1903), who was Niebuhr's successor as the leader of critical historiography and a giant of nineteenth-century German classical studies. Mommsen's approach thoroughly dominated the professionalized discourse of ancient history and was seriously opposed only by relative cranks like Bachofen. Freud's personal exposure to Niebuhr's ideas was mostly likely indirect, and could have begun either with his reading of Livy in the fifth class of Gymnasium, or in the history lectures on early Rome which occurred in the same year.

5. Freud's reference to his own Hannibal fixation can be found in the *Interpretation of Dreams* (4:196–197). In the *Psychopathology of Everyday Life*, he refers to a Livian anecdote about Tarquin the Proud (*Ab urbe condita* 1.54) in reference to an analysis of a twelve-year-old boy, who "failed to recall it, although he must have learnt it so much more recently than I" (SE 6:198–199). In addition to Livy's account of Hannibal, it is worth mentioning that Freud would also have been familiar with the life of Hannibal from the biographical works of Cornelius Nepos, one of the first texts in Latin he would have read (Schmidt and Gehlen, 1865).

6. The addition of his material in 1907 is significant, as that was around the time Freud was working on "Delusions and Dreams in Jensen's *Gradiva*" as well as "Creative Writers and Day-Dreaming." These two works explicitly analyze the connection between historical analysis, memory, and fantasy, and formed the basis for Rank's investigation of the epic tradition (1917). Rank's own study, in turn, is clearly behind Freud's references in *Moses and Monotheism*. This circularity of influence must be taken into account, and for that reason we probably ought to refer to the Freudian *bottega* instead of just "Freud" or "Rank" in such discussions.

7. Livy *Ab urbe condita* 1.48.7: "There followed an act of bestial inhumanity—history preserves the memory of it in the name of the street, the Street of Crime. The story goes that the crazed woman, driven to frenzy by the avenging ghosts of her sister and husband, drove the carriage over her father's body. Blood from the corpse stained her clothes and spattered the carriage, so that a grim relic of the murdered man was brought by those gory wheels to the house where she and her husband lived. The guardian gods of that house did not forget; they were to see to it, in their anger at the bad beginning of the reign, that as bad an end should follow" ([1960] 2002, 89).

8. For a very sensitive reading of Livy's early history of Rome that overturns many stereotypes of Livian criticism, see Miles (1995), who also treats the linkage of tradition (things heard, *fama, fabula*) and remains (*monumenta*) in Livian discourse. Freud's view of Livy, however, was no doubt far more conventional.

9. There are other reasons to suspect the details of the narrative. The Hellenization of the Tarquin saga has long been taken as proof that it was concocted in order to correspond to Athenian history, namely, the end of the Pisistratid dynasty in the sixth century BCE.

10. See Niebuhr [1811–1832] 1853, 145–148. Niebuhr was convinced of his thesis in large part because of the wealth of attention folk balladry was receiving among his contemporaries, such that he declared confidently: "*Wer in dem Epischen der römischen Geschichte die Lieder nicht erkennt, der mag es: er wird immer mehr allein stehen: hier ist Rückgang für Menschenalter unmöglich*" (1853, 146). On the historical value of the ballad thesis, see Momigliano 1977, 231–251.

11. Niebuhr [1811–1832] 1853, 218: "*So fabelten nach der Herstellung der alten Litteratur italiänische Historiker, welche sich der barbarischen Herrschaft schämten, daß Narses die Gothen, Karl der Große die Longobarden aus ganz Italien vertrieben, und den Römern ihr Land von Fremden und fremden Gesezen gereinigt zurückgegeben haben.*"

12. Niebuhr later softened this thesis, particularly after the advent of Karl Otfried Müller's work (*Die Etrusker*, 1828), a man whom Niebuhr personally disliked and from whom he sought to distance himself (see Cornell 1995, 152). He later held that the Tarquinii were in fact a Latin *gens*, and not Etruscan.

13. For example, Ogilvie in his famous commentary says (1965, 142): "The Etruscans led by Tarquins came to Rome towards the end of the seventh century. Salt and the passage of the Tiber led them on. They created the city and, by whatever means, controlled it." For a discussion of *etruscheria* and a very different kind of hypothesis on Etruscan influence, see T. J. Cornell 1995, chapter 6.

14. Freud mentions in *The Psychopathology of Everyday Life* the "golden rule" of Darwin, which was to note down whatever he discovered in violation of his theory lest he should conveniently forget it (SE 6:148, parts added in 1912). He also cites approvingly Nietzsche's aphorism from *Beyond Good and Evil* (4.68): "'I did this,' says my Memory. 'I cannot have done this,' says my Pride and remains inexorable. In the end—Memory yields" (cited in SE 6:147, note 2 [added in 1910]).

15. On Niebuhr's connection to Macaulay, see Vance 2000. Freud was an avid reader of Macaulay's essays during the 1870s, and may owe his familiarity to the *Lays* from that time. He certainly knew Otto Rank's article on epic poetry from 1917, which discusses Macaulay's *Lays* (378–381). There is an 1884 Longman's edition of the *Lays* in his library at Maresfield Gardens (as reported to me by Michael Molnar). From Macaulay's preface, we can see the garden-variety hermeneutics of suspicion that characterizes the source-critical consciousness of the age. The wise man, he says, will admit that the most important parts of the early Roman narratives "have some foundation in truth. But he will distrust almost all the details, not only because they seldom rest on any solid evidence, but also because he will constantly detect in them, even when they are within the limits of physical possibility, that peculiar character, more easily understood than defined, which distinguishes the creations of the imagination from the realities of the world in which we live" ([1842] 1997, xx).

16. In a compelling analogy, one of a great many in his works, Freud once compared the mental preserve of fantasy to the natural preserve of Yellowstone Park ("Formulations on the Two Principles of Mental Functioning," SE 12:222, note 1). Like the wilderness preserve, fantasy retains its "natural" condition of domination by the pleasure principle.

17. Niebuhr's hypothesis had clear romantic underpinnings: the ballads were the alternative history of the plebs, whereas the annals were the history of the patricians. This is very hard to maintain, however, given the very content of these supposed "ballads."

18. Goethe to Niebuhr, December 17, 1811 (Bunsen et al. 1852, 229); German text in Goethe (1985–, 33:719).

19. On the importance of the date of these additions, see above note 6.

20. Eisler lectured in Oxford during WWII and was active among the Austrian exile community. Michael Molnar of the Freud Museum London has reported to me that Freud's Austrian address book contains Eisler's Vienna address, but to date there is no evidence of personal contact between them, though it is possible that they were somehow in contact, either in Vienna or in England. However, it is also possible that they were not on friendly terms, since Eisler attended the 1935 *Eranos* conference held by Jung, which assembled psychologists with scholars of religion and anthropology. In his extraordinary work *Man into Wolf* (1951), Eisler shows clear indebtedness to Jung and posits a theory of human culture easily as daring as *Totem and Taboo*. No such daring was deployed in his reconstructed life of Jesus.

21. It bears mentioning that most scholars agree the text of Josephus is likely to be corrupt at this passage, but most also reject Eisler's reconstruction.

22. Freud made it clear to Arnold Zweig that his Moses researches were a reaction against the developing anti-Semitism of Germany, particularly after the accession to power of the Nazis in 1933. The genesis of *Moses* is tied to Freud's reading of Zweig's *Bilanz der deutschen Judenheit 1933: Ein Versuch* ([1933] 1998; see also Arnold Zweig 1996). His first mention of the material is in a letter to Zweig of August, 18, 1933, but the draft of the initial Moses study begins August 9, 1934 and Freud's diary records its completion on September 23, 1934 (Molnar 1992, 176).

23. On the relationship between collections, museums, and historical consciousness, see especially Crane 2000, Bennett 1995, and Elsner and Cardinal 1994.

24. Friedrich August Wolf, the founder of an "analytic" Homeric philology ([1795] 1985), was the one to suggest the term divination, which Niebuhr also took up; see Rytkönen 1968, 194 note 1.

25. On the German tradition of "self-cultivation" or *Bildung*, see Bruford 1975.

26. Burckhardt's criticisms of German historicism stem from the cultural difference of his milieu in Basel, as has been argued at great length in Lionel Gossman's magisterial *Basel in the Age of Burckhardt: A Study in Unseasonable Ideas* (2000). See also Hinde 2000 and Howard 2000.

9. The Archaeology of Freedom

1. My own approach obviously takes the view that the archaeological analogy was in a sense a creative alternative to traditional approaches to the self and sexuality. However, its pernicious lingering in the practice of psychotherapy has been attacked by Donald Spence, who comes from the clinical perspective (1982, 1987, 1994). A defense of the analogy has been mounted by Mertens and Haubl (1996). On the force of this figure of thought, see Kuspit 1989, Reinhard 1996, and Stockreiter 1998.

2. In addition to the role of the analyst, Freud also makes reference to the fact that cathartic therapy, through verbalizing the patient's experience, can have an effect similar to confession "In other cases speaking is itself the adequate reflex, when, for instance, it is a lamentation or giving utterance to a tormenting secret, e. g. a confession [in the original German, this was put more emphatically in a parenthetical aside: (*Beichte!*)]" (*Studies in Hysteria*, SE 2:8).

3. In this regard, his analogy with the reconstructions of the "conscientious archaeologist" from the Dora case is instructive ("Fragment of an Analysis of a Case of Hysteria," SE 7:12).

4. In "Analysis Terminable and Interminable," Freud states that the greatest obstacle an analyst faces with a female analysand is penis envy (SE 23:250–253). This leads us to suspect that this moment in the analysis was a clever way of getting H.D. to confront the fact that her anatomy shaped her destiny.

5. On the *Nationalgeschenk*, I follow Jones interpretation of the term ([1953–1957] 1981, 2:389–390).

6. Brabant et al. 1993–2000, 1:136–137.

7. See his letter to Fliess of December 6, 1896 (Masson 1985, 207–214), in which he discusses his assumption that "our psychic mechanism has come into being by a process of stratification" (207); see also Derrida's commentary in "Freud and the Scene of Writing" ([1967] 1978, 200–215). Note, however, that this is a *dynamic* stratification, as is quite evident in his pronouncement: "*the architectonic principle of the mental apparatus lies in a stratification—a building up of superimposed agencies [der Aufbau aus einander überlagernden Instanzen]*" (*The Psychopathology of Everyday Life*, SE 6:147, original emphasis).

10. Uncanny Understanding and a Grave Philosophy

1. On von Kraus, see Knoepfmacher 1979, 293. Freud describes their relationship as "indifferent, even comfortable" to Fliess on Oct. 15, 1897 (Masson 1985, 271). He later often dreamed of being examined by him on history for the *Matura* examination (*The In-*

terpretation of Dreams, SE 4:275). From a comment at SE 4:17, it seems Freud still met von Kraus from time to time in the 1890s, when he was a prominent member of the German National Party.

2. Frazer's stages are magic, religion, and science, but Freud essentially treats magic as the *technique* of animism. In this tripartition, Freud claims to follow "the authorities" (SE 13:77), whom he does not name, though throughout he cites Frazer in his notes. A letter from Jones written in 1914 suggests that there was some concern about originality here. "I find that Comte's three stages of mental development in mankind (which we searched for in vain last year) are: religious, metaphysical, positivist, *so your originality still holds the field*" (Paskauskas 1993, 260; my emphasis). Freud's familiarity with Comte was mediated through his contact as a university student with Franz Brentano, and also through at least one lecture at his student union (Boehlich 1990, 96, 104). However, it seems his scheme in *Totem and Taboo* is more indebted to Frazer.

3. Freud constantly deploys characterizations of childishness versus maturity in his polemic with religion in *The Future of an Illusion*, but this one citation can suffice, "But surely infantilism is destined to be surmounted. Men cannot remain children forever; they must in the end go out into 'hostile life.' We may call this '*education to reality*'" (SE 21:49).

4. Freud comments that Feuerbach is the philosopher "I revere and admire above all other philosophers" in a letter to Eduard Silberstein on March 7, 1875 (Boehlich 1990, 96). It is worth noting this is in reference to a lecture at the student union on the three stages of the human spirit (clearly redolent of Comte) "which culminated in a glorification of modern science and of our most modern saints, such as Darwin and Haeckel, promising the students blessing upon blessing" (Boehlich 1990, 96). See also Stepansky 1986.

5. A similar tendency to find greater affinities with the "practical savage" and his magic than with the Church runs throughout *The Golden Bough* ([1922] 1993, 322): "We may smile at [the savage's] vain endeavours if we please, but it was only by making a long series of experiments, of which some were almost inevitably doomed to failure, that man learned from experience the futility of some of his attempted methods and the fruitfulness of others. After all, magical ceremonies are nothing but experiments which have failed and which continue to be repeated merely because [. . .] the operator is unaware of their failure." Thus the "savage" turns out to be a plucky empiricist in the good old English style.

6. The best treatment of the topic of history and freedom in Freud's thought to date is Roth 1987, though Herbert Marcuse's neglected lectures deserve a wider reading still (1970, especially chapter 1).

7. Like Niebuhr's erotic gazing, Droysen's immediate intuition is couched in sexualized terms. "This act results, under the conditions above explained, as an immediate intuition, wherein soul blends with soul, creatively, after the manner of conception in coition" ([1881] 1967, 14). Freud would no doubt have taken this sexualized formulation as a hint of unconscious understanding.

8. This essay is responsible, in fact, for the common impression that German historicism and English historical positivism are utterly alien to each other. Current research, however, is dismantling this hard dichotomy, and this in itself has implications for understanding Freud. See Stuchtey and Wende 2000.

9. See "The Question of a *Weltanschauung*" in the *New Introductory Lectures* (SE 22:158–182).

10. I borrow this coinage from Ernest Gellner ([1985] 1993, 111).

11. Sándor Ferenczi understood that this unconscious understanding would in effect set phylogenetic concerns to the side. "I find new and outstanding the idea of transmission by means of *unconscious understanding*, which to a certain extent forces the phyloge-

netic theories into the background" (Brabant et al. 1993–2000, 1:494). This is thus one of the possible loopholes for those who wish to save Freud from his Lamarckian sympathies (cf. Bernstein 1998, chapter 2).

12. See for example his dismissal of philosophers as abstract and non-empirical ("The Resistance to Psycho-Analysis," SE 19:216–217); enamored of totalizing systems (*New Introductory Lectures on Psycho-Analysis*, SE 22:160–161); and unable to conceive of unconscious mentation (*The Ego and the Id*, SE 19:14). His dismissive attitude toward German philosophy was—paradoxically—encouraged by his philosophy teacher, Franz Brentano, who in a frank conversation with Freud and other students dismissed Schelling, Fichte, and Hegel as "swindlers" (Boehlich 1990, 104).

13. For thoughtful comments on the "myth of Freud as anti-philosopher," see Herzog 1988.

14. On Freud's contentment to think without ultimate unities, see the interesting conversation about philosophy he had with Lou Andreas-Salomé as reported in her journal (February 23, 1913–1987, 104–106).

15. See his 1915 essay "Thoughts for the Times on War and Death" (SE 14:275–302).

11. The Myth of Ur

1. Freud's comment to Karl Abraham in this regard is quite succinct about the problem of psychoanalysis's Jewish origins: "Our Aryan comrades are really completely indispensable to us, otherwise psychoanalysis would succumb to anti-Semitism" (Abraham and Freud 1965, 64).

2. I say here *historical* armature, but there are those who feel Freud's interpretive art is profoundly Jewish, namely, Susan Handelman (1982). I am not attempting an exclusion of a Jewish thematics so much as calling into question why that thematics must be rooted exclusively in rabbinical or cabbalistic thought which, unlike the historiographical and archaeological intertexts I have been examining, is not formally present in the corpus of Freud's works. That Freud's interpretive verve might be a dynamic cross-fertilization of Jewish and gentile traditions would in fact please me all the more. But any such *rapprochement* would take another book to establish.

3. A more ambitious exploration of "multiple marginality" and cultural creativity is made by Hanák (1998, chapter 7); see also Homans 1989.

4. There are many thoughtful investigations of Freud's relationship to Jewish tradition (Bakan 1958; Robert 1977; Handelman 1982; Gay 1987; Homans 1989; Bloom 1989, chapter 6; Frieden 1990; Feldman 1994) and the Jewish community (Cuddihy 1974; Klein 1981; Diller 1991; Gresser 1994), his relationship to discourses of Jewishness (Gilman 1986, 1993a, 1993b), and his rather ambivalent return to an interest in his own Jewish origins toward the end of his life (Rice 1990; Yerushalmi 1991; Blum 1994; Bernstein 1998). I wish to stress that my own attempt to trace a heterogeneous "Jewish trajectory" for Freud's interests is neither an attempt to undermine his claim to Jewishness (or the claim others make to call him a Jew) nor to "solve" the issue of his status as a European Jew by declaring him blandly universal. I seek the specificity of his Jewish experience through the interactions with the ancient archive, even when those interactions are not archetypical of a monolithic Jewish culture. In this regard, his attendance at the Leopoldstadt *Gymnasium* qualifies as part of a Jewish trajectory (in an historical, sociological sense), even if it is a mainstreaming event in his life and not a separating rite of passage like circumcision or the bar mitzvah. This may seem an unusual approach, but I find it has certain affinities with new ways of articulating Jewishness (i.e., beyond the repetition of ritual practices and tra-

ditional folkways) as well as with new views of identity. See, for example, Jonathan Boyarin's "Yiddish Science and the Postmodern" and "Before the Law There Stands a Woman" (1996); Silberstein 2000; and Richard Handler's "Is Identity a Useful Cross-Cultural Concept?" (in Gillis 1994, chapter 1), which flatly declares that "Groups are not bounded objects in the natural world. Rather, 'they' are symbolic processes that emerge and dissolve in particular contexts of action" (30). I find myself perhaps most sympathetic with the approach of José Brunner 1995, especially chapter 3, and Gilman 1993b.

5. I am admittedly narrowing the focus to Freud and his immediate Viennese followers for ease of presentation. One should also account for the departures from Christian tradition on the part of people like Ernest Jones and Carl Jung, but for the moment I have restricted this analysis.

6. Freud stated this perhaps most clearly to the journalist George Sylvester Viereck. "My language . . . is German, my culture, my attainments are German. I considered myself German intellectually, until I noticed the growth of anti-Semitic prejudices in Germany and German Austria. Since that time, I prefer to call myself a Jew." Cited in Gilman 1993b, 16.

7. Boyarin 1997 represents perhaps the most elaborate and eloquent historical interrogation of Jewish male identity to date, though Gilman 1993b is very rich in detail concerning the scientific background.

8. Hengel (1980, 7) describes this as a Palestinian folk tale that had worked its way into a literary version composed in Alexandria by the first century CE; Bickerman (1988, 4–5) refers to it as a "silly tale"; see also Graetz [1894] 1941, 1:412–413; Green 1991, 266; and Gruen 1998, 189–199.

9. Rice (1990, 20) cites another Talmudic legend that Simon the Just deftly evaded Alexander's request for his own image to be placed near the altar in the Jerusalem Temple by having all the sons born to Levites in that year named "Alexander," thus honoring the king through future generations of Jews.

10. The strongest ancient statement that Alexander's cause was essentially that of civilization itself can be found in Plutarch's "On the Fortune or the Virtue of Alexander" (*Moralia* 326d–345b). At 328e, in particular, Plutarch holds the imperialist line that the barbarians conquered by Alexander were happier than those who escaped his hand, for they were led out of their native savagery to civilization. Green argues that these works were written by a very young Plutarch, who had changed his attitude considerably when writing his *Life of Alexander* (1991, 445–446). Among modern scholars, the idea that Alexander ushered in the cosmopolitan era of the "brotherhood of man" has persisted. The equation of Hellenistic culture with the "cause" of European culture at large was made by Gilbert Murray as late as 1954; see Murray 1954.

11. See the letter to Fliess of October 15, 1897 (Masson 1985, 272–273) in which Freud's reading of *Hamlet* follows upon his reading of Oedipus. Though originally a footnote, this reading is later incorporated into the main text of the *Interpretation of Dreams* after 1914 (SE 4:264–266). It was expanded by Ernest Jones into an entire monograph ([1949] 1976). One might say that Freud's reading of Sophocles must be understood in a triangular relationship with *Hamlet* and Goethe's *Faust* — all performed on the Burgtheater's stage during the directorship of Adolf Wilbrandt. It is important to note, however, that the more obvious comparison is between Hamlet and Orestes, undertaken by Gilbert Murray (1914). In this regard we might ask why there is such a silence on the topic of matricide in Freud's works, given its foundational status in Athenian myth.

12. See Freud's letters to Schnitzler of May 8, 1906 (Ernst Freud 1960, 251) and May 14, 1922 (339).

13. Beller ([1989] 1993, 167–168) relates how Vienna, as opposed to other cities and towns with long-standing Jewish communities under their traditional governance, lacked "patriarchal regimentation" and was therefore a center for assimilation.

14. The term *imago*, like the term "complex," came to Freud via Jung. Jung, in fact, coined the term *imago* explicitly in reference to the Roman *imagines et lares* used in the patriarchal home religion; on the relation of this term to his more famous "archetype," he clarifies that "In my later writings, I use the term 'archetype' instead, in order to bring out the fact that we are dealing with impersonal, collective forces" ([1912] 1956, 44, note 4).

15. A thorough critique of Cohen's argument was offered in the pages of *Der Jude* by Jacob Klatzkin ([1917–1918] 1980). One should point out that since Cohen's time, the emergence of considerable evidence for Hellenistic Judaism of a more syncretic sort has greatly softened the antagonisms assumed to exist between Hellenism and the Jewish populations of the Mediterranean. See the classic study by Goodenough ([1953–1968] 1988) and the more recent work by Bickerman (1988), Gruen (1993, 1998) and John Collins (2000). As always, the crucial text on modern Jewish Hellenism is Shavit 1999, a weakness of which is its lack of attention to psychoanalysis; see my review, Armstrong 2001a.

16. Needless to say, I do not agree with David Bakan that the first Moses essay is "a symbolic Sabbatian assertion of freedom against the severe restrictions of thought and action which had been the life strategy of the Eastern European Jews" (1958, 128). To take Moses *tout court* as the symbol of orthodoxy, as Bakan does, seems to miss entirely the heroic dimension of self-mastery, which Freud explicitly formulates in the essay. This seems to fit much more simply into a Platonic paradigm of rational hegemony than into the tradition of Jewish mysticism, and is more suitable for the plastic form of the statue itself (which is Freud's *point*, after all). Michelangelo's "muscle Jew" Moses, as a work of gentile figural art, is by its mere existence a violation of Jewish orthodoxy and can hardly be the *symbol* of it.

17. On Nietzsche's influence in the reception of antiquity, see O'Flaherty et al. [1976] 1979; Cancik and Cancik-Lindemeier 1999.

18. Nietzsche's attitude toward the Jews is rather complex, and often quite complimentary. See Walter Kaufmann 1974, chapter 10. Though there is a Nietzschean climate among Freud's followers, I am not making the reductive argument that Freud is executing a purely Nietzschean plan. Freud's deferred reading of Nietzsche makes such a simple causal argument impossible. On Freud's knowledge of Nietzsche, see Lehrer 1995 and Assoun 2000. However, Freud's deployment of sexuality has a powerful affinity with Nietzsche's view of the Hellenic, and one could say that it was diffused through other sources at the time. In point of fact, Nietzsche is not fair to Goethe's appraisal of antiquity, which quite often is deeply sexualized (as in the *Roman Elegies*).

19. See Freud's classic statement to Karl Abraham. "Please be tolerant and do not forget that it is really easier for you than it is for Jung to follow my ideas, for in the first place you are completely independent, and then you are closer to my intellectual constitution because of racial kinship, while he as a Christian and a pastor's son finds his way to me only against great inner resistances. His association with us is the more valuable for that. I nearly said that it was only by his appearance on the scene that psychoanalysis escaped the danger of becoming a Jewish national affair" (Abraham and Freud 1965, 34). See also Gilman 1993b, chapter 1.

20. For a fuller picture of Freud's use of anthropology, see Edwin Wallace 1983; on the primitivist current of thought at the time, see Robertson 1990. One might fancifully see in the scholarship of *Totem and Taboo* the interaction of Freud's Anglophilia—his "Cromwell complex" (he named one of his sons "Oliver" after all!)—with his "Hannibal complex," as represented by the secular Jewish scholars he cites.

21. See his defensive footnote in *Totem and Taboo* (SE 13:155, note 1): "No one familiar with the literature of the subject will imagine that the derivation of Christian communion from the totem meal is an idea originating from the author of the present essay."

22. There are reasons to see the filicidal dynamic of the Akedah as simply one end of a
spectrum, the other end of which is the patricidal dynamic of Oedipus. See Paul 1996, 54–
55. Paul has no problem using the primal horde scenario to read the central narrative of
the entire Judeo-Christian tradition, which shows the remarkable staying power of Freud's
"scientific myth."

23. For Jung's "ceremony of atonement," see his letters to Freud of April 27 and May
8, 1912 (McGuire 1974, 502–503).

24. An assumed early stage of totemism became the foundation for virtually all religions in the eyes of many European scholars at the time, and the ancient Greeks were held
to be no exception here, particularly by the Cambridge Ritualists. Jane Ellen Harrison in
her *Themis* (first edition 1912) stated the position. "We do not claim for Greece a fully developed totemistic social system, but rather that totemistic habit of thought, which is, we
believe, common to all peoples in an early phase of their epistemology" ([1927] 1962, 128).
Gilbert Murray made totemism part of the first stage in his "five stages of Greek religion"
([1925] 1976, chapter 1), and Francis Cornford ([1912] 1957, chapter 2) discusses it at
length in relation to Moira in a chapter that bears comparison to Freud's "The Theme of
the Three Caskets" essay from around the same time (1913; SE 12:297–298).

25. Durkheim saw religious experience as the source of "nearly all the great social institutions" including science itself. "If religion gave birth to all that is essential in society,
that is so because the idea of society is the soul of religion" ([1912] 1995, 421). Freud's
main difference in this regard would be his tendency to see large social relations as regressive—particularly in the case of religious organizations—and historically determined
through trauma. For his brief mention of Durkheim's theory of the totem symbol, see
Totem and Taboo, SE 13:113. Fields (1995) provides an excellent introduction to Durkheim's
use of totemism.

26. In point of historical fact, the supposed close rivalry between Mithraism and Christianity is misconceived since the two religions did not have the same aims, as Manfred
Clauss explains ([1990] 2001, chapter 14). But this "competition" had become a topic of
lively discussion, in large part as a response to the writings of Ernest Renan.

27. On the connection between the bull and the Jewish God, see Freud's letter to Fliess.
"Have you read that the English have excavated an old palace in Crete (Knossos), which
they declare to be the real labyrinth of Minos? Zeus seems originally to have been a bull.
Our old god, too, is said to have been worshiped as a bull prior to the sublimation imposed
by the Persians. This is cause for all sorts of thoughts too premature to write down" (Masson 1985, 445).

28. In his memoirs, Jones was quite candid about his unusual status as virtually the only
gentile among the members of the psychoanalytic movement. "After a quarter of a century's such experience I came to feel that I knew their characteristics with an intimacy that
must have fallen to the lot of few Gentiles, and I have reflected much on them and the social problems that surround their lives" ([1959] 1990, 200). He ascribed this affinity for his
Jewish colleagues to his "Celtic mind," which responded readily to their mental qualities,
so different from "Anglo-Saxon placidity, complacency, and slowness of imagination"
([1959] 1990). One can see how his Welsh difference dovetailed with Jewish alienation.

29. Paul Vitz (1988) has tried to plot what he terms "Freud's Christian unconscious,"
based on his childhood experiences with his Czech nanny in Freiberg. Freud's early disillusionment with this figure of his past supposedly formed the basis for his uncompromis-

ing atheism. But Vitz ultimately wants to use his reading of the Freud scenario to found a more sympathetic approach to religious belief, and it seems to me he greatly underestimates the secular intellectual climate of the times.

30. Freud explains the origin of the verse in a letter to Werner Achelis, in which he states, "I had borrowed the quotation from Lassalle, in whose case it was probably meant personally and relating to social—not psychological—classifications. In my case it was meant merely to emphasize the most important part in the dynamics of the dream. The wish rejected by the higher mental agencies (the repressed dream wish) stirs up the mental underworld (the unconscious) in order to get a hearing" (Ernst Freud 1960, 375).

31. The Cumean Sibyl also casts Aeneas' Italian destiny in terms of historical repetition; see *Aeneid* 6.86–90.

32. What makes the line difficult is that the verb is in the second person singular, a colloquialism in Latin put here to serious use. The line may in fact echo a line of Aeschylus' Cassandra (*Agamemnon* 1279–80). See Austin 1955, 182 and 625, and for a refutation of Freud's reading of this parapraxis from a philological point of view, see Timpanaro 1985. Peter Swales suggests that this Latin verse too was taken by Freud via Lassalle (1982, 5).

33. On the nature of Vergilian narration and its psychological depth with regard to the historical Other, see Conte 1986, chapter 5, and Quint 1993, chapter 2. For readings of the *Aeneid* in relation to gender studies, see McManus 1997, chapter 4; Keith 2000; Desmond 1994. Also relevant vis-à-vis Freud's use of the mother goddess within a patriarchal history is the Roman use of such cults to support the patriarchal conception of power under the Principate. See Zanker 1988 and Fischler 1998.

34. Two years after the publication of *Psychopathology*, Otto Weininger went to greater lengths to compare "the Jew" to women in *Sex and Character* ([1903] 1975, chapter 13), and Freud commented that Weininger "treated Jews and women with equal hostility and overwhelmed them with the same insults" ("Analysis of a Phobia in a Five-year-old Boy," SE 10:36, note 1). There as elsewhere, however, Freud himself admits that "what is common to Jews and women is their relation to the castration complex," that is, through the Jew's circumcised member and the woman's lack of one. On the connections between femininity and Jewishness, see Gilman 1993b, Boyarin 1997, and Jonte-Pace 2001, chapter 3.

35. The characterization of the rule of the sons as a restoration of the primal patriarchy exposes the patriarchal teleology of Freud's argument, since the primal patriarchy by definition excludes the sons: "The family was a restoration of the former primal horde and *it gave back to fathers a large portion of their former rights*" (*Totem and Taboo*, SE 13:149).

36. One could say, however, that feminists went to the opposite extreme in alleging a unitary mother goddess cult along the lines of a kind of primitive utopia. For a balanced assessment of what can genuinely be known of such goddesses, see Goodison and Morris 1998. For a well argued feminist perspective, see Lerner 1986, chapter 7.

37. Jan Assmann, the eminent Egyptologist, corroborates Freud's view of the rationalistic aspects of Aten cult, but does not agree with Freud's assessment of its ethical character (1997, 190 and 210).

38. For Abraham's study, see Abraham 1955, chapter 3. Freud rejected Abraham's characterization of Akhenaten as neurotic, "which is in sharp contrast with his exceptional energy and achievements" (Abraham and Freud 1965, 118). It is very odd that Freud nowhere cites Abraham's study in *Moses and Monotheism*.

39. Hitler stated his educational ideals already in *Mein Kampf*, which were based on the notion that the German citizen soldier should have an education "so ordered as to give him the conviction that he is absolutely superior to others. Through his physical strength and dexterity, he must recover his faith in the invincibility of his whole people" ([1925]

1999, 411). He clearly called for a return to the Greek ideal. "Above all, in our present education a balance must be created between mental instruction and physical training. The institution that is called a *Gymnasium* today is a mockery of the Greek model" ([1925] 1999, 253).

40. I am touching upon the secularization thesis that holds that secular culture still applies non-secular categories and modes of thought as it emerges. For such an approach to religion and the rise of historicism, see Howard 2000, especially chapter 5, which deals with the works of Jacob Burckhardt, whose historical vision was very influential on Freud, as argued in chapter 8.

41. See *The Posterity and Exile of Cain* 101 (= Philo 1993, 142) and *On the Unchangeableness of God* 159 (= Philo 1993, 171).

42. For Christian uses of the phrase *basilikê hodos*, see, for example, Clement of Alexandria, *Stromata* 1.7.38, 4.2.6, 7.12.73, and 7.15.91. The statement I have made above about its use is based on an electronic analysis done with the *Thesaurus Linguae Graecae*, from which I have learned that the vast majority of citations for the phrase are in fact metaphorical.

WORKS CITED

Abraham, Hilda C., and Ernst L. Freud, eds. 1965. *A Psycho-Analytic Dialogue: The Letters of Sigmund Freud and Karl Abraham, 1907–1926*. New York: Basic Books.

Abraham, Karl. 1955. *Clinical Papers and Essays on Psycho-Analysis*. Translated by Hilda C. Abraham and D. R. Ellison. London: Hogarth Press.

Ackerman, Robert. 1991. *The Myth and Ritual School: J. G. Frazer and the Cambridge Ritualists*. Theorists of Myth 2. New York: Garland.

Ahl, Frederick. 1991. *Sophocles' Oedipus: Evidence and Self-Conviction*. Ithaca: Cornell University Press.

Albrecht, Paul. 1920. *Arminius-Sigurfrid: Der Roman des deutschen Volkes*. Leipzig: Matthes und Thost.

Allen, Susan Heuck. 1999. *Finding the Walls of Troy: Frank Calvert and Heinrich Schliemann at Hisarlik*. Berkeley: University of California Press.

Allen, Thomas George, trans. 1974. *The Book of the Dead, or Going Forth by Day*. Prepared for publication by Elizabeth Blaisdell Hauser. The Oriental Institute of the University of Chicago Studies in Ancient Oriental Civilization 37. Chicago: University of Chicago Press.

Andreas Salomé, Lou. 1987. *The Freud Journal*. Translated by Stanley A. Leavy. London: Quartet Books.

Armstrong, Richard H. 1999a. "The Archaeology of Freud's Archaeology: Recent Work in the History of Psychoanalysis." *The International Review of Modernism* 3 (1999): 16–20.

——. 1999b. "*Oedipus* as Evidence: The Theatrical Background to Freud's Oedipus Complex." *Psyart: An Online Journal for the Psychological Study of the Arts*. URL:http://web.clas.ufl.edu/ipsa/journal/1999_armstrong01.shtml.

——. 1999c. "Oedipus in Performance: 1881–1912." *Psyart: An Online Journal for the Psychological Study of the Arts*. URL: http://www.clas.ufl.edn/ipsa/journal/articles/psyart1999/oedipus/oedipus.html.

——. 2001a. "Japheth in the Tents of Shem." *Classical and Modern Literature* 21.2 (2001): 109–120.

——. 2001b. "Unreal City: Freud on the Acropolis." *Psychoanalysis and History* 3.1 (2001): 93–108.

Artemidorus of Daldus. [Second century ce] 1881. *Symbolik der Träume*. Translated by Friedrich S. Krauss. Vienna: [n.p.].

——. [n.d.] "Erotische Träume und ihre Symbolik." Translated by Hans Licht [Paul Brandt]. *Anthropophyteia* 9:316–328.

——. 1963. *Artemidori Daldiani onirocriticon libri v.* Edited [Greek text] by Roger Pack. Leipzig: Teubner.

——. 1975. *The Interpretation of Dreams.* Translated by Robert J. White. Park Ridge, N.J.: Noyes Press.

Assmann, Jan. 1992. *Das kulturelle Gedächtnis: Schrift, Erinnerung und politische Identität in frühen Hochkulturen.* Munich: Beck.

——. 1997. *Moses the Egyptian.* Cambridge: Harvard University Press.

——. 2000a. *Herrschaft und Heil.* Darmstadt: Wissenschaftliche Buchgesellschaft.

——. 2000b. *Religion und kulturelles Gedächtnis.* Munich: Beck.

——. [1996] 2002. *The Mind of Egypt.* Translated by Andrew Jenkins. New York: Henry Holt.

Assoun, Paul-Laurent. 2000. *Freud and Nietzsche.* London: Athlone.

Austin, R. G. 1955. *P. Vergili Maronis Aeneidos Liber Quartus.* Oxford: Clarendon Press.

——. 1977. *P. Vergili Maronis Aeneidos Liber Sextus.* Oxford: Oxford University Press.

Bachofen, J. J. [1861] 1948. *Das Mutterrecht: Eine Untersuchung über die Gynaikokratie der alten Welt nach ihrer religiösen und rechtlichen Natur.* 2 vols. Basel: Benno Schwabe.

Badian, Ernst. 1963. "The Death of Philip II." *Phoenix* 17 (1963): 244–50.

Baguley, David. 2000. *Napoleon III and His Regime: An Extravaganza.* Baton Rouge: Louisiana State University Press.

Bakan, David. 1958. *Sigmund Freud and the Jewish Mystical Tradition.* Princeton: Van Nostrand.

Balmary, Marie. [1979] 1982. *Psychoanalyzing Psychoanalysis: Freud and the Hidden Fault of the Father.* Translated by Ned Lukacher. Baltimore: Johns Hopkins University Press.

Bambach, Charles R. 1995. *Heidegger, Dilthey, and the Crisis of Historicism.* Ithaca: Cornell University Press.

Bapty, Ian, and Tim Yates, eds. 1990. *Archaeology after Structuralism.* London: Routledge.

Barkan, Leonard. 1999. *Unearthing the Past: Archaeology and Aesthetics in the Making of Renaissance Culture.* New Haven: Yale University Press.

Barker, Stephen, ed. 1996. *Excavations and Their Objects: Freud's Collection of Antiquity.* Albany: State University of New York Press.

Bastéa, Eleni. 2000. *The Creation of Modern Athens: Planning the Myth.* Cambridge: Cambridge University Press.

Beer, Gillian. 2000. *Darwin's Plots: Evolutionary Narrative in Darwin, George Eliot, and Nineteenth-Century Fiction.* 2d ed. Cambridge: Cambridge University Press.

Belgum, Kirsten. 1998. *Popularizing the Nation: Audience, Representation, and the Production of Identity in Die Gartenlaube, 1853–1900.* Lincoln: University of Nebraska Press.

Beller, Steven. 1990. "Why Was the Viennese Liberal *Bildungsbürgertum* Above All Jewish?" In Don and Karady 1990, 155–171.

——. [1989] 1993. *Vienna and the Jews 1867–1935.* Reprint, Cambridge: Cambridge University Press.

Benndorf, Otto, and George Niemann. 1884. *Reisen in Lykien und Karien.* Vienna: Druck und Verlag von Carl Gerold's Sohn.

Bennett, Tony. 1995. *The Birth of the Museum: History, Theory, Politics.* London: Routledge.

Beneke, A. 1911. *Siegfried ist Armin!* Dortmund: Ruhfus.

Bergmann, Martin S. 1989. "Science and Art in Freud's Life and Work." In Gamwell and Wells 1989, 173–183.

Bernal, Martin. 1987. *Black Athena: The Afro-Asiatic Roots of Classical Civilization.* Vol. 1. New Brunswick, N.J.: Rutgers University Press.

Bernays, Anna Freud. [1940] 1973. "My Brother, Sigmund Freud." In *Freud as We Knew Him,* edited by Hendrik M. Ruitenbeek, 140–147. Detroit: Wayne State University Press.

Bernays, Jacob. [1858] 1970. *Grundzüge der verlorenen Abhandlung des Aristoteles über Wirkung der Tragödie.* Breslau. Reprint, Hildesheim: Olms.

Bernstein, Richard J. 1998. *Freud and the Legacy of Moses.* Cambridge: Cambridge University Press.

Bianchi Bandinelli, Ranuccio. 1978. *Klassische Archäologie: Eine kritische Einführung.* Munich: Beck.

Bickerman, Elias J. 1988. *The Jews in the Greek Age.* Cambridge: Harvard University Press.

Bloom, Harold. 1989. *Ruin the Sacred Truths: Poetry and Belief from the Bible to the Present.* Cambridge: Harvard University Press.

Blum, Harold P. 1994. "Freud and the Figure of Moses." In Gilman et al. 1994, 109–128.

Blumenberg, Hans. [1979] 1985. *Work On Myth.* Translated by Robert M. Wallace. Cambridge: MIT Press.

Boehlich, Walter, ed. 1989. *Sigmund Freud: Jugendbriefe an Eduard Silberstein 1871–1881.* Frankfurt am Main: Fischer Verlag.

———. 1990. *The Letters of Sigmund Freud to Eduard Silberstein, 1871–1881.* Translated by Arnold J. Pomerans. Cambridge: Harvard University Press.

Botting, Wendy, and J. Keith Davies. 1989. "Freud's Library and An Appendix of Texts Related to Antiquities." In Gamwell and Wells 1989, 184–192.

Bourdieu, Pierre. [1972] 1977. *Outline of a Theory of Practice.* Translated by Richard Nice. Cambridge: Cambridge University Press.

———. [1984] 1988. *Homo Academicus.* Stanford: Stanford University Press.

———. 1993. *The Field of Cultural Production.* New York: Columbia University Press.

Bouveresse, Jacques. 1995. *Wittgenstein Reads Freud: The Myth of the Unconscious.* Translated by Carol Cosman. Princeton: Princeton University Press.

Boven, William. 1922. "Alexander der Große." *Imago* 8 (1922): 418–439.

Boyarin, Daniel. 1997. *Unheroic Conduct: The Rise of Heterosexuality and the Invention of the Jewish Man.* Berkeley: University of California Press.

Boyarin, Jonathan. 1996. *Thinking in Jewish.* Chicago: University of Chicago Press.

Boyer, John W. 1981. *Political Radicalism in Late Imperial Vienna: Origins of the Christian Social Movement 1848–1897.* Chicago: University of Chicago Press.

———. 1994. "Religion and Political Development in Central Europe around 1900: A View from Vienna." *Austrian History Yearbook* 25: 13–57.

Brabant, Eva, Ernst Falzeder, and Patrizia Giampieri-Deutsch, eds. 1993–2000. *The Correspondence of Sigmund Freud and Sándor Ferenczi.* 3 vols. Cambridge: Belknap Press of Harvard University Press.

Breger, Louis. 2000. *Freud: Darkness in the Midst of Vision.* New York: John Wiley.

Brein, Friedrich, ed. 1998. *Emanuel Löwy: Ein vergessener Pionier.* Kataloge der archäologischen Sammlung der Universität Wien, Sonderheft 1. Vienna: Verlag des Clubs der Universität Wien.

Brenkman, John. 1993. *Straight Male Modern: A Cultural Critique of Psychoanalysis.* New York: Routledge.

Breuer, Leopold. [1860] 1869. *Biblische Geschichte und Geschichte der Juden und des Judenthumes bis zum Abschlusse des Talmuds, nebst einem kurzen Ueberblicke der weitern Geschichte der Juden bis auf unsere Tage.* Part 1. Third revised and expanded edition. Vienna: Wilhelm Braumüller.

Bronnr, Stephen Eric, and F. Peter Wagner, eds. 1997. *Vienna: The World of Yesterday (1889–1914).* Atlantic Heights, N.J.: Humanities Press International.

Brooks, Peter. 1984. *Reading for the Plot: Design and Intention in Narrative.* New York: Alfred A. Knopf.

Bruford, W. H. 1975. *The German Tradition of Self-Cultivation: "Bildung" from Humboldt to Thomas Mann.* Cambridge: Cambridge University Press.

Brunner, José. 1995. *Freud and the Politics of Psychoanalysis.* Oxford: Blackwell.

Buckle, Henry Thomas. [1857] 1934. *History of Civilization in England.* Vol. 1. New York: D. Appleton-Century Company.

Bunsen, Christian Karl Josias, et al. 1852. *The Life and Letters of Barthold George Niebuhr with Essays on his Character and Influence.* New York: Harper and Brothers.

Burckhardt, Jacob. [1898–1902] 1998. *The Greeks and Greek Civilization.* Edited by Oswyn Murray. Translated by Sheila Stern. New York: St. Martin's Press.

Burkert, Walter. 1979. *Structure and History in Greek Mythology and Ritual.* Berkeley: University of California Press.

Burn, A. R. 1962. *Alexander the Great and the Hellenistic World.* Second revised edition. New York: Collier.

Butler, E. M. [1935] 1958. *The Tyranny of Greece Over Germany.* Boston: Beacon Press.

Callies, Horst. 1975. "Arminius—Held der Deutschen." In Engelbert 1975, 33–42.

Cancik, Hubert, and Hildegard Cancik-Lindemaier. 1999. *Philolog und Kultfigur: Friedrich Nietzsche und seine Antike in Deutschland.* Stuttgart and Weimar: J. B. Metzler.

Carabelli, Giancarlo. 1996. *In the Image of Priapus.* London: Duckworth.

Cassirer Bernfeld, Suzanne. 1951. "Freud and Archaeology." *American Imago* 8 (1950): 107–128.

Chase, Cynthia. [1986] 1994. "Oedipal Textuality: Reading Freud's Reading of *Oedipus.*" Reprinted in *Psychoanalytic Literary Criticism,* edited by Maud Ellman, chapter 2. London: Longman.

Cioffi, Frank. 1998. *Freud and the Question of Pseudo-Science.* Chicago: Open Court.

———. [1970] 1998. "Freud and the Idea of a Pseudo-Science." Originally in *Explanation and the Behavioral Sciences,* edited by Robert Borger, 471–499. Cambridge: Cambridge University Press.

Clarke, G. W, ed. 1989. *Rediscovering Hellenism.* Cambridge: Cambridge University Press.

Clauss, Manfred. [1990] 2001. *The Roman Cult of Mithras.* Translated by Richard Gordon. New York: Routledge.

Cohen, Gary B. 1996. *Education and Middle Class Society in Imperial Austria, 1848–1918.* West Lafayette, Ind.: Purdue University Press.

Cohen, Hermann. [1915–1916] 1924. "Deutschtum und Judentum." In *Hermann Cohens Jüdische Schriften,* edited by Bruno Strauss, 2: 237–318. Berlin: Schwetschke & Sohn. Reprint, New York: Arno Press, 1980.

Collins, Bradley. 1997. *Leonardo, Psychoanalysis, and Art History.* Evanston, Ill.: Northwestern University Press.

Collins, John J. 2000. *Between Athens and Jerusalem: Jewish Identity in the Hellenistic Diaspora.* 2nd ed. Grand Rapids, Mich.: Eerdmans.

Constans, Léopold Eugène. 1881. *La légende d'Oedipe. Étudiée dans l'antiquité, au moyen-âge et dans les temps modernes en particulier dans le Roman de Thèbes, texte français du XIIe siècle.* Paris: Maisonneuve.

Conte, Gian Biagio. 1986. *The Rhetoric of Imitation: Genre and Poetic Memory in Virgil and Other Latin Poets.* Translated by Charles Segal, Susan George, Anthony Johnson, and Sylvia Notini. Ithaca: Cornell University Press.

Cornell, T. J. 1995. *The Beginnings of Rome: Italy and Rome from the Bronze Age to the Punic Wars (c. 1000–263 BC).* Routledge History of the Ancient World. London: Routledge.

Cornford, Francis. [1912] 1957. *From Religion to Philosophy: A Study in the Origins of Western Speculation.* Harper Torchbooks. New York: Harper Brothers.

Cotti, Patricia. 2004. "The History of the Libido's Development: Evidence from Freud's Case Studies." *Psychoanalysis and History* 6 (2004): 237–251.

Crane, Susan A. 2000. *Collecting and Historical Consciousness in Early Nineteenth-Century Germany.* Ithaca: Cornell University Press.

Crews, Frederick. 2003. Letter to the Editor of *PMLA* in response to Marshall 2002. *PMLA* 118 (2003): 615–616.

Crews, Frederick, et al. 1995. *The Memory Wars: Freud's Legacy in Dispute.* New York: New York Review of Books.

Crews, Frederick, ed. 1998. *The Unauthorized Freud.* New York: Viking.

Cuddihy, John Murray. 1974. *The Ordeal of Civility: Freud, Marx, Lévi-Strauss, and the Jewish Struggle with Modernity.* New York: Basic Books.

D'Agata, Anna Lucia. 1994. "Sigmund Freud and Aegean Archaeology: Mycenaean and Cypriote Material from his Collection of Antiquities." *Studi micenei ed egeo-anatolici* 34 (1994): 7–44.

Daly, C. D. 1927. "Hindu-Mythologie und Kastrationskomplex." Translated by Peter Mendelsohn. *Imago* 13 (1927): 145–198.

Davidson, Arnold I. 2001. *The Emergence of Sexuality: Historical Epistemology and the Formation of Concepts*. Cambridge: Harvard University Press.

Davidson, James N. 1998. *Courtesans and Fishcakes: The Consuming Passions of Classical Athens*. New York: St. Martin's.

Davis, Robert Con. 1993. *The Paternal Romance*. Urbana: University of Illinois Press.

Davis, Russell H. 1993. *Freud's Concept of Passivity*. Psychological Issues 60. Madison, Conn.: International Universities Press.

Davis, Whitney. 1996. *Replications: Archaeology, Art History, Psychoanalysis*. University Park: Pennsylvania State University Press.

Decker, Hannah. 1991. *Freud, Dora, and Vienna 1900*. New York: Macmillan International.

Derrida, Jacques. [1967] 1978. *Writing and Difference*. Translated by Alan Bass. Chicago: University of Chicago Press.

——. 1995. *Archive Fever: A Freudian Impression*. Translated by Eric Prenowitz. Chicago: University of Chicago Press.

Desmond, Marylinn. 1994. *Reading Dido: Gender, Textuality, and the Medieval Aeneid*. Medieval Cultures 8. Minneapolis: University of Minnesota Press.

Devereux, George. [1953] 1988. "Why Oedipus Killed Laius: A Note on the Complementary Oedipus Complex in Greek Drama." In Pollock and Ross 1988, chapter 7.

Diller, Jerry Victor. 1991. *Freud's Jewish Identity: A Case Study in the Impact of Ethnicity*. London: Associated University Presses.

Dodds, E. R. 1977. *Missing Persons: An Autobiography*. Oxford: Clarendon Press.

Don, Yehuda, and Victor Karady. 1990. *A Social and Economic History of Central European Jewry*. New Brunswick, N.J.: Transaction.

Dover, Kenneth. 1978. *Greek Homosexuality*. Cambridge: Harvard University Press.

Dörner, Andreas. 1997. 1993. "Die Inszenierung politischer Mythen. Ein Beitrag zur Funktion der symbolischen Formen in der Politik am Beispiel des Hermannsmythos in Deutschland." *Politische Vierteljahresschrift* 34 (1993): 199–218.

——. 1997. "Der Mythos der nationalen Einheit: Symbolpolitik und Deutungskämpfe bei der Einweihung des Hermannsdenkmals im Jahre 1875." *Archiv für Kulturgeschichte* 79 (1997): 389–416.

Droysen, Johann Gustav. [1833] 1943. *Geschichte Alexanders des Grossen*. Edited by Helmut Berve. Reprint of the original 1833 edition. Stuttgart: Alfred Kröner Verlag.

——. [1877] 1952–53. *Geschichte des Hellenismus*. Edited by Erich Bayer. Special edition. Tübingen: Wissenschaftliche Buchgemeinschaft.

——. [1881] 1967. *Grundriss der Historik*. 3rd ed. Translated by E. Benjamin Andrews as *Outline of the Principles of History*. Reprint, New York: Howard Fertig.

Durkheim, Emile. [1912] 1995. *The Elementary Forms of the Religious Life*. Translated by Karen E. Fields. New York: Free Press.

Eagleton, Terry. 1990. *The Ideology of the Aesthetic*. Oxford: Basil Blackwell.

Edmunds, Lowell, and Alan Dundes. [1983] 1995. *Oedipus: A Folklore Casebook*. Madison: University of Wisconsin Press.

Edwards, Catharine. 1999. *Roman Presences: Receptions of Rome in European Culture, 1789–1945*. Cambridge: Cambridge University Press.

Eisler, Robert. 1929–1930. Ἰησοῦς βασιλεύς οὐ βασιλεύσας: *Die messianische Unabhängigkeitsbewegung vom Auftreten Johannes des Täufers bis zum Untergang Jakobs des Gerechten nach der neuerschlossenen eroberung von Jerusalem des Flavius Josephus und den christlichen Quellen*. 2 vols. Heidelberg: Carl Winter.

——. 1931. *The Messiah Jesus and John the Baptist*. Edited by Alexander Haggerty Krappe. New York: Dial Press.

———. [1951] 1969. *Man into Wolf: An Anthropological Interpretation of Sadism, Masochism, and Lycanthropy.* New York: Greenwood Press.

Eisner, Robert. 1987. *The Road to Daulis: Psychoanalysis, Psychology, and Classical Mythology.* Syracuse: Syracuse University Press.

Eissler, Kurt. 1961. *Leonardo da Vinci: Psychoanalytic Notes on the Enigma.* New York: International Universities Press.

Eliot, T. S. [1920] 1967. *The Sacred Wood.* University Paperbacks Edition. London: Methuen.

Elon, Amos. 2002. *The Pity of It All: A History of Jews in Germany, 1743–1933.* New York: Metropolitan Books.

Elsner, John, and Roger Cardinal, eds. 1994. *The Cultures of Collecting.* Cambridge: Harvard University Press.

Engelbert, Günther. 1975. *Ein Jahrhundert Hermannsdenkmal 1875–1975.* Sonderveröffentlichungen des naturwissenschaftlichen und historischen Vereins für das Land Lippe. Detmold: Naturwissenschaftlicher und Historischer Verein für das Land Lippe.

Engelman, Edmund. 1993. *Sigmund Freud Wien IX. Berggasse 19.* Vienna: Verlag Christian Brandstätter.

Ephraim, Charlotte. [1936] 1970. *Wandel des Griechenbildes im achtzehnten Jahrhundert: (Winckelmann, Lessing, Herder).* Nendeln/Liechtenstein: Kraus Reprint.

Ernst, Wolfgang. 2002. *Das Rumoren der Archive.* Berlin: Merve Verlag.

Farrell, John. 1996. *Freud's Paranoid Quest: Psychoanalysis and Modern Suspicion.* New York: New York University Press.

Feldman, Yael S. 1994. "'And Rebecca Loved Jacob,' But Freud Did Not." In Rudnytsky and Spitz 1994, 7–25.

Ferenczi, Sándor. [1912] 1956. "The Symbolic Representation of the Pleasure and Reality Principles in the Oedipus Myth." Reprinted in *Sex in Psycho-analysis*, 214–227. Translated by Ernest Jones. New York: Dover Publications.

———. [1924] 1989. *Thalassa: A Theory of Genitality.* Translated by Henry Alden Bunker. London: Karnac Books.

———. 1988. *The Clinical Diary of Sándor Ferenczi.* Edited by Judith Dupont. Translated by Michael Balint and Nicola Zarday Jackson. Cambridge: Harvard University Press.

Ferris, David. 2000. *Silent Urns: Romanticism, Hellenism, Modernity.* Stanford: Stanford University Press.

Feuerbach, Ludwig. [1841] 1960. *Das Wesen des Christentums.* Stuttgart: Frommann Verlag.

———. [1848] 1967. *Lectures on the Essence of Religion.* Translated by Ralph Manheim. New York: Harper and Row.

Fields, Karen E. 1995. "Religion as an Eminently Social Thing." Introduction to Durkheim [1912] 1995.

Fischler, Susan. 1998. "Imperial Cult: Engendering the Cosmos." In Foxhall and Salmon 1998, chap. 8.

Fish, Stanley. [1986] 1998. "The Primal Scene of Persuasion." In Crews 1998, chap. 15.

Fitton, J. Lesley. 1996. *The Discovery of the Greek Bronze Age.* Cambridge: Harvard University Press.

Flaig, Egon. 1998. *Ödipus: Tragischer Vatermord im klassischen Athen.* Munich: Beck.

Foucault, Michel. [1969] 1972. *The Archaeology of Knowledge.* Translated by A. M. Sheridan Smith. New York: Pantheon Books.

———. [1969] 1979. "What Is an Author?" In *Textual Strategies*, edited by Josué Harari, 141–160. Ithaca: Cornell University Press.

———. [1976] 1980. *The History of Sexuality: Volume 1: An Introduction.* Translated by Robert Hurley. Vintage Books edition. New York: Random House.

Forrester, John. 1980. *Language and the Origins of Psychoanalysis.* New York: Columbia University Press.

———. 1994. "'*Mille e tre*': Freud and Collecting." In Elsner and Cardinal 1994, 224–251.

Foxhall, Lin, and John Salmon, eds. 1998. *When Men Were Men: Masculinity, Power, and Identity in Classical Antiquity.* London: Routledge.

Fraenkel, Josef, ed. 1967. *The Jews of Austria.* London: Valentine, Mitchell.

Fraenkel, Michael, ed. 1932. *Jacob Bernays: Ein Lebensbild in Briefen.* Breslau: M. and H. Marcus.

Frattaroli, Elio. 2001. *Healing the Soul in the Age of the Brain: Becoming Conscious in an Unconscious World.* New York: Viking.

Frazer, Sir James. [1922] 1993. *The Golden Bough: A Study in Magic and Religion.* Abridged by the author. Reprint, Ware, UK: Wordsworth Editions.

Freud, Ernst L., ed. 1960. *The Letters of Sigmund Freud.* Translated by Tania Stern and James Stern. New York: McGraw Hill.

——, ed. 1968. *Sigmund Freud–Arnold Zweig: Briefwechsel.* Frankfurt am Main: Fischer Verlag.

——, ed. 1970. *The Letters of Sigmund Freud and Arnold Zweig.* Translated by Elaine Robson-Scott and William Robson-Scott. New York: New York University Press.

——, ed. 1988. *Sigmund Freud: Brautbriefe.* Frankfurt am Main: Fischer Verlag.

Freud, Martin. 1967. "Who Was Freud?" In Josef Fraenkel 1967, 197–211.

——. [1958] 1983. *Sigmund Freud: Man and Father.* New York: Jason Aronson.

Freud, Sigmund. 1953–1974. *The Standard Edition of the Complete Psychological Works of Sigmund Freud* [SE]. Edited and translated by James Strachey et al. London: Hogarth Press.

——. 1940–1968. *Gesammelte Werke chronologisch geordnet.* Edited by E. Bibring, W. Hoffer, E. Kris, O. Isakower, with the collaboration of Marie Bonaparte. London: Imago.

——. 1969–1975. *Sigmund Freud Studienausgabe.* Edited by Alexander Mitscherlich et al. Frankfurt am Main: Fischer Verlag.

——. [1900] 1999. *The Interpretation of Dreams.* Translated by Joyce Crick. Oxford: Oxford University Press.

Friedell, Egon. [1931] 1954. *Kulturgeschichte der Neuzeit: Die Krisis der europäischen Seele von der schwarzen Pest bis zum ersten Weltkrieg.* 3 vols. Munich: Beck.

Frieden, Ken. 1990. *Freud's Dream of Interpretation.* Albany: State University of New York Press.

Gamwell, Lynn. 1989. "The Origin's of Freud's Antiquities Collection." In Gamwell and Wells, 1989, 21–32.

Gamwell, Lynn, and Richard Wells, eds. 1989. *Sigmund Freud and Art: His Personal Collection of Antiquities.* London: Freud Museum, in association with Abrams, New York.

Gantz, Timothy. 1993. *Early Greek Myth: A Guide to Literary and Artistic Sources.* Baltimore: Johns Hopkins University Press.

Gardiner, Muriel, ed. 1971. *The Wolf-Man by the Wolf-Man: The Double Story of Freud's Famous Case.* New York: Basic Books.

Gay, Peter. 1975. *The Enlightenment: An Interpretation.* Vol. 1: *The Rise of Modern Paganism.* New York: Alfred A. Knopf.

——. 1987. *A Godless Jew: Freud, Atheism, and the Making of Psychoanalysis.* New Haven: Yale University Press in conjunction with Hebrew Union College Press, Cincinnati.

——. 1995. *The Naked Heart.* The Bourgeois Experience Victoria to Freud, Vol. 4. London: HarperCollins.

Gelfand, Toby, and John Kerr, eds. 1992. *Freud and the History of Psychoanalysis.* Hillsdale, N.J.: Analytic Press.

Gellner, Ernest. [1985] 1993. *The Psychoanalytic Movement: The Cunning of Unreason.* Evanston, IL: Northwestern University Press.

Gillis, John R. 1994. *Commemorations: The Politics of National Identity.* Princeton: Princeton University Press.

Gilman, Sander L. 1986. *Jewish Self-Hatred: Anti-Semitism and the Hidden Language of the Jews.* Baltimore: Johns Hopkins University Press.

——. 1993a. *The Case of Sigmund Freud: Medicine and Identity at the Fin de Siècle.* Baltimore: Johns Hopkins University Press.

———. 1993b. *Freud, Race, and Gender.* Princeton: Princeton University Press.

Gilman, Sander L., Jutta Birmele, Jay Geller, and Valerie Greenberg. 1994. *Reading Freud's Reading.* New York: New York University Press.

Goethe, Johann Wolfgang. 1985–. *Sämtliche Werke.* 40 vols. Frankfurt am Main: Deutscher Klassiker Verlag.

Goetz, Christopher G., Michel Bonduelle, and Toby Gelfand. 1995. *Charcot: Constructing Neurology.* New York: Oxford University Press.

Goldhill, Simon. 1995. *Foucault's Virginity: Ancient Erotic Fiction and the History of Sexuality.* Cambridge: Cambridge University Press.

Gomperz, Theodor. 1896. *Griechische Denker: Eine Geschichte der Antiken Philosophien.* 3 vols. Leipzig: Veit.

———. [1905] 1931. *Greek Thinkers: A History of Ancient Philosophy.* 4 vols. Translated by G. G. Berry. Reprint, London: John Murray.

Goodenough, Erwin R. [1953–1968] 1988. *Jewish Symbols in the Greco-Roman Period.* Edited and abridged by Jacob Neusner. Princeton: Princeton University Press.

Goodhart, Sandor. 1978. "Ληστὰς ἔφασκε: Oedipus and Laius' Many Murderers." *Diacritics* (1978) 8: 55–71.

Goodison, Lucy, and Christine Morris. 1998. *Ancient Goddesses: The Myths and the Evidence.* London: British Museum Press.

Gossman, Lionel. 2000. *Basel in the Age of Burckhardt: A Study in Unseasonable Ideas.* Chicago: University of Chicago Press.

Gössmann, Wilhelm. 1977. "Deutsche Nationalität und Freiheit: Die Rezeption der Arminius-Gestalt in der Literatur von Tacitus bis Heine." *Heine Jahrbuch* 16: 71–95.

Gould, Stephen J. 1977. *Ontogeny and Phylogeny.* Cambridge: Harvard University Press.

Gourgouris, Stathis. 1996. *Dream Nation: Enlightenment, Colonization, and the Institution of Modern Greece.* Princeton: Princeton University Press.

Goux, Jean-Joseph. 1993. *Oedipus, Philosopher.* Translated by Catherine Porter. Stanford: Stanford University Press.

Graetz, Heinrich. [1894] 1941. *History of the Jews.* Translated by Bella Löwy et al. Philadelphia: Jewish Publication Society of America.

Green, Peter. 1991. *Alexander of Macedon 356–323B.C.: A Historical Biography.* Berkeley: University of California Press.

Greenberg, Jay. 1991. *Oedipus and Beyond: A Clinical Theory.* Cambridge: Harvard University Press.

Gresser, Moshe. 1994. *Dual Allegiance: Freud as a Modern Jew.* Albany: State University of New York Press.

Griffin, Jasper, ed. 1999. *Sophocles Revisited: Essays Presented to Sir Hugh Lloyd-Jones.* Oxford: Oxford University Press.

Groh, Otto Emmerich, ed. 1934. *Aufruf ans Volk: Worte der Führer an die Deutschen von Arminius bis Hitler. Mahnrufe deutscher Männer in den Tagen der Entscheidung.* Leipzig: Nothung Verlag.

Grubrich-Simitis, Ilse. [1993] 1996. *Back to Freud's Texts: Making Silent Documents Speak.* Translated by Philip Slotkin. New Haven: Yale University Press.

Grubrich-Simitis, Ilse, ed. 1971. *Selbstdarstellung, Schriften zur Geschichte der Psychoanalyse.* Frankfurt am Main: Fischer Verlag.

———, ed. 1987. *A Phylogenetic Fantasy: An Overview of the Transference Neuroses.* Translated by Axel Hoffer and Peter T. Hoffer. Cambridge: Harvard University Press.

Gruen, Erich S. 1993. "Hellenism and Persecution: Antiochus IV and the Jews." In *Hellenistic History and Culture,* edited by Peter Green, 238–274. Berkeley: University of California Press.

———. 1998. *Heritage and Hellenism: The Reinvention of Jewish Tradition.* Berkeley: University of California Press.

Gubel, Eric, ed. [n.d.] *Le sphinx de Vienne: Sigmund Freud, l'art et l'archéologie.* Liege: Ludion.

Guilland, Antoine. [1915] 1970. *Modern Germany and Her Historians.* Reprint, Westport, Conn.: Greenwood Press.

Habermas, Jürgen. [1968] 1971. *Knowledge and Human Interests.* Translated by Jeremy J. Shapiro. Boston: Beacon Press.

Haeckel, Ernst. 1905. *Die Welträthsel: Gemeinverstandliche Studien über monistische Philosophie.* 9th ed. Stuttgart: Alfred Kröner Verlag.

Hale, Nathan G., ed. 1971. *James Jackson Putnam and Psychoanalysis.* Cambridge: Harvard University Press.

Hall, G. Stanley. [1904] 1969. *Adolescence.* 2 vols. Reprint, New York: Arno Press.

Hallett, Judith P., and Marilyn B. Skinner. 1997. *Roman Sexualities.* Princeton: Princeton University Press.

Halperin, David M. 1990. *One Hundred Years of Homosexuality.* New York: Routledge.

Hammond, N. G. L. 1997. *The Genius of Alexander the Great.* Chapel Hill: University of North Carolina Press.

Hanák, Péter. 1998. *The Garden and the Workshop: Essays on the Cultural History of Vienna and Budapest.* Princeton: Princeton University Press.

Handelman, Susan. 1982. *The Slayers of Moses: The Emergence of Rabbinic Interpretation in Modern Literary Theory.* Albany: State University of New York Press.

Harrison, Jane Ellen. [1927] 1962. *Epilogomena to the Study of Greek Religion and Themis: A Study of the Social Origins of Greek Religion.* Reprint, New Hyde Park, N.Y.: University Books.

Hartnack, Christiane. 2001. *Psychoanalysis in Colonial India.* Oxford: Oxford University Press.

H. D. [Hilda Doolittle]. [1956] 1974. *Tribute to Freud.* New York: New Directions Books.

Hegel, Georg Wilhelm Friedrich. [1899] 1956. *The Philosophy of History.* Translated by J. Sibree. New York: Dover Publications.

Hengel, Martin. 1980. *Jews, Greeks, and Barbarians: Aspects of the Hellenization of Judaism in the pre-Christian Period.* Translated by John Bowden. Philadelphia: Fortress Press.

Herding, Klaus. 2000. "Freud's Leonardo: A Discussion of Recent Psychoanalytic Theories." *American Imago* 57 (2000): 339–368.

"Hermann der Cherusker und sein Denkmal." 1925. Detmold: Verlag der Meyerschen Hofbuchhandlung.

Herrmann, Hans Peter. 1995. "Arminius und die Erfindung der Männlichkeit im 18. Jahrhundert." *Der Deutschunterricht* 47 (1995): 32–47.

Herzog, Patricia. 1988. "The Myth of Freud as Anti-philosopher." In Stepansky 1988, 163–189.

Hess, Jonathan M. 2002. *Germans, Jews and the Claims of Modernity.* New Haven: Yale University Press.

Himmelfarb, Martha. 1998. "Elias Bickerman on Judaism and Hellenism." In *The Jewish Past Revisited: Reflections on Modern Jewish Historians,* edited by David Myers and David Ruderman, chap. 9. New Haven: Yale University Press.

Hinde, John R. 2000. *Jacob Burckhardt and the Crisis of Modernity.* McGill-Queen's Studies in the History of Ideas 29. Kingston: McGill-Queen's University Press.

Hirschmüller, Albrecht. [1978] 1989. *The Life and Work of Josef Breuer: Physiology and Psychoanalysis.* New York: New York University Press.

———. 2002. "Kritische Glosse: Wer war 'Herr Aliquis'?" *Psyche* 56 (2002): 396–402.

Hitler, Adolf. [1925] 1999. *Mein Kampf.* Translated by Ralph Manheim. Boston: Houghton Mifflin.

Hodder, Ian, et al. 1995. *Interpreting Archaeology: Finding Meaning in the Past.* London: Routledge.

Hollinger, David A. [1986] 1994. "The Knower and the Artificer, with Postscript 1993." In *Modernist Impulses in the Human Sciences, 1870–1930,* edited by Dorothy Ross, 26–53. Baltimore: Johns Hopkins University Press.

Holt, Robert. 2001. Review of Louis Breger, *Freud: Darkness in the Midst of Vision* (New York: Wiley, 2000). *American Imago* 58 (2001): 739–743.

Homans, Peter. 1989. *The Ability to Mourn: Disillusionment and the Social Origins of Psychoanalysis*. Chicago: University of Chicago Press.

Horkheimer, Max, and Theodor W. Adorno. [1944] 1972. *Dialectic of Enlightenment*. Translated by John Cumming. New York: Continuum.

Howard, Thomas Albert. 2000. *Religion and the Rise of Historicism*. Cambridge: Cambridge University Press.

Hudson, Kenneth. 1981. *A Social History of Archaeology: The British Experience*. London: Macmillan Press.

Humboldt, Wilhelm von. [1793] 1968. "Über das Studium des Alterthums, und des Griechischen insbesondere." *Wilhelm von Humboldts Gesammelte Schriften*. Vol. 1. Berlin: B. Behr's Verlag.

Iggers, Georg C. 1968. *The German Conception of History*. Middletown, Conn.: Wesleyan University Press.

Inwood, Brad. 2001. *The Poem of Empedocles*. 2nd rev. ed. Toronto: University of Toronto Press.

Janik, Allan, and Stephen Toulmin. 1973. *Wittgenstein's Vienna*. New York: Simon and Schuster.

Jenkyns, Richard. 1980. *The Victorians and Ancient Greece*. Cambridge: Harvard University Press.

Jensen, Wilhelm. [1903] 1956. *Gradiva: A Pompeiian Fancy*. Translated by Helen M. Downey. Reprinted in *Sigmund Freud: Delusion and Dream and Other Essays*, edited by Philip Rieff, 147–235. Boston: Beacon Press.

Johns, Catherine. 1982. *Sex or Symbol: Erotic Images of Ancient Greece and Rome*. Austin: University of Texas Press.

Johnson, Lawrence. 2001. *The Wolf Man's Burden*. Ithaca: Cornell University Press.

Jones, Andrew. 2002. *Archaeological Theory and Scientific Practice*. Cambridge: Cambridge University Press.

Jones, Ernest. [1949] 1976. *Hamlet and Oedipus*. Reprint. New York: W. W. Norton.

———. [1953–1957] 1981. *The Life and Work of Sigmund Freud*. 3 vols. Reprint. New York: Basic Books.

———. [1959] 1990. *Free Associations: Memories of a Psycho-analyst*. New Brunswick, N.J.: Transaction.

Jonte-Pace, Diane. 2001. *Speaking the Unspeakable: Religion, Misogyny, and the Uncanny Mother in Freud's Cultural Texts*. Berkeley: University of California Press.

Joyce, Rosemary. 2002. *Languages of Archaeology: Dialogue, Narrative and Writing*. Oxford: Blackwell.

Jung, Carl Gustav. [1961] 1983. *Memories, Dreams, Reflections*. Recorded and edited by Aniela Jaffé. Translated by Richard and Clara Winston. Rev. ed. New York: Vintage Books.

———. [1912] 1956. *Symbols of Transformation*. Translated by R. F. C. Hull. Bollingen Series 20. Princeton: Princeton University Press. [Note: this is a much later reworking of Jung's original *Wandlungen und Symbole der Libido*, first published in two parts in the *Jahrbuch für psychoanalytische und psychopathologische Forschungen* 3–4, then together as a book in 1912 by Deuticke Verlag, Leipzig and Vienna.]

Kain, Philip J. 1982. *Schiller, Hegel, Marx: State, Society, and the Aesthetic Ideal of Ancient Greece*. McGill-Queen's Studies in the History of Ideas 4. Kingston: McGill-Queen's University Press.

Kaufmann, Thomas Dacosta. 1994. "From Treasury to Museum: The Collections of the Austrian Habsburgs." In Elsner and Cardinal 1996, 137–154.

Kaufmann, Walter. 1974. *Nietzsche: Philosopher, Psychologist, Antichrist*. 4th ed. Princeton: Princeton University Press.

Keith, A. M. 2000. *Engendering Rome: Women in Latin Epic*. Roman Literature and Its Contexts. Cambridge: Cambridge University Press.

Kerr, John. 1993. *A Most Dangerous Method: The Story of Jung, Freud, and Sabina Spielrein.* New York: Vintage Books.

Keuls, Eva. 1985. *The Reign of the Phallus: Sexual Politics in Ancient Athens.* New York: Harper and Row.

Kirk, G. S. 1970. *Myth: It Meaning and Functions in Ancient and Other Cultures.* Sather Lectures Series 40. Cambridge: Cambridge University Press; Berkeley: University of California Press.

Klein, Dennis B. 1981. *The Jewish Origins of the Psychoanalytic Movement.* New York: Praeger Publishers.

Knoepfmacher, Hugo. 1979. "Sigmund Freud in High School." *American Imago* 36 (1979): 287–300.

Knox, Bernard. 1957. *Oedipus at Thebes.* New Haven: Yale University Press.

Kofman, Sarah. [1974] 1991. *Freud and Fiction.* Translated by Sarah Wykes. Cambridge, UK: Polity Press.

Korfmann, Manfred, and Dietrich Mannsperger. 1998. *Troia: Ein historischer Überblick und Rundgang.* Stuttgart: Theiss.

Kraenkel, Franz H. 1893. *Hermann der Befreier: Ein vaterländisches Festspiel für die deutsche Jugend.* Litterarische Beilage zum Programm des Grossh. Gymnasiums in Lahr. Lahr: J. H. Geiger.

Kramer, Fritz. 1977. *Verkehrte Welten: Zur imaginären Ethnographie des 19. Jahrhunderts.* Frankfurt am Main: Syndikat.

Krapf, Ludwig. 1979. *Germanenmythus und Reichsideologie: Frühhumanistische Rezeptionsweisen der taciteischen Germania.* Studien zur deutschen Literatur, 59. Tübingen: Max Niemeyer Verlag.

Krebs, Roland. 1992. "Hermann au temps des lumières: A propos du motif germanique dans le théâtre allemand et français du XVIIIᵉ siècle." *Cahiers d'études germaniques* 22 (1992): 179–190.

Krieger, Leonard. 1977. *Ranke: The Meaning of History.* Chicago: University of Chicago Press.

Krüll, Marianne. [1979] 1986. *Freud and His Father.* Translated by Arnold J. Pomerans. New York: Norton.

Kuspit, Donald. 1989. "A Mighty Metaphor: The Analogy of Archaeology and Psychoanalysis." In Gamwell and Wells 1989, 133–151.

Lacan, Jacques. [1966] 1977. *Écrits: A Selection.* Translated by Alan Sheridan. New York: Norton.

Lamm, Leonard Jonathan. 1993. *The Idea of the Past: History, Science, and Practice in American Psychoanalysis.* New York: New York University Press.

Langholf, Volker. 1990. "'Die kathartische Methode': Klassische Philologie, literarische Tradition und Wissenschaftstheorie in der Frühgeschichte der Psychoanalyse." *Medizinhistorisches Journal* 25 (1990): 5–39.

Larmour, David H. J., Paul Allen Miller, and Charles Platter, eds. 1998. *Rethinking Sexuality: Foucault and Classical Antiquity.* Princeton, N.J.: Princeton University Press.

Latacz, Joachim. 2001. *Troia und Homer: Der Weg zur Lösung eines alten Rätsels.* Munich: Koehler & Amelang.

Latour, Bruno. 1993. *We Have Never Been Modern.* Translated by Catherine Porter. Cambridge: Harvard University Press.

Lehrer, Ronald. 1995. *Nietzsche's Presence in Freud's Life and Thought.* Albany: State University of New York Press.

Lerner, Gerda. 1986. *The Creation of Patriarchy.* New York: Oxford University Press.

Lesko, Barbara S. 1999. *The Great Goddesses of Egypt.* Norman, Okla.: University of Oklahoma Press.

Levin, Harry. 1931. *The Broken Column: A Study in Romantic Hellenism.* Cambridge: Harvard University Press.

Licht, Hans [Paul Brandt]. [n.d.] "Artemidorus aus Daldis: Erotische Träume und ihre Symbolik. Aus dem Griechischen übersetzt von Dr. Hans Licht." *Anthropophyteia* 9: 316–328.

——. 1924. *Beiträge zur antiken Erotik.* Dresden: Paul Aretz Verlag.

——. 1926. *Sittengeschichte Griechenlands.* 3 vols. Dresden: Paul Aretz Verlag.

——. [1930] 2000. *Sexual Life in Ancient Greece.* Edited by Lawrence H. Dawson. Translated by J. H. Freese. London: Kegan Paul International.

Lincoln, Bruce. 1999. *Theorizing Myth: Narrative, Ideology, and Scholarship.* Chicago: University of Chicago Press.

Livy [Titus Livius]. [1960] 2002. *The Early History of Rome.* Translated by Aubrey de Sélincourt. London: Penguin Books.

Lloyd-Jones, Hugh. 1982. *Blood For the Ghosts: Classical Influences in the Nineteenth and Twentieth Centuries.* London: Duckworth.

——. 1990. *Greek Comedy, Hellenistic Literature, Greek Religion, and Miscellanea: The Academic Papers of Sir Hugh Lloyd-Jones.* Oxford: Clarendon Press.

Loraux, Nicole. 1995. *The Experiences of Tiresias: The Feminine and the Greek Man.* Translated by Paula Wissing. Princeton: Princeton University Press.

Luschan, Felix von. 1889. *Reisen in Lykien, Milyas, und Kibyratis.* Vienna: Druck und Verlag von Carl Gerold's Sohn.

Macauly, Thomas Babington. [1842] 1997. *Lays of Ancient Rome.* Gateway Editions. Washington, D.C.: Regnery.

Mahony, Patrick. 1980. "Towards the Understanding of Translation in Psychoanalysis." *Journal of the American Psychoanalytic Association.* 28 (1980): 461–475.

Malcolm, Janet. 1984. *In the Freud Archives.* New York: Knopf.

Malinowski, Bronislaw. [1927] 1955. *Sex and Repression in Savage Society.* New York: Meridian Books.

——. [1967] 1989. *A Diary in the Strict Sense of the Term.* Translated by Norbert Guterman. London: Athlone.

Marchand, Suzanne. 1996. *Down From Olympus: Archaeology and Philhellenism in Germany, 1750–1970.* Princeton: Princeton University Press.

Marcuse, Herbert. 1970. *Five Lectures: Psychoanalysis, Politics, and Utopia.* Translated by Jeremy J. Shapiro and Shierry M. Weber. Boston: Beacon Press.

Marinelli, Lydia, and Andreas Mayer. 2002. *Träume nach Freud: Die Traumdeutung und die Geschichte der psychoanalytischen Bewegung.* Vienna: Turia + Kant.

Marinelli, Lydia, ed. 1998. *"Meine . . . alten und dreckigen Götter." Aus Sigmund Freuds Sammlung.* Vienna: Sigmund Freud-Museum.

Marshall, Cynthia. 2002. "Psychoanalyzing the Prepsychoanalytic Subject." *PMLA* 117 (2002): 1207–1216.

Marx, Karl. [1852] 1978. *The Eighteenth Brumaire of Louis Napoleon.* In *The Marx-Engels Reader,* edited by Robert C. Tucker, 594–617. 2nd ed. New York: Norton.

Masson, Jeffrey Moussaieff. 1984. *The Assault on Truth: Freud's Suppression of the Seduction Theory.* New York : Farrar, Straus and Giroux.

——, ed. and trans. 1985. *The Complete Letters of Sigmund Freud to Wilhelm Fliess, 1887–1904.* Cambridge: Harvard University Press.

Maylan, Charles E. 1929. *Freuds tragischer Komplex: Eine Analyse der Psychoanalyse.* Munich: Reinhardt.

McCaffrey, Phillip. 1984. *Freud and Dora: The Artful Dream.* New Brunswick, N.J.: Rutgers University Press.

McCagg, William O. 1989. *A History of Habsburg Jews, 1670–1918.* Bloomington: Indiana University Press.

McGrath, William J. 1974. *Dionysian Art and Populist Politics in Austria.* New Haven: Yale University Press.

——. 1986. *Freud's Discovery of Psychoanalysis: The Politics of Hysteria.* Ithaca: Cornell University Press.

McGuire, William, ed. 1974. *The Freud/Jung Letters.* Translated by Ralph Manheim and R. F. C. Hull. Princeton: Princeton University Press.

McManus, Barbara F. 1997. *Classics & Feminism: Gendering the Classics.* New York: Twayne.

Mertens, Wolfgang, and Rolf Haubl. 1996. *Der Psychoanalytiker als Archäologe: Eine Einführung in die Methode der Rekonstruktion.* Stuttgart: W. Kohlhammer.

Michler, Werner. 1999. *Darwinismus und Literatur: Naturwissenschaftliche und literarische Intelligenz in Österreich, 1859–1914.* Literaturgeschichte in Studien und Quellen, vol. 2. Vienna: Böhlau.

Miles, Gary B. 1995. *Livy: Reconstructing Early Rome.* Ithaca: Cornell University Press.

Milns, R. D. 1968. *Alexander the Great.* New York: Pegasus.

Mitchell, Juliet. 1974. *Psychoanalysis and Feminism.* New York: Vintage Books.

Mitchell-Boyask, Robin N. 1994. "Freud's Reading of Classical Literature and Classical Philology." In Gillman et al. 1994, 23–46.

Mollon, Phil. 2000. *Freud and False Memory Syndrome.* Duxford, UK: Icon Books.

Molnar, Michael, ed. 1992. *The Diary of Sigmund Freud: 1929–1939.* London: Freud Museum.

Momigliano, Arnaldo D. 1977. *Essays in Ancient and Modern Historiography.* Middletown, Conn.: Wesleyan University Press.

Mommsen, Theodor. [1854–1856] 1933. *Römische Geschichte.* 4 vols. 14th ed. Berlin: Weidmann.

Murray, Gilbert. 1914. *Hamlet and Orestes: A Study in Traditional Types.* Annual Shakespeare Lecture 1914. London: Oxford University Press.

———. [1925] 1976. *Five Stages of Greek Religion.* Reprint, Westport, Conn.: Greenwood Press.

———. 1954. *Hellenism and the Modern World.* Boston: Beacon Press.

Nandy, Ashis. 1995. *The Savage Freud and Other Essays on Possible and Retrievable Selves.* Princeton: Princeton University Press.

Nauck, August. 1964. *Tragicorum Graecorum Fragmenta.* Reprint, Hildesheim: Georg Olms.

Niebuhr, Barthold Georg. [1811–1832] 1853. *Römische Geschichte.* Vol. 1. 5th ed. Berlin: Georg Reimer.

Niederland, William G. 1965a. "An Analytic Inquiry Into the Life and Work of Heinrich Schliemann." *Drives, Affects, Behavior* 2 (1965): 369–396.

———. 1965b. "Analytische Studie über das Leben und Werk Heinrich Schliemanns." *Psyche* 18/10 (1965): 563–590.

Nietzsche, Friedrich. [1889] 1968. *Twilight of the Idols* and *The Anti-Christ.* Translated by R. J. Hollingdale. Harmondsworth, UK: Penguin Books.

Nunberg, Herman, and Ernst Federn, eds. 1967. *Minutes of the Vienna Psychoanalytic Society.* Translated by M. Nunberg. 5 vols. New York: International Universities Press.

Nussbaum, Martha. "The *Oedipus Rex* and the Ancient Unconscious." In Rudnytsky and Spitz 1994, chap. 3.

Ogilvie, R. M. 1965. *A Commentary on Livy, Books 1–5.* Oxford: Oxford University Press.

O'Flaherty, James C., Timothy F. Sellner, and Robert M. Helm, eds. [1976] 1979. *Studies in Nietzsche and the Classical Tradition.* Chapel Hill: University of North Carolina Press.

Parker, Harold Talbot. [1937] 1965. *The Cult of Antiquity and the French Revolutionaries.* New York: Octagon Books.

Parker, Robert. 1999. "Through a Glass Darkly: Sophocles and the Divine." In Griffin 1999, 11–30.

Parsons, William B. 1999. *The Enigma of the Oceanic Feeling.* New York: Oxford University Press.

Paskauskas, R. Andrew, ed. 1995. *The Complete Correspondence of Sigmund Freud and Ernest Jones, 1908–1939.* 1993. Cambridge: Harvard University Press.

Pateman, Carole. 1989. *The Disorder of Women: Democracy, Feminism, and Political Theory.* Stanford: Stanford University Press.

Paul, Robert A. 1996. *Moses and Civilization.* New Haven: Yale University Press.

Payne Knight, Richard. [1786] 1894. *Discourse on the Worship of Priapus.* Reprint of the 1865 edition, n.p.: Kessinger.

Phillips, Adam. 2000. *Darwin's Worms.* New York: Basic Books.

Philo of Alexandria. 1993. *The Works of Philo Complete and Unabridged.* Translated by C. D. Yonge. New updated edition. Peabody, Mass.: Hendrickson.

Pokorny, Alois, ed. 1864–1874. *Jahresberichte des Leopoldstädter Communal-Real- und Obergymnasiums in Wien.* Vienna: Verlag des Leopoldstädter Real- und obergymnasiums.

Pollock, George H., and John Munder Ross, eds. 1988. *The Oedipus Papers.* Classics and Psychoanalysis, 6. Madison, Conn.: International Universities Press.

Potts, Alex. 1994. *Flesh and the Ideal: Winckelmann and the Origins of Art History.* New Haven: Yale University Press.

Prager, Jeffrey. 1998. *Presenting the Past: Psychoanalysis and the Sociology of Misremembering.* Cambridge: Harvard University Press.

Quint, David. 1993. *Epic and Empire.* Princeton: Princeton University Press.

Rank, Otto. [1912] 1992. *The Incest Theme in Literature and Legend: Fundamentals of a Psychology of Literary Creation.* Translated by Gregory C. Richter. Baltimore: Johns Hopkins University Press.

——. [1914] 1995. *Traum und Dichtung, Traum und Mythos: Zwei unbekannte Texte aus Sigmund Freuds Traumdeutung.* Reprint, Vienna: Turia & Kant.

——. 1917. "Homer: Psychologische Beiträge zur Entstehungsgeschichte des Volksepos." *Imago* 5 (1917): 133–169 (pt. 1), 372–392 (pt. 2).

——. 1919. *Psychoanalytische Beiträge zur Mythenforschung.* Internationale Psychoanalytische Bibliothek, 4. Leipzig: Internationaler Psychoanalytischer Verlag.

——. [1924] 1993. *The Trauma of Birth.* Reprint of 1929 English translation [no translator cited]. New York: Dover.

——. [1932] 1989. *Art and Artist: Creative Urge and Personality Development.* Translated by Charles Francis Atkinson. New York: W. W. Norton.

——. 1932. *Modern Education: A Critique of Its Fundamental Ideas.* Translated by Mabel E. Moxon. New York: Alfred A. Knopf.

——. [1941] 1958. *Beyond Psychology.* New York: Dover.

Reik, Theodor. 1957. *Myth and Guilt: The Crime and Punishment of Mankind.* New York: Grosset and Dunlap.

Reinach, Salomon. 1912. *Cults, Myths, and Religions.* Translated by Elizabeth Frost. London: David Nutt.

Reinhard, Kenneth. 1996. "The Freudian Things: Construction and the Archaeological Metaphor." In Barker 1996, chap.4.

Rehm, Walther. 1969. *Griechentum und Goethezeit: Geschichte eines Glaubens.* Bern: Francke.

Rice, Emanuel. 1990. *Freud and Moses: The Long Journey Home.* Albany: State University of New York Press.

Richlin, Amy. [1983] 1992. *In the Garden of Priapus: Sexuality and Aggression in Roman Humor.* Rev. ed. New York: Oxford University Press.

——. 1998. "Foucault's *History of Sexuality:* A Useful Theory for Women?" In Larmour, Miller, and Platter 1998, chap. 6.

Ritvo, Lucille. 1990. *Darwin's Influence on Freud: A Tale of Two Sciences.* New Haven: Yale University Press.

Robert, Carl. 1915. *Oidipous: Geschichte eines poetischen Stoffs im griechischen Altertum.* Berlin: Weidmann.

Robert, Marthe. 1977. *From Oedipus to Moses: Freud's Jewish Identity.* Translated by Ralph Manheim. Littman Library of Jewish Civilization. London: Routledge and Kegan Paul.

Robertson, Ritchie. 1990. "Primitivism and Psychology: Nietzsche, Freud, Thomas Mann." In *Modernism and the European Unconscious,* edited by Peter Collier and Judy Davies, chap. 5. New York: St. Martin's Press.

Rohrwasser, Michael, Gisela Steinlechner, Juliane Vogel, Christiane Zintzen. 1996. *Freuds pompejanische Muse*. Vienna: Sonderzahl.

Ross, John Munder. [1982] 1988. "Oedipus Revisited: Laius and the 'Laius Complex.'" In Pollack and Ross 1988, chap. 19.

Roth, Michael S. 1987. *Psycho-Analysis as History: Negation and Freedom in Freud*. Ithaca: Cornell University Press.

Roustang, François. [1976] 1982. *Dire Mastery: Discipleship from Freud to Lacan*. Translated by Ned Lukacher. Baltimore: Johns Hopkins University Press.

Rozenblit, Marsha L. 1983. *The Jews of Vienna, 1867–1914: Assimilation and Identity*. Albany: State University of New York Press.

Rudnytsky, Peter. 1987. *Freud and Oedipus*. New York: Columbia University Press.

——. 1992. "Introductory Essay" to Otto Rank [1912] 1992, xi–xxxv.

——. 1994. "Freud's Pompeian Fantasy." In Gilman et al. 1994, chapter 10.

Rudnytsky, Peter, and Andrew M. Gordon, eds. 2000. *Psychoanalyses / Feminism*. Albany: State University of New York Press.

Rudnytsky, Peter, and Ellen Handler Spitz, eds. 1994. *Freud and Forbidden Knowledge*. New York: New York University Press.

Ruperti, Paul, ed. 1925. *Armin, Deutschlands Befreier*. Bielefeld: Velhagen & Klasing.

Rytkönen, Seppo. 1968. *Barthold Georg Niebuhr als Politiker und Historiker*. Annales Academiae Scientiarum Fennicae 156. Helsinki: Suomalainen Tiedeakatemia.

Sachs, Hanns. 1946. *Freud: Master and Friend*. Cambridge: Harvard University Press.

Sadger, Isidor. 1909. *Heinrich von Kleist: eine pathographisch-psychologische Studie*. Wiesbaden: Bergmann.

——. 1912. "Von der Pathographie zur Psychographie." *Imago* 1 (1912): 158–175.

Safranski, Rudiger. [1987] 1990. *Schopenhauer and the Wild Years of Philosophy*. Translated by Ewald Osers. Cambridge: Harvard University Press.

Said, Edward W. 2003. *Freud and the Non-European*. London: Verso.

Santas, Gerasimos. 1988. *Plato and Freud: Two Theories of Love*. Oxford: Blackwell.

Savage, Kirk. 1994. "The Politics of Memory: Black Emancipation and the Civil War Monument." In Gillis 1994, 127–149.

Schäfer, Peter. 1997. *Judeophobia: Attitudes Toward the Jews in the Ancient World*. Cambridge: Harvard University Press.

Schama, Simon. 1996. *Landscape and Memory*. New York: Alfred A. Knopf.

Schapiro, Meyer. 1956. "Leonard and Freud: An Art-Historical Study." *Journal of the History of Ideas* 17 (1956): 147–178.

Schleifer, Ronald. 2000a. *Modernism and Time: The Logic of Abundance in Literature, Science, and Culture 1880–1930*. Cambridge: Cambridge University Press.

——. 2000b. *Analogical Thinking: Post-Enlightenment Understanding in Language, Collaboration, and Interpretation*. Ann Arbor: University of Michigan Press.

Schliemann, Heinrich. [1875] 1994. *Troy and Its Remains; A Narrative of Researches and Discoveries Made on the Site of Ilium, and in the Trojan Plain*. Reprint, Mineola, N.Y.: Dover.

——. [1881] 1968. *Ilios: The City and Country of the Trojans*. Reprint, New York: Benjamin Blom.

Schmidt, C. and O. Gehlen, eds. 1865. *Memorabilia Alexandri Magni et aliorum virorum illustrium selectasque fabulas Phaedri*. Vienna: Sommer.

Schmidt, Hans. [n.d.] *Das Hermannsdenkmal im Spiegel der Welt*. Detmold: Hermann Bösmann.

Schmidt, Robert A., and Barbara L. Voss. 2000. *Archaeologies of Sexuality*. London: Routledge.

Schönau, Walter. 1968. *Sigmund Freuds Prosa: Literarische Elemente seines Stils*. Germanistische Abhandlungen 25. Stuttgart: Metzler.

Schoeps, Julius. 1996. *Deutsch–jüdische Symbiose, oder Die mißglückte Emanzipation*. Darmstadt: Wissenschaftliche Buchgesellschaft.

Schorske, Carl E. 1981. *Fin-de-Siècle Vienna*. Vintage Books edition. New York: Random House.

———. 1998. *Thinking with History*. Princeton: Princeton University Press.

Schumann, Michael. 1997. "Arminius Redivivus: Zur literarischen Aneignung des Hermannsstoffs im 18. Jahrhundert." *Monatshefte für deutsche Unterricht* 89 (1997): 130–147.

Seeba, Hinrich C. 1993. "'Hermanns Kampf für Deutschlands Not': Zur Topographie der nationalen Identität." In *Deutsche Nationaldenkmale 1790–1990*. Bielefeld: Verlag für Regionalgeschichte.

Seidl, Wolf. 1981. *Bayern in Griechenland*. Munich: Süddeutscher Verlag.

Shavit, Yaacov. 1999. *Athens in Jerusalem: Classical Antiquity and Hellenism in the Making of the Modern Secular Jew*. Translated by Chaya Naor and Niki Werner. London and Portland, Oregon: Littman Library of Jewish Civilization.

Sichtermann, Hellmut. 1996. *Kulturgeschichte der klassischen Archäologie*. Munich: Beck Verlag.

Sigmund Freud-Museum Wien. 1995. *Internationaler Psychoanalytischer Verlag*. Sondernummer 1/1995, Sigmund Freud House Bulletins. Vienna: Sigmund Freud-Museum.

Silberstein, Laurence J, ed. 2000. *Mapping Jewish Identities*. New Perspectives on Jewish Studies. New York: New York University Press.

Skues, Richard A. 2001. "On the Dating of Freud's *aliquis* Slip." *International Journal of Psychoanalysis* 82 (2001): 1185–1204.

Spector, Jack J. 1972. *The Aesthetics of Freud: A Study in Psychoanalysis and Art*. New York: McGraw-Hill.

Spence, Donald P. 1982. *Narrative Truth and Historical Truth: Meaning and Interpretation in Psychoanalysis*. New York: Norton.

———. 1987. *The Freudian Metaphor: Toward Paradigm Change in Psychoanalysis*. New York: Norton.

———. 1994. *The Rhetorical Voice of Psychoanalysis: Displacement of Evidence by Theory*. Cambridge: Harvard University Press.

Spengler, Oswald. 1923. *Der Untergang des Abendlandes: Umrisse einer Morphologie der Weltgeschichte*. 2 vols. Munich: C. H. Beck.

Sprengnether, Madelon. 1990. *The Spectral Mother: Freud, Feminism, and Psychoanalysis*. Ithaca: Cornell University Press.

———. 2000. "Mourning Freud." In Rudnytsky and Gordon 2000, chapter 1.

Stannard, David E. 1980. *Shrinking History: On Freud and the Failure of Psychohistory*. New York: Oxford University Press.

Stepansky, Paul E. 1986. "Feuerbach and Jung as Religious Critics—With a Note on Freud's Psychology of Religion." In Stepansky, ed., 1986, 215–239.

Stepansky, Paul E, ed. 1986. *Freud: Appraisals and Reappraisals*. Vol. 1. Hillsdale, N.J.: Analytic Press.

———, ed. 1988. *Freud: Appraisals and Reappraisals*. Vol. 2. Hillsdale, N.J.: Analytic Press.

Stern, Bernard H. [1940] 1969. *The Rise of Romantic Hellenism in English Literature, 1732–1786*. New York: Octagon Books.

Stockreiter, Karl. 1998. "Am Rand der Aufklärungsmetapher: Korrespondenzen zwischen Archäologie und Psychoanalyse." In Marinelli 1998, 81–93.

Stuchtey, Benedikt, and Peter Wende, eds. 2000. *British and German Historiography 1750–1950*. Oxford: Oxford University Press.

Sugarman, Susan. 1998. *Freud on the Acropolis*. Boulder, Colo.: Westview Press.

Sulloway, Frank J. [1979] 1992. *Freud, Biologist of the Mind: Beyond the Psychoanalytic Legend*. Cambridge: Harvard University Press.

Swales, Peter J. 1982. "Freud, Minna Bernays, and the Conquest of Rome." *New American Review* (Spring/Summer 1982): 1–23.

———. 1986. "Freud, His Teacher, and the Birth of Psychoanalysis." In Stepansky 1986, 3–82.

Tarn, W. W. 1948. *Alexander the Great*. 2 vols. Cambridge: Cambridge University Press.

Terdiman, Richard. 1993. *Present Past: Modernity and the Memory Crisis.* Ithaca: Cornell University Press.

Thion, Edmond, ed. 1877. *Arminius, dialogue par Ulrich von Hutten.* Translated by Edmond Thion. Paris: Liseux.

Tilley, Christopher. 1999. *Metaphor and Material Culture.* Oxford: Blackwell.

Timms, Edward. 2001. "Freud's Imagined Audience: Dream Text and Cultural Context." *Psychoanalysis and History* 3.1: 3–17.

Timpanaro, Sebastiano. [1976] 1985. *The Freudian Slip: Psychoanalysis and Textual Criticism.* Translated by Kate Soper. Reprint, London: Verso.

Timpe, Dieter. 1970. *Arminius-Studien.* Heidelberg: Carl Winter Universitäts Verlag.

Tögel, Christfried. 1989. *Berggasse — Pompeji und Zurück.* Tübingen: Edition Diskord.

Tögel, Christfried, ed. 2002. *"Unser Herz zeigt nach dem Süden."* Reisebriefe 1895–1923. Berlin: Aufbau Verlag.

Traill, David A. 1995. *Schliemann of Troy: Treasure and Deceit.* New York: St. Martin's Press.

Trevelyan, Humphrey. [1941] 1972. *Goethe and the Greeks.* Reprint, New York: Octagon Books.

Trigger, Bruce G. 1989. *A History of Archaeological Thought.* Cambridge: Cambridge University Press.

Trosman, H. 1976. "Freud's Cultural Background." *Psychological Issues* 46–70.

Turner, A. Richard. 1993. *Inventing Leonardo.* New York: Alfred A. Knopf.

Turner, Frank M. 1981. *The Greek Heritage in Victorian Britain.* New Haven, Yale University Press.

——. 1989. "Why the Greeks and Not the Romans in Victorian Britain?" In *Rediscovering Hellenism,* edited by G. W. Clarke, 61–81. Cambridge: Cambridge University Press.

Tylor, Edward Burnett. [1871] 1958. *The Origins of Culture* [originally *Primitive Culture*]. Reprint, Harper Torchbook Edition. New York: Harper & Row.

Vance, Norman. 2000. "Niebuhr in England: History, Faith, and Order." In Stuchtey and Wende 2000: 83–98.

Veddeler, Peter. 1975. "Nationale Feiern am Hermannsdenkmal in früherer Zeit." In Engelbert 1975, 167–181.

Vermorel, Henri, and Madeleine Vermorel. 1993. *Sigmund Freud et Romain Rolland: Correspondance 1923–1936.* Paris: Presses Universitaires de France.

Vernant, Jean Pierre and Pierre Vidal-Naquet. 1990. *Myth and Tragedy in Ancient Greece.* Translated by Janet Lloyd. New York: Zone Books.

Vidal-Naquet, Pierre. 1990. *La démocratie grecque vue d'ailleurs.* Paris: Flammarion.

Vitz, Paul C. 1988. *Sigmund Freud's Christian Unconscious.* New York: Guilford Press.

Wain, Martin. 1998. *Freud's Answer.* Chicago: Ivan R. Dee.

Wallace, Edwin R. 1983. *Freud and Anthropology: A History and Reappraisal.* Psychological Issues Monograph 55. New York: International Universities Press.

——. 1985. *Historiography and Causation in Psychoanalysis: An Essay on Psychoanalytic and Historical Epistemology.* Hillsdale, N.J.: Analytic Press.

Wallace, Jennifer. 1997. *Shelley and Greece: Rethinking Romantic Hellenism.* New York: St. Martin's Press.

Webster, Richard. 1995. *Why Freud Was Wrong: Sin, Science, and Psychoanalysis.* New York: Basic Books.

Weininger, Otto. [1903] 1975. *Sex and Character.* Authorized translation from the sixth German edition. Reprint, New York: AMS Press.

Weissl, Michael. 1998. "Löwys These von den Ursprüngen der bildenden Kunst." In Brein 1998, 72–80.

Wells, Peter S. 2003. *The Battle That Stopped Rome.* New York: W. W. Norton.

West, Martin. 1999. "Ancestral Curses." In Griffin 1999, 31–45.

Williams, Craig. 1999. *Roman Homosexuality.* Oxford: Oxford University Press.

Winckelmann, Johann Joachim. [1764] 1993. *Geschichte der Kunst des Altertums.* Reprint, Darmstadt: Wissenschaftliche Buchgesellschaft.

Winkler, John. 1990. *The Constraints of Desire*. New York: Routledge.

Winter, Sarah. 1999. *Freud and the Institution of Psychoanalytic Knowledge*. Cultural Memory in the Present. Stanford: Stanford University Press.

Wiplinger, Gilpert, and Gudrun Wlach. 1996. *Ephesus: 100 Years of Austrian Research*. Translated by Claudia Luxon. Vienna: Böhlau Verlag.

Wistrich, Robert S. 1989. *The Jews of Vienna in the Age of Franz Joseph*. Littman Library of Jewish Civilization. Oxford: Oxford University Press.

Wittgenstein, Ludwig. 1966. *Lectures and Conversations on Aesthetics, Psychology and Religious Belief*. Edited by Cyril Barrett. Berkeley: University of California Press.

———. [1977] 1984. *Culture and Value*. Edited by G. H. von Wright. Translated by Peter Winch. Chicago: University of Chicago Press.

Wittels, Fritz. 1904. *Der Taufjude*. Vienna: Breitenstein.

———. 1912. *Alles um Liebe: Eine Urweltdichtung*. Berlin: Egon Fleischel.

———. [1924] 1971. *Sigmund Freud: His Personality, His Teaching, & His School*. Translated by Eden Paul and Cedar Paul. Reprint, Freeport, N.Y.: Books for Libraries Press.

———. 1931. *Freud and His Time*. Translated by Louise Brink. New York: Horace Liveright.

———. 1995. *Freud and the Child Woman: The Memoirs of Fritz Wittels*. Edited by Edward Timms. New Haven: Yale University Press.

Wolf, Friedrich August. [1795] 1985. *Prolegomena to Homer*. Translated by Anthony Grafton, Glenn W. Most, and James E. G. Zetzel. Princeton: Princeton University Press.

Wolf, Harald. 1998. "Emanuel Löwy. Leben und Werk eines vergessenen Pioniers." In Brein 1998, 15–62.

Wortis, Joseph. [1954] 1975. *Fragments of an Analysis with Freud*. New York: MacGraw-Hill.

Wright, M. R. [1981] 1995. *Empedocles: The Extant Fragments*. London: Duckworth.

Yerushalmi, Yosef Hayim. 1982. *Zakhor: Jewish History and Jewish Memory*. Seattle: University of Washington Press.

———. 1991. *Freud's Moses: Judaism Terminable and Interminable*. New Haven: Yale University Press.

Zanker, Paul. 1988. *The Power of Images in the Age of Augustus*. Translated by Alan Shapiro. Ann Arbor: University of Michigan Press.

Zanuso, Billa. 1986. *The Young Freud: The Origins of Psychoanalysis in Late Nineteenth-Century Viennese Culture*. Translated anonymously. Oxford: Basil Blackwell.

Zeitlin, Froma. 1990. "Thebes: Theater of Self and Society in Athenian Drama." In *Nothing to Do with Dionysus? Athenian Drama in Its Social Context*, edited by John Winkler and Froma Zeitlin, 130–167. Princeton: Princeton University Press.

Zweig, Arnold. [1933] 1998. *Bilanz der deutschen Judenheit 1933: ein Versuch*. Arnold Zweig Berliner Ausgabe, Essays 3/2. Berlin: Aufbau Verlag.

———. 1996. *Freundschaft mit Freud: Ein Bericht*. Berliner Ausgabe, Essays 5. Berlin: Aufbau Verlag.

Zweig, Stefan. [1944] 1997. *Die Welt von Gestern*. Reprint, Frankfurt am Main: Fischer Verlag.

———. 1989. *Über Sigmund Freud: Porträt, Briefwechsel, Gedenkworte*. Frankfurt am Main: Fischer Verlag.

INDEX

∎

Harrison, Jane Ellen, 123
Hatshepsut, 74
H.D. (Hilda Doolittle, analysand), 194–197, 216
Hegel, G. W. F., 15–16, 18, 104, 206, 211
Heine, Heinrich, 75
Hellenism, 104–109, 225–233, 247
Herzl, Theodor, 227
Hirschfeld, Otto, 172
historical consciousness, 2, 21, 160, 200, 202–216; Jewish, 224–225. *See also* prehistory
"historical truth," 31, 204, 235
historicism, 132, 172–173, 175–176, 202–216
historiography, 36, 106, 160, 162–182. *See also* analogy: historiographical
history and psychoanalysis, 130–134, 157–158, 192
Hitler, Adolf, 97
Homans, Peter, 148–149
homosexuality, 61–62, 66, 69, 72, 76, 78
Horai (Seasons), 22, 81
Horapollo, 66
Horkheimer, Max, 147–148
Humboldt, Wilhelm von, 16

imperialism, 104–109, 120–125
improvisation, 4, 27–28, 44, 82, 116–117, 224, 248
India, 97–101, 122–123
Ingres, Jean-Auguste-Dominique, 52–55
instinct. *See* drive
Italy, 20. *See also* Freud, Sigmund: Travels: Aquileia *and* Rome; Rome

Jensen, Wilhelm, 12–25, 64, 84–85, 92, 115, 140
Jesus, 7, 66, 77, 169–170, 236–238
Jewish law, 50, 229, 250
Jews in antiquity, 49–50, 78–79, 83, 107, 225–226, 229–230, 244–247. *See also* Josephus; Philo of Alexandria; Talmud
Jones, Ernest, 44, 149, 154, 237–238, 242
Jonte-Pace, Diane, 75–76,
Josephus, 170
Jung, C. G., 35–36, 48, 69–70, 91, 101, 107–108, 123, 143–144, 146, 149, 151, 219, 221, 229, 233–235, 237–238
Juno, 239–240

"Katharina" (analysand), 187–189
Klenze, Leopold von, 2
Krafft-Ebing, Richard von, 130
Kraus, Victor von, 106, 201

Lacan, Jacques, 5, 57–58, 132–134, 259n6
Laius, 50, 61, 72
Leopoldstadt (district in Vienna), 29, 118
Livy, 162–168
Löwy, Emanuel, 117–120, 172, 268n21

Macaulay, Thomas Babington, 166
Malinowski, Bronislaw, 123
Marcuse, Herbert, 215
Marx, Karl, 7, 135, 145, 206–207, 211
matriarchy, 241–244
Medea (of Euripides), 28
memory, 72–73, 132, 135–146, 160–162, 167, 183–194, 198–200
Mithras, 236–237
mnemohistory, 3
modernity, 31
Moirai (Fates), 22, 80–81
Mommsen, Theodor, 202, 272n4
Moses, 6, 7, 50, 148, 165, 169–170, 229–230, 236, 238, 244, 247, 249
mother: great, goddess, 22, 76, 81–82, 243–244, 246 (*see also* Mut); law of, 80–83; Leonardo's, 65–67, 69, 72, 75–77, 80, 82, 148, love, 75–76; primal fear of, 59. *For Freud's mother see* Freud, Amalie. *See also* matriarchy; nature
Murray, Gilbert, 28
Mut (Egyptian goddess), 66–67, 70, 72–74, 76, 78–79, 82–83, 91, 110, 148, 163, 246, 262n3
mythology, Freud's general use of, 41–42, 47–58, 66–69, 72–73, 80–83, 101, 108, 141–142, 146–153, 162

Napoleon I, 104–105, 225
Napoleon III, 105
Narcissus, 4, 76–77
narrative and psychoanalysis, 134–146, 166–167
nature, 18, 43, 52, 68–69, 74, 78–83, 100, 140–141, 241
Niebuhr, Barthold Georg, 162–168, 170–174, 176, 183, 185, 199, 211
Nietzsche, Friedrich, 29, 96, 156, 231–232, 236

Oedipus, 4, 5, 42, 47–62, 73, 76–78, 80, 82–83, 95–96, 104, 140–143, 146, 151, 154, 210, 213, 226–228, 235
Oedipus complex, 1–2, 42, 45, 47–62, 76–83, 95, 100, 108, 121, 135, 140–143, 152–156, 181, 226–228, 235, 242
orient, 16, 18, 99–101

Adolf Wölfli: Draftsman, Writer, Poet, Composer
EDITED BY ELKA SPOERRI

Sublime Surrender: Male Masochism at the Fin-de-Siècle
BY SUZANNE R. STEWART